GRINGOLANDIA

Latin American Silhouettes
Editors: William H. Beezley and Judith Ewell

The Origins of Mexican National Politics, 1808–1847
Jaime E. Rodríguez O.

Integral Outsiders: The American Colony in Mexico City, 1876–1911
By William Schell, Jr.

The French in Central America: Culture and Commerce
By Thomas D. Schoonover

The Tale of Healer Miguel Perdomo Neira: Medicine, Ideologies, and Power in the Nineteenth-Century Andes
By David Sowell

Based on a True Story: Latin American History at the Movies
Edited by Donald F. Stevens

Cuban and Cuban-American Women: An Annotated Bibliography
Edited and Compiled by K. Lynn Stoner, with Luis Hipólito Serrano Pérez

Patriotism, Politics, and Popular Liberalism in Nineteenth-Century Mexico: Juan Francisco Luca and the Puebla Sierra
By Guy P. C. Thomson with David G. LaFrance

Argentina: The Challenges of Modernization
Edited by Joseph S. Tulchin with Allison M. Garland

Cuba and the Caribbean: Regional Issues and Trends in the Post-Cold War Era
Edited by Joseph S. Tulchin, Andrés Serbín, and Rafael Hernández

State and Society in Spanish America during the Age of Revolution
Edited by Victor M. Uribe-Uran

Nicaragua without Illusions: Regime Transition and Structural Adjustment in the 1990s
Edited by Thomas W. Walker

Repression, Resistance, and Democratic Transition in Central America
Edited by Thomas W. Walker and Ariel C. Armony

Vagrants and Citizens: Politics and the Masses in Mexico City from Colony to Republic
By Richard A. Warren

On the Border: Society and Culture between the United States and Mexico
Edited by Andrew Grant Wood

Revolution in the Street: Women, Workers, and Urban Protest in Veracruz
By Andrew Grant Wood

GRINGOLANDIA
Mexican Identity and Perceptions
of the United States

Stephen D. Morris

An SR Book
Rowman & Littlefield Publishers, Inc.
Lanham • Boulder • New York • Toronto • Oxford

An SR Book
Rowman & Littlefield Publishers, Inc.
A wholly owned subsidiary of The Rowman & Littlefield Publishing Group, Inc.
4501 Forbes Boulevard, Suite 200
Lanham, MD 20706

PO Box 317, Oxford OX2 9RU, UK

British Library Cataloguing in Publication Information Available

Library of Congress Cataloging-in-Publication Data

Morris, Stephen D., 1957–
   Gringolandia : Mexican identity and perceptions of the United States / Stephen D. Morris.
      p.   cm.— (Latin American silhouettes)
   Includes bibliographical references and index.
   ISBN 0-8420-5146-5 (cloth : alk. paper)—ISBN 0-8420-5147-3 (pbk. : alk. paper)
   1. United States—Foreign public opinion, Mexican.   2. Public opinion—Mexico.
3. Group identity—Mexico.   I. Title.   II. Series.
E183.8.M6M84   2005
973—dc22   2004018386

Printed in the United States of America

⊗ ™ The paper used in this publication meets the minimum requirements of American National Standard for Information Sciences—Permanence of Paper for Printed Library Materials, ANSI/NISO Z39.48-1992.

To my bi-cultural *hijos* David and Tania,
con cariño,
and in loving memory of my Mother, Gaye Wilson Morris

Contents

Tables and Figures

Tables

Figures

Preface

FOR OVER TWENTY YEARS, I have traveled into and throughout Mexico. During that time, I have had the privilege of teaching and learning from Mexicans at Mexican institutions, conducting research on contemporary political, economic, and cultural topics, participating in summer study programs for U.S.-based institutions as student, teacher, and director, and being integrated by marriage into a Mexican family. My fascination of, respect for, and curiosity about the country and the people have never waned. But despite my intimate knowledge of the country and its culture, I recognize that my understanding will always be limited by my U.S. origin. Not only does it color my perceptions, but it also influences the treatment I receive and the visions presented to me by others.

Inspiration to explore Mexican perceptions of the U.S. and their impact on views of self and nation was partly professional, but mainly personal. At the professional level, my research during the early nineties resulting in *Political Reformism in Mexico* (1995) pointed to the U.S. as a critical factor behind the impressive longevity of the PRI-based regime. That study showed, however, that it was not merely direct U.S. influence, but the institutions and thinking forged by living beside such a powerful neighbor. In exploring the litany of explanations for Mexico's stability, I often ran across references to the role of the U.S. Certainly, many saw the concern about the U.S. expressed within the Revolutionary ideology as merely a political ploy to maintain the regime's grip on political power, but such views begged even more questions about how perceptions of the U.S. are made, used, and even misused within the political setting.

But much of the drive behind this project was personal. My long struggle to understand Mexico demanded a better knowledge of what it means to be Mexican and that required a better sense of the Mexican view of the world, of others, of their country, and of themselves. The project was shaped by the need to better understand my wife's view of the world and particularly her view of the country where we reside most of the year. It was shaped by the fascinating process of change I witnessed when my sister-in-law came to live with us to attend the university: a process that involved fundamental and complex changes in her perceptions of both Mexico and the U.S. And, finally, the research stems from a desire to help in some way my now virtually grown children better understand and negotiate their cultural heritages. Both have grown to embrace the two cultures, appreciate aspects of both, and reject hierarchical formulas. At the same time, both have run into prejudice and misperceptions on both sides of the border. Of course, for them, neither Mexico nor the U.S. is a foreign country. For this reason, I dedicate this book to David and Tania, who in many ways represent part of the *raza cosmica* of the twenty-first century, the hope of a true partnership between Mexico and the U.S., and the seeds of a uniquely binational identity.

Work on this project took a number of years in part because it took me further afield than I had ever ventured in the past. Research into nationalism and national identity led me deep into the bailiwick of anthropology and history, while literature on perceptions of difference took me into the fascinating and mysterious world of postmodernism, complete with its own unique jargon and radical, sometimes nonempirical, propositions. I also spent considerable time acquainting myself with the amorphous and unruly literature on globalization. I have no doubt that I am better off for these journeys into neighboring camps, and what many colleagues consider unorthodox realms. Thankfully, throughout the period I was able to develop ideas, put together conference presentations, develop seminars, and publish articles on the subject. Articles in the *Journal of Latin American Studies* (1999), *Carta Economica Regional* (1999), *Mexican Studies/Estudios Mexicanos* (2000), *Latin American Perspectives* (2001), and *National Identities* (2001) all represent pieces in the development of this work.

Of course, many people and institutions assisted in the time-consuming task. These range from anonymous reviewers of manuscripts and panel discussants at conferences to our library staff burdened with constant requests to locate materials. In particular, the University of South Alabama provided a research grant to fund the public opinion poll in Guadalajara and sabbatical leave. Charles Davis, University of Kentucky, lent invaluable assistance in putting together the data on public opinion. Fara Ferguson, a student in one of my Thunderbird classes in Mexico, assisted in researching franchises and the consumer market as did my son, David Morris-Díaz. Cesar Morones, *Centro de Estudios de Opinion Público*, collaborated on the development of the poll and its implementation. My longtime friend and colleague John Passe-Smith, University of Central Arkansas, provided helpful comments and feedback from the conceptualization of the project on, and worked with me on putting together and analyzing the local poll. Bruce Willis, now at the University of Tulsa, took time to read and comment on the chapter on Mexican movies. Sam Fisher, at the University of South Alabama, helped at each step of the data analysis and read and commented on that chapter. Richmond Brown, also at the University of South Alabama, read and commented on the entire manuscript, more than once. Finally, I thank my wife Celina for always helping me try to comprehend the way Mexicans think and view the world. She not only helped me understand the meanings behind the cartoons or translate the occasional unrecognized word, but has taught me hundreds of Mexican sayings over the years and always shared her perspective on the U.S., even when it seemed to offend. Indeed, being by her side to watch the Mexican and U.S. soccer teams battle it out has always been part of this research endeavor. To her and all my friends and colleagues, I am forever grateful for their assistance and willingness to lend a hand. Even so, I alone am responsible for the content, interpretations, and translations. As always, this study is offered in the noblest of spirits to further our understanding; it in no way is meant to offend anyone on either side of the imaginary line that unites and divides us.

1

Introduction: Analyzing Perceptions of Self and Other

THE UNITED STATES "presence . . . in Mexican life is a historical fact that needs no demonstration," according to Nobel laureate Octavio Paz.[1] From the direct and personal (i.e., visiting the U.S., having family or friends in or from the U.S., or working with people from the U.S.) to the more abstract and impersonal (i.e., working for a U.S. company, producing or consuming U.S. products), Mexicans encounter *los Estados Unidos* on a daily basis, at virtually every turn, without having to leave the country.[2] Mexicans find the U.S. in their school texts, in newspapers, on television, in novels and magazines, on billboards, or while listening to *políticos* debate national issues. "Foreign capital for the most part means United States capital," just as cinema for the most part means Hollywood.[3] And though seemingly intensified by recent trends, this staggering presence or penetration is nothing new, as seen in Jules Davids's depiction of the early years of the twentieth century: "Many Mexican cities could almost be said to be American, such as Monterrey, and even the capital . . . wherever one went there were American names, American goods, American customs, the American language and Americans themselves. By 1910, the prediction that Mexico would be acquired by the gradual process of Americanization through the immigration of colonists and capital slowly neared completion."[4] Indeed, Julia Tuñón illustrates how by just opening the newspaper in the 1940s one "encounters U.S. influence at many levels": an ad for "un *ham sandwich lunch*," radio workers demanding censorship to protect the Spanish language, the promotion of American football, baseball, and movies.[5]

Few question the extent of U.S. influence over Mexican politics, the economy, or society. As Mario Ojeda notes, the U.S. "has cost Mexico an open and declared war, the loss of more than half of its original territory, various military interventions, constant interference in internal political matters, and economic penetration at all levels."[6] But as Mexico's predominant "other," the U.S. goes beyond direct influence to shape Mexico's historical memory, its sense of self and nation, and its perceptions of the national interest. Social observer Carlos Monsiváis, for example, locates the U.S. behind the out-pouring of nationalist feelings and the booing of the U.S. anthem during a Julio César Chávez fight. Not only does the American challenger embody anti-Mexican attributes, he notes, but "there is never lacking someone who remembers the loss of Texas, California, and New Mexico."[7] Popular dis-course goes even further by hinting that the U.S. may in some way figure in the country's propinquity to God: "Poor Mexico, so far from God, and so close to the United States" is a common saying attributed to such historic figures as Porfirio Díaz and Lucas Alaman.[8] But despite the (omni)presence of the U.S. in the country or in the minds of the people, despite references in the literature to "anti-Americanism" among the elite[9] or popular notions of a "love-hate" feeling, and despite even the nation's long historic struggle to define its own identity, few have seriously explored Mexican views of the U.S. Little is known about the nature of Mexicans' complex sentiments toward their northern neighbor (*sus primos del norte*), the role such images play in shaping national identity or public policy, or how recent policy som-ersaults (the North American Free Trade Agreement [NAFTA]) or political changes (democratization) contest past images or what might be emerging in their place.

This study addresses these questions as it seeks to contribute to a better understanding of contemporary Mexico, the future of Mexican-U.S. rela-tions, and the dynamics of nationalism amid globalization. Specifically, the study concentrates on three fundamental questions:

1. How do Mexicans view the U.S.?
2. How do these images contribute to Mexican identity and perceptions of the national interest?
3. Are Mexican perceptions of the U.S. changing in the contemporary period, the age of NAFTA? And, if so, how are these changes altering previous conceptualizations or meanings of the nation and of being Mexican?

As the wording suggests, each question fastens to a host of theoretical approaches and assumptions. This introductory chapter reviews each query, sets out the theoretical framework and scope of the current study, elaborates on the methodological approach, and demonstrates the questions' relevance to the broader issues.

Question 1: How do Mexicans view the U.S.?

The study's fundamental question centers on identifying and understanding Mexican images of the U.S. during the contemporary period. The question can be rephrased in many provocative ways. For example, what meanings do Mexicans attach to terms like *Estados Unidos, gringo, gabacho, los Americanos,* or *los norteamericanos?* What attributes do they stress or downplay? What narratives do Mexicans use to describe the U.S.? How, according to Mexicans, does the U.S. view them? Where and how does the U.S. fit within the Mexican narrative of its own history, an individual's personal situation, or the general political or economic climate facing the country? What is the perceived impact the U.S. has on the country or the Mexicans who live and work there?

Indicative of the ambiguity attached to Mexican perceptions of the U.S. is the confusion surrounding what term to use to refer to people from the U.S., along with the recognition that what may be considered appropriate for a Mexican is different when used by someone from the U.S. Objectively, the term *Americano* is inappropriate since all people from the hemisphere are Americans, including Mexicans. Though this term is often employed by people on both sides of the border to refer to the people of the U.S., it can, when used by a person from the U.S., provoke a certain degree of resentment among Mexicans who read into it a pinch of U.S. arrogance in appropriating the term. America, they will remind the person, refers to the entire hemisphere. The same is basically true of the term *norteamericano* (spatially, Mexicans reside within North America), though it too is commonly used by Mexicans to refer to those from the U.S. Even the commonly used *estadounidense* or *estadunidense* (both spellings seem to coexist) is not entirely proper since Mexicans also match the label, being citizens of the United Mexican States, though I have never heard a Mexican refer to his or her copatriots as such. The term *gringo,* of course, exclusively refers to people from the U.S. and is used throughout Mexico. Though once considered derogatory, the term has lost that power. Generally, two explanations of the origin of the term can be found. One account refers to U.S. soldiers who sang the old ballad "Green Grow the Rushes, Oh!" while marching through the dry deserts of the north during the war. The other, and more likely, explanation is that it comes from the old word meaning "gibberish" once used to describe anyone who could not speak proper Spanish. Other terms like *gabacho* or *bolillo* also refer exclusively to people from the U.S. though they are used much less frequently than *gringo*. The term *gabacho* also has two explanations: one, that in French it means a "bad act"; the other, that it is an adaptation of the word *gabacha,* which refers to an "apron" and thus to the unmasculine tendency for U.S. males to help their wives in the kitchen.[10] Of course, each of these terms embodies a distinct narrative and hence relates directly to the issue at the heart of this study. Referring to *gringos* as *primos del norte* [cousins of the north] or as being *del otro lado* [the other side], for example—both terms are commonly used—invokes strikingly different images. One characterizes the *gringo* as a member of the family, while the other is a double entendre meaning a homosexual, as someone lacking in macho qualities. While recognizing and acknowledging these points is important, throughout this study I will tend to use the terms North American or *gringo* to refer to people from the U.S., though quotes from others may use other terms.

Prior research projects into Mexican perceptions of the U.S. have focused on specific areas or time periods, and none of them comprehensively explores the topic. Some works examine survey data to assess Mexicans' basic attitudes toward the U.S., with the more recent works concentrating on the public's support or opposition to NAFTA.[11] Beyond these, Gene Hanrahan concentrates on anti-American sentiments during the Revolution; Alice Coote and John Merrill on the attitudes of Mexican journalists toward the U.S.; Américo Paredes on the images contained in Mexican *corridos*; Jorge Bustamante and Pablo Vila on the views of border residents; David Wilt on Mexican cinema; and Dennis Gilbert and Josefina Vázquez on Mexican school texts.[12] Studies on Mexican national identity, nationalism, and Mexican-U.S. relations also tend to highlight anti-American sentiments and the rhetoric of the post-Revolutionary elite, but rarely do they concentrate much attention on the overall question or look beyond "official" statements or policy.[13]

The fact that prior studies look at only one particular area begs the question of what is meant here by "Mexican perceptions" of the U.S. Perhaps it is better to ask, "Whose image?" First, I start from the assumption that no simple, straightforward answer to the research question exists: there is no one, singular, authentic "Mexican" perception of anything (much less the U.S.). Instead a plurality of images or discourses on the U.S. coexist and compete to forge broader social meanings. The images are complex, multidimensional, and contextualized, shaped by and reflected within a variety of social and spatial settings. Hence, the reference here to Mexican images is in the plural, not the singular. In addition, it is assumed here that Mexican images of the U.S. are not static or fixed, but fluid, shaped continuously by a complex interaction with reality and other social and psychological discourses. Social identity, as Vila contends, "is the complex interplay of narratives about others, history, the present and the future, constantly activated and actualized through narrative identities."[14]

Of course, these assumptions regarding "images" rule out the behavioralist's dream of empirically locating "it" (the authentic Mexican image of the U.S.) with precision. Even a nicely crafted opinion poll would merely tap one dimension of the broader image at just one point in time. It would fail to probe the deeper meanings, the specific contexts that give the images their meaning, and how the images interact and influence the broader discourse on self and nation, or tell us whether that particular temporal moment was "unique" or "typical." Therefore, in an effort to overcome some of these problems, the current study seeks to examine Mexican perceptions of the U.S. as found within different contexts. Or, to put it differently, the current inquiry explores the images contained within narratives produced by a diverse set of social agents: narratives that both express and influence the overall political culture. These distinct contexts include:

Political Leaders. Given the weight of the U.S. in Mexican society, it is of little surprise that the theme of the U.S. inundates the statements and speeches of the nation's political leaders. As many studies have shown, public policy rests on certain assumptions and perceptions that the culture and policy makers make regarding other countries. What do Mexican politicians say or think about the U.S.? What traits or assumptions about the U.S. do they echo in support of their proposed policy solutions? (chapter 2)

School Textbooks. As in any nation, Mexicans learn who they and others are at an early age in the schools. The textbook is thus an important agent nurturing Mexican images of the U.S and nation. How do schoolbooks depict the U.S.? What lessons do they teach regarding the U.S. as Mexico's neighbor? (chapter 3)

Political Cartoons. Political caricaturists offer poignant and politicized images of the U.S. Due perhaps to the unique nature of the medium, cartoons have a specific power to illustrate underlying perceptions, images, and associations and, in turn, to influence society. How do Mexican caricatures portray the U.S.? What messages do the images convey? (chapter 4)

Intellectual Writings. Like school texts and the politicians' rhetoric, the writings of such nationally acclaimed thinkers as Octavio Paz, Carlos Fuentes, Carlos Monsiváis, Samuel Ramos, and others contain many references to the U.S. How do these thinkers portray and use the U.S.

to define and explain Mexico? To what extent do these images differ from those expressed by the more "official" version? (chapter 5)

National Cinema. Like the writings of the intellectuals and the drawings of the caricaturists, Mexican motion pictures also contain meaningful images of the U.S. Movies construct and represent nationalist themes and images that feed on and nurture the political culture. How is the U.S. portrayed in Mexican movies? Are characters from the U.S. treated as heroes, villains, or idiots? What lessons regarding the U.S. and Mexico vis-à-vis the U.S. do the movies provide the viewer? (chapter 6)

Consumption and Marketing. Two general approaches are taken here with regard to "the public." The first centers on consumption and the consumer market. As cultural analyst Nestor García Canclini notes, it is in the context of consumption that rich and poor countries come into contact with one another and where one learns about the "other."[15] What images and meanings underlie Mexican consumption of U.S. products? Do Mexicans prefer U.S. products to Mexican products? What images of the U.S. inform advertising in Mexico? (chapter 7)

Opinion Surveys. The second approach focusing on the public utilizes opinion polls. Certainly the most direct method to explore Mexican views of the U.S. is to ask Mexicans, and a host of surveys have done precisely that. The polls also provide information on political preferences, feelings of Mexicanness, and other related areas, and hence a means to assess demographic and social determinants of these views. (chapter 8)

Each of these areas brims with rich and nuanced images of the U.S. But while each represents a component of the overall equation, I wish to stress that neither alone nor in unison do they add up to what would mistakenly be termed the "true" Mexican image of the U.S. First, no particular image is treated here as more "authentic" or "real" than others. Even though the various contexts are probably linked causally and some may be more influential than others in shaping the broader image (though neither question is explored here), I do not attempt to privilege any single context or agent. For example, the rhetoric of the State elite, what many often refer to as the "hegemonic discourse," may go a long way in shaping the general political culture by setting the parameters of public debate, and by making policies that structure U.S. penetration of the market or that determine the content of movies and the school texts. But gauging how influential the State is in shaping political culture remains a matter of contentious debate among historians, and I do not wish to enter that debate here.[16] The same can be asked of other agents as well: how influential are textbooks, the writings of the intellectual elite, the political cartoons, or even the national cinema in shaping political culture? To what extent do people really pay enough attention? The number of people exposed to Mexican movies is really quite limited compared to the numbers forced to read the textbooks, but does that really make them less influential or less representative of the broader culture from which they emerge? Again, such questions, while intriguing, lie beyond the scope of this study. In short, this study does not concentrate on the causes behind Mexican images of the U.S. or try to explain why Mexicans harbor these images; instead, the task is simply to examine the different dimensions of the images. Such an approach ensures that no one discourse is presented as or confused with the authentic view.

But even taken together the various images studied here can only hope to approach something akin to the "true" Mexican image of the U.S. This is because the current study delves into only a handful of the almost unlimited range of social contexts rich with images of the U.S. The U.S, for instance, looms heavily in the discourse of Mexican migrants, Mexican-Americans, and *fronterizos*,[17] within the written press, in Mexican *telenovelas*, or in business meetings, to mention just a few areas; yet none of these will be examined here. Of course it would be impossible to cover all social contexts. And then of course not all Mexican perceptions of the U.S. originate just from Mexican sources. Arguably an important ingredient shaping Mexicans' perceptions of the U.S. comes from U.S. agents. Hollywood images of the U.S., for example, may possibly go further in molding Mexican perceptions of the U.S. than Mexican movies since they attract more viewers. But analyzing exported U.S. images of itself and their impact on Mexico lies even further beyond the original question regarding *Mexican* images of the U.S. So, like other unexplored contexts, U.S. images of the U.S. in Mexico will not be incorporated into this analysis.

This study then explores the many Mexican images of the U.S. as presented by Mexicans in a variety of contexts. It builds on the understanding that Mexican perceptions of the U.S. are multidimensional, contested, and fluid, and that no single, authentic view exists. As such, this initial question is essentially descriptive, void of much theoretical meaning. So, what will Mexican images of the U.S. really tell us about Mexico? The answer to this question, in turn, resides within a set of theoretical ideas linking perceptions of others to identity (personal, cultural, national), nationalism, and public policy: the essence of the second research question.

Question 2: How do Mexican images of the U.S. contribute to identity and perceptions of the national interest?

Like the opening research question, this query lends itself to more specific variations. How are Mexican perceptions of the U.S. related to perceptions of the nation and culture? Do Mexican perceptions of the U.S. in some way relate to and define what Samuel Ramos once called the country's inferiority complex,[18] or what Octavio Paz portrays as the people's deep-rooted sense of solitude,[19] or perhaps even Mexican *machismo*? How important is anti-Americanism in confirming Mexicanness? Is it possible for a Mexican not to be anti-American and yet still consider her- or himself or be considered by others as a pronationalist? Put differently, to what extent do Mexicans see the two in strictly oppositional terms? Or is anti-Americanism not the opposite of pro-Mexicanism, but rather the flip side of a desire to imitate the U.S.? To what extent do Mexicans associate the U.S. with modernity or differentiate between the two? What connotations dangle from the term "Americanization"? To what degree do these images of the U.S. determine views regarding the national interest or the role of the State? In what ways and contexts is the U.S. considered a threat and what interests or objectives are expendable to counter the threat? Questions such as these are rooted in theories tying perceptions of others to culture, national identity, and policy, concerns that take us into the realm of nationalism.

The themes of national identity and nationalism have enjoyed substantial attention over the years from anthropologists, historians, literary analysts, political scientists, psychologists, and sociologists. While many emphasize endogenous variables, such as language, ethnicity, culture, or political ideology, in anchoring and defining a national community,[20] others highlight difference—and the discourse on difference—in forging the nation, a people's sense of belonging, and their culture.[21] According to Edward Said, "All societies acquire their identities through juxtaposition to another: an alien, a foreigner, or an enemy."[22] In fact, "identity is what 'differs,' i.e., those symbolic marks that a person constructs to delineate differences from the 'others.'"[23] Jorge Castañeda echoes the point: "Belonging is intimately tied to nonbelonging: there is no national consciousness without the identification of 'another' that is characterized by its alien qualities or exclusion."[24] Even culture, according to Arjun Appadurai, is considered "less a property of individuals and groups and more a heuristic resource that we can use to talk about differences."[25]

Linking perceptions of others to national identity or culture—difference over essence—is of relatively recent vintage and it still seems to dance outside the main hall in disciplines like political science. But tying one's perceptions of others to behavior, specifically public policy behavior, is neither new, nor particularly unorthodox. Stereotype theory in psychology dates back to the early decades of the twentieth century. It holds that people utilize codes to understand and interpret others and that such codes in turn influence people's reactions to others.[26] Even within the field of international relations, image theory builds on the basic assumption that personal and national perceptions of others shape foreign policy behavior.[27] As Kenneth Boulding notes, "It is what we think the world is like, not what it is really like, that determines our behavior."[28] This view not only underpins international relations research on the Cold and Vietnam Wars, but is actually shared by postmodernist studies that root the behavior of the imperialist powers on their Manichean (ideologically crafted stereotypical) perceptions of self (civilized) and others (barbarians).[29] This premise also underlies recent analyses of U.S. Latin American policy.[30] And while such studies focus on foreign policy behavior, there is no reason to believe that such perceptions do not also affect domestic policy. After all, a key part of domestic politics is the intense competition to "appropriate the national identity dynamic."[31] Consequently, perceiving or casting a neighbor as hostile or friendly, weak or powerful, straightforward or hypocritical can be instrumental in determining a wide range of domestic policies, from policies seeking to define and strengthen national culture to the repression of certain domestic groups and outright authoritarianism.

While national identity and policy can be easily tied to perceptions of others, crucial conceptual gaps still remain. One (national identity) refers to sentiments, the other (policy) to behavior; one (national identity) to the populace, the other (policy) to the State. I will use the concept of "national interest" to bridge these lacunae. As used here, "national interest" builds on past treatments of nationalism as a political doctrine stressing that: (1) a unique people or nation exists (often in a primordial sense), (2) its interests take precedence over all others, (3) an independent State is needed to promote and protect those interests, and (4) these principles are universal.[32] But the nationalist doctrine is incomplete. Though it holds that a State should be independent to protect the interests of the nation, it says little about what those interests are, what specifically the State should do on behalf of the nation, or what might be considered acceptable trade-offs in its pursuit of that objective. In short, the nationalist doctrine enshrines national interest, but does not define it. This distinction is crucial since societies do not confront a decision over whether or not to cede national sovereignty, but how much, in what ways, and in what areas? Consequently, the idea of national interest is used to refer to the ongoing discourse or debate to define the nation's interests, to define the threats to the nation, and to determine what should be done to protect or promote the nation's interests (policy preferences). Given the contradictory nature of nationalism—in which "people paradoxically attempt both to become modern and to defend themselves against modernity"—national interest is employed here to refer to the space where ideas, interpretations, and images, all flowing from and sustaining the sentiments of belonging, struggle to negotiate the paradoxes.[33] In the end, national interest refers to that component of nationalism relating to the "imagined community's" discursive struggle to define "legitimacy."[34] National interest is tied, on the one hand, to national identity since it flows from the sense of belonging, and to policy, on the other hand, by representing the preferences for State activity.

As indicated, the current study borrows from the vast literature on nationalism, differentiates national identity, national interest, and policy, and ties all three to perceptions of self and others. But up to this point, little has been said about the question of causality. Of particular theoretical importance is whether national identity (sentiment) shapes national interests (preferences) and policy (State behavior) or the other way around. There is substantial disagreement on this point. The primordialist view tends to emphasize the role of national identity in shaping ideology (national interest) and State policies.[35] It stresses the fact that a sense of "we" must precede the demands for a State to represent "we the people" or pursue policies to "our" benefit. The instrumentalist view, by contrast, underscores the role of the State in constructing a people's sense of identity and their perceptions of the nation's interests.[36] In the case of Mexico, for example, this widely held view holds that the nationalistic ideology of the Mexican Revolution, including its anti-American strands, represents merely a political device: what Peter Calvert calls a "camouflage for the real powers and forces within."[37]

Given the intensity of the primordialist versus instrumentalist debate, it is important to begin from the assumption that though all three variables (national identity, national interest, and policies) are linked theoretically to perceptions of the "other," the causal linkages are neither straightforward nor unidirectional. This study thus assumes a mutual cause-and-effect relationship with sentiments (through perceptions of the national interest) influencing State policy just as the State (through education, etc.) influences national identity. This therefore leaves the causality question aside, at least for now. Images of others can still play a role in shaping policy (primordialist view) just as the smoke screen (instrumentalist view) cast by the elite can influence political culture.

Couched within this nationalist framework, to reiterate, Mexican perceptions of the U.S. are considered important factors shaping Mexican national identity, the debates over national interest, and public policy. As upcoming chapters will show, Mexican identity, the essence of being Mexican, has often been defined and crafted by traits that serve to distinguish it from the U.S. Similarly, the public debate over Mexican policies has long pivoted upon particular perceptions of or assumptions made regarding the U.S, particularly in terms of its potential to help or to harm the nation. As Octavio Paz puts it, "The question about us is always revealed as a question about them."[38]

Question 3: Are Mexican perceptions of the U.S. changing? And, if so, how do such changes affect perceptions of self, nation, and policy?

Mexico, particularly in its relationship to the U.S., has undergone significant changes since the mid-eighties. Briefly, three closely interwoven changes should be noted. First, the degree of Mexico-U.S. integration has expanded, magnifying the depth of U.S. penetration into Mexican society. On the economic front, Mexican trade with the U.S. climbed from about 18% of Mexico's GDP in 1985 to almost 47% by 1999 (see figure 1.1).[39] During the eighties, the ratio of exports to output in manufacturing jumped from just 3.9% to 23.9%, with over 85% of that servicing the U.S. market.[40] With over 75% of this trade in intermediate goods, most of the bilateral trade is intra-industry and about 40% of it is intrafirm trade, reflecting the sizable U.S. investments in the auto, computer, and pharmaceutical industries, and integrated production schemes.[41] The explosive growth in the *maquiladora*

Figure 1.1.   Mexico-U.S. Economic Integration since 1980

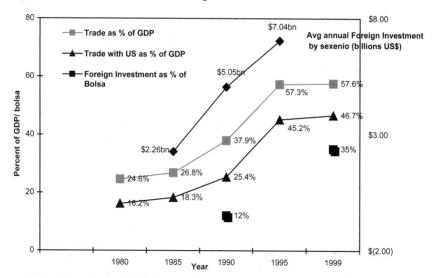

Sources: Bulmer-Thomas (1994); Heyman (1999; 18, 173); IMF Direction of Trade Yearbooks (various years).

industry illustrates this tightly woven pattern. From 12 plants and 3,000 workers in 1965 (roughly 0.008% of the population) and just 130,973 workers (0.01% of the population) in 535 plants in 1982, the *maquiladora* sector grew to employ 1.2 million workers in 3,465 plants by the year 2000 (1.2% of the population).[42] Though as of 1997 just 37% of *maquiladora* plants were wholly U.S.-owned, all remain intimately tied to the U.S. through their reliance on U.S. inputs, production for the U.S. market, or contractual agreements with U.S. firms.[43]

Foreign investment in Mexico, particularly that coming from the U.S., has also grown during this period. From $8.6 billion under President José López Portillo (1976–1982) and $13.6 billion under Miguel de la Madrid (1982–1988), foreign direct investment (FDI) grew to $30.3 billion and $44.4 billion under Carlos Salinas (1988–1994) and Ernesto Zedillo (1994–2000), with roughly 65% of that coming from the U.S. From 1970 to 1990 alone, foreign investment as a proportion of GDP increased from 12% to 32%.[44] While most of the capital has gone into manufacturing, feeding the dramatic growth in integrative production and trade noted above, a large portion has also fed an increase in the number of U.S. franchises, like McDonald's, Burger King, Domino's Pizza, and Mail Boxes Etc., that now dot the Mexican urban and suburban landscape. Indeed, by the end of the twentieth century, Mexico represented the largest market for U.S. franchises.[45] So while investments in manufacturing are turning parts of Mexico into "America's" new industrial belt, the explosion of franchises could be seen as transforming urban space, enhancing the resemblance between Mexican and U.S. cities. Portfolio investments and foreign loans, also predominantly from the U.S., have similarly increased, capturing an ever-increasing portion of the market and the economy. In 1990, foreign investment accounted for just 12% of market capitalization in the Mexican *bolsa*, equaling about 1.7% of GDP; by 1998 it had grown to 35% of the market and 8.5% of GDP.[46] Mexico's foreign debt, about 65–70% of which is held by U.S. banks, also climbed from 17.5% of GDP in 1970 to 57.9% in 1995, before falling to 42.3% in 1998.[47]

The scope and extent of Mexico-U.S. integration by century's end reaches well beyond the easily quantifiable economic realm, however, to encompass social, cultural, and political dimensions. Based on U.S. census figures, the number of Mexican-born residents in the U.S. as a percentage of the total Mexican population jumped from 6.3% in 1970 to 14.2% in 1990, a figure that does not include the estimated 2 million Mexicans residing "illegally."[48] The Gallup-Mexico poll of 1998 found that 60% of the Mexican urban public had relatives in the U.S., 25% had traveled to the U.S., and 45% had met and spoken with at least one North American (see chapter 8). In 1999, Mexicans working in the U.S. transferred an estimated $5.9 billion to relatives back home, tying millions more Mexicans to the U.S.[49] In the same year, U.S. citizens spent $7.6 billion shopping in Mexico, while Mexicans forked out $4.5 billion doing likewise in the U.S., making the U.S.-Mexico border clearly the most porous border in the world.[50] Even within Mexico the degree of integration (or U.S. penetration)—and hence familiarity—has been enhanced in recent years by the spread of cable and satellite television stations, videos exhibiting U.S. programs and movies, the Internet, and U.S.-produced motion pictures. According to Javier Flores, Monterrey now has the highest level of satellite dish ownership per capita in the world, with most devices pulling in U.S. programs.[51] Meanwhile, millions across the country flock to see U.S. movies, which account for over 70% of box-office receipts and over 80% of video rentals.[52] That the country's top-grossing films as of 1999— "Titanic," "Tarzan," "Godzilla," "Star Wars: Episode I"—were all U.S. productions is no surprise.[53]

   Political and social interactions linking Mexican and U.S. governmental and nongovernmental organizations have also skyrocketed in recent years. "Compared to where U.S.-Mexico civil society relations stood a decade ago, there is no question that a wide range of networks, coalitions and alliances have emerged that would once have been hard to imagine."[54] The range and degree of collaboration among social organizations on both sides of the border are impressive. This includes a wide range of state-to-state linkages in virtually every area of the government, including NAFTA institutions, and meetings by parliamentarians and regional governors. In contrast to past decades, truly binational and trinational (along with Canada) institutions now exist. They encompass links between Mexican civil society and the U.S. government such as AID, NED, and the Inter-American Foundation programs supporting electoral observation, community-based projects and organizations, and environmental causes. Collaboration also features links between the Mexican State and U.S. civil society. These range from electoral campaigns in the U.S. to extensive lobbying efforts and programs targeted at the Mexican Diaspora. Finally, many civil society linkages have emerged, ranging from religious institutions and private foundations to media, environmental, and women's organizations, labor unions, and so on. Indeed, "the past decade witnessed an upsurge of binational civil society discussion, beginning before the NAFTA debate but then rapidly expanding."[55]

   Besides increasing levels of integration, a second change involves shifts in State policy and the accompanying political rhetoric. In contrast to the nationalistic, State-oriented policies of prior decades, governments since the early 1980s (Miguel De la Madrid 1982–1988, Carlos Salinas 1988–1994, Ernesto Zedillo 1994–2000, and Vicente Fox 2000–2006) have substantially reduced or eliminated tariffs, scrapped industrial policies, lifted restrictions on foreign investments and technology transfers, and ended preferential treatment of national businesses and the domestic market. Capped by Mexico's entrance into GATT (now the WTO) in 1986 and the trilateral NAFTA in 1994, tariffs and other restrictions on trade and foreign investment have been reduced to almost nothing, giving Mexico one of the most open economies in the world. Though some restrictions remain (e.g., foreign ownership of television and radio stations, and the petroleum sector), foreigners can now own 100% of a business in most sectors of the economy. They are no longer required to use local inputs in the production process and are essentially free to import technology, including foreign brand names. Even in the cultural realm, recent governments have diluted the State's ability to define and shape national identity by reducing or eliminating scores of programs and regulations relating to control of language, education, the media, and consumption. Salinas, for example, ended quotas on the importation of books in Spanish. He removed the stipulation under the *Ley de la Industria Cinematografica* that required theaters to devote 50% of screen time to Mexican movies. He altered the *Ley de Fomento para la Proteccion de la Propiedad Intelectual* to pave the way for the proliferation of U.S. franchises. He eased restrictions on foreign participation in radio and television and passed reforms that broadened the role of the Church, the private sector, and even foreigners in education.[56]

Recent governments have also shifted the nation's foreign policy away from one stressing independence vis-à-vis the U.S. to one based more on cooperation and collaboration. In contrast to earlier decades, the Mexican government now accepts an array of U.S. programs of assistance, including military training programs and foreign election observers. And through NAFTA, the government actually has given both the U.S. and Canada certain authority to at least evaluate whether Mexico abides by its own domestic laws. Such policies, which have paved the way for the heightened U.S. economic penetration or integration noted earlier, do have their limits, to be sure, as evidenced by the Mexican government's criticism of U.S. policy toward Cuba and its opposition to the Iraq war.[57] Overall, Mexico's relationship with the U.S. is closer than at perhaps any period in the history of the two nations.

Certainly the State has altered its rhetoric in conjunction with these policy shifts. In contrast to the nationalistic "metanarrative" of the Mexican Revolution that long provided answers to questions about the nature of being Mexican, the identity and interests of the nation, and the traits and motives of others,[58] the nation's political leaders since the eighties have played down nationalistic goals and means, sung the praises of the neoliberal ideology championed by the U.S., and touted economic integration with the U.S. as the yellow brick road to development and modernization. In a phrase, the ruling elite began to view the U.S. as the solution to Mexico's problems rather than the cause of those problems. From "Poor Mexico" the new version seemed to be "Fortunate Mexico . . . So close to the United States." Indeed, most analysts tend to characterize recent policy shifts as dramatic departures from the past. Jorge Chabat, for instance, refers to a "radical redefinition of Mexico's traditional understanding of national sovereignty" under Salinas.[59] Historian Lorenzo Meyer similarly labels the new policies *"un viraje histórico."*[60] Rodolfo de la Garza dramatizes the shift even more by noting that under Salinas "nationalism and sovereignty were redefined so that the United States became an ally rather than the enemy."[61]

The third and final trend sweeping Mexico in recent years represents in some ways the sum of these two forces: fundamental shifts in the relative strength and influence of the various actors determining Mexican political culture. Consistent with the neoliberal ideology, there has been a decline in the role and capacity of the State as an agent capable of influencing the meaning of national identity and national interest—or, stated differently, of offering a "hegemonic" discourse—and a corresponding increase in the influence of the private sector, the media, and private consumption.[62] Widespread privatization and deregulation of State enterprises have shifted many of the State's powers to shape national identity and determine perceptions of the national interest to the private sector, just as the spread of multinational (predominantly U.S.) entities throughout the country has enhanced the reach and potential influence of those expressing a discourse on the U.S. and the nation contrary to the views once embraced by the Revolutionary State or even Mexicans themselves. Though the State continues to be an important player in forging political culture, the sources of nationalism are today rooted much more in society than they were in the past.

These changes underpin the third research query, giving rise to a variety of more specific questions. To what extent does this heightened integration alter Mexican perceptions of the U.S.? Do Mexicans believe that the increased U.S. penetration into Mexican society is promoting an American "way of life" and values to the detriment of Mexican values?[63] And if so, is that a matter of great concern? To what extent are increasing person-to-person, organization-to-organization exchanges altering previous images of the "other" and "nation," contributing to broader mutual understanding? According to Keck and Sikkink, broadening cross-cultural exchanges and experiences can lead to the creation of "a common frame of meaning."[64] Is this occurring or are these changes, perhaps, feeding what Jurgen Habermas calls a "crisis of identity"? In terms of policy, what discursive devices have leaders used to explain the new policies and their turn from the past? To what degree have they truly distanced themselves from the "traditional" (past) views on the U.S., national identity, and the national interest? Has the State lost what little control it once had over the culture, national identity, or perceptions of the U.S.? Or is the State's new discourse effectively altering perceptions of self and other? Is the once seemingly homogenous Mexican culture and identity, held together perhaps by the State's hegemonic discourse, a thing of the past, transformed into a pluralistic culture that is increasingly decentered and detached from the national territory? To what extent is NAFTA, to borrow from García Canclini, "accelerating Mexico's process of reorientation in relation to both North America and Latin America?"[65] Do Mexicans, for instance, share Samuel Huntington's assessment of NAFTA as representing Mexico's attempt to become a North American country rather than a Latin American one?[66]

Questions such as these are intensely debated throughout Mexico. And while it would be impossible to fully explore the competing views here, suffice it to say that there is little agreement or consensus.[67] Generally, three camps can be identified. The first contends that the recent changes are eroding Mexican culture, identity, and economic or political sovereignty. Proponents warn of the loss of culture and tradition, Americanization, the *maquiladorization* of the economy, and political subordination of the country to U.S. interests.[68] Even the relatively pro-U.S. National Action Party (PAN) highlighted "the risk of losing values of *mexicanidad*" in its 1994 presidential platform.[69] A second perspective takes the opposite view: rather than weakening national identity, greater contact has actually strengthened it, giving it new outlets of expression, even to the point of reinforcing traditional Mexican values and anti-American sentiments. In some cases this position attaches to the view that integration is actually going both ways, providing fresh opportunities for the expression of Mexican identity, including its cultural penetration of U.S. society. North Americans, after all, are said to spend more on *salsa* these days than ketchup. In other cases, those supporting this conclusion emphasize the fact that integration not only enhances contact, but also magnifies the asymmetries, thereby polarizing perceptions of the "other" and bolstering the sense of nation and the need to defend one's interests.[70] Accordingly, the increasing contact actually strengthens rather than weakens national identity. A third group positions itself somewhere between these two extremes. Like the first camp, it agrees that recent changes are changing Mexican nationalism and sentiments toward the U.S., but sees these changes as contained or natural, and essentially nonthreatening. The political elite, for example, argue that the effects of NAFTA are limited solely to the economic sphere and thus in no way threaten Mexican culture or identity—a view often echoed by the U.S. media and government officials. Others, like Carlos Monsiváis, stress the idea that culture and identity inevitably change and modernize and that languishing over the loss of traditional Mexican values because of heightened integration with the U.S. is futile. Mexico is today more amorphous and variable than in the past, a representation of postnationalist culture.

But while the changes in Mexico mapped out here are clearly dramatic, fathering intense debate and sustaining the current inquiry, it is important to step back and ask how significant these recent changes truly are. How dramatic a departure is the current period from the past? Looking back further in time than we did earlier shows that the extent and even direction of these recent changes may be somewhat exaggerated. The current period, in short, is not the only period featuring intense Mexican-U.S. integration, policies of collaboration, or intense national debate over their impact. A brief historical detour is thus important in helping to place the current trends in broader context, and important to help locate historic foundations of Mexico's debates over its national interests. Cue the flashback.

A Brief Historical Detour

From almost the beginning, Mexico has lived in the shadow of a country larger, richer, more powerful, and fundamentally different from itself (Mexico was larger until 1848).[71] This geographic reality has fed an ongoing national debate over how to handle the U.S. At the time of national independence, Mexican leaders were strongly concerned about U.S. domination and erected stiff trade barriers to keep the U.S. at bay. And yet just a few decades later the government embraced trade and cooperation with the U.S. and abolished many of those barriers out of a concern for progress.[72] This policy of openness and collaboration reached its ultimate fruition during the dictatorship of Porfirio Díaz (the *Porfiriato*) when the regime, though tentatively at first, gradually strengthened the nation's economic ties to the U.S.[73] As Davids notes, "By 1884, Díaz had come to the realization that cooperation with the United States, and the entrance of foreign capital into the country would contribute to the increase of wealth and the development of Mexico."[74] In addition to a new tariff law in 1887 that gave special advantage to frontier trade with the U.S., the government also made numerous concessions to American investors, particularly in rail, banking, mining, land, and oil, and even passed a colonization law to encourage U.S. development of Mexican territory.[75] As a result, exports to the U.S. in 1887 reached a record level of $20.3 million, roughly equal to total trade in 1876: a growth comparable to the 1982–1995 period.[76] And though early prospects of developing railroads had been retarded by the fear of "Yankee influence," the Mexican minister in the U.S. believed that "both countries would benefit by being connected by a railroad."[77] U.S. companies thus built most Mexican railroads, holding 80% of Mexico's railroad stock by 1902.[78] Díaz also encouraged U.S. companies in mining. From 40 concessions in 1884, U.S. mining operations grew to over 13,000 by 1904. According to historian John Mason Hart, by the end of the Porfiriato U.S. companies held 81% of the industry's total capital.[79] One report dated 1912 shows the value of U.S.-owned mines and smelters at $249 million compared to just $14.5 million for Mexican-owned mines.[80] In banking as well, by 1900 U.S. capital owned controlling interest in three of the largest banks in Mexico. The U.S. also owned huge tracts of Mexican land, over 100 million acres, "more than 22 percent of Mexico's land surface."[81] By 1910, American investors also held 46% of the foreign capital in agricultural companies.[82] As Davids notes, "Within a short period of time, Mexico was invaded by a number of American ranchmen, planters, land speculators, and small farmers. [By 1910, the U.S. owned] a considerable portion of Mexican land. Sisal, coffee, Tabasco, tobacco, chicle plantations, cotton gins, timber lands, numerous farms, ranches and cattle in Mexico were all owned completely by Americans. . . . The discovery of Mexico's oil deposits climaxed the American economic invasion of the country."[83] Indeed, the situation was such that by 1910, as cited in the introduction, "the prediction that Mexico would be acquired by the gradual process of Americanization through the immigration of colonists and capital, slowly neared completion."[84]

Many opposed these moves of course. Even Díaz was labeled xenophobic and anti-imperialistic in the early days.[85] Others remained so. Commenting on the proposed commercial reciprocity treaty and a treaty of alliance with the U.S. in the 1880's, for example, the press "feared that the United States had something up its sleeve" and claimed that the proposed treaty of alliance "aimed at establishing an American protectorate over Mexico with the ultimate aim of annexation."[86] The Mexican Congress was also hostile to U.S. advancement. Chamber of Deputy Alfren Chavero in 1878, for instance, quipped, "Border nations are natural enemies. . . . They may appear to be very friendly in their relations, because one fears the power of the other on account of its superior diplomacy or it peculiar policy; but . . . naturally, in conformity with the laws of history, border nations are enemies."[87] Indeed, throughout the early Díaz period, opposition in the Mexican Congress to U.S. economic penetration was so intense that it often voided concessions granted by the Díaz administration. "The Mexican Congress declared that the country must be free from being made a colony or kind of dependency of the United States . . . which . . . would cause only the scorn and indignation of future generations."[88] Even key advisors within the regime grew concerned about the level of U.S. influence. Noting the "tremendous growth of economic power of Americans in Mexico," Minister Limantour convinced the president to adopt a more restrictive railroad policy, which between 1902 and 1909 led to a policy of converting a large part of railroads to national control.[89] Díaz also encouraged British capital as a means to check the influence of the U.S. companies. According to one observer, "President Díaz became very concerned at the rapidly increasing power of the American oil companies."[90]

The conviction that "President Díaz and his administration had sold out the country to the Americans" forever wedded anti-Americanism with political opposition to the Díaz regime.[91] Hart characterizes U.S. penetration during the period as a key factor in the Revolution, particularly in offending the national pride of the *pequeña* bourgeoisie.[92] Initially, this perception set the stage for a series of anti-American incidents during the Revolution, while U.S. intervention (backing counterrevolutionary Victoriana Huerta in 1913, the occupation of Veracruz in 1914, and General Pershing's pursuit of Francisco Villa in 1917–1918) fanned the flames of the nation's sentiments. According to Mexican historian Daniel Cosio Villegas, U.S. treatment of Mexico prior to and during the Revolution fundamentally altered the relationship: "The United States lost something much more important and more permanent than the expansion of its economic interests and its political influence: it lost the admiration and the trust of the Mexicans . . . [the U.S. obtained] economic preponderance at the price of losing esteem and admiration."[93] Such sentiments thus set the stage for post-Revolutionary regimes to embrace a different perspective and policy approach toward the U.S. and to incorporate anti-Americanism into the official Revolutionary ideology.

Reversing the Díaz policy, the post-Revolutionary elite pursued a more nationalistic program designed specifically to protect the nation against foreign economic interests (read the U.S.), while privileging the interests of Mexican workers and peasants.[94] The 1917 Constitution and the statutes of the *Partido Nacional Revolucionario* (PNR—the forerunner of the PRI) both explicitly made economic nationalism a guiding principle of the nation.[95] During the 1930s, the regime "featured policies that were hostile to foreigners and culminated in the nationalization of foreign oil companies in 1938."[96] Arguing that the oil companies were not benefiting the nation, President Lázaro Cárdenas touted nationalization as involving the "very sovereignty of the nation."[97] He nationalized not only oil, but also the railroads, and created a State-owned electric company.

On the cultural level as well, the new elite sought to create and use State power to give meaning to "being Mexican," a phase President Calles once called the psychological revolution.[98] Governments of the time refashioned and redeployed the policies designed to curb the influence of the Church, and through education and public art programs, they enshrined *mestizaje* as the racial ideal of the nation. At the same time, the regime glorified the nation's Indian roots while converting the real-life indigenous into cultural "Mexicans." The State, in short, defined the Mexican culturally as "a moral Mestizo" and socially as a worker or peasant, while all the time casting itself (the State) as the great protector.[99] Fundamental to this ideological campaign was to depict the U.S. as culturally different, distant, and essentially a danger to the interests of the nation: a danger that could only be tamed through national unity and a strong State.

Yet by the end of the Cárdenas period, public policy again shifted, this time subtly to include more open discussions with the U.S. in response to the global war. This produced an "era of good feelings" under President Avila Camacho and U.S. President Franklin Roosevelt that wrought the 1941 General Agreement ending claims going back to the Revolution: a move that "swept old issues away at one grand stroke—or so it seemed."[100] The era also witnessed the 1942 Trade Treaty that lowered duties on a list of manufactured items entering Mexico from the U.S. and gave Mexican goods similar treatment going north. Accordingly, Mexico intensified its production of primary materials for the war effort and obtained machinery from the U.S. in return as North American technicians and experts "swarmed into Mexico."[101] As a result, trade and dependence between the two skyrocketed, with 87.8% of Mexican exports going to and 86.4% of imports coming from the U.S.: a level, again, comparable to and even surpassing the figures of recent years.[102] The two even signed an agreement for Mexico to supply the U.S. with labor—the *bracero* program—providing many Mexicans with jobs and firsthand contact with the U.S. The two nations even cooperated on the military front through the Mexican-North American Joint Defense Committee.[103] Even in the realm of culture, according to Rafael Segovia, the government modulated its rhetorical tune, playing down both class conflict and its openly hostile opposition to the U.S.[104]

Most perceived the moment as unique. During his first *Informe*, for example, President Miguel Alemán stated: "Never have our relations with the North American Union reached the broad cordiality of which the presidential visits were public testimony," a description that would seem equally appropriate coming from Salinas or Zedillo.[105] Even attacks on the U.S. in the "radical Mexican press became muted [and finally] disappeared during the era of Good Feelings."[106] Indeed, Howard Cline sums up the relationship during this period in terms reminiscent of the both the *Porfiriato* and the present: "Mexico and the United States are interacting more vigorously, more extensively, and more intensely than at any earlier time. Contacts between the republics, 'international relations,' have multiplied. The deep reservoir of good will that has been thus accumulated displaces many of the hidden resentments, which formerly poked above the surface to founder the unwary."[107]

The conclusion of the global war and the outbreak of the Cold War, however, brought a return to some of the more "traditional" policies of distance. Mexico, for instance, refused to sign a military assistance program (MAP) agreement with the U.S., refused to participate in "*misiones de defensa del hemisferio occidental*," and refused to break relations with Cuba.[108] Meanwhile, efforts to extend and revise the wartime trade treaty died. By now, Mexicans were complaining that the U.S. drive for free trade "is merely a device to increase its markets at the expense of local Mexican industry that has developed since the war."[109] In contrast to the previous epoch, the government thus erected a series of tariff barriers and related policies as part of a broader strategy of import substitution industrialization. Though the regime began in the postwar period "to seek foreign capital aggressively" for the purpose of development, it nonetheless returned to a policy of protecting sovereignty and limiting the scope and influence of foreign investment. In fact Weinert describes Mexico's stance as "one of the most aggressively nationalistic policies toward foreign capital."[110] This was coupled with tax policy and jawboning to encourage foreign investors to partner with Mexican firms. By the 1960s, discriminatory taxation favored companies with majority Mexican ownership and selective granting of tax exemptions. By the early 1970s, the government sported a trade-licensing regime covering over 8,000 items, severely limiting foreign trade.[111] Further strengthening policies favoring Mexican companies, President Echeverría instituted the so-called Mexicanization law in 1973, requiring 51% national ownership of new companies and creating the National Commission on Foreign Investment to approve or reject foreign investment. Mexico also took the lead during the period in promoting the New International Economic Order (NIEO), in signing international agreements, and in embracing policies designed to lessen its trade dependence on the U.S.[112]

But even within this context, the ebbs and flows of policy toward the U.S. are striking. For instance, stressing economic development as the primary objective of the Revolution, President López Mateos in the late 1950s and early 1960s sought to strengthen Mexico's "special relationship" with the U.S.[113] Ant yet the pendulum moved back a few years later under Luis Echeverría (1970–1976), who, doubting "the suitability of concentrating on the bilateral relationship with the United States, discredited the idea that Mexico could obtain advantages from a 'special relationship.' "[114] Later, in contrast to the nationalistic policies of Echeverría, President López Portillo (1976–1982) embraced a more conciliatory approach, "a new government attitude toward national and foreign businessmen."[115] He decreased the nation's enthusiasm for the "Third World" approach and sought to "establish a climate of harmonious relations with the U.S."[116] But when newfound oil wealth wrought a new emphasis on export promotion and selective import substitution, López Portillo maintained or rediscovered the desire to diversify "away from Mexico's traditionally high dependence on the United States."[117]

Figure 1.2 attempts to capture and depict some of these historic trends. Perhaps most strikingly, it shows that foreign investment—the biggest proportion of which has long come from the U.S.—equaled 155% of GDP in 1900 and 183% by 1913, levels far greater than those of today. It also indicates that while trade as a proportion of the economy has remained somewhat consistent through the years, the proportion of total trade with the U.S. has not. During the war years, 87.8% of Mexican exports went to and 86.4% of imports came from the U.S., a level, again, comparable to and even surpassing the figures of today. Trade with the U.S. subsequently fell to the 50–60% range in the ensuing decades of import substitution before climbing once again in the current period. In terms of people, the proportion of the total population living in the border states has increased substantially over the years (indicating the growing importance of the U.S. and increased contact), but it did not increase markedly during the 1980–1990 period. Similarly, despite the increases in absolute and relative numbers of Mexicans living in the U.S., the number of undocumented persons apprehended as a percentage of the Mexican population has remained somewhat stable, from 1.9% in 1951 to 1.1% in 1964 and 1.2% in 1990. Even remittances of workers in the *bracero* program from 1954 to 1964, when measured as a percentage of GDP, are not different from the estimated remittances of the early or late 1990s (estimated as 1.13% to 1.5%).[118]

Besides the ebbs and flows in the nature of Mexico-U.S. integration and the policy debates over how to deal with the U.S., another relevant historical factor in the relationship centers on the asymmetries separating the two countries. Above and beyond the level of contact, part of the real or imagined U.S. dominance over Mexico reflects the relative size and strength of the country. But to what extent have these changed in recent years, feeding perhaps new images of the U.S.? Figure 1.3 shows Mexico's size and dependence relative to the U.S. over the century. As it indicates, the relative size of the U.S. in terms of population has fallen considerably over the years, such that today Mexico's population has grown to roughly a third of that of the U.S. Yet in terms of the size of the economy, the level of development as measured by GDP per capita, and even the level of mutual dependence as measured by

Figure 1.2. Historical Trends in Mexico-U.S. Integration

Sources: Bulmer-Thomas (1994); Inter-American Development Bank (1974); IMF Direction of Trade Year-books; UN (1959).

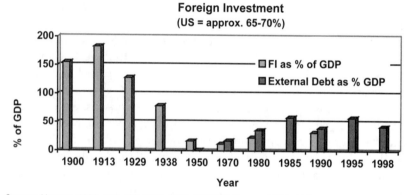

Sources: Heyman (1999; 110); IDB (1974; 1990; 1998/99); Twomey (1998: 188).

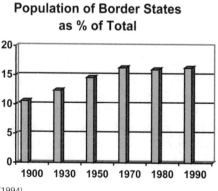

Source: Pick and Butler (1994)

Chapter 1

Figure 1.3. Asymmetries Mexico-U.S.

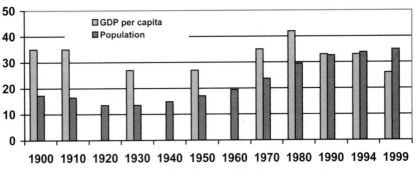

Sources: New York Times 1998 Almanac; Pick and Butler (1994: 24); www.geographic.org.

trade dependence, the relative weight of Mexico vis-à-vis the U.S. has remained about the same or fallen. By the 1990s, the Mexican economy was smaller and its level of development lower relative to the U.S. compared to the beginning of the twentieth century. And its relative level of dependence was greater than at any time in the past.

This brief historical detour is important for three reasons. First, the trends demonstrate that Mexican policies toward the U.S. have not been consistent, and that Mexico's pattern of integration with or penetration by the U.S. has not been linear. Past periods of close collaboration, despite predictions at the time, eventually eased or faded rather than flourished. This suggests the possibility of inherent limits in the nature of any policy approach. This is important given the difficulties many see today in reversing the current policies or the pattern of integration. Second and closely related to this conclusion, the historic evidence suggests that periods of closeness and collaboration, despite predictions of historic breaks, have never truly eliminated deep sentiments or images of the U.S. In fact, the sentiments rooted in the past—as expressed through the policy debates—seem to recrystallize at various periods of time, becoming the source of political mobilization. This raises the question, if closer contact in the past did not effectively and fundamentally alter Mexican perceptions of the U.S., why should it do so today? Finally, the evidence shows that despite the current political interpretations, the new policies toward the U.S. and the national debate over Mexico's position vis-à-vis the U.S. are really not all that new, but rather rooted in Mexican history. This is important since, as we see in chapter 2, the discourse regarding policy approaches toward the U.S. and the nation by proponents and opponents of the current policies draws on and echoes many of these historical themes. In other words, current policy debates parallel those of the past.

But despite this important historic caveat, recent changes nonetheless remain significant, driving home the third research question plotted here: how have Mexican images of the U.S., national identity, and perceptions of the national interest changed in recent years? In many ways, this third research question represents the most compelling, certainly the most timely, of the three guiding questions; and yet it builds on the other two since it would be impossible to answer the question of change without a clear understanding of the overall nature of Mexican images of the U.S. or the linkages to perceptions of nation and national interest.

Significance of the Study: The Broader Context

So far we have reviewed the three guiding research questions. To complete this overview it is important now to ground these questions in a broader framework by addressing the issue of theoretical relevance. Exploring Mexican images of the U.S. in the current period is important at three distinct levels. First, addressing these questions should help contribute to a better understanding of the dynamics of Mexican society and politics. In so many ways, Mexico is changing, contesting views of the past and our understanding of its society. And though Mexicans have a rich and long history of debating the nature of the nation and national identity, the challenges of today seem to give that debate new meaning and urgency. How people negotiate, respond to, and influence the rapid changes of today and tomorrow depends in many ways on what it means to be Mexican, whether one or many Mexicos do or can (co)exist, whether Mexico coincides with a specific territory, and what interests the Mexican State is expected to protect or support. At heart, all political debates and struggles pivot on competing perceptions of the nation and the national interest. Or, is the concept of the nation itself becoming obsolete in Mexico?

In addition to understanding the dynamics of the world's largest Spanish-speaking country, an exploration of these questions also contributes to a better understanding of Mexico-U.S. relations. Mexico's importance to the U.S. is undeniable. It is the U.S.' second-largest trading partner, arguably the country with the greatest impact on domestic issues like drugs, immigration, and economic prosperity, and the "homeland" to a growing portion of the U.S. population. Most studies of Mexico-U.S. relations, of course, concentrate on direct U.S. influence, the countries' cultural, economic, or political ties, or inter-State relations. By contrast, the current study tries to take a broader view, concentrating more on the indirect influence that occurs through the Mexican psyche. By exploring how Mexican perceptions of the U.S.—as Mexico's predominant other—might be changing and how these changes may be reconstructing Mexico's sense of who it is and what it aspires to be or not to be, the current study addresses the context within which the international and intercultural relationship unfolds. Arguably, the future of NAFTA or the course of Mexico-U.S. integration rests more on how, within a historically informed and nationally charged context, trends are perceived rather than the actual operation of binational institutions or the economic ups and downs.

Finally, in addition to Mexico and Mexico-U.S. relations, the suppositions and questions posed here stand atop a much broader theoretical concern relating to globalization and nationalism. García Canclini makes the immediate link: "Understanding globalization requires . . . an exploration of how the images in Latin America of Europe and the United States are changing . . . what stories about the others persist (obstructing new opportunities of integration) . . . and which new ones are being formed by recent migratory, commercial, and tourist interchanges."[119] With one seemingly steeped in the past and the other in the future, nationalism and globalization have become the two most important phenomena of our times. Many see twenty-first-century globalization—defined by Anthony Giddens as "the intensification of worldwide social relations which link distant localities in such a way that local happenings are shaped by events occurring many miles away and vice versa"—as fundamentally contesting the foundations of nineteenth-century nationalism, stripping the nation of much of its meaning and the State of much of its function.[120] To date, globalization *cum* economic integration has rendered almost meaningless the idea of a "national" product, while forcing the State to relinquish layers upon layers of sovereignty in order to enjoy the fruits of the global economy.[121] In some areas, the State seems to acknowledge the "benefits" of ceding sovereignty, like the economic benefits of signing NAFTA; but in other areas, the State seems to simply recognize the "futility" of using its power to try to dam the tide. To paraphrase Eric Hobsbawm, nationalism has failed "because economic and political transformations have made it obsolete."[122] At the same time, globalization *cum* advances in communications and the spread of multinational cultural industries has fundamentally altered the basic idea of the nation in a cultural sense. Many see these trends as weakening territorial-based restrictions, rendering meaningless territorial-based thinking, while at the same time fostering a universal culture.

But questions regarding the impact of globalization are many. Rather than forging a universal culture, for instance, some see globalization as synonymous with the spread of American influence (Americanization), or as simply the cultural expression of late capitalism.[123] Still others, like Michael Featherstone and García Canclini, see globalization as creating hybrid, postmodernist cultures by providing new outlets for the expression of the subaltern.[124] Fredric Jameson captures this difference when he asks whether globalization is "a matter of transnational domination and uniformity or, on the other hand, the source of the liberation of local culture from hidebound State and national forms."[125] This latter view emphasizes that communities, defined by interactive communication patterns and a shared identity, are no longer restricted to a common physical space. Indeed, individuals within a diaspora today can easily maintain contact with loved ones "back home," read the newspaper from "home" via the Internet, purchase products from "home," watch movies and television programs from "home" via satellite, and travel relatively cheaply to and fro, thus creating and reinforcing their cultural identity rather than replacing it with another. By the same token, of course, "nationals" can partake of the same technological devices to become part of a "nonnational" community, reading "foreign" papers, watching "foreign" movies, and listening to "foreign" music, thus creating a new identity that replaces the old. In the end, both forces allow individuals to form more complex identities partially delinked from territory and the State. Again Jameson recognizes these dual patterns within the cultural belly of globalization, concluding with how one can envision "the worldwide Americanization or standardization of culture, the destruction of local differences" or the inverse.[126]

Many, however, question the nature of globalization's impact. They stress the view that, paraphrasing Mark Twain, tales of nationalism's death are premature. Not only is globalization unable to fill the vacuum created by the weakening of nationalism because of the basic human need for identity and a feeling of belonging,[127] but opposition to globalization's assault on the nation and the State is strong, deep, and wide. Rather than burying nationalism and national culture, the record shows globalization at times stirring it, re-creating it, and reinforcing it, triggering renewed ethnic political movements and violence, and even horror stories of a coming "Clash of Civilizations."[128] The fact that the benefits of globalization have remained highly concentrated, or that national-based perceptions of "us" and "them" resist change, may be reinforcing this tendency.[129]

The importance of nationalism and globalization today is matched only by the relevance of the Mexican case in shedding some light on both. Indeed, few countries embody the themes of nationalism and globalization, hegemony and counterhegemony, dominance and subalternity like Mexico. For good or ill, Mexico lives in the shadow of the most powerful country on earth, a country considered by most to be the main architect of globalization and whose culture is often confused or conflated as universal. Mexico is the only developing country to enter into a free trade agreement with a developed one, and the only country to partner up with a country so different from itself culturally, economically, and politically. At the same time, Mexico also suffers (or enjoys) a degree of dependence on—or interdependence with, or penetration by—an outside power (the U.S.) that remains virtually unmatched in the world—all unmistakable signs of globalization. And yet, Mexico's history features the loss of more territory to a foreign invader (the U.S.) than any other nation in history, repeated interventions and humiliations at the hands of its powerful neighbor (the U.S.), and a strident nationalism and sense of national unity imbued with what many have considered a "paradigmatic" "anti-Americanism."[130]

Methodological Approach

Prior to exploring Mexican images, certain additional methodological points should be addressed. Like the theoretical focus, the methodological strategy used here is somewhat eclectic. The major tool is discourse analysis. This imitates similar studies on images of self and others.[131] Stuart Hall defines discourse as "a particular way of representing—a particular kind of knowledge about a topic."[132] Analyzing discourse on the nation thus entails a type of qualitative content analysis wherein one seeks to uncover the definitions, descriptions, and narrative linkages employed by the speakers themselves to describe and explain a given situation: to unearth the meanings of the nation contained in the "stories which are told about it, memories which connect its present with its past, and images which are constructed of it."[133] Discourse analysis is the primary method used here to assess the images expressed by the politicians, the school texts, the cartoons, the writings of the intellectuals, and the movies. More traditional, orthodox empirical methods are used to analyze the consumer market and public opinion. Analysis of marketing trends relies on empirical data measuring consumption patterns, while the chapter on public opinion draws on survey data.

In addition to blending these research methods, this study also combines original research with interpretation and synthesis. Part of the purpose of this study is to bring together the various dimensions of Mexican images of the U.S., some of which have been explored and presented by others, as noted at the outset. Though all research draws on secondary materials to some extent, chapters here on the political elite, the intellectual elite, the textbooks, and the cartoons build primarily on original research, while those pertaining to marketing, the movies, and to a lesser extent public opinion, center on a review and interpretation of existing research. The chapter on public opinion includes a combination of the review of previous surveys, the reanalysis of the data from prior polls, and data from one original regional survey conducted early on during the research process.

Each chapter strives to address each of the three research questions, though I am unable to address all three equally or as systematically as one might hope. (To reiterate, they are: (1) How do Mexicans view the U.S.? (2) How do perceptions of the U.S. shape perceptions of the nation? and (3) Are Mexican perceptions of the U.S. and the nation changing?) The first two questions are invariably linked since it is difficult to locate Mexican images of the "other" without finding parallel and related references to self or nation. In many cases, the images of other and self are explored simultaneously. The question of change, however, presents a particular methodological challenge that is addressed in part by combining primary and secondary source materials. Relying on one opinion poll, for example, cannot truly address the question of change, so the only way to gauge change in this area is to compare results from a series of polls taken at different points in time. Though this approach raises problems about sampling differences, it nonetheless provides some insight regarding possible changes in public opinion. My review of Mexican school texts also exemplifies this approach. My original research centers on the analysis of Mexican texts produced since the 1960s; but by comparing the results to Vázquez's comprehensive review of texts dating back to the nineteenth century, it is possible to assess the nature of change over the years. Still, not all chapters are able to address each question equally or as systematically as one might hope. Discourse analysis, for instance, brings into better focus the complex relationships between images of the other and nation than, say, surveys, which tend to be more superficial. In the area of marketing as well, few studies on Mexican perceptions of U.S. products were conducted prior to the 1980s, complicating the analysis of long-term change in that area.

Both the research questions and the sources consulted relate to very general periods of time and in many cases no effort is made to truly differentiate the temporal component. This complicates the look at change since no clear benchmark period is ever identified. Instead, the search is for general trends suggesting change from the past. In exploring textbooks, for instance, I draw on texts covering a relatively broad period dating as far back as 1960 and treat all as part of a collection of "contemporary" texts. This approach is taken in other areas as well in an effort to characterize contemporary images. To explore the issue of change, this image is then compared to clearly historical texts or references. In some ways, this approach may seem somewhat ahistoric since the specific historic context is really never taken into account. Like other areas of interest, however, understanding how the historic situation influences images of the U.S. is largely beyond the scope of the study.

Since each chapter looks at a distinct social context or the images of the U.S. as presented by different social agents, and since no attempt is being made here to privilege one view over another, the chapters are in many ways independent one from the other. This means that the order of the presentation is somewhat arbitrary, though it does progress from State-based agents (political discourse, textbooks) to intellectuals and popular culture (cartoons, writings of the intellectual elite, movies) and ends with the public (consumption and public opinion). The reader is welcome to jump around or follow some other logic-imposed progression, however. Following the presentations of each substantive area, the concluding chapter seeks to summarize the findings, highlight areas of agreement and disagreement among the various dimensions, and draw out the broader implications.

Finally, it is important to reiterate that there are many questions and nuances that are not addressed here and are considered beyond the scope of this study. With some very minor exceptions, I do not explore the reasons why Mexicans view the U.S. or the nation in a particular way. By the same token, even if perceptions of self and other are different today than in the past, I make no systematic effort to explain the changes or link them to historic contexts. The study, as noted, focuses on images arising or expressed within specific contexts, leaving out many others that could be selected, including U.S. sources that may influence Mexican perceptions and opinion. Even so, no effort is made to determine which contexts are the most influential or authentic.

Conclusion

This introductory chapter poses the major research questions, highlights their theoretical roots and relevance, and thus provides the framework for the current study. To recap, each of the succeeding chapters draws on primary and secondary materials to explore within different social contexts: (1) Mexican images of the U.S., (2) their links to perceptions of the nation and the national interest, and (3) changes in these that might reflect or inform recent transformations in the country. The analytical journey begins by focusing on the political discourse.

Notes

1. Octavio Paz, *Labyrinth of Solitude and Other Essays* (New York: Grove Press, 1985), 385.

2. Barbara Carol Gorka, *Images of the United States in the Literature of Octavio Paz, Carlos Fuentes, and Jose Emilio Pacheco* (Ph.D. diss., University of Pennsylvania, 1993), 8.

3. Richard S. Weinert, "Foreign Capital in Mexico," *Proceedings of The Academy of Political Science* 34 (1) (1981): 115; Nestor García Canclini, *Consumidores y Ciudadanos: Conflictos multiculturales de la globalización* (Mexico City: Grijalbo, 1995), 137.

4. Jules Davids, *American Political and Economic Penetration of Mexico, 1877–1920* (New York: Arno Press, 1976), 190.

5. Julia Tuñón, "Una Mirada al vecino. Estadounidenses de celuloide en el cine mexicana de la edad de oro," in *México Estados Unidos: Encuentros y desencuentros en el cine*, edited by Ignacio Duran, Iván Trujillo, and Monica Verea (Mexico City: Imcine, 1996), 106.

6. Mario Ojeda, *Alcances y limites de la política exterior de México* (Mexico City: El Colegio de México, 1976), 87.

7. Carlos Monsiváis, *Los rituales del caos* (Mexico City: Procuraduría Federal del Consumidor y Ediciones Era, 1995), 25–30.

8. Ojeda, *Alcances y limites*, 87.

9. Paul Hollander, *Anti-Americanism: Critiques at Home and Abroad, 1965–1990* (New York: Oxford University Press, 1992).

10. Boye Lafayette de Mente, *NTC's Dictionary of Mexican Cultural Code Words* (Lincolnwood, IL.: NTC Publishing Group, 1996), 122–24.

11. See Ralph L. Beals, "The Mexican Student Views the United States," *Annals of the Academy of Political and Social Science* 295 (1954): 108–15; Charles Davis, "Mass Support for Regional Integration," *Mexican Studies/Estudios Mexicanos* 14 (1) (1998): 105–30; Hollander, *Anti-Americanism*; Norman J. Humphrey, "The Mexican Image of Americans," *The Annals of the American Academy of Political and Social Sciences* 295 (1954): 116–25; Ronald F. Inglehart, Neil Nevitte, and Miguel Basañez, *The North American Trajectory: Cultural, Economic, and Political Ties among the United States, Canada, and Mexico* (New York: Aldine de Gruyter, 1996).

12. See Gene Z. Hanrahan, ed. *¡Abajo el Gringo! Anti-American Sentiment during the Mexican Revolution* (Salisbury, NC: Documentary Publications, 1982); Alice H. Coote, *The Images of the Good Neighbor: The Mexican view of the United States as seen in selected Mexican newspapers and periodicals, 1940–1962* (Masters thesis, University of Maryland, 1962); John C. Merrill, *Gringo: The American as Seen by Mexican Journalists* (Gainesville: University of Florida Press, 1963); Américo Paredes, "The Anglo-American in Mexican Folklore," in *New Voices in American Studies*, edited by Ray B. Browne, Donald M. Winkelman, and Allen Hayman (Lafayette, IN.: Purdue University Studies, 1966), 113–28; Jorge Bustamante, "Identidad nacional en la frontera norte: hallazgos preliminares," in *Impacts regionales de las relaciones economicas Méx-ico–Estados Unidos*, edited by A. Carona Renteria (Mexico City: El Colegio de Méx-ico, 1984), "Frontera México-Estados Unidos. Reflexiones para un Marco Teórico," in *Decadencia y auge de las identidades*, edited by José Manuel Valenzuela Arce (Tijuana: El Colegio de la Frontera Norte, 1992), and "The Mexico-U.S. Border: A Line

of Paradox," in *Identities in North America: The Search for Community*, edited by
Robert L. Earle and John D. Wirth (Stanford, CA.: Stanford University Press, 1995),
180–94; Pablo Sergio Vila, *Everyday Life, Culture and Identity on the Mexican-American Border: The Ciudad Juarez-El Paso Case* (Ph.D. diss.: University of Texas at Austin, 1994); David Edward Wilt, *Stereotype Images of United States Citizens in Mexican
Cinema, 1930–1990*, (Ph.D. diss.: University of Maryland, College Park, 1991); Dennis Gilbert, "Rewriting History: Salinas, Zedillo, and the 1992 Textbook Controversy," paper presented at the XIX Congress of the Latin American Studies
Association, Washington, D.C., September 28–30, 1995, subsequently published in
Mexican Studies/Estudios Mexicanos 13 (2) (1997): 271–98; and Josefina Vázquez de
Knauth, *Nacionalismo y Educacion en Mexico* (Mexico City: El Colegio de México,
1975).

    13. See, for instance, Roger Bartra, "Culture and Political Power in Mexico,"
Latin American Perspectives 16 (2) (1989): 61–69, and *The Cage of Melancholy: Identity and Metamorphosis in the Mexican Character* (New Brunswick, NJ: Rutgers University Press, 1992); Agustin F. Basave Benitez, *México Mestizo: Análisis del
nacionalismo mexicano en torno a la mestizofília de Andrés Molina Enríquez* (Mexico
City: Fondo de Cultural Económica, 1992); Ilan Bizberg, ed. *México ante el fin de la
Guerra Fría* (Mexico City: El Colegio de México, 1998); David Brading, *Los orígenes
del nacionalismo mexicano* (Mexico City: Ediciones Era, 1980); Rodolfo O. de la Garza
and Jesus Velasco, ed. *Bridging the Border: Transforming Mexico-U.S. Relations* (New
York: Rowman and Littlefield, 1998); John Mason Hart, *Revolutionary Mexico: The
Coming and Process of the Mexican Revolution* (Berkeley: University of California
Press, 1989); Alan Knight, "Peasants into Patriots: Thoughts on the Making of the
Mexican Nation," *Mexican Studies/Estudios Mexicanos* 10 (1) (1994): 135–61, and
"Popular Culture and the Revolutionary State in Mexico, 1910–1940," *Hispanic
American Historical Review* 743 (3) (1994): 393–444; Ojeda, *Alcances y limites*; Robert
A. Pastor and Jorge G. Castañeda, *Limits to Friendship: The United States and Mexico*
(New York: Vintage Books, 1989); Samuel Ramos, *Profile of Man and Culture in Mex-
ico* (Austin: University of Texas, 1962); Jaime E. Rodríguez O. and Kathryn Vincent,
*Common Border, Uncommon Paths: Race, Culture, and National Identity in U.S.-Mex-
ican Relations* (Wilmington, DE.: Scholarly Resources, 1997); Henry C. Schmidt, *The
Roots of Lo Mexicano: Self and Society in Mexican Thought, 1900–1934* (College Station: Texas A & M University Press, 1978); Frederick C. Turner, *The Dynamics of
Mexican Nationalism* (Chapel Hill: University of North Carolina Press, 1968); Gustavo Vega, ed. *México–Estados Unidos* (Mexico City: El Colegio de México, 1992).

    14. Vila, *Everyday Life, Culture and Identity*, 4.

    15. García Canclini, *Consumidores y Ciudadanos*, 26.

    16. For a glimpse into this debate see William H. Beezley, Cheryl English Martin,
and William E. French, eds. *Rituals of Rule, Rituals of Resistance* (Wilmington, DE:
Scholarly Resources, 1994); Knight, "Peasants into Patriots," and "Popular Culture
and the Revolutionary State."

    17. See Bustamante, "Identidad nacional," "Frontera México-Estados Unidos,"
and "The Mexico-U.S. Border"; and Vila, *Everyday Life, Culture and Identity*.

    18. Ramos, *Profile of Man*.

    19. Paz, *Labyrinth of Solitude*.

    20. On nationalism see Benedict Anderson, *Imagined Communities: Reflections on*

the Origin and Spread of Nationalism (London: Verso, 1991); John Breuilly, *Nationalism and the State* (Chicago, IL: The University of Chicago Press, 1994); Ernest Gellner, *Nations and Nationalism* (Ithaca, NY: Cornell University Press, 1983); Eric J. Hobsbawm, *Nations and Nationalism since 1780: Programme, Myth, Reality* (London: Cambridge University Press, 1990); and Anthony Smith, *National Identity* (Reno: University of Nevada Press, 1993).

21. For postmodern views of nationalism see Arjun Appadurai, "Disjuncture and Difference in the Global Cultural Economy," in *Global Culture: Nationalism, Globalization and Modernity*, edited by Michael Featherstone (London: Sage, 1990), 295–310; Arjun Appadurai, *Modernity at Large: Cultural Dimensions of Globalization* (Minneapolis: University of Minnesota Press, 1996); John Beverley, José Oviedo, and Michael Aronna, eds. *The Postmodernism Debate in Latin America* (Durham, NC: Duke University Press, 1995); M. Boroujerdi, *Iranian Intellectuals and the West: The Tormented Triumph of Nativism* (New York: Syracuse University Press, 1996); Mike Featherstone, *Global Culture: Nationalism, Globalization and Modernity* (London: Sage, 1990); David C. Gordon, *Images of the West: Third World Perspectives* (New York: Rowman and Littlefield, 1989); Ernesto Laclau, ed. *The Making of Political Identities* (London: Verso, 1994); Jan Nederveen Pieterse and Bhikhu Parekh, "Shifting Imaginaries: Decolonization, International Decolonization, Postcoloniality," in *The Decolonization of Imagination: Culture, Knowledge, and Power*, edited by Pieterse and Parekh (Atlantic Highlands, NJ: Zed Books, 1995), 1–20; Sarah Radcliffe and Sallie Westwood, *Remaking the Nation: Place, Identity and Politics in Latin America* (London: Routledge, 1996); Edward Said, *Orientalism* (London: Routledge, 1978), and *Culture and Imperialism* (New York: Alfred A. Knopf, 1993); Vila, *Everyday Life, Culture and Identity*; and Kathryn Woodward, ed. *Identity and Difference* (London: Sage, 1997).

22. Cited in Boroujerdi, *Iranian Intellectuals and the West*, 6.

23. Vila, *Everyday Life, Culture and Identity*, 3.

24. Jorge G. Castañeda, *Utopia Unarmed: The Latin American Left After the Cold War* (New York: Alfred A. Knopf, 1993), 284.

25. Appadurai, *Modernity at Large*, 12–13.

26. Walter Lippmann, *Public Opinion* (New York: Hartcourt, Brace and Company, 1922), 89–90, cited in William Buchanan, "How Others See Us," *The Annals of the American Academy of Political and Social Science* 295 (1954): 2.

27. See William Bloom, *Personal Identity, National Identity and International Relations* (London: Cambridge University Press, 1990).

28. Kenneth Boulding, "National Images and International Systems," in *International Politics and Foreign Policy: A Reader in Research and Theory*, edited by James N. Rosenau (New York: The Free Press, 1969), 423.

29. For an overview of research in international relations using this approach see Michael P. Sullivan, *International Relations: Theories and Evidence* (Englewood Cliffs, NJ: Prentice Hall, 1976). For examples of research from the postmodernist perspective see Gordon, *Images of the West*; and Said, *Orientalism*, and *Culture and Imperialism*.

30. Mark T. Berger, *Under Northern Eyes: Latin American Studies and U.S. Hegemony in the Americas, 1898–1990* (Bloomington: Indiana University Press, 1995); Eldon Kenworthy, *America/Americas: Myth in the Making of U.S. Policy toward*

Latin America (University Park: Pennsylvania State University Press, 1995); James William Park, *Latin American Underdevelopment: A History of Perspectives in the United States, 1870–1965* (Baton Rouge: Louisiana State University Press, 1995); and Fredrick B. Pike, *The United States and Latin America: Myths and Stereotypes of Civilization and Nature* (Austin: University of Texas Press, 1992).

31. Bloom, *Personal Identity*, 81.

32. Breuilly, *Nationalism and the State*, 2; Smith, *National Identity*, 19.

33. Gregory Jusdanis, "Beyond National Culture?" *Boundary 2* 22 (1) (1995): 42.

34. Stephen D. Morris, "Reforming the Nation: Mexican Nationalism in Context," *Journal of Latin American Studies* 31 (2) (1999): 363–97.

35. See, for example, Smith, *National Identity*.

36. See, for example, Breuilly, *Nationalism and the State*; and Hobsbawm, *Nations and Nationalism since 1780*.

37. Peter Calvert, *The Mexican Revolution, 1910–1914: The Diplomacy of the Anglo-American Conflict* (London: Cambridge University Press, 1968), 67; Bartra, "Culture and Political Power in Mexico" and *The Cage of Melancholy* also present this view.

38. Cited in Gorka, *Images of the United States*, 53.

39. *Country Profile Mexico* (London: Economist Intelligence Unit, 2000).

40. Manuel Pastor and Carol Wise, "State Policy, Distribution and Neoliberal Reform in Mexico," *Journal of Latin American Studies* 29 (1997): 419–56.

41. Sidney Weintraub, "Mexico's Foreign Economic Policy: From Admiration to Disappointment," in *Changing Structure of Mexico*, edited by Laura Randall (New York: M. E. Sharpe, 1996), 50.

42. Van R. Whiting, Jr., "Markets and Bargains: Foreign Investment and Development Strategies in Mexico," in *Mexico's Economic Crisis: Challenges and Opportunities*, edited by Donald L. Wyman (Center for US-Mexican Studies, University of California, San Diego, 1983), 57–78. INEGI figures reported in *Público* (Guadalajara, Mexico), June 26, 2000.

43. *El Mercado de Valores*, Mexico, July–August 1997.

44. Michael J. Twomey, "Patterns of Foreign Investment in Latin America in the Twentieth Century," in *Latin America and the World Economy since 1800*, edited by John H. Coatsworth and Alan M. Taylor (Cambridge, MA: Harvard University, David Rockefeller Center for Latin American Studies, 1998), 188.

45. "Comidas Rapidas," *US/Latin Trade*, October, 1993.

46. Timothy Heyman, *Mexico for the Global Investor: Emerging Markets Theory and Practice* (Mexico City: Editorial Milenio, 1999), 18, 173.

47. Heyman, *Mexico for the Global Investor*, 110; Inter-American Development Bank, *Economic and Social Progress in Latin America* (Washington, D.C.: Inter-American Development Bank, 1974, 1990), *Facing Up to Inequality in Latin America: Economic and Social Progress in Latin America* (Washington, D.C.: Inter-American Development Bank, 1998/99).

48. U.S. Census Bureau, Department of Commerce [www.census.gov]; Peter Andreas, "U.S.-Mexico: Open Markets, Closed Border," *Foreign Policy* 103 (1996): 51–69.

49. *Link with Mexico* 1 (2) (2000): 23.

50. *Country Profile Mexico.*

51. Javier Flores, *The Industry Sector Analysis: Mexico—Satellite Services* (Washington, D.C.: U.S. State Department, 01/95, 1995).

52. García Canclini, *Consumidores y Ciudadanos*, 136. See also "Reel Renaissance," *Business Mexico,* April 2000.

53. "Life comes back into Mexican Video Market," *Screen Digest,* November 1999, 284.

54. Jonathan Fox, "Assessing Binational Civil Society Coalitions: Lessons from the Mexico-US Experience," paper presented at Latin American Studies Association Congress, Miami, Florida, March 16–18, 2000, 1.

55. Fox, "Assessing," 4.

56. Rafael Tóvar y de Teresa, *Modernización y política cultural: Una visión de la modernización de México* (México: Fondo de Cultura Económica, 1994); Mauricio de Maria y Campos, "Las industrias culturales y de entretenimiento en el marco de las negociaciones del tratado de libre comercia," in *La educación y la cultura ante el Tratado de Libre Comercio*, edited by Gilberto Guevara Niebla and Nestor García Canclini (Mexico City: Nueva Imagen, 1992), 279; and Luis González Sousa, *Soberanía Herida: México-Estados Unidos en la hora de la globalización.* Tomo 2 (Mexico City: Nuestro Tiempo, 1994).

57. The current study was completed prior to the 2003 Iraq war so it is not incorporated into the discussion of political issues in chapter 2. Numerous polls showed the Mexican public in strong opposition to the war. The Mexican government, enjoying a seat on the U.N. Security Council for the first time in its history, similarly opposed the U.S. action though Fox did attempt to soften his opposition. The lack of support, however, probably costs the Fox administration the immigration reform it had sought from the Bush administration.

58. Andrian A. Bantjes, "Burning Saints, Molding Minds: Iconoclasm, Civic Ritual, and the Failed Cultural Revolution," in *Rituals of Rule, Rituals of Resistance*, 261–84; Bartra, "Culture and Political Power in Mexico"; Marjorie J. Becker, "Black and White and Color: *Cardenismo* and the Search for a Campesino Ideology," in *Constructing Culture and Power in Latin America*, edited by Daniel H. Levine (Ann Arbor: University of Michigan Press, 1993), 155–70; Beezley et al., *Rituals of Rule, Rituals of Resistance*; and Knight, "Peasants into Patriots," and "Popular Culture and the Revolutionary State."

59. Jorge Chabat, "Mexico's Foreign Policy after NAFTA: The Tools of Interdependence," in *Bridging the Border*, edited by de la Garza and Velasco, 37.

60. Lorenzo Meyer, "Las crisis de la elite mexicana y su relación con Estados Unidos. Raíces históricas del tratado de libre comercio," in *México–Estados Unidos*, edited by Gustavo Vega (Mexico City: El Colegio de México, 1992), 73.

61. Rodolfo O. de la Garza, "Foreign Policy Comes Home: The Domestic Consequences of the Program for Mexican Communities Living in Foreign Countries," in *Bridging the Border*, edited by de la Garza and Velasco, 71.

62. Nestor García Canclini, *Culturas Hibridas: Estrategias para Entrar y Salir de la Modernidad* (Mexico City: Grijalbo, 1989), *Consumidores y Ciudadanos,* and *La Globalización Imaginada.*

63. See Jose Carlos Lozano, "Media Reception on the Mexican Border with the

US," in *Mass Media and Free Trade*, edited by Emile G. McAnay and Kenton T. Wilkinson (Austin: University of Texas, 1996), 157–86.

64. Margaret E. Keck and Kathryn Sikkink, *Activists Beyond Borders: Advocacy Networks in International Politics* (Ithaca, NY: Cornell University Press, 1998), cited in Fox, "Assessing Binational Civil Society Coalitions," 5.

65. Nestor García Canclini, "North Americans or Latin Americans? The Redefinition of Mexican Identity and the Free Trade Agreements," in *Mass Media and Free Trade*, edited by McAnay and Wilkinson, 142.

66. Samuel P. Huntington, "The Clash of Civilizations?" *Foreign Affairs*, Summer (1993): 22–49.

67. See, for instance, Roberto Gutiérrez López and José Luis Gutiérrez E., "En torno a la redefinición del nacionalismo mexicano," *Sociología* 8 (21) (1993): 87–101; Alejandra Lajous Vargas, "Mexico: Culture and Identity in the Information Age," in *Identities in North America*, edited by Earle and Wirth, 102–14; Soledad Loaeza, "The Changing Face of Mexican Nationalism," in *The NAFTA Debate: Grappling with Unconventional Trade Issues*, edited by M. Delal Baer and Sidney Weintraub (Boulder, CO: Lynne Rienner, 1994), 145–57; Carlos Monsiváis, "Muerte y resurrección del nacionalismo mexicano," *Nexos* 109 (1987): 13–22; and Juán Manuel Valenzuela Arce, "Las identidades culturales frente al TLC," *Sociología* 8 (21) (1993):103–29.

68. Guillermo Bonfil Batalla, "Dimensiones Culturales del Tratado de Libre Comercio," in *La educación y la cultura ante el Tratado de Libre Comercio*, edited by Guevara Niebla and García Canclini, 168.

69. *Proceso* 915 (1994).

70. Bustamante, "Identidad nacional," "Frontera México-Estados Unidos," and "The Mexico-U.S. Border."

71. On the different paths taken by the two societies since independence see Jaime E. Rodríguez O., ed., *The Independence of Mexico and the Creation of the New Nation* (Los Angeles: University of California, Los Angeles, 1989).

72. Richard J. Salvucci, "Texas, 'Tyrants,' and Trade with Mexico," reprinted in *Latin America and the World Economy: Dependency and Beyond*, edited by Richard J. Salvucci (Lexington, MA: D.C. Heath, 1996).

73. Daniel Cosío Villegas, *The United States versus Porfirio Díaz*. Translated by Nettie Lee Benson (Lincoln: University of Nebraska Press, 1963).

74. Davids, *American Political and Economic Penetration*, 171.

75. See Cosio Villegas, *The United States versus Porfirio Díaz*; Davids, *American Political and Economic Penetration*; and Hart, *Revolutionary Mexico*.

76. Davids, *American Political and Economic Penetration*, 171.

77. Davids, *American Political and Economic Penetration*, 173.

78. Hart, *Revolutionary Mexico*, 134.

79. Hart, *Revolutionary Mexico*, 142.

80. Marvin Bernstein, *The Mexican Mining Industry 1890–1950* (Albany: Suny, 1964), 75, cited in Wilt, *Stereotype Images*, 310.

81. Hart, *Revolutionary Mexico*, 158.

82. Hart, *Revolutionary Mexico*, 159.

83. Davids, *American Political and Economic Penetration*, 187, 189, 199.

84. Davids, *American Political and Economic Penetration*, 190.

85. Cosio Villegas, *The United States versus Porfirio Díaz.*

86. Davids, *American Political and Economic Penetration,* 166–67.

87. Cited in Davids, *American Political and Economic Penetration,* 169.

88. Cited in Davids, *American Political and Economic Penetration,* 176.

89. Davids, *American Political and Economic Penetration,* 180; and Hart, *Revolutionary Mexico,* 139.

90. Davids, *American Political and Economic Penetration,* 197.

91. Davids, *American Political and Economic Penetration,* 224.

92. Hart, *Revolutionary Mexico.*

93. Cosio Villegas, *The United States versus Porfirio Díaz,* 237–38.

94. See Linda B. Hall, *Oil, Banks and Politics: The United States and Postrevolutionary Mexico, 1917–1924* (Austin: University of Texas Press, 1995); and Hart, *Revolutionary Mexico.*

95. Rafael Segovia, "El nacionalismo mexicano: los programas politicos revolucionarios 1929–1964," in *Lecturas de Política Mexicana* (Mexico City: El Colegio de México, 1977), 41.

96. Weinert, "Foreign Capital in Mexico," 116.

97. Howard Cline, *The United States and Mexico* (New York: Atheneum, 1973), 140, 239.

98. Bantjes, "Burning Saints, Molding Minds," 265; María García Castro, "Identidad nacional y nacionalismo en México," *Sociología* 8 (21) (1993): 38.

99. Julie A. Erfani, *The Paradox of the Mexican State: Rereading Sovereignty from Independence to NAFTA* (Boulder, CO: Lynne Rienner, 1995), 43; Lajous, "Mexico: Culture and Identity," 112.

100. Cline, *United States and Mexico,* 248.

101. Cline, *United States and Mexico,* 389, 273.

102. Ojeda, *Alcances y limites,* 26.

103. Cline, *United States and Mexico,* 277.

104. Segovia, "El nacionalismo mexicano."

105. Cited in Cline, *United States and Mexico,* 316.

106. Cline, *United States and Mexico,* 266–67.

107. Cline, *United States and Mexico,* 388.

108. Ojeda, *Alcances y limites,* 57, 58, 52.

109. Cline, *United States and Mexico,* 389.

110. Weinert, "Foreign Capital in Mexico," 115.

111. It is important to note that during much of this time—the period of the Mexican miracle, 1940–1970—there was really no trade-off. Mexico maintained its nationalistic policies, successfully fostering Mexican ownership and a domestic orientation, while receiving substantial foreign investment. According to Weinert ("Foreign Capital in Mexico," 121), "Mexico has both imposed tough restrictions on foreign capital and attracted most of the foreign capital it has desired."

112. Ojeda, *Alcances y limites,* 180, 188–89.

113. Leopoldo Solis, "La política económica y el nacionalismo mexicano," in *Lecturas de Política Mexicana* (Mexico City: El Colegio de México, 1977), 55–75; and Olga Pellicer de Brody, "Viente Años de Política Exterior Mexicana: 1960–1980," *Foro Internacional* 21 (1980): 149–60.

114. Pellicer, "Viente Años," 154.

115. Maria del Rosario Green, "Mexico's Economic Dependence," *Proceedings of the Academy of Political Science*, 34 (1) (1981): 109; and Weinert, "Foreign Capital in Mexico," 121.

116. Pellicer, "Viente Años," 156.

117. Gary Clyde Hufbauer, W. N. Harrell Smith IV, and Frank G. Vukmanic "Bilateral Trade Relations," *Proceedings of The Academy of Political Science*, 34 (1) (1981): 141.

118. Juán Ramón García, *Operation Wetback: The Mass Deportation of Mexican Undocumented Workers in 1954* (Westport, CT: Greenwood Press, 1980), 236; and Peter Andreas, "The Making of Amerexico: (Mis) Handling Illegal Immigration," *World Policy Journal* 11 (2) (1994): 45–56.

119. García Canclini, *Globalización Imaginada*, 33.

120. Anthony Giddens, *The Consequences of Modernity* (Stanford, CA: Stanford University Press, 1990), 64.

121. See Robert J. Holton, *Globalization and the Nation-State* (New York: St. Martin's Press, 1998).

122. Cited in Carlos A. Parodi, "Nationalism and Globalization," paper presented at the meeting of the Latin American Studies Association, Chicago, Ill., September 24–26, 1998: 15.

123. Fredric Jameson, "Notes on Globalization as a Philosophical Issue," in *The Cultures of Globalization*, edited by Fredric Jameson and Masao Miyoshi (Durham, NC: Duke University Press, 1998), 56–57; and Leslie Sklair, "Social Movements and Global Capitalism," in *The Cultures of Globalization*, edited by Jameson and Miyoshi, 291–311.

124. Featherstone, *Global Culture*; and García Canclini, *Culturas Hibridas* and *Consumidores y Ciudadanos*.

125. Fredric Jameson, "Preface," in *The Cultures of Globalization*, edited by Jameson and Miyoshi, xiii.

126. Jameson, "Notes on Globalization."

127. Parodi, "Nationalism and Globalization," 2 makes this point.

128. Huntington, "Clash of Civilizations?"

129. Stuart Hall, "The West and the Rest: Discourse and Power," in *Modernity: An Introduction to Modern Societies*, edited by Stuart Hall, David Held, Don Hubert, and Kenneth Thompson (Cambridge, MA: Blackwell, 1996), 224.

130. Hollander, *Anti-Americanism*.

131. See, for example, Gordon, *Images of the West*; Kenworthy, *America/Americas*; Pike, *United States and Latin America*; and Said, *Orientalism*.

132. Hall, "The West and the Rest," 201.

133. Hall, "The West and the Rest," 213.

2

Gringolandia in the Political Discourse

T‍HE BRIEF HISTORICAL FLASHBACK in chapter 1 indicated how Mexico's approach to the U.S. has varied over the years. Though usually noted for its nationalist, anti-U.S. posture and policies, Mexico has also at certain times and historic contexts embraced policies solidifying and taking advantage of the country's proximity to the U.S. How do contemporary politicians view the U.S. and the nation? To what extent do their views draw on or break with past images?

This chapter explores political discourse to cull contemporary Mexican images of the U.S., related perceptions of nation, the national interest, and policy, and the degree of change in recent years. The chapter begins, however, by setting out a theoretical framework containing two polar narratives on the U.S. and the nation. The framework facilitates comparison of the various contemporary discourses, and of the present with the past. The next section then analyzes statements, speeches, and writings from a small yet diverse set of national political figures. The analysis highlights the way these political actors depict the U.S., how they explain the bilateral relationship, and how they justify their policy prescriptions. The concluding section draws out the similarities and differences among the actors and compares contemporary images to those of the past.

Competing Political Discourses on the U.S. and Nation: A Framework

The U.S. has long been a topic of concern for Mexican policy makers. Both foreign and domestic policy debates—and analyses—contain substantial references to the U.S. Just as Mario Ojeda characterizes Mexican foreign policy as "more a response to the North American [U.S. foreign policy] than an action that comes alive through its own initiative,"[1] Rodolfo de la Garza suggests that cultural policy pivots on the U.S.: "Many if not most of the battles revolutionary leaders waged to create the Mexican nation involved the United States."[2]

History suggests two broad narratives related to the U.S. Each narrative emphasizes a distinct image of the U.S. and a distinct assessment of the relationship, each supports a particular policy approach, and each envisions the State and nation in different ways. One view sees the U.S. as a powerful, interventionist, and anti-Mexican agent and, hence, a threat to the nation's interests. This view emphasizes historic events and the traditionally heavy-handed treatment of the U.S. toward Mexico, frequently offering both as reminders that "the United States is the only enemy that modern Mexico has had."[3] It depicts the U.S. as not only a foreign policy concern, but also as a domestic matter as a challenge to national identity. According to Ojeda, "the massive cultural influence [from the U.S.] has eroded the bases of national identity and set the stage for ideological penetration."[4] Couched within this context of threat, this narrative depicts the relationship as conflict-prone due primarily to the cultural, political, and economic differences separating the two countries. In sum, it portrays Mexico as vulnerable to a country far more powerful than itself. This image, in turn, supports policies that seek to temper U.S. influence by promoting and insuring distance, while demonstrating or strengthening components of the nation and national identity, further sharpening the differences separating the two nations. This includes a foreign policy that asserts Mexican independence vis-à-vis the U.S., an economic policy favoring national over foreign entities and interests, and a cultural policy defending the national culture. Almost by definition, this narrative underscores the need for a strong and activist State charged with protecting and promoting the nation's interest vis-à-vis the powerful U.S.

The counternarrative envisions the U.S. as essentially an opportunity for Mexico. Rather than portraying the U.S. as a danger to its national interests, this approach stresses the advantages of engaging the U.S.: the benefits of proximity. According to this logic, the amenities range from economic prosperity through trade and investment, assistance in the drug war, and even democratization to an enrichment of the national culture. Even statements as to how Mexico implicitly relies on the U.S. as an escape valve to relieve demographic, economic, and political pressures through immigration play on this image of the U.S. as an opportunity: a mechanism to help the nation overcome its internal problems. Rather than portraying the relationship as conflictual, this narrative depicts the relationship as peaceful and cooperative, based on interdependence, mutual benefits, and mutual respect, not dependence. As such, it sees the U.S. "as the central element of the long-term solution of the problems of the stagnation and obsolescence of the Mexican productive apparatus,"[5] or what García Canclini refers to as "the friendly neighborhood under U.S. tutelage."[6] At the same time, this narrative portrays the Mexican nation as relatively strong, particularly in the cultural or nationalist realm, thus making the country less vulnerable to U.S. influence. This view embraces policies of collaboration, economic engagement and integration, and cultural openness. It builds on the (hegemonic) discourse of comparative advantage founded to support the notion that nondiscriminatory (nonnationalistic) policies in the economic and cultural fields promote development. Consequently, it offers an image of a far less activist State, relieved in a sense of the burden of having to mobilize to defend the nation against U.S. influence or to create and assert nationalist identity. Indeed, this view downplays difference. Maria García Castro nicely describes this tendency in the policies marking the end of the twentieth century: "In the last few years the State has begun erasing the nationalist discourse . . . the references of identification that underline our differences with 'the other,' the foreigner."[7]

These competing narratives can be located in most explanations of Mexican policies over the years. The *Porfiriato*, for instance, is often described as a period when the dangers of foreign influence were offset by arguments stressing the economic benefits of allowing foreigners, including the U.S., to control the nation's economic resources. World War II is also depicted as a period of close collaboration and friendship: a time when not only did the government ease up on the anti-American rhetoric, but a time when Mexico enjoyed substantial trade benefits. Yet other events and periods in Mexican history are presented as reactions to U.S. influence. For example, David Brading depicts the intellectual movement underpinning the Revolution as a reaction not only to positivism's denial of national tradition and its privileging of foreign interests, but also as a reaction to the U.S. itself.[8] Knight similarly characterizes the idea of a powerful State during the thirties and forties as one crafted "vis-a-vis the foreigner,"[9] while Ojeda associates Mexican opposition to the OAS in the fifties with the country's concern over U.S. interventionism.[10]

While the two narratives offer mirror images of one another, they are nonetheless linked in three important ways. First, both images and the policies they sustain are embedded within and thus share a nationalist discourse. Regardless of differences in perceptions of or policies toward the U.S., the political elite (and analysts) have long assumed that such a thing as the nation exists. They have privileged the "national interest" as an ultimate good, seen the State's *razon d' etat* as being to protect and promote those interests (sovereignty), employed the oppositional categories that distinguish foreign and domestic realms with national unity a presumption of the former (politics stops at the water's edge), and envisioned foreign relations as primarily a matter of inter-State affairs. Above all, this means that arguments for and against a particular policy—even policies diametrically opposed such as whether to have free trade or not with the U.S., for instance—center on whether the policy can be shown to be in the "national interest" (the point of agreement), not whether such a thing as the nation or the national interest actually exists, or why it may be less important than some other category of interests. In true paradoxical fashion, then, the idea of promoting national sovereignty provided the ultimate justification for post–World War II policies of economic self-determination just as it has done for the postcrisis policies supporting integration with the U.S.[11]

The two views are also connected in a hierarchical arrangement wherein the "U.S. as threat" narrative enjoys a superior position. This relates perhaps more to history than anything else and can best be seen by differences in the treatment of the competing assessments of the relationship. Labeling the relationship as conflictual—thus sustaining policies of distance—is generally seen by the elite as historically consistent, as almost the normal state of affairs. Describing the relationship as harmonious, by contrast, featuring policies of collaboration, is thus presented as a break with the past. Such views consequently carry a heavier burden of justification. Ojeda captures this point, for example, when he describes the agreement over petroleum in the 1920s as a sign of "The *new* style of political relation with the United States based on cooperation [which has relegated] to history the threat of military intervention on their part" (emphasis added).[12] As we see later, Carlos Salinas and Vicente Fox as presidents amply illustrate this tendency, frequently peppering their policy statements and assessments of the relationship with references to historical ruptures and dramatic breakthroughs. How they explain these dramatic departures, as we will see, becomes a further guide to understanding the perceptions of self and other.

Finally, the two discourses are connected in that they seem to define each other's boundaries. On the one hand, a policy of distance and independence rooted in the image of the U.S. as a threat is limited by the inherent dangers of actually triggering U.S. intervention (an internal limit) or of losing the opportunities represented by engagement (an external limit). Both limits check how far the policies of distance can really go, guaranteeing in a sense that they never go "too far." Leopoldo Solis nicely demonstrates the first limit when he argues that the nationalism of the Revolution remained "limited" precisely because it sought to avoid "confrontation with the United States."[13] Meanwhile, Bernardo Mabire points to the second limit: "The anti-

U.S. ingredient in official Mexican nationalism has always been unique more for its ambivalence than its radicalism, perhaps because of the expectation of the Mexican elite to obtain support from the United States . . . has been a recurring phenomenon in the national history."[14] In a similar way, the risks of ceding too much political sovereignty (herein "subordination"), economic sovereignty ("maquiladorization"), or culture and identity ("Americanization"), concerns only meaningful within a nationalist narrative, limit how far the policies of collaboration can go. Here, going "too far" implies a relinquishing of sovereignty, thereby undermining the foundations of the State's legitimacy.

Of course, precise limits or boundaries are contested, and many of the recent policy changes, as we see later, can be characterized as a shifting of these boundaries. Collaboration is limited by the danger of ceding "too much" sovereignty; but how much is "too much" can vary. The issue of free trade provides a good example. Collaboration with the U.S., though it has existed at important periods in the past, never stretched to the level of a free trade agreement until the nineties. President Díaz Ordáz, for instance, despite the nation's close economic ties with the U.S., made it clear in 1967 that Mexico was and should remain a part of Latin America, not "North" America: "The integration of Latin America is, and we should struggle so that it continues to be, an exclusively Latin American process."[15] Fifteen years later, amid deep economic crisis (usually a catalyst to change), President de la Madrid made a similar point, stating in *The Economist* that a free trade zone with the U.S. was not possible because Mexicans were not prepared to surrender their economy and society to U.S. hegemony. As late as mid-1989, even Salinas, the eventual architect of NAFTA, claimed that Mexico did not want to belong to a free trade zone.[16]

One consequence of this linkage is an inherent tension between the two narratives: a tension that often feeds the appearance of policy cycles. Policies of collaboration, in other words, at a particular point in time come to be seen—discursively through the "U.S. as dangerous" discourse—as "too close," thus prompting a policy reversal and the adoption of policies of distance. Policies of distance, likewise, eventually come to be interpreted as a loss of an opportunity or as protecting something (nation) that is not really being threatened, thereby fostering the adoption of policies of collaboration. In broad terms then, just as the collaborationism during the *Porfiriato* gave way to xenophobia following the Revolution, so too did the "excesses" of the Echeverría period—according to Jorge Castañeda, "the Echeverria government decided that its predecessors had gone too far in accommodating the United States"—set the stage for the "excesses" of the Salinas years.[17]

This framework suggests a simple continuum marked by policies of distance (nationalistic) at one end and collaboration (nonnationalistic) on the other. This continuum, in turn, facilitates comparison of policy areas, styles, concerns, and presidential administrations. In terms of policy, for example, most would consider economic policy as historically more collaborationist (less distance-oriented) than foreign policy or cultural policy, both of which have usually stressed distance.[18] As Jorge Bustamante notes, "Facing the impossibility of efficiently confronting the asymmetry of power in like terms, the Mexican State has responded with actions or omissions of a political character."[19] Alan Knight makes a similar point regarding cultural policies: "the Mexican Revolution provided the government with the discursive weapons with which to resist U.S. cultural hegemony, even as U.S. economic hegemony was consolidated."[20] The framework also makes it possible to differentiate rhetoric from reality. The literature on Mexican foreign policy, for example, often draws this basic distinction, noting how the Mexican government has historically employed an anti-American rhetoric rooted in images of the U.S. as dangerous, while simultaneously pursuing policies that ensure closeness and collaboration. Lorenzo Meyer, for example, notes how Presidents Obregón and Calles both used Carranza's nationalistic rhetoric (foreign policy narrative), while pursuing a distinct (less nationalistic) policy in practice.[21] Ojeda also notes how independence vis-à-vis the U.S. is stressed only "at the margins" and not in areas considered critical to the U.S., what he terms "nationalistic intransigence at the margins."[22] The framework also facilitates a comparison or ranking of the perceived levels of U.S. influence or perceptions of threat, which can be phrased as the question, Which is greater: the perceived danger of Americanization, economic *maquiladorization*, or political subordination? Soledad Loaeza offers one response, arguing that "the risk of subordination seems greater than the risk of Americanization."[23] Certainly allowing foreigners [read the U.S.] to run a company invites a different reaction than allowing them to run the schools or the government.

Implicit here is the idea that the policy approaches rooted in the two narratives can and often do coexist even during the same presidential term. So while change from one administration to another may be noticeable, suggesting policy cycles, these shifts are never absolute. It may be somewhat accurate, in other words, to label the Cárdenas and Echeverría periods as basically anti-U.S. (distance) and those of, say, Ruíz Cortines and Salinas as pro-U.S. (collaborationist), but such labels overplay the extent of change and hide the coexistence of the two competing images of the U.S. Indeed, the historical record offers examples of pro-U.S. policies and statements by Cárdenas and Echeverría (i.e., Cárdenas created the free trade zone along the border) and anti-U.S. policies by Ruíz Cortines or Salinas (i.e., the Alvarez Machaín case under Salinas).[24]

Figure 2.1 sketches the two narratives. It attempts to show the components as well as the tension that pulls and connects the two. The model is proposed as a framework to help evaluate contemporary discourse, compare the views of some of the nation's more important leaders, and compare the contemporary debate with the past.

The Contemporary Political Discourse

The current exploration of the contemporary political discourse is based on a review of a sample of writings and speeches by four important political actors: President Carlos Salinas de Gortari (1988–1994); Vicente Fox, governor of Guanajuato (1995–2000) for the center-right PAN, and the first non-PRI president (2000–2006); Cuauhtémoc Cárdenas, cofounder of the center-left PRD, mayor of Mexico City (1997–2000), and three-time presidential candidate; and the EZLN, the guerrilla-political-indigenous organization concentrated in the southern state of Chiapas and led by the enigmatic Sub-

Figure 2.1.   Two Narratives of the U.S. and the Nation

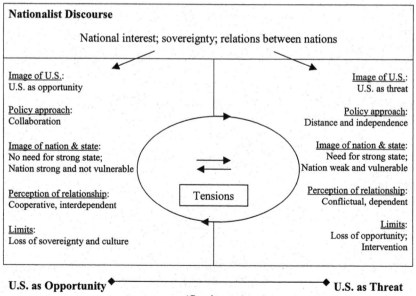

comandante Marcos. Why these individuals? Carlos Salinas was selected because of his role in mapping out a new policy direction and posture toward the U.S. in the early part of the 1990s. Though some of what has been described as a "radical" policy shift began in the mid-1980s—unilateral tariff reductions, entrance into the GATT—Salinas is generally credited as the primary author of these types of changes (he fathered more Constitutional changes than any of his predecessors, for instance). The sample includes the president's annual *informes* (or State of the Union addresses) to the Mexican Congress and people, a speech to the U.S. Congress in 1989, and his address marking the anniversary of the PRI on March 4, 1992 (his famous social liberalism speech), as well as secondary sources analyzing the ideas of Salinas. Here, Salinas's views represent the "official" or PRI-system discourse.

Fox, Cárdenas, and the EZLN, by contrast, were selected because they offer different forms and expressions of a counterhegemonic discourse contesting the State's. Collectively, the arguments of these high-profile actors compete in the public space to offer the nation political meaning, to define the nation, its interests and threats. Analysis of the discourse by Vicente Fox is based on a review of the following speeches and writings offered during his presidential campaign in 2000: *"Propone una Segunda etapa al TLC donde se facilite el libre tránsito de trabajadores"* (*Boletin No. 012/99*) (October 17, 1999); *"Discurso al Instituto Tecnológico Autónomo de México"* (September 22, 1999); *"Discurso a la Federación Nacional de Colegio de Abogados"* (September 29, 1999); *"Discurso durante la celebración de 189 aniversario de la independencia de México, en el Angel"* (September 15, 1999); *"Mensaje despues de ser declarado candidato oficial del PAN"* (September 12, 1999); his book *A Los Pinos: Recuento autobiografico y politico,* and three speeches since becoming president in December of that year.[25] Analysis of the Cárdenas-PRD position is based on an article by Cárdenas in *New Perspectives Quarterly,*[26] his interview with Carlos Gil,[27] a series of speeches reprinted in *Cuauhtémoc Cárdenas: Palabras de Cárdenas,*[28] as well as basic documents and platforms of the party and secondary sources. EZLN documents examined include: *"Chiapas: el Sureste en dos vientos, una tormenta y una profecia"*; *"Composición del EZLN"*; *"Ayuda Militar de EU a México"*; *"México: Entre el Sueño, la Pesadilla y el depertar"*; *"Carta de Marcos sobre el Avance del Ejército Mexicano"*;[29] *The First Declaration from the Lacandon Jungle,* January 1994; *Third Declaration from the Lacandon Jungle,* January 1995; *Fourth Declaration from the Lacandon Jungle,* January 1996; *Fifth Declaration from the Lacandon Jungle,* July 1998; Letter to *Proceso* and others dated March 11, 1995; Letter to *"Encuentro intercontinental por la humanidad y contra el neoliberalismo,"* July 1997, and two letters to the press dated April 9 and 10, 1999. In many cases, these documents were selected based on Kathleen Bruhn's analysis of EZLN political thought.[30]

Carlos Salinas de Gortari

President Salinas's image of the U.S. can be gauged through a series of statements delivered to the Mexican public, the PRI, and even the U.S. While offering a range of statements on the U.S., Salinas generally depicts the U.S. kindly, consistent with the "U.S. as opportunity" narrative noted above. What can be considered terms of admiration punctuate his 1989 address to the U.S. House of Representatives. He alludes here to the "Nation's greatness," which he locates in its "spirit of work and its commitment to freedom." He refers to the U.S. as "the promise that all men in this land are born free and have a right to the pursuit of happiness. In essence," he contends, "it is a premise that has given shape to the American soul. It is the soul of the common people, and therein lies its greatness; of a people that love their rights, and are sensitive to human suffering and to the value of liberty; of an ingenious and creative people who are pioneers in human association and espouse mankind's highest values." In anointing the U.S. with such qualities, he stresses the similarities, not the differences, with the people of Mexico. He does this by suggesting that Mexicans are like-minded and love freedom just as much as the *gringos*.

Not all is admiration, to be sure, even when addressing the *gringos*. During the same speech, for instance, Salinas lashes out against U.S. stereotypes of Mexicans: "Let's get rid of myths: Mexican workers do not push anyone out of a job; they work efficiently and with dignity for wages, in many cases, below the market wage, doing jobs that are not done by American citizens . . . we fail to understand why the 'American dream' must be harsh for the Mexican immigrants who have decided to share it, and why the productive and cultural potential of the ever-growing Mexican-American community is not taken advantage of to benefit the United States and, unquestionably, our bilateral relations." He punctuates this image by employing such terms as "discrimination" and "exploitation."

The *Quinto Informe* also expresses a critical image of some in the U.S., though he does not mention the country by name. Here, Salinas argues that "when voices are being raised in other countries to single out our country's shortcomings [it is] merely reflecting a profound ignorance of our innate vitality." The *Sexto Informe* similarly portrays local political interests in the U.S. who "tend to blame Mexican workers for the evils of the society" as part of a xenophobic campaign. At heart, then, he suggests that at least some in the U.S. do not understand that Mexicans are as freedom-loving and hardworking as they are.

In addition to such periodic statements of praise for the internal strengths of the U.S. or of condemnation of their views and treatment of Mexicans,

Salinas clearly depicts the U.S. as an opportunity for Mexico, downplaying any threat. This view, in turn, sustains a policy approach rooted in collaboration. He refers, for instance, to "the rich opportunities that are offered to find together the paths full of mutual benefit"[31] as well as the need to "stress the similarities."[32] After all, he notes, "The agreements and similarities are much greater than the differences."[33] And despite occasional problems, it is more important to work together for mutual gain: "above [the differences], there exist many similarities to work together."[34] It is clear, furthermore, that by rich opportunities, Salinas essentially means economic ones: "we derive internal economic strength from active participation in the regions that concentrate the dynamic of world growth";[35] "growth requires greater and more secure access to the world's largest market, the United States."[36] Salinas's *Plan Nacional de Desarrollo* makes this privileging of the economic even more explicit by subordinating foreign policy to the role of "support[ing] the economic, political and social development of the country through a better insertion of Mexico [into the world]."[37]

Most importantly, if the U.S. stands as an [economic] opportunity for Mexico, then it is not envisioned by Salinas as a danger to the country. The downplaying of the U.S. threat is conspicuous by both its presence and its absence in the Salinas discourse. The *Segundo Informe* specifies, for example, that the purchase of foreign technology is "no longer" a threat to national sovereignty, but rather a means of strengthening sovereignty. The *Quinto Informe* similarly contends that promoting greater relations with the U.S. actually better defends than weakens Mexico. Consistent with this view, the narrative depicts the relationship as cooperative and respectful, again essentially nonthreatening to Mexico. Salinas praises the cooperative relationship exemplified by the International Water and Boundary Commission and the Bi-National Commission in his *Primer Informe* and on other occasions refers to a relationship based on "respect," "friendship," and "cooperation."[38] In the *Cuarto Informe*, he describes a "climate of *firmeza* and cooperation" wherein the two governments have agreed to conduct the relation "with respect, dignity and friendship." Even in the difficult area of drugs, Salinas states in the *Sexto Informe* that Mexico no longer blames others—the end of "reciprocal recrimination"—but enjoys a "mature and responsible understanding." Clearly, Salinas paints cooperation as the rule and conflict as the exception: "The complex relation with the United States found a constructive and respectful course, thereby preventing differences in particular matters from complicating the broad agenda of cooperation."[39]

Consistent with the narrative described earlier, such "good" relations with the U.S. are defined by Salinas not only in contrast to the "poor" relations of the past, but also as a historic break, as something essentially "new." References are commonly made to the "*new* chapter of respect and friendship in our relations," or the "*new* era of cooperation and friendship."[40] The *Quinto Informe*, for instance, notes how "With the United States we have achieved a climate of intergovernmental cooperation and mutual respect that seeks to *modify* the difficult relations of the past" (emphasis added). The *Sexto Informe* makes a similar though perhaps less direct point: "We have proved that the complex and on occasion historically traumatic relation with the United States can have spaces of respect, cooperation and mutual benefit."

According to the Salinas narrative, this new relationship is distinct from the past in a number of ways: it (the new friendship) "does not attribute the cause of the problems to others"; it entails the end of "reciprocal recrimination"; it features "mature and responsible understanding";[41] and it is "free of myths and prejudices."[42] The use of the powerful term "rapprochement" during his 1989 address to the U.S. House of Representatives to describe the "new era" hints at the magnitude of the change envisioned by Salinas.

Underpinning the portrayals of the relationship as shifting from bad to good are the reasons why relations were bad to begin with. As the previous quotes indicate, Salinas acknowledges that the old relationship was difficult: a situation that stemmed in part from the existence of "myths and prejudices," as noted—a point we will return to in a moment. But in addition to this, Salinas also attributes the poor relations of the past to the very nature of proximity. The *Primer Informe*, for example, refers to "the small and big problems that our neighboring constantly generates." The *Cuarto Informe* cites "the diverse problems generated by our neighboring." And the address to the U.S. House of Representatives posits that "it is natural that differences should exist" in any border situation, "but particularly in this highly dissimilar one." The use of the term "natural" here suggests how Salinas seems to blame a neutral parameter for the poor relations, rather than placing any blame on the U.S. (its arrogance, imperialism, thirst for power, or racism). Of course, any historic blame on the U.S. would weaken the fundamental interpretation that the U.S. does not constitute a threat to Mexico. The use of the term "dissimilar" (rather than unequal) is also interesting in that it implies a fundamental level of equality: a nominal rather than an ordinal difference between the two nations.

As indicated, Salinas clearly acknowledges decisive change in the relationship. Two questions emerge: first, how far does Salinas really go in breaking with the past? And second, how does he present and explain the changes? First, despite the clear policy shifts, Salinas offers both real and rhetorical limits to those changes. Mindful of criticisms of the "U.S. as opportunity" narrative, he stresses that cooperation and a good relationship with the U.S. do not mean that Mexico just blindly imitates the U.S. With a subtle refer-

ence to national identity and independence, the *Quinto Informe* (1993) is
quite clear on this point: "It would be best to recall that we have no desire to
be like others, nor to share their deficiencies. We learn from the world, we
do not imitate it; we want to improve ourselves, not become assimilated."
Nor do good relations imply a full relinquishing of Mexico's autonomy. They
do not extend, for instance, to the level of support for political integration
with the U.S. (and implicitly foreign observers of Mexican elections), a bor-
derless nation, the old bipolar world, unilateral action by the U.S. in the drug
war, foreign military on Mexican soil,[43] or privatization of strategic economic
sectors like petroleum, basic petrochemicals, railroads, or electricity.[44]

Salinas couples such real limits of cooperation with rhetorical limits. He
establishes these by placing his policies upon a nationalist screen, by bowing
to the approaches of the past, and by playing down or disguising the extent
of change. Consistent with the framework noted earlier, Salinas marshals the
supreme values of sovereignty, independence, and the national interest to
judge his approach toward the U.S. In fact, he wraps the entire narrative in
the context of the essential principles of Mexican foreign policy. His *Primer
Informe* explicitly states that the changes (part of, recall, the "new era" of the
relationship) do not represent real changes in "our principles." So while he
praises "interdependence," he also, in the same sentence, ratifies "Our character as a sovereign and independent nation: We open our economy and we
have a universal vocation, but we ratify our profound nationalism. We con-
cede as a supreme value the self-determination of our Fatherland, the invia-
bility of our territory, the respect of our traditions and costumes."[45]
Nationalism also rings clearly as the primary and the unifying theme of the
Tercer Informe, where the term is mentioned 31 times compared to only six
references to the U.S. In providing the context to discuss foreign relations,
his address to the U.S. House of Representatives also opens by stressing
respect for sovereignty: "Mexico, therefore, is loyal to the principles that gov-
ern its coexistence with the rest of the world: Self-determination of peoples
and nonintervention; cooperation and solidarity among nations; peaceful
coexistence for growing development that translates into more and better
freedom, and a better quality of life for all . . . [indeed] true independence
can only take place among independent nations."

In addition to wrapping the policy changes in nationalist banners, Salinas
also at times bows to earlier approaches in an effort to disguise or at least
downplay the extent of the policy somersault. In the *Tercer Informe,* for
instance, he does this by touting closer relations with the U.S. as merely a
part of a much broader pattern of diversification (a historical objective associated with distance vis-à-vis the U.S.): "Our fundamental strategy," he
notes, "has been that of diversifying foreign relations." In fact, before even

mentioning Mexico's relations with the U.S. or NAFTA, Salinas discusses Mexico's less significant ties with other Latin American countries, Europe, the Pacific, and even the nations of the Caribbean. Indeed, despite the centrality of the U.S. to Mexico and NAFTA to the economic reform program, Salinas devotes surprisingly little attention to the new posture toward the U.S.: approximately 16 lines of the 134 devoted to foreign relations. The U.S. is only mentioned six times, as noted, while Latin America is referenced seven times. Even in the *Primer Informe* (1989) Latin America receives 11 mentions (usually in the sense of solidarity or working together) and the U.S. just 6. The *Cuarto Informe* similarly touts "diversification" as the policy goal, and after mentioning progress on NAFTA, it provides a statement on relations with Latin America. It contains four references to Latin America compared to three for the U.S. Two years later in the *Sexto Informe* Salinas alters the approach somewhat, however. No longer does he portray diversification as the broader strategy that *includes* the relationship with the U.S., but as something separate from and a response to it: "When it is decided to have more intense relations with one nation so powerful, it is necessary at the same time to become closer to distant friends. With this strategy we are diversifying our international relations." Nonetheless, the *Sexto Informe* still discusses the nation's relations with Latin America prior to those with the U.S.[46]

Together, these two points (employing nationalist rhetoric and bowing to the principles of the past) echo the findings of Mabire that "The official rhetoric continues insisting, in fact, in the advantages of diversification and does not want to discard other classical themes of the political discourse."[47] This, he concludes, may be due to the need to use traditional means to affirm political legitimacy or the difficulties of filling the vacuum left by the absence of an external enemy: "It is so difficult to fill the gap left by the official disappearance of the external threat, that the diplomatic discourse continues talking—although without the hostility and dispassionately—about diversifying the country's international relations and defending its sovereignty."[48]

So if the nationalist doctrine continues to provide the guiding principles, and, according to Salinas, the principles remain the same, what factors have altered the relationship? What explains this "new chapter"? Indeed, how "new" is it? As noted earlier, the basic hierarchy of the two narratives is such that a policy of collaboration requires justification, much more so than a policy of distance, and Salinas does depict the relationship as a historic rupture. But how does he justify this shift? Generally, Salinas justifies his policy alteration through a two-step process that weaves together a reconstructed view of nationalism with changes that are both global and specific to both countries. First, Salinas contends that what has changed is the means (not the

goals) of achieving the nationalistic objectives. In this subtle reconstruction
of the meaning of nationalism, Salinas embraces a historicist view that differentiates the impulse of nationalism today from that of yesterday: "Historically, the impulse for nationalism has been in response to an external
challenge. Today, that challenge is the risk of being on the outside."[49] As a
result, "Defending Mexico," he contends in the *Quinto Informe*, comes "by
promoting greater relations" and not with "protective barriers, nor . . .
aggressive rhetoric." Under this setting, then, the new challenge of nationalism requires Mexico "to open new and better defined economic ties with the
new poles of world development."[50] The *Tercer Informe* thus defines nationalism itself as variable and changing, and the failure to recognize this change
as the major threat to the nation, not the U.S.: "Nationalist is that which
strengthens the nation, and not the longing for formulas and traits from
other times that in the context of the current world, rather than strengthening the nation, weakens it."[51] Salinas's *Segundo Informe* makes a similar
point: "Sovereignty founded on stagnation, self-marginalized from the international centers of technology and resources, under the ingenuous argument
that these create unfair rules of interchange detrimental to developing countries, is not firm. Sovereignty never meant self-sufficiency or autarky, lack of
influences or of relations."

In the second step, Salinas attributes this fundamental shift in the means
to achieve nationalist goals to a combination of global developments (globalization) and changes in the two countries. The address to the U.S. House of
Representatives, for instance, attributes the "era of new friendship" to
changes sweeping the world, including the technological revolution and the
end of bipolarity. The *Quinto Informe* stresses the fact that "the world has
undergone far-reaching changes, and so has Mexico." Such changes are manifested in a shift from "poor" to "better thinking" on the part of both countries. References cited earlier to the new relationship as one free of "myths
and prejudices" or "mutual recrimination," of course, suggest that the poor
relations in the past were due to the existence of "myths and prejudices" and
that these now have been overcome. When Salinas describes, for example,
the need within the relationship to "recognize dispassionately, objectively,"
he is of course positing that the historical relationship was passionate and
subjective.[52] The *Tercer Informe* also sees changes in both countries. It justifies
closer relations with the U.S. because the U.S. now exhibits an "attitude of
respect" toward Mexico and because Mexico now enjoys a "new disposition,
free of myths and prejudices." Not only does his view illustrate "good thinking," but Salinas also acknowledges, rather paternalistically, how "on occasion, our political and social organizations do not seem to understand this."[53]

Fundamental to this approach then is a narrative that characterizes nationalistic ideas as historical constructs: dependent variables, the meanings of which are shaped by the times. This device accomplishes a number of crucial rhetorical tasks, as the *Tercer Informe* handsomely illustrates. By arguing that a (nationalistic) strategy is appropriate only to a particular time in history ("Every moment of our history needs . . . a response."), Salinas is able to substitute the demands of the current global juncture for those of the past so that the real crux of the argument centers on demonstrating how the times demand the actions he has taken or proposes to take rather than anything related to nationalist ideology per se or historical consistency. This allows Salinas to present change as palpable without necessarily completely denouncing the past. Moreover, by viewing ideas as historical constructs, as the product of the times, this erodes the value of ideals or at least makes them only historically relative. At the same time, this elevates the value of change itself, and makes the current situation (rather than ideals) the determining factor. The hegemonic narrative on globalization readily encompasses these devices. As Salinas posits, "principles have never been a pretext for declining to take a position before the facts."[54] Consequently, it is acceptable to adapt the ideas to the current realities or to "modernize." Prominently placed in this and other presidential addresses, "modernization"—defined by Salinas as "a strategy to change in response to our needs and the rhythm of the beat of the world"—is used repeatedly instead of the word "change" (i.e., to "modernize the armed forces," "modernize education," "modernize relations with the Church," etc.) since it offers an underlying and crucial strand of historical continuity. Salinas thus contends that these changes are nationalist policies for *our moment* (ideas are historically based), nationalist in the *same sense* that other approaches were nationalist for their time and, with certainty, equally decisive for the permanence of Mexico (the new ideas have equal validity to those of the past) (emphasis mine).

Implicit in the narrative is Salinas's underlying image of Mexico. Three strands are noteworthy. First, Salinas depicts Mexico as strong nationally with a great cultural heritage and sense of unity. The *Quinto Informe* notes: "History has taught us to be profoundly zealous of our territorial integrity, of our will to endure as a sovereign nation." This image is also cast in the opening of Salinas's address to the U.S. House of Representatives, where he depicts Mexico as having a long and rich heritage, great "cultural wealth," and a strong nationalism that "cost us the struggle and the blood of generations." Consistent with the model outlined in the opening section, this image anchors the broader discourse by providing a mechanism to downplay the U.S. as a threat to the nation. In other words, the U.S. is not a threat because Mexico is not vulnerable. The *Segundo Informe* (1990) is quite clear on this, referring to the "healthy confidence in the strength and permanence of our culture [and how such cultural strength] gives us every day the security and firmness to cross borders and go out into the world."[55] He also uses this image of a strong nation to denounce the idea that Mexico wishes to imitate or be like the U.S., as noted earlier.[56]

Second, privileging change, Salinas envisions Mexico as "modernizing," by which he seems to mean being able to overcome the ideas of the past. Contesting the popular image of Mexico as a country tied to tradition and the past, Salinas portrays Mexico as no longer influenced by dogmas and sharing a new faith in the future: a new spirit of optimism.[57] Such views fit nicely within the context of Mexico's "new" relationship with the U.S., free from the "myths and prejudices of the past."

A third image regarding the nation relates to migration. Salinas depicts Mexican migrants to the U.S. in highly dignified terms: as individuals seeking employment[58] who "deserve and seek" the well-being that their homeland cannot provide.[59] As such, it is their homeland that has heretofore abandoned them, not the opposite. He does not criticize or condemn the migrants, nor portray them as any less or more Mexican than others. This view, moreover, sets the stage for arguments specifying the State's responsibility to protect the rights of these conationals and to condemn, noted earlier, the violence against them: "Mexico has in effect a broad system of legal protection for the human and labor rights of our nationals that immigrate in search of opportunities for employment. We reject categorically the violent actions that are committed against them."[60]

Taken as a whole, Salinas portrays the U.S. rather kindly, depicting the country as strongly democratic and hard-working, as a potential economic partner, and as nonthreatening to Mexico. He envisions the relationship as cooperative and respectful, and, as such, a distinct break from the past. Though he acknowledges problems and is especially critical of those in the U.S. who discriminate against Mexicans (anti-Mexican image of the U.S.), he nonetheless treats these as essentially secondary. He goes to great lengths to explain the change in approach, and though he drapes the new approach in the nationalistic terms of the past, he reconstructs nationalism for the current, globalist period to mean collaboration, not distance. Within this discourse, Mexico is portrayed as strong culturally, modernizing, and not vulnerable to outside influence.

Vicente Fox

In a series of statements and writings as a presidential candidate and governor of the state of Guanajuato, Vicente Fox, the man who would go on to become the first non-PRI president, offers what can be considered a more limited and pragmatic image of the U.S. His view is limited in part by the absence of many direct references to the U.S., particularly references to the U.S. in any stridently nationalistic context or tone. During his Independence Day speech, for instance, in which he praises Mexican national pride and the nation's history, the U.S.—the "eternal enemy" that in a sense defines Mexican nationalism, according to others—is not even mentioned. During his *Mensaje al ser candidato official del PAN*, the future president similarly makes no mention of the country's relation with the U.S., foreign relations in general, or external threats to the nation. He does refer to the U.S., along with Europe and Canada, to compare and thus demonstrate Mexico's low levels of education and the country's slow economic progress: in macroeconomic terms, he states that Mexico went from 19.2% of the per-capita GDP of the U.S. in 1985 to 9.8% in 1994 (my figures in chapter 1 differ).[61] To an extent, this statement hoists the U.S. up as a benchmark and a country to imitate.

But like the Salinas narrative, the main image of the U.S. contained in the statements by Fox sees the U.S. as a potential partner and an economic opportunity for Mexico: a means to help close the development gap just noted. At one point, for instance, Fox refers "to the enormous potential represented by the closeness to the largest market in the world." He supports taking advantage of this opportunity, which clearly offsets any danger to the *"patria"* posed by the U.S. or by collaboration. To dismiss critics, he reassures them that resources from trade have been channeled into the development of Mexico and that this has been accomplished without having to "lower our pants, or blemish our honor."[62] Fox makes clear this overwhelming vision of "opportunity": "What would others give to sit down . . . with German Volkswagen or U.S. Chrysler to negotiate a billion dollar investment that would create five thousand jobs."[63] He reiterates this point by noting that it would almost be impossible to create jobs with internal resources alone, thus making economic openness and trade agreements the only means to economic recovery and development. He even labels his visits to California as governor as an effort to "globalize the state economy."[64] With the emphasis on globalization, of course, he is able to stress that it is not a change in attitude toward the U.S only., but also the world: indeed, Guanajuato, he notes as justification in this speech, has offices in Asia, Europe, and Canada.

While envisioning the U.S. as an (economic) opportunity, Fox also acknowledges the historic nature of the relationship, though in the end, like Salinas, he discounts the historic threats. Prior to stressing the "potential," for instance, he refers to the fact that "When you just mention the idea of sitting down to negotiate with them [the U.S.], you are immediately accused of 'selling out' the Fatherland." Even so, he dismisses this problem since not dealing with the U.S. means renouncing the opportunities. One passage begins by referring to the importance of distance: "It is true that a safe distance must be maintained."[65] But again he follows this empty statement by minimizing the dangers of foreign involvement. Not only does he envision external electoral observers as part of the democratic process—and thus not as foreign intervention[66]—but he contends that even a common market would have virtually no impact (threat) on the nation: "we do not think that it [a common market with the U.S.] would affect sovereignty, nor that advancing on these themes would result in the loss of our roots, our history or our culture."[67] He notes that unfortunately when it comes to relations with the U.S., "we are invaded by a sense of inferiority." But he dismisses this by arguing that *he* can have a good relationship with the *gringos* because he has the experience: "Having worked in a transnational company and having had direct contact with people from the U.S. gives me the sufficient elements to guarantee that a professional and beneficial relationship can be maintained. The last thing I intend is to establish a submissive relation or to give in to U.S. imperialism, but we cannot 'kick the crib' and fight with the greatest opportunity that Mexico has."[68] The use of the word imperialism to dramatize the "historical relation" here is interesting especially since he treats the threat today not only as less than the opportunities, but as easily amenable to someone with experience.

While the dominant vision of the U.S. within the Fox discourse is one of economic partnership and hence a relationship advantageous to Mexico, he does, like Salinas, acknowledge the negative side of the relationship. Following a review of trade and investment (offered as the "good" side), he reminds his readers that it is important to also look at the "bad" side of the relationship: "You cannot push aside the enormous list of negative aspects: the repression and violation of the human rights of immigrants, commercial limits on avocados or cement, the slow tariff reductions in shoes and clothes. . . . The list is endless."[69] And yet, though endless, the "mentioned" part of the list is noteworthy for still being loaded with mainly economic issues (trade in avocados, cement, shoes, clothes). While he fails here to mention the conflictual issue of drug trafficking, he does point to it as a problem at a different juncture in the same speech, even alluding to corruption in the U.S. as a factor in the equation and one the U.S. fails to acknowledge.[70] Again, like Salinas, Fox thus points to some in the U.S. who fail to understand Mexico. Still, overall these criticisms come across as largely secondary, lost behind criticism that the collaborative relationship with the U.S. does not go far enough, not that it goes too far. In fact, Fox states that the two are not "true partners" because NAFTA does not permit the free flow of workers, which would show "that we are true partners and all three countries benefit."[71] "*La realidad*," he contends, "is that Mexico receives investments and exports because of cheap labor and that if the country maintains that strategy it ensures 'permanent depression' of salaries."[72]

But rather than blaming the U.S. or U.S. imperialism for any of these shortcomings, what distinguishes the Fox narrative is that he tends to blame the bad features of the relationship—made through implicit references to "a submissive relation and giving in to U.S. imperialism" and explicit nods to "the negative features"—on the Mexican government. After referring for example to the "mistreatment of eighteen million countrymen" in the U.S, he shifts the blame, stating that "we should not forget that the true cause of the problem is the Mexican government's inability to provide employment." Echoing the theme of the U.S. as an opportunity from a somewhat different vantage point, he then asks rhetorically: "I wonder how these countrymen would have fed themselves had they remained in national territory." He concludes: "Illegal immigration is not a problem of the U.S., but Mexico."[73] Fox even reduces the conflicts with the U.S. over drug trafficking to failures of the Mexican government: "We have let them subject us and point to us as the only ones responsible and there is the constant threat from the U.S. Congress of not granting certification. We have not known how to balance the discussion and make them see their own problems of corruption."[74] In fact, Fox attributes virtually all the failures to take full advantage of the enormous opportunity represented by the U.S. to the nature of the Mexican government rather than any inherent qualities of the U.S. Though acknowledging the importance of "maintaining a safe distance," he nonetheless states that "the principal problem of our governments is that they have lacked the moral authority and legitimacy gained through authentic democratic processes."[75]

Fox's image of the nation and nationalism is relatively clear in the materials examined. He envisions Mexico equal to the U.S. in terms of economic potential though not results, as patriotic and with a strong culture unthreatened by integration. While he posits the U.S. as representing development and modernity (and thus defining Mexico's lack thereof) and an opportunity for Mexico as noted earlier, he suggests that this does not make the U.S. a "superior" country: while the U.S. may be a large country with many resources, "they do not surpass us in ingenuity and capacity."[76] But rather than refer to Mexico's cultural superiority (a contrast to the material know-how of the U.S.), here he supports the point by citing the competitive quality of Mexican goods, that is, that Mexico can compete with the U.S. on what many might consider U.S. (economic) terms. Fox also sees Mexico as having an immense love and pride in the country and a strong culture unthreatened by closer relations.[77] Though he criticizes the Mexican government for failing to erect a fully beneficial relationship with the U.S., Fox does not go too far in stressing the role of the State in protecting the "nation's" interests. He

rejects selling the petroleum business to foreigners and supports the continued role of the State in controlling the resource. Even so, he does endorse
nationalization (what he denotes as a "second nationalization"): that is, selling parts of PEMEX to the Mexican private sector. Interestingly he does not
couch this idea of not "selling the enterprise internationally" in strong
nationalistic terms, but simply because Mexico has capable administrators.[78]
He does, however, emphasize the importance of the State in protecting the
rights and interests of Mexican immigrants in the U.S.: rights that presumably are not protected because of the anti-Mexican nature of the U.S.

Though he offers some references to concepts borrowed from the nationalistic narrative, the overall discourse offered by Fox is not strongly wedded
to it, particularly when compared to the Salinas narrative. The discourse,
instead, is strikingly pragmatic, privileging economic growth and development, and stressing the need to take advantage of the opportunities represented by Mexico's proximity to the world's largest market. The Fox
discourse uses terms like sovereignty, autonomy, and national interest spar-
ingly; it rarely poses the U.S. as a threat to Mexican identity; and it hardly
ever invokes the nationalistic need for a strong independent and powerful
State to promote the nation's interests, with the exception of Mexican immigrants abroad. Basic objectives usually refer to domestic matters and are not
expressed or couched in nationalistic terms. The three main objectives set
out during his speech at ITAM in 1999 were economic growth and work,
human development, and security and justice. At times, Fox even seems to
hint at a somewhat deterritorialized vision of the nation. In referring to the
importance of maintaining contact with migrants, for instance, he stresses,
"The roots, the culture and the values of the nation are not lost by betting
on globalization and commercial opening."[79] By the same token, lying
behind this implicit concern for the deterritorialized nation is the pragmatic
concern for investments that migrants in the U.S. can make in their home
country.

Fox as President

Vicente Fox ended seven decades of PRI rule when he assumed the presidency on December 1, 2000. This postdated my initial analysis of the Fox
discourse on the U.S., raising questions as to how his perceptions might have
changed as a result. In an effort to provide at least a preliminary answer,
I looked at three speeches during the period: the two presidential *informes*
(September 2001 and 2002)[80] and the president's address to the U.S. House
of Representatives on September 6, 2001.[81] As might be expected, the dis-

course combines key elements of the Salinas discourse (the government perspective) with themes from the Fox repertoire but taken to a new level.

The two presidential *informes* are largely consistent with Fox's tendency to concentrate on domestic issues. They provide limited attention to the U.S. The first *Informe* mentions the U.S. just twice. On one occasion, like Salinas, he points to the importance of opening new lines of cooperation with Europe, Asia, and Latin America, which is in addition to strengthening ties to the U.S. and Canada. The other time he mentions the U.S. is in relation to his proposal for a new migratory agreement to legalize Mexicans residing there. The second *Informe* also provides limited references to the U.S. It too notes the need for broadening foreign ties, a subtle call for diversification: a notion perhaps rooted in the sense that the country is too closely tied to the U.S. And the speech harps even more on the issue of immigration and the need for change. Here he criticizes the U.S. for its treatment of Mexicans in its country: "We have firmly pushed the idea that immigrants no longer be considered as delinquents, and that they be recognized and that their worker and human rights be respected." After stating how Mexico demonstrates its support for humanitarian and just causes by offering hospitality and refuge to those forced to leave their lands, Fox then seems to suggest that the U.S. does not offer hospitality or share the humanitarian and just causes that Mexico believes in.

President Fox's address to the U.S. House of Representatives focuses almost exclusively on the Mexico-U.S. relationship. Here, Fox, like Salinas, strongly emphasizes the theme of a "new relationship" based now on trust. In three of the opening paragraphs, for instance, Fox notes how "this is an historic moment between our two nations in which the governments of Mexico and the United States have decided to begin a new era of friendship and cooperation to benefit both our peoples." He claims that the current period "may represent the beginning of the most promising chapters in our common history." Later he posits that "it is our very firm wish as Mexicans and Americans to establish a new relationship, a more mature, full and equitable relationship based on mutual trust." As alluded to earlier when looking at the Salinas discourse, this latter point suggests that the relationship of the past was not mature, equitable, or based on trust. Even in concluding the speech, he returns to this theme, quoting Kennedy's "New Frontier" speech regarding "new beginnings."

The second major theme of this speech is trust. Indeed, Fox calls this the "key element of our new relationship." Consistent with the notion of historic rupture, Fox acknowledges that for many "trusting their neighbor may seem risky" and that this "perception has deep roots in history." He then blames the Mexican side of this on a "long-held sense of suspicion and apprehension about its powerful neighbor." And then in an adaptation of the previous theme of blaming the Mexican government found in the discourse of Fox as opposition leader, he attributes the U.S.'s part of the blame for not trusting its neighbor to the authoritarian regime in Mexico. "And in the United States, they [not trusting the neighbor] stem from previous experiences with a political regime governing Mexico which for the most part was regarded as undemocratic and untrustworthy."

Finally, Fox ties these two themes together rather neatly by suggesting that what has fundamentally changed in the relationship, thereby crafting a "historic opportunity" rooted in a relationship of trust, is the political change in Mexico: "The relationship between Mexico and the United States has changed in one fundamental way. True democracy in Mexico, for decades an unfulfilled dream, is now a reality." And since both are now democratic, sharing values of democracy and freedom, they can trust one another: "Thanks to those democratic changes inaugurated in Mexico last year on July 2, the time has come for Mexico and the United States to trust each other." He then describes how trust means greater cooperation, that "one partner not be judged unilaterally by the other," exploring immigration issues, and so on.

Cuauhtémoc Cárdenas (and the PRD)

In contrast to the statements by Salinas and Fox, Cárdenas and the PRD use somewhat harsher terms to describe the U.S. and the contemporary relationship. At times, they portray the U.S. as essentially a threat, and Mexico as vulnerable and weakened by the prevailing linkages to the U.S. At other times, however, they speak more in class than national terms, siding with many in the U.S. who, like the Mexicans, are also hurt by NAFTA. They tend to attribute blame for this situation in part to the U.S., but like Fox, also to the Mexican regime. Though stressing a more historical vision of the U.S., the nation, and their relationship than Salinas or Fox, Cárdenas and the PRD acknowledge the potential for a better relationship with the U.S., recognize recent global developments, and underscore the need to alter Mexico's historic policy toward the U.S.

To begin with, Cárdenas and the PRD clearly do not see the then-current Mexico-U.S. relationship as a good one. Cárdenas, in fact, labels the relationship a "façade": the two countries, he notes, only "pretend to be embraced by a new spirit of friendship." The reality is "of a subordinated government which, without pride, surrenders to the economic and political demands of an embattled yet abrasive northern neighbor."[82] At one end, the relationship entails significant costs for Mexico, illustrating the image of the U.S. as a threat to the nation's interests. It [the relationship] "comes at the expense of Mexico's pride and dignity [and] . . . is based on self-inflicted vulnerability;"[83] it has led to a loss of control of the national economy to multinationals;[84] and it has led to an increase in dependency and the loss of national sovereignty. According to a 1989 statement by the party, "If before there had been a pronounced dependence of Mexico on the outside, by embracing without limit the cause of globalization it [the government] has not only renounced in large part national sovereignty, but also a political project whose historic compromise was for social justice."[85] Cárdenas, in fact, blames the economic opening (implicitly attributable to the U.S.) for shutting people behind a "wall of political intolerance, human rights abuses, electoral fraud and growing social inequality" and criticizes the free-trade agenda as being "simple and narrow" because it feeds authoritarian survival by exchanging cheap labor for foreign capital.[86] More specifically, he notes that while economic integration benefits certain sectors within Mexico, most do not benefit from it. In this he contends that Mexico represents the contradictions inherent within the current pattern of globalization wherein certain sectors do well (here he mentions NAFTA), while the majority remains poor.[87]

Consistent with this view, of course, Cárdenas characterizes the relationship as advantageous to the U.S. This is implied just in the simple statement: "We think that our relations should be advantageous to both countries." When asked directly to elaborate he notes how "some [aspects] [of the relationship] are favorable to us, . . . [but] most are not . . . especially the economic ones."[88] This poor view of the relationship is also seen in the PRD's basic recommendations not to eliminate NAFTA, but to revise it so as to "strengthen the advantages and reduce the negative effects on our economic development and institutional strength."[89]

Within this context of portraying the U.S. as a threat, Cárdenas and the PRD, like Fox, tend to assign most of the blame to the Mexican government and not the U.S. or U.S. imperialism. The underlying message within the Cárdenas discourse is that the government has abandoned its historic responsibility of representing the interests of the nation and now serves the interests of those outside the nation or a select and privileged group within it. The PRD Document contends almost euphemistically, for example, that "the State has been redesigned to serve the global scheme." Cárdenas is more direct. He characterizes the policies of both de la Madrid and Salinas— though at one point he calls Salinas the *"principal responsable"*[90]—as carbon copies of IMF and World Bank formulas. He employs such phrases as "cede national sovereignty, lose autonomy, and encourage the submission of the country to decisions made abroad concerning our interest and our welfare" to describe these policies. Accordingly, "their objective is to give away the country and to dismantle the Mexican economy and subject the masses to ever-greater levels of exploitation."[91] He characterizes deregulation as leaving Mexico unprotected, creating a situation where only the strong survive.[92] On a separate occasion, he draws a discursive parallel between the announcement of Zedillo's proposal to privatize the energy sector—an idea he blames on the World Bank—and the 151st anniversary of the Treaty of Guadalupe Hidalgo: such a move, he contends, would eliminate the possibility of exercising sovereignty.[93] He also refers to the "disadvantageous conditions under which this agreement [NAFTA] was negotiated and signed by the Mexican government."[94] Later he refers to "the promised integrative possibilities in the negotiation of NAFTA that were not kept."[95] The PRD Document also echoes this point, noting the need for a new government "that knows how to negotiate in better terms the country's insertion into the globalization process." The party is particularly critical of the government paying the foreign debt, which it sees as privileging the interests of foreigners over those of the people.[96] In essence, both draw on historic principles to basically accuse Salinas of treason.

In assigning the bulk of the blame to the Mexican government, the Cárdenas-PRD discourse tends to depict the U.S. as an accomplice, providing support to the PRI-led government. For example, Cárdenas refers to the U.S. in terms of how "the Mexican government has found strong allies and obtained new sources of political support and funding."[97] The PRD Document, meanwhile, notes how the "emergency megacredit" by the U.S. government saved the Mexican regime from financial disaster. It also highlights how neoliberalism and globalization (the Mexico-U.S. relation) block the nation's democratic development because "the powers support a government that guarantees the continuity of the economic opening project . . . for transnational enterprises . . . [and] from outside they support politics of repression against the demands of a society made poor by neoliberalism and the Market economy."[98]

Contending that the U.S. sustains an authoritarian regime that pursues policies beneficial to the U.S. fits the image of the U.S. taking advantage of Mexican weakness: a part of the "U.S. as threat" narrative. Of course, the discourse contains more direct statements attributing Mexico's problems to the U.S., highlighting the inherent threat posed by the U.S. Most cast the U.S. and U.S. behavior in historic terms, with NAFTA and globalization as basically old wine in new bottles. Cárdenas characterizes the Brady Plan (early phase), for instance, as not only being to the benefit of the U.S., but "yet another opportunity for the United States to interfere with our sovereignty."[99] Yet, even here he still returns the blame to the Mexican government by noting later how the government "is going beyond the demands of the IMF."[100] He also refers to the U.S. as "a military hegemonic power," and as having a major concentration of economic power through which it "seeks to exert hegemony over the processes of globalization which we are living."[101] In a similar vein, the PRD Document portrays globalization as the new model of world domination, one in which by becoming buyers of products made abroad, developing countries have started "assuming a new function within the scheme of political subordination and financial dependency." Part of this image of the U.S. also entails a perception of the U.S. as contradictory in its posture toward others, including Mexico. It demands a limited democracy that avoids violence, but one that does not permit an economic change that benefits the people.

And yet despite these images, there are also some rather clear images of the U.S. as an example of an admirable political system, and as being capable of having a good relationship with other countries, including Mexico. The PRD Document, for instance, cites the U.S. as providing an example, along with Europe and Japan, of how an active State can play an effective role in promoting economic development. It uses this "evidence" to support the party's recommendations for a proactive State. Cárdenas, similarly, in explaining the effects of globalization contends that the benefits from globalization have gone to developed economies because of their "proven and legitimate" democratic institutions, strong judicial systems, and so on. And though he specifically cites the European Union as an example, the U.S. is certainly implicit within the statement.[102] The "success" of such countries, he continues, contrasts to those lacking these internal structural factors, like Mexico, where the effects of globalization are negative. Though he contends that one finds increasing dependence in these latter cases, the blame is squarely focused more on domestic structures as opposed to the nature of the foreign imperialist powers.[103]

In a similar vein, Cárdenas also argues that the U.S. is capable of having a good relationship with other countries, including Mexico, though heretofore this has not been the case. "The United States has developed advantageous relations with other countries," he states, so "there is no reason why it can't have the same kind of relationship with us."[104] At one point, in referring to the relation between the U.S. and the European Union, he notes how Europe in fact "speaks to the U.S. using the *tu* [informal] form of [the word] 'you.'"[105] Once again, implicit within this view resides the tendency to attribute the poor relationship to the Mexican government rather than the U.S. per se. Even the idea that the U.S. views Mexico in a position of inferiority is somewhat discounted by his contention that there is no reason why Mexico cannot have a good relationship with the U.S.

Within this context, one senses a playing down of "U.S. imperialism" and a far more differentiated and even sympathetic view toward the U.S. Of course it is hard to show the absence of something (a traditional U.S. imperialism discourse), but it is noteworthy that in a speech on Chilean president Salvador Allende, Cárdenas refers simply to the coup leader's accomplices, but does not outright condemn or even mention the U.S.[106] For a "leftist" to discuss that historic event without taking the opportunity to take a stab at the U.S. is, I believe, quite significant. Even more noticeable within the Cárdenas discourse, however, is a tendency to differentiate his images of the U.S. This can be seen at two levels. First, the discourse often speaks in nonnational terms and thus avoids blaming the U.S. or envisioning the U.S. monolithically. This is something we see more pronounced in the EZLN narrative. Though at times referring to the relationship as beneficial to the U.S. (as a nation) as noted above, Cárdenas speaks more often in terms of benefits going to certain groups rather than nations (a privileging of class over nation). In criticizing privatization, for example, the PRD Document argues that "privatizations . . . benefit a few, but not the national treasury nor the majority of Mexicans." Cárdenas similarly argues that the free-trade agreement is not only not in Mexico's interest, but "neither will it favor the interests of the majority of the inhabitants of the U.S."[107] Here one can easily see the tendency to differentiate the U.S. government from the U.S. people, suggesting the desire not to paint the two with the same brush. When asked how the U.S. would see his proposals, for example, Cárdenas argues that the "American people will view our proposals in a realistic way"; that "If Americans take a close look at the grave reality that faces us, then they will better understand our proposals."[108] Implicit here then is the assumption that the U.S. people can think reasonably though they may be uninformed. Fully consistent with this image, Cárdenas later depicts the U.S. people as very sympathetic toward Mexico and vice versa. Clarifying that Mexico is not "trying to fashion policies contrary to the interests of the American people," he characterizes the attitude of the U.S. people toward Mexico as "one of collaboration and sympathy, feelings that the Mexican people hold toward the American people, speaking at the level of people to people."[109]

Fundamental to the Cárdenas discourse on the U.S. and Mexico-U.S. relations is his view of the nation and globalization. In many ways, the Cárdenas-PRD discourse remains firmly rooted in nationalist soil. Fears, objectives, and recommendations are all spelled out in terms borrowed from the nationalist doctrine. The PRD Document, for instance, states in almost frightening terms that if the petroleum sector is not strengthened it could end up in the hands of foreigners: a move, like other privatizations, that only benefits a select few. It also stresses the need to "defend national sovereignty by attending to the fundamental values that give the Mexican people their sense of unity, their sense of belonging and their attachment to their millennial culture." Cárdenas also speaks in terms of promoting the interests of Mexicans both within and outside the country. He stresses the need to create a government that "affirms and defends national sovereignty like the other great nations of our times do," and one that prioritizes the needs of Mexicans (clearly nationalistic and implying that current policies are nonnationalistic).[110]

Consistent with the framework set out earlier, both Cárdenas and the PRD envision the need for an activist State to pursue such nationalistic goals and defend the country against the U.S. The PRD Document holds, for instance, that the State must participate in strategic areas for national sovereignty, touting education as the key to preventing the loss of sovereignty: "If the participation of Mexico in globalization is not intended as an act of giving-in or surrender, then one of the most urgent challenges is to elevate the average level of education of the people from six to 12 years." But going beyond education, the discourse portrays democracy as the *sine qua non* for the State to effectively pursue these nationalistic goals.[111] According to the PRD Document, "The contradiction between a party and a government that gives in to outside interests, and a people who demand progress and well-being can only be overcome by preventing the party's permanence in power, substituting in its place another party and another government that knows how to negotiate the country's insertion into the process of globalization." In other words, according to this logic, the failure of the regime to effectively pursue the nation's interests, particularly in its relationship with the U.S., stems from the lack of democracy in Mexico, not anything inherent to the U.S.

And yet, despite the sense of nationalism underlying the rhetoric, Cárdenas and the PRD also seem to recognize and embrace the changes of globalization, and therefore never fully accept what could be considered the "traditional" nationalistic position. The PRD Document, for example, refers to the "neoliberal and globalization imperative," while Cárdenas defines globalization as a "contemporary reality, not an ideology" marked by a greater intensity, density, extension, and velocity of "*intercambios*" among countries.[112] Not only do they not reject globalism, but they also acknowledge that there is no escape from it. As Cárdenas argues, "We can neither free ourselves from it [globalization, the U.S.], nor should we try to escape it. Isolating ourselves will only deepen the problems."[113] As such, he does not preach autarky or reversing NAFTA, as his critics often contend, but rather the need to strengthen cooperation and free trade with Europe, "renegotiate and revitalize democratically NAFTA," and pursue a continental project.[114] Departing even further from the old nationalistic narrative of "us" versus "them," he criticizes (rather than praises) the fact that people (viewed as labor) "remain prisoners of national borders" while the regulations on labor are eliminated (this is not a view that praises nationalist autonomy).[115] He thus proposes, like Fox, "the free circulation of people and labor as an indispensable requirement of a truly global economy."[116] Again not seeing the situation in solely nationalistic terms, Cárdenas notes how "we aspire to a more integrated world."[117] He stresses within this vision "the sharing of scientific and technological progress," and even concludes his piece to the *U.S. audience* by stating that free trade must "not work against *our* common future" (emphasis added).

So rather than rejecting globalization, Cárdenas and the PRD question the specific route it has taken thus far. This approach helps complete the narrative by retargeting blame once again on the Mexican government and, secondarily, on the U.S. At the same time it provides a backdrop for offering "sound" recommendations. Cárdenas is quite explicit in rejecting the form globalization has taken, which he calls the "Washington Consensus."[118] It is this "form" of globalization, he contends, that has led to periodic crises worldwide (he cites the Russian, Asian, and Brazilian financial crises in addition to the Mexican version). More specifically, it is this "form" of globalization, he argues, that contains two contradictory processes: one that integrates and the other that pulls apart. The one that integrates relates to free trade and the more dynamic sectors of the economy, while the one that pulls apart relates to "less dynamic sectors and activities with less capacity to augment the levels of productivity."[119] Though at one point he suggests that the negative effects follow national lines as noted earlier (that countries with democratic structures enjoy the benefits), he contends at another juncture that they do not follow national boundaries: a clear departure from the nationalist discourse. In fact, he notes that disintegration is occurring in all societies (not just the less developed ones): what he refers to as the "new disorder within our societies."[120] Through this differentiation he can posit that globalization is partial and incomplete, and therefore recommend continental trade and a pact under a different model: "Trade must be seen as an instrument of development and that a new kind of development model must be at the core of any continental trade negotiations." Such a new pact would include a social charter and labor, social, and environmental rights and would strengthen internal democracy—and still "guarantee the sovereign rights of each nation to develop its own natural resources."[121] Through this differentiation he can also pitch NAFTA as opposed to the interests of the people in the U.S., Mexico, and Canada, as noted earlier, not just the Mexicans. By the same token, this differentiation allows Cárdenas to reject the counterview that portrays the discourse as overly nationalistic and tied to the past: "We cannot accept the argument whereby any criticism of free-trade agreements is disqualified as being against world trends . . . or that we are simply trying to preserve anachronistic structures."[122]

This image of globalization, finally, seems to parallel broad criticisms of modernity and fold nicely within Mexico's broader image of the U.S. This broader image holds that modernity, often associated with the U.S., may contain certain beneficial features (progress), but it also leads to certain evils. According to Cárdenas, globalization leads to lawlessness and "In a world without law two things occur: one, there is the only universal law, that of survival of the fittest; the other, the existence of private agreements between parties whose only and last guarantee of compliance is, one again, through force."[123] This view, moreover, parallels visions of the U.S. domestically as representing both positive (progress) and negative features (loss of culture, racism, materialism), and the U.S. externally as using force against weaker countries like Mexico in pursuit of its "modernizing" objectives. These themes will crop up in other chapters.

The Ejército Zapatista de Liberación Nacional

Since its emergence onto the national stage in 1994, the EZLN has been engaged in a war of position to create a counterhegemony and undermine the ideas supporting the ruling class. And yet in a content analysis of the organization's political thought, Kathleen Bruhn finds little mention of the U.S. and a "surprising absence of references" to NAFTA. According to Bruhn, "even direct references to the United States are startlingly low, at an average of just 0.3 in 16 percent of documents, failing to rank among the top 15 themes."[124] This finding contrasts references to neoliberalism, present in 29% of the documents examined, with a mean of 1.1 mentions per document (ranking 14th); and *patria* with a mean of 0.9 per document (ranking 15th), present in 31.9% of the documents. Bruhn contends that the relative absence of references to the U.S. may be due to the organization's "concern with building international as well as domestic alliances."[125] Indeed, it is interesting where the EZLN conspicuously does not mention the U.S. The *Third Declaration from the Lacandon Jungle*, for example, criticizes Salinas and the economic farce in 1994, notes the need to take back the Motherland from the federal government, and even mentions the French intervention twice, but does not mention the U.S., the U.S. intervention, or NAFTA.

Still, a review of a sample of writings by the EZLN shows that direct references to the U.S., like the more indirect ones, generally portray the U.S. as a threat to the nation's interests, consistent with the narrative discussed earlier. At times, the EZLN uses history to make the point. "*Composición del EZLN*," for example, refers to the fact that the EZLN learned military tactics from

Mexican history, including "resistance to the Yankee invasion in 1846–1847."[126] The *First Declaration from the Lacandon Jungle* similarly casts the "EZLN [as the] product of 500 years of struggle," including the struggle to "avoid being absorbed by North American imperialism." At other times, the reference is more explicit and refers to the contemporary period. The EZLN letter to *Proceso* in 1995 depicts the U.S. as a clear and present danger to Mexican sovereignty by asking, "If the Mexican Federal Army exists to guarantee national sovereignty, why does it not accompany Ortiz to Washington instead of chasing the dignity of the indigenous in Chiapas?"

Beyond the few explicit references, the EZLN narrative nonetheless incorporates the U.S. implicitly within other, broader contexts. This includes frequent references to the capitalist system, modernity, and the "accomplices" of the Mexican government. First, and perhaps the most overriding theme within the EZLN narrative, is the U.S. as an agent of global capitalism. *Chiapas: El Sureste en dos vientos*, for example, rather than referring to the U.S. by name employs such abstract, nonnationalist terms as "the insatiable beast" or "*el imperio*" to refer to the agents of global capitalism. Reference at one point is made to the U.S. by name, but as just one of many countries in a capitalist camp that includes Canada, Holland, Germany, Italy, and Japan.[127] Though it refers to the U.S. as the principal destiny for the products from Chiapas, the statement also refers to Europe and the E.U. as important destinations, again extending the reference beyond the U.S. alone. Within this context, the EZLN depicts the capitalist system—and thus indirectly the U.S.—as a threat to Mexico, though more specifically a threat to Chiapas. The discourse refers, for example, to the "sacking" of Chiapas or the "tribute charged by capitalism." And the answer to the rhetorical question, "What does the beast leave in return for all that it takes?" is poverty and the lack of infrastructure.[128]

In addition to capitalism, the U.S. also implicitly represents "modernity" and hence is a factor shaping in part Mexican nationalism. But unlike the Fox reference where the U.S. is held up as a benchmark of development, the EZLN portrays the U.S. model in less admirable terms. *México: Entre el Sueño, la Pesadilla y el Despertar*, for example, tells a story about three Mexicos located at different levels. It describes the wealth of those "*de arriba*" (a term that can have the double geographic and political-economic meaning) in dollars, foreign investment, and trade (hence the association with the U.S.), and then questions their Mexicanness. It contends that at this level "the Fatherland and dignity have no weight," the people misguidedly imitate the U.S. and believe in the "fallacy of the *American dream*."[129] Later, under a subheading on how to be named "Man of the Year," the narrative posits that this fictional country (of modernity) "has no Fatherland."[130] The story thus sets up a simple dichotomy such that those closer to the U.S., in geographic and economic terms, are less Mexican: that the U.S. represents modernity and modernity is fundamentally antinational. Indeed, this image of modernity seems to go beyond wealth to include merely accepting foreign perspectives, to accept "their" (centered) view of things. "To triumph in Mexico one must go abroad. Not necessarily to go in the physical sense, but in the history, in the desires. This vocation of exile being synonymous with triumph has nothing to do with physical crossing of borders. There are those who even by going, stay. And there are those who even by staying, go." Such people have not only forgotten the nation, the statement suggests, but history itself: they suffer from "historic ignorance."[131] We will return to this story letter.

As an opposition group, it is no surprise that the EZLN targets blame and anger at the Mexican government, in a similar tone to the statements of Fox and Cárdenas. The *Fourth Declaration from the Lacandon Jungle* is quite clear in stating that "bad government" is the reason igniting the guerrilla struggle. In this context, the EZLN tends to portray the U.S. as an accomplice to the Mexican government, though nonetheless a threat to the nation's interests. The document *Ayuda Militar de EU a México*, for example, specifically calls the U.S. "an accomplice of the Mexican government," while *Composición del EZLN* credits the U.S. for facilitating repression: "With the support that the people and the government of the U.S. provide the federal government they do nothing but soil their own hands with indigenous blood." This view of the U.S. as an accomplice can also be seen in the reference to a mountain called the "*Extranjero*" ["foreigner"], so noted because of the presence of U.S. military personnel teaching their Mexican "*pares*" [equals] to work the radar.[132] The use of the term *pares* here suggests a sense of equality between U.S. and Mexican military personnel with no implication that the U.S. is in charge or actually giving the orders. The *First Declaration from the Lacandon Jungle* makes a similar point, ordering the EZLN army to "initiate summary judgments against all soldiers of the Mexican federal army and the political police that have received training or have been paid by foreigners." Again, the statement does not seem to blame the U.S. for Mexican ills; instead, it characterizes the U.S. as supportive of the regime, but not the cause of the problems. The *Fourth Declaration* highlights this supportive role and its effects on the nation as well by referring to the "technical assistance of foreigners" to the Mexican military and how the true loss of sovereignty lies in the "secret pacts . . . with the owners of money and foreign governments."

The EZLN is also clear in depicting NAFTA as a selling-out of the country, as a return to the *Porfiriato*, and hence as anti-Zapata.[133] *México: Entre el Sueño, la Pesadilla y el Despertar* criticizes President Zedillo, for instance, for "repeating the fallacy of the American dream."[134] The *First Declaration* also refers to those making up the "70 year dictatorship" as traitors, sell-out groups, equating them to those who "sold half our country to the foreign invader" many years ago. The use of the term "sold" here is instructive since it posits the Mexican government as the historic agent. The *Fourth Declaration* blames "the Powerful" for "the total destruction of the Mexican nation, the negation of its history, the sale of its sovereignty, treachery, and so on. Even the "Letter to the Press" dated April 9, 1999 uses the word "treason" to describe the proposed privatization of the electric industry.

Within the narrative of the U.S. as an accomplice, the EZLN, like Cárdenas, also seems to offer a more nuanced view of the U.S. and to differentiate the U.S. society and people from the government. *Composición del EZLN*, for example, calls on the world to demand that "the U.S. government suspend all economic and military aid to the Mexican federal government because it deals with a dictatorial government that does not respect human rights and because such help will be used to massacre the Mexican people." This appeal suggests the belief not only that the U.S. is not fully to blame for the problem and does not control the Mexican government (U.S. as accomplice), but that the U.S. could be persuaded to "do the right thing." The assumption is that the U.S. can be reasonable; the implication is that the policy of supporting the Mexican government is not evil, but misguided, rooted in erroneous information. This position and image of the U.S. are reiterated in the EZLN open letter to President Clinton, the U.S. Congress, and the U.S. people, which seeks simply enough to *"decirles"* [tell them] how the Mexican government is using U.S. economic and military assistance to massacre Chiapan Indians.[135] Showing knowledge of what historically motivates the U.S., the letter clarifies that the rebels receive no foreign assistance. This vision of parts of the U.S. as potential allies in the struggle against the Mexican government can also be seen in the *Fourth Declaration*. Without specifically mentioning the U.S., it contains a vague reference to "international society" which, along with national society, it credits for forcing the Mexican government to open a dialogue and suspend military operations during the initial days of the armed uprising in 1994. The same document also refers to an intercontinental dialogue in opposition to neoliberalism. Implicitly, such views portray the U.S. as part of international society, as an opportunity (not solely a threat) that can benefit the "cause."

Moving beyond references of the U.S. or the relationship to references to the nation, the broader narrative of the EZLN is deeply nationalistic. The *Third Declaration* uses such terms and phrases as "The Motherland lives," the "sacred fire of patriotism," and the "national banner." The *Fourth Declaration* refers to the objective of making the land "our own." And the 1999 "Letter to the Press" defines the struggle as a defense of the national sovereignty against those who want to "sell the sovereignty." But the EZLN's image of the nation is unique, laced at times with implicit references to the U.S. In *México: Entre el Sueño, la Pesadilla y el Despertar*, the EZLN describes a nation seriously divided, marked by a rich and middle class wedded to the U.S. and the ideas of modernity. Completing the "story" of the three Mexicos referred to earlier, the document touts the Mexico *"de abajo"* as the true Mexico, using such nationalistic modifiers as solidarity, *raza, cúate*, and indigenous (a term, it notes, that is excluded in NAFTA). The EZLN thus envisions the Mexican nation not only as the opposite of the modernity represented by those *"de arriba,"* but as containing indigenous features that heretofore have been excluded from the official version of the nation: features that must therefore be reincorporated if the nation is to survive. The only means of incorporating the indigenous of the nation with justice and dignity, according to this logic, is to recognize the characteristics of their own social, political, and cultural organization, though it clarifies that "Autonomy is not separation."[136] Only "when the homeland speaks its Indian heart," the *Fourth Declaration* concludes, "will [it] have dignity and memory."

Similarities and Differences, Change and Continuity

As expressed through the narratives of Salinas, Fox, Cárdenas, and the EZLN, the contemporary political discourse encompasses a range of images and views on the U.S. and the nation. Consistent with the model presented earlier, the contemporary discourse contains images of the U.S. as both threat and opportunity. It exhibits the basic hierarchy privileging distance and conflict, remains rooted in a nationalistic narrative, and shows the inherent limits to any policy approach. Generally, Salinas, Fox, and to a lesser extent Cárdenas all stress policies of collaboration rooted in an image of the U.S. as an opportunity for Mexico. "Opportunity," of course, is expressed primarily in economic terms as the key to modernity or progress, though Fox and Cárdenas in supporting foreign electoral observers also see U.S. involvement as contributing to the country's democratic development.

Salinas and Fox clearly go the furthest in minimizing the U.S. threat to Mexico (politically, culturally, and economically) and in portraying the relationship as cooperative and mutually beneficial. They depict the relationship as "new" and a rupture with the past. And though both acknowledge the principles of the past—and Salinas even envelops his image in a somewhat traditional rhetoric—they nonetheless present cooperation and integration as the new (and only) model for the nation. They tend then to see a uniform market as "the only means of thinking" and disqualify other ideas as anachronistic and nostalgic for nationalism.[137] Building on this perspective, they also tend to downplay the role of the State, while privileging the role of market forces.

Though Cárdenas expresses the possibility and the desire for an economic relationship with the U.S. that would be beneficial to Mexico, he, along with the EZLN, seems to stress the dangers or the negative consequences of U.S. involvement, at least in terms of the current involvement. Both speak often about the elite "selling out" the country to foreigners and the exclusion of millions from the benefits of "free trade." Their discourse is more historically grounded than that of Salinas and Fox, playing on and reiterating the "lessons of history." Both also are critical of market forces and emphasize the need for a powerful State capable of defending and promoting the nation's interests. In contrast to Cárdenas, the EZLN goes further in emphasizing the impact of U.S. involvement specifically on Chiapas and the indigenous.

But despite the differences among them, a substantial portion of the underlying nationalistic narrative remains, providing all with a common underlying logic. Even what appear to be radically and historically inconsistent policies—whether expressed by Salinas, Fox, Cárdenas, or the EZLN—are still couched within a broadly nationalistic rhetoric.[138] Sovereignty is still valued and neither Salinas nor Fox go so far as to denounce the idea. So what becomes contested is the means to achieve the objectives, not the overall goals.

Similarly, the competing images still entertain and recognize basic limits. None offers blanket statements of the U.S. as an opportunity or a threat, and none extends collaboration or distance to the extreme. Despite Salinas's embrace of the U.S. as a friend and ally, he nonetheless continues to see the U.S. as engaging at times in anti-Mexican behavior with regards to the immigrants, and he rules out a full extension of his policy of collaboration to encompass political integration or U.S. military on Mexican soil. Even statements on the left remain limited. Despite Cárdenas's desire to privilege the national economy or protect strategic sectors, he never suggests a policy of autarky or complete independence. Cárdenas and the PRD even support NAFTA, albeit with revisions. Overall, the contested image of the U.S. as a threat or opportunity relates not so much to immigration or drug trafficking as it does to economic matters. All seem to agree, as Andrés Rozental claims, that the U.S. treatment of Mexican immigrants shows "that xenophobia and racism still prevail in some sectors of a society which should have already overcome these types of expressions."[139]

Much of this, of course, suggests certain similarities to the past. As noted earlier, history reveals the coexistence of both discourses—the U.S. as opportunity, supporting policies of collaboration; and the U.S. as a threat, sustaining policies of distance. The two have long coexisted, competed, and in certain respects complemented one another. So despite the hierarchy, which makes cooperative relations "new" by definition, the competing contemporary images can in some way be linked to parallel views and arguments from the past. What is historically distinct in the current discourse, however, is the relative weight of the two images, the shifting of the limits, the enhanced weight of the economy and economic matters, a political tendency to target blame not abroad but to the Mexican government, and a more nuanced view of the U.S. and the world.

First, there has been a clear shift in the relative weight of the two narratives and their policy boundaries. For the better part of the twentieth century, the meganarrative of the Revolution as well as the nation's foreign, economic, and cultural policies all seemed strongly rooted in a nationalistic discourse stressing the U.S. as a threat. Supported, as we see in chapter 3, by textbook lessons, this State-sponsored vision prompted many to characterize Mexico as essentially anti-American. Such a position is clearly an exaggeration and a simplification as a review of policy shows, but it nonetheless captures a basic tendency. The contemporary discourse, by contrast, has moved away from that earlier image. But the change seems one of degree and not of kind. In other words, the discourse of Salinas and Fox does not fully break with the past, nor does the Cárdenas or EZLN discourse fully embrace it. Salinas and Fox have undoubtedly gone the furthest in embracing collaboration and promoting a cooperative view of the U.S.; but even on the left, Cárdenas now accepts closer integration, rejects stridently nationalistic postures, and views the U.S. as a potential partner capable of having a relationship that can be mutually beneficial. Even the "guerrilla" left represented by the EZLN offers a narrative that seems at times far less anti-American than their counterparts in the past or even the Mexican government of the past.

In addition to a shifting in the relative weight, it is also clear that the limits have moved. While many administrations have pursued policies to solidify the economic relationship with the U.S. over the years, this always stopped short of a free trade agreement. Even as late as the early days of the Salinas *sexenio*, such a policy was considered beyond the boundaries of acceptable policy: a threat to the nation's interests. Salinas, of course, reversed his position: a shift Monsiváis interprets as an effort to eliminate "the meaning of critical nationalism."[140] But not only did Salinas revise his position on the issue of free trade, but Fox and Cárdenas also came to support NAFTA at least in principle, despite their criticism that that the agreement does not go far enough to protect the nation's interests. So despite efforts by some to portray the Cárdenas narrative as anachronistic, it too shows clear signs of change, suggesting that the general boundaries of the discourse have shifted in the direction of U.S. as opportunity.

Such a shift can also be seen in their position on the State and U.S. and foreign involvement in Mexican "internal" affairs and vice versa. For years, the ruling elite employed a discourse that associated any foreign involvement, including foreign election or human rights observers, with a threat to sovereignty. But it eventually lost this discursive battle.[141] As the issue became incorporated into a democratic as opposed to a nationalistic narrative, the ruling elite, along with the opposition who led the change, came to accept foreign electoral observers. This particular boundary shift, to be sure, has gone both ways as seen in increased Mexican involvement in U.S. domestic politics. Mexicans now accept a degree of involvement in the "internal" affairs of the U.S. once considered unacceptable.[142] This ranges from the massive Salinas-orchestrated lobbying in the U.S. for the passage of NAFTA to the many campaign visits by Fox and Cárdenas to the U.S. as well as the numerous urgings that the U.S. government protect Mexican nationals residing in the U.S. As Rozental puts it, "we are utilizing the specific characteristics of the U.S. system now to promote our interests."[143]

A second important difference centers on the economy and economic policy. Arguably, the Mexican political elite has long privileged economic concerns over foreign policy or cultural issues, and this remains true. The contention, therefore, that economic policy "determined the logic of the foreign policy of the administration of Carlos Salinas de Gortari" is probably not historically unique.[144] What has changed, however, is the nature of the economic approach and, especially for Salinas and Fox, its fit with other policies. In other words, a critical delinking or hollowing out of the economic from the nationalist narrative has occurred. For years, Mexico pursued a successful economic policy rooted in a domestic and nationalistic orientation. Such a policy—known as import substitution—fit neatly within a broader ideology stressing the dangers of the U.S., a foreign policy stressing distance and independence, a cultural policy protecting cultural industries, and a strong, authoritarian, and paternalistic State. There was a good fit between the policies. According to Meyer, the success of the Mexican Miracle period (sustained economic growth from 1940s to the 1970s) permitted Mexico "to leave aside the idea of the development and modernization of Mexico depending on too close a relationship with the U.S."[145] But the new neoliberal economic policy centers on a different vision of cooperation with and openness toward the U.S. Economic progress remains a superior value as it always has, but only now the means of obtaining it have changed. As Erfani emphasizes, a strong economy is now defined as integration with the U.S., not national economic autonomy.[146] This economic approach of integration, however, does not mesh well with a foreign policy stressing distance, a cultural policy protecting cultural industries, or even a strong State. It produces disharmony. Indeed, Monsiváis posits that this inconsistency forced Salinas and others to abandon the idea of the Mexican Revolution and replace it with Modernization, and to replace the idea of Nationalism with productivity.[147]

While the change in economic policy goes a long way in accounting for a general change in the overall approach to the U.S., parallel to this there has also been an effort, most notable within the discourse of Salinas and Fox, to separate the economic from the cultural: to delink the two. This can be seen in many areas. At one level, the leaders argue that economic integration is not a threat to culture and identity.[148] Monsiváis recognizes this: "One by one, from the president of the republic to the most recalcitrant governor toward the theory, they all assure that NAFTA will have no affect on our identity, it cannot affect the indestructible."[149] A few years later, he cites Jaime Serra Puche, the main negotiator of NAFTA, declaring that Mexicans are "untouched" in culture because of economic integration: "We will not become North Americans: McDonald's and Domino's Pizza are here and for that we will not stop being Mexicans, and what is to be done is to strengthen our culture, cling to it so that it will survive."[150] Of course whether and how economic integration influences culture is a hotly contested issue throughout the country[151]

Delinking the economic and the cultural spheres parallels attempts by some to separate the ideas of "modernity" (understood in economic terms) from "nationalism" (understood in cultural terms). Indeed, Gutierrez and Gutierrez posit this view by arguing that there is no longer any opposition between nationalism and the modern in Mexico: that the modern is no longer rejected simply because it is identified with the foreign.[152] This contrasts clearly with the EZLN position that associates modernity with the U.S. and, in turn, with anti-Mexicanness. This tendency to differentiate the two spheres and strip the economic of much of its nationalistic attire can also been seen in the efforts of Salinas and others to insulate the economic relationship from other areas so that conflict in areas like immigration or border conflicts does not affect the (priority) commercial negotiations.[153] It can also be seen in the view and treatment of the State. In the economic realm, the new posture downplays the need for a strong State, positing instead that international market forces—specifically, competition and integration with the U.S.—best protect a strong economy.[154] And yet, in terms of protecting the interests of Mexicans in the U.S.—the area where the image of the U.S. is one of racism and xenophobia—there seem to be much greater demands for the State to assert itself. This divorce provides an institutional division, as well, with the economic dimension of the relationship being under the economic ministries (Secretariat of Industry [SECOFI], later Secretariat of the Economy [SE]) and the other areas being handled by the foreign ministry.[155]

A third difference separating the contemporary discourse from that of the past relates to the role of the opposition, the growing power of its discourse, and a concomitant weakening in the State's hegemonic discourse: a clear reflection of contemporary political changes in Mexico. Narratives by Fox, Cárdenas, and the EZLN all concurred in targeting the bulk of the blame for society's ills on the PRI-led government or the authoritarian system rather than the U.S. Though they differ in fundamental ways, they all envision the U.S. as an accomplice either sustaining the authoritarian PRI regime or taking advantage of its weaknesses. This makes sense given the fact that all three were at the time engaged in domestic opposition to the PRI government. Still, this position seems a far cry from the historic position generally echoed by the Revolutionary ruling elite, who attributed many societal ills to the U.S. and depicted any peripheral government, including Mexico's, as subject rather than agent. And yet, there is an important strand of historical consistency here. It is common, within the nationalistic narrative, to attack opponents by tying them to nonnational (foreign) powers. But in the past, it was the Revolutionary elite who used the idea of foreign threat, anti-U.S. rhetoric, and the myth of unity to block domestic dissent.[156] As the government began to use foreign involvement to further its political and economic ends, however, it undermined the "unwritten rule" among political groups not to invite American involvement, and the utility of this approach changed.[157] The tables turned. Now it is the opposition that accuses the government not just of dealing with foreigners, but of dealing with them in a way contrary to the nation's interests.

Finally, the contemporary political discourse differs in that it contains a seemingly more nuanced and sophisticated image of the U.S. and the world. Facilitated in part by the delinking of the economy from the culture and national identity, all the narratives explored here tend to see the U.S. in less than monolithic or one-dimensional terms. Salinas and Fox, who go the furthest in stressing cooperation with the U.S. for economic gain, and Cárdenas and the EZLN, who tend to highlight the negative side of the relationship, all see the U.S. as combining both pro-Mexican (cooperative, partnerlike, believers in freedom and supporters of democracy) attributes and anti-Mexican (racist, xenophobic, arrogant in treatment of drug trafficking or Mexican immigrants) features. Moreover, in many cases, they draw a distinction between the U.S. people and the government, with the greatest sympathy and the most positive image usually reserved for the U.S. people. Even Cárdenas and the EZLN seek to reach out to the U.S. people to enlist their support and cooperation in their struggles against government repression and injustice. This reflects what Rozental describes as Mexico's "better understanding of its neighbor, of its institutions, of its peculiar features of the government, of its enormous decentralization that characterizes its federal regime. This has permitted us a better comprehension of certain phenomena that we often misinterpreted."[158]

Though to differing degrees, all the political actors studied here also acknowledge the changing nature of the world itself and Mexico's place in it. Though never truly relinquishing the metanarrative of nationalism, Salinas, Fox, Cárdenas, and the EZLN nonetheless modulate the traditional version by incorporating globalism into their political discourse. Deemed at one point an "imperative," globalism represents the common denominator linking the changes in the political discourse listed above. Globalization entails the privileging of the economic and general acceptance of economic integration and openness as well as a more deterritorialized view of the nation where Mexicans in the U.S. are still thought of as Mexican (and therefore should be able to vote and enjoy the protection of the Mexican State). As the foreign minister under Zedillo, José Angel Gurría, notes, "the Mexican nation surpasses the physical borders."[159] This view of globalization also incorporates the idea that *gringos* can now be considered potential allies in domestic political struggles. It supports the idea that Mexico can actually influence the U.S. through participation in its political system. And it encompasses the idea of a more decentered diffusion of culture.

A component and illustration of this can be seen in the new discourse regarding the border. According to Eduardo Barrera, the old discourse (what would here be labeled U.S. as threat) envisioned the border as the site of U.S. penetration. This view not only saw the nation as threatened, but saw the level of threat varying with proximity to the U.S. Accordingly, like a tent, Mexicanness was considered stronger at the center and weaker along the border. The post-NAFTA discourse, by contrast, reconstructs the border. "The selling of NAFTA in Mexico required a substantive change in the collective imaginary of Mexico, to one where the border became a key trope, serving as the paradigm of what Mexico was going to be like once the trilateral agreement was in place."[160] The new discourse on the border does not define U.S. influence as threatening or lament the loss of Mexican culture; instead, the border represents the image of modernity. This reconstruction reflects the privileging of the economic and the privileging of modernity, noted earlier. And yet, despite this view, recent governments have sought to use policy— for example, the *Programa Cultural de las Fronteras* established under President de la Madrid—to help bolster and ensure the continued Mexicanness of border residents.

To be sure, many questions emerge or remain. How influential, for example, are these political discourses in constructing or reconstructing Mexican public images of the U.S. and the nation? Did the Salinas discourse, which detaches anti-Americanism from the State, truly persuade the people, leading to an overall shift in the public's perceptions of the U.S. and the nation? Or did the new discourse merely broaden the gap separating the State and a public still wedded to the rhetoric of the past? Two basic positions can be identified. The first view suggests that the public's views have changed in conjunction with those of Salinas and the ruling elite. Gutierrez and Gutierrez, who see in the lack of opposition to Salinas and NAFTA a weakening of Mexican nationalism in recent years, offer one example of this view.[161] The other position, however, holds that the elite has left the public behind, thus forging a widening gap between the two with respect to their views of the U.S. and the nation. Sálazar, for instance, points to "the weak linkage that exists between the official nationalist discourse and the daily culture of the people . . . the distance between that which intellectuals define as national character and how the people really are."[162] This position supports the view that popular images, shaped by the rhetoric and policies of the past, remain vibrant, available for political mobilization by the political opposition, and that such images may effectively limit the extent to which the ruling elite can alter the historic stance. Mabire seems to take this position when he warns that "the inert resistance to change in this baggage of antique beliefs that the State has cultivated for many decades before trying to dismantle it . . . has become an obstacle to the reverses in Mexican foreign policy."[163]

While some of these questions are explored when attention turns to public opinion in chapter 8, it is important to reiterate that the contemporary political discourse is only one of many expressing and shaping images of the U.S. and the nation. We turn now to the one area where the State clearly plays the dominant role in offering a particular image of the U.S. and nation, a role generally uncontested by opponents: education and the school texts.

Notes

1. Ojeda, *Alcances y limites,* 8.

2. Rodolfo O. de la Garza, "Foreign Policy Comes Home: The Domestic Consequences of the Program for Mexican Communities Living in Foreign Countries," in *Bridging the Border: Transforming Mexico-U.S. Relations,* edited by Rodolfo de la Garza and Jesus Velasco (New York: Rowman and Littlefield, 1998), 70.

3. De la Garza, "Foreign Policy Comes Home," 71.

4. Ojeda, *Alcances y limites,* 88.

5. Lorenzo Meyer, "La crisis de la elite mexicana y su relación con Estados Unidos. Raíces históricas del tratado de libre comercio," in *México–Estados Unidos,* edited by Vega, 75–76.

6. García Canclini, *Globalización Imaginada,* 98.

7. Maria García Castro, "Identidad nacional y nacionalismo en México," 38.

8. Brading, *Orígenes del nacionalismo mexicano*, 11, 129.

9. Knight, "Peasants into Patriots," 154.

10. Ojeda, *Alcances y limites*.

11. Loaeza, "Changing Face of Mexican Nationalism," 151; Erfani, *Paradox of the Mexican State*.

12. Ojeda, *Alcances y limites*, 38, 30.

13. Solis, "Política económica y el nacionalismo mexicano," 61.

14. Bernardo Mabire, "La utilidad del nacionalismo en el México de hoy," in *México ante el fin de la Guerra Fría*, edited by Ilan Bizberg (Mexico City: El Colegio de México, 1998), 126.

15. Cited in Ojeda, *Alcances y limites*, 71.

16. Both the de la Madrid and Salinas statements are cited in Chabat, "Mexico's Foreign Policy after NAFTA," 44.

17. Pastor and Castañeda, *Limits to Friendship*, 128.

18. Pellicer de Brody, "Viente Años," 149.

19. Bustamante, "Frontera México-Estados Unidos," 101.

20. Alan Knight, "Dealing with the American Political System: An Historical Overview, 1910–1995," in *Bridging the Border*, edited by de la Garza and Velasco, 13–14.

21. Meyer, "Crisis de la elite mexicana."

22. Ojeda, *Alcances y limites*, 79.

23. Loaeza, "Changing Face of Mexican Nationalism," 156.

24. These two discourses parallel and fit neatly within some broader theoretical paradoxes. First, the two discourses reflect the basic paradox of the nation-state system wherein the State seeks to be part of the modern world (collaborationism— world as opportunity) and yet to defend itself from modernity (distance—national interest) (Jusdanis, "Beyond National Culture?" 42). The two discourses also reflect the gap separating the principles of the international system (sovereignty and equality) from the reality of power differentials or realism. National sovereignty, enshrined in the nationalist doctrine, is only equal in theory, not in practice. So Mexico, like any country, must bow discursively to the hegemony of the nation-state ideology and perhaps rely on foreign policy to assert its national identity, while it maneuvers within a world shaped by power politics and inequality. Third, the two discourses reflect an essential gap separating the nationalist doctrine of equality and the meta-narrative on modernity. The one envisions Mexico, like any nation-state, as autonomous and equal; but the other casts Mexico as "backward," "underdeveloped," or in some way less "something valuable" (modern, developed) than the U.S. Combined these gaps craft what Erfani (*Paradox of the Mexican State*, 5) calls "Mexico's inferior cultural-legal status in international relations" (which she associates with the U.S.-Mexican war), and this creates a situation in which Mexico may collaborate in an effort to achieve development, but at other times rejects the discourse that locates the country in an inferior status. According to Carlos Fuentes ("The Decay of Nations," *New Perspectives Quarterly* [Fall, 1991]: 11), the nation rejected positivism (a cosmopolitan view rooted in a modernist discourse that placed Mexico low on the scale) in response to the "cultural discrimination that identified civilization with Europe, whites, and positivism."

25. Vicente Fox Quezada, *A Los Pinos: Recuento autobiográfico y político* (Mexico City: Oceano, 1999).

26. Cuauhtémoc Cárdenas, "Free Trade Is Not Enough," *New Perspectives Quarterly* 8 (1) (1991): 21–22.

27. Carlos B. Gil, ed. *Hope and Frustration: Interviews with Leaders of Mexico's Political Opposition* (Wilmington, DE: Scholarly Resources, 1992).

28. Cuauhtémoc Cárdenas, *Cuauhtémoc Cárdenas: Palabras de Cárdenas,* prologue by Miguel Ángel Granados Chapa (Mexico City: Grijalbo, 1999).

29. "Chiapas: el Sureste en dos vientos, una tormenta y una profecia" in *EZLN: Documentos y comuncados.* Vol. 1 (Mexico City: Ediciones Era, 1994), 49–66; "Composición del EZLN" in *EZLN: Documentos y comuncados.* Vol. 1, 72–79; "Ayuda Militar de EU a México" in *EZLN: Documentos y comuncados.* Vol. 1, 85; "México: Entre el Sueño, la Pesadilla y el depertar" in *EZLN: Documentos y comuncados.* Vol. 2 (Mexico City: Ediciones Era, 1995), 50–80; and "Carta de Marcos sobre el Avance del Ejército Mexicano" in *EZLN: Documentos y comunicados* Vol. 2, 215–18.

30. Kathleen Bruhn, "Antonio Gramsci and the *Palabra Verdadera*: The Political Discourse of Mexico's Guerilla Forces," *Journal of Interamerican Studies and World Affairs* 41 (2) (1999): 29–55.

31. *Primer Informe Presidencial* (1989).

32. *Tercer Informe* (1991).

33. *Cuarto Informe* (1992).

34. Address by the Honorable Carlos Salinas de Gortari, President of the United Mexican States, on October 4, 1989, to the U.S. House of Representatives, 101st Cong., *Congressional Record,* H6562, cited in Victor Arriaga, "El Manejo de la Relación con Estados Unidos, 1990–1994," *Foro Internacional* 34 (4) (1994): 581.

35. *Address on the Occasion of the Anniversary of the PRI,* March 4, 1992 (aka "Social liberalism speech").

36. Address by the Honorable Carlos Salinas de Gortari.

37. Cited in Arriaga, "Manejo de la Relación," 582.

38. Address by the Honorable Carlos Salinas de Gortari; *Tercer Informe* (1990).

39. *Sexto Informe* (1994).

40. Address by the Honorable Carlos Salinas de Gortari.

41. Address by the Honorable Carlos Salinas de Gortari.

42. *Tercer Informe* (1991).

43. Address by the Honorable Carlos Salinas de Gortari.

44. Gil, *Hope and Frustration,* 36.

45. Cited in Mabire, "La utilidad del nacionalismo," 549–550, 554.

46. It is interesting to contrast Salinas's depictions of Latin America and the U.S. In his "Address" to the U.S. House of Representatives he refers to Mexico's relations with Latin America as a "priority" because of "common origins and sensitivities." He says nothing about a new chapter or a friendship with Latin America free from the past, but rather a relationship made fragile by the conditions of the region. The *Primer Informe* (1989) likewise acknowledges ties to Latin America in cultural terms but admits that they have been weak: "Because of the extensive cultural and friendly ties that unite Mexico with the countries of Latin American and the Caribbean, and for the similar problems that they confront, we have sought to elevate step by step

the cooperation that in many respects has been left behind in constituting a Latin American community."

47. Bernado Mabire, "El fantasma de la antigua ideología y su resistencia al cambio de la política exterior en el sexenio de Salinas de Gortari," *Foro Internacional* 34 (4) (1994): 546–47.

48. Mabire, "El fantasma de la antigua ideología," 568.

49. *Tercer Informe* (1991).

50. *Tercer Informe* (1991)

51. Cited in Mabire, "El fantasma de la antigua ideología," 566.

52. Address by the Honorable Carlos Salinas de Gortari.

53. Address by the Honorable Carlos Salinas de Gortari.

54. *Tercer Informe* (1991).

55. Cited in Mabire, "El fantasma de la antigua ideología," 565.

56. Address by the Honorable Carlos Salinas de Gortari.

57. Address by the Honorable Carlos Salinas de Gortari.

58. *Cuarto Informe* (1992).

59. Address by the Honorable Carlos Salinas de Gortari.

60. *Cuarto Informe* (1992).

61. Fox, *A Los Pinos,* 134, 149.

62. Fox, *A Los Pinos,* 136.

63. Fox, *A Los Pinos,* 137.

64. Fox, *A Los Pinos,* 137.

65. Fox, *A Los Pinos,* 138.

66. Fox, *A Los Pinos,* 123.

67. *Boletín No. 012/99.*

68. Fox, *A Los Pinos,* 136, 138.

69. Fox, *A Los Pinos,* 139.

70. Fox, *A Los Pinos,* 144.

71. *Boletín No. 012/99.*

72. Fox, *A Los Pinos,* 141.

73. Fox, *A Los Pinos,* 139.

74. Fox, *A Los Pinos,* 144.

75. Fox, *A Los Pinos,* 138.

76. Fox, *A Los Pinos,* 136.

77. Fox, *Independence Day speech.*

78. Fox, *A Los Pinos,* 132.

79. Fox, *A Los Pinos,* 141.

80. *Primer Informe Presidencial* (September 1, 2001), *Segundo Informe Presidencial* (September 1, 2002), downloaded from the presidential Web site, www.presidencia .gob.mx.

81. Address by His Excellency Vicente Fox, President of the United Mexican States, on September 6, 2001, to the U.S. House of Representatives, 106th Cong., *Congressional Record,* H5411. [http://thomas.loc.gov/cgi-bin/query/D?r107:5:./temp/ ~r107bsT5XW::]

82. Cárdenas, "Free Trade Is Not Enough."

83. Cited in Laurence Whitehead, "Mexico and the 'Hegemony' of the US: Past,

Present and Future," in *Mexico's External Relations in the 1990s,* edited by Riordan Roett (Boulder, Colo: Lynne Rienner, 1991), 259.

84. Partido de la Revolución Democrático (PRD), *1989: Informe de la situación nacional* (Mexico City, 1989).

85. PRD, *1989.*

86. Cárdenas, "Free Trade Is Not Enough."

87. *Cuauhtémoc Cárdenas,* 95.

88. Gil, *Hope and Frustration,* 170.

89. Partido de la Revolución Democrático (PRD), *Programa para el desarrollo económico con justicia social* (electronic versión) (n.d.).

90. *Cuauhtémoc Cárdenas,* 98.

91. Gil, *Hope and Frustration,* 162.

92. *Cuauhtémoc Cárdenas,* 101.

93. *Cuauhtémoc Cárdenas,* 71.

94. *Cuauhtémoc Cárdenas,* 95.

95. *Cuauhtémoc Cárdenas,* 96.

96. Partido de la Revolución Democrático (PRD), *Propuestas Basicas* (Mexico City, 1997).

97. Cárdenas, "Free Trade Is Not Enough."

98. PRD, *Programa para el desarrollo económico con justicia social.*

99. Gil, *Hope and Frustration,* 163.

100. Gil, *Hope and Frustration,* 164.

101. *Cuauhtémoc Cárdenas,* 108.

102. *Cuauhtémoc Cárdenas,* 93.

103. *Cuauhtémoc Cárdenas,* 93–94.

104. Gil, *Hope and Frustration,* 169.

105. *Cuauhtémoc Cárdenas,* 108.

106. *Cuauhtémoc Cárdenas.*

107. Cárdenas, "Free Trade Is Not Enough."

108. Gil, *Hope and Frustration,* 166, 167.

109. Gil, *Hope and Frustration,* 171.

110. *Cuauhtémoc Cárdenas,* 81, 103.

111. *Cuauhtémoc Cárdenas,* 81.

112. *Cuauhtémoc Cárdenas,* 85.

113. *Cuauhtémoc Cárdenas,* 108.

114. *Cuauhtémoc Cárdenas,* 82, 104, 107–8.

115. *Cuauhtémoc Cárdenas,* 91.

116. *Cuauhtémoc Cárdenas,* 92.

117. Cárdenas, "Free Trade is Not Enough."

118. *Cuauhtémoc Cárdenas,* 86.

119. *Cuauhtémoc Cárdenas,* 87.

120. *Cuauhtémoc Cárdenas,* 89.

121. Cárdenas, "Free Trade Is Not Enough."

122. Cárdenas, "Free Trade Is Not Enough."

123. *Cuauhtémoc Cárdenas,* 91.

124. Bruhn, "Antonio Gramsci and the *Palabra Verdadera,*" 38.

125. Bruhn, "Antonio Gramsci and the *Palabra Verdadera*," 40.

126. "Composición del EZLN," 74.

127. "Chiapas: El Sureste en dos vientos," 51.

128. "Chiapas: El Sureste en dos vientos," 52.

129. "México: Entre el Sueño," 52.

130. "México: Entre el Sueño," 53.

131. "México: Entre el Sueño," 54.

132. "Composición del EZLN," 55.

133. "Chiapas: El Sureste en dos vientos," 65.

134. "México: Entre el Sueño," 52.

135. "Ayuda Militar de EU a México."

136. *Third Declaration from the Lacandon Jungle* (mimeo).

137. García Canclini, *Globalización Imaginada*, 10.

138. See Javier Treviño, "Principios e intereses de la politica exterior de Mexico," in *México ante el fin de la Guerra Fría*, edited by Ilan Bizberg, 39–48.

139. Andrés Rozental, "La nueva etapa en las relaciones México-Estados Unidos," *Revista Mexican de Política Exterior* 44 (1994): 9.

140. Carlos Monsiváis, "Will Nationalism Be Bilingual?" in *Mass Media and Free Trade*, edited by McAnay and Wilkinson, 132–33.

141. See Jacqueline Mazza, "The Dilemma of National Sovereignty in Mexico: The Case of Foreign Electoral Observation," paper presented at the American Political Science Association meeting, Atlanta, Georgia, September 2–4, 1999.

142. Bernardo Sepulveda Amor, "Objetivos e intereses de la política exterior mexicana," in *México ante el fin de la Guerra Fría*, edited by Ilan Bizberg, 49–76.

143. Rozental, "Nueva etapa," 12.

144. Emilio Zebadúa, "Del plan Brady al TLC: La lógica de la política exterior mexicana, 1988–1994," *Foro Internacional* 36 (4) (1994): 628; Mabire, "El fantasma de la antigua ideología," 546.

145. Meyer, "Crisis de la elite mexicana," 91.

146. Erfani, *Paradox of the Mexican State.*

147. Monsiváis, "Will Nationalism Be Bilingual?" 132–33.

148. Mabire, "El fantasma de la antigua ideología," 565.

149. Carlos Monsiváis, "De la Cultura Mexicana en Visperas del Tratado de Libre Comercio," in *La educacion y la cultura ante el Tratado de Libre Comercio*, edited by Gilberto Guevara Niebla and Nestor García Canclini (Mexico City: Nueva Imagen, 1992).

150. Monsiváis, "Will Nationalism Be Bilingual?" 131.

151. To be sure, this has become a major point of contention with many analysts stressing the opposite point. Gustavo del Castillo Vera, "The Cultural Dimension of a Free Trade Agreement: The Case of Mexico," in *North America without Borders?: Intergrating Canada, the United States and Mexico*, edited by Stephen J. Randall, Herman Konrad, and Sheldon Silverman (Calgary: University of Calgary Press, 1992, 85), for instance, holds that neoliberalism has a clear impact on culture, including the harmonization of social policy and the transference of values: "in the face of commercial opening and the negotiations between Mexico and the United States . . . the acculturation of Mexico can take larger proportions." This view is particularly common in the literature focusing on the media and consumption.

152. Gutiérrez López and Gutiérrez E., "En torno a la redefinición del nacionalismo mexicano," 94.

153. Rozental, "Nueva etapa," 12.

154. Erfani, *Paradox of the Mexican State,* 163.

155. Arriaga, "Manejo de la Relación."

156. Mabire, "Utilidad del nacionalismo," 127; Pastor and Castañeda, *Limits to Friendship,* 36.

157. Pastor and Castañeda, *Limits to Friendship,* 36.

158. Rozental, "Nueva etapa," 12.

159. José Angel Gurría, "La nueva estrategia diplomática de México," in *México ante el fin de la Guerra Fría,* edited by Bizberg, 24.

160. Eduardo Barrera, "The US-Mexico Border as Post-NAFTA Mexico," in *Mass Media and Free Trade,* edited by McAnay and Wilkinson, 207.

161. Gutierrez and Gutierrez, "En torno a la redefinición del nacionalismo mexicano," 94.

162. Sotelo Sálazar, "Nación y nacionalismo en México," *Sociologia* 8 (21) (1993): 61.

163. Mabire, "Utilidad del nacionalismo," 129.

3

Gringolandia in the School Texts

E DUCATION IS A CRITICAL SITE in the construction of self and nation.[1] Through schools the State seeks to nurture identity and loyalty, create the nation's heroes and villains, privilege certain values, define and mold the "good" citizen, and even engage in ideological revisionism. To paraphrase Ernest Renan, it is in the schools where the State "gets the history wrong" for the sake of the nation.[2] Textbooks, particularly social science and history texts, are central to this constructive process. One fourth-grade text clearly establishes the nationalistic purpose in a page-one message: "This book proposes to help you understand your Fatherland, since by knowing it you will better understand why you love it and how and why you should be prepared to serve it."[3]

Since 1959 the Mexican government has controlled the content of texts at the primary level through its free textbook program, enabling "succeeding Mexican governments . . . to promote their respective political-social philosophies."[4] This makes the images and messages contained in the texts all the more important. Of course interpretations and perceptions of the U.S. constitute an important strand of such philosophies. As Sarah Corona shows, the narration of history related to the U.S. in the texts helps construct national identity and define the relationship between the two countries: "What is ultimately at play in the image of the U.S. in the textbooks is the construction, through opposition, of the identity of Mexico and the Mexicans."[5]

This chapter explores the Mexican narrative on the U.S. in Mexican primary and secondary (middle school) social science and history texts.[6] It builds on a body of works focusing on Mexican texts[7] and analyzes six elementary texts, all from the free textbook program, and six secondary school textbooks. The primary texts include: *Mi libro de Cuarto Año: Historia y Civismo* (herein referred to as fourth-grade 1960 text); *Mi libro de Quinto Año:*

Historia y Civismo (herein fifth-grade 1964 text); *Mi libro de Sexto Año: Historia y Civismo* (sixth-grade 1966 text); Josefina Vázquez, *Ciencias Sociales: Sexto Grado* (sixth-grade 1974 text); *Mi libro de Historia de Mexico Cuarto Grado* (fourth-grade 1992 text); and *Mi libro de Historia de Mexico Sexto grado* (sixth-grade 1992 text).[8] As part of the free text program, these volumes were mandatory throughout the nation at different times during the contemporary period. Prior studies helped identify some of these volumes. Going beyond previous analyses, I also examine six middle school books from the nineties.[9] Middle school texts are not part of the government's free text program; instead, the Secretary of Education produces a list of approved secondary texts for use in both the public and the private middle schools. To locate these volumes, I simply sought "the current secondary texts on history" from bookstores in Guadalajara and Mexico City. Though perhaps not a fully systematic or random selection, it is assumed that the texts under analysis represent a good cross sample of the texts in use at both the elementary and secondary levels, with the primary texts actually reaching back a few years.

In conducting the analysis, I began by locating all references to the U.S. and then comprehensively examined the discussion to identify the characteristics used to describe the U.S., the factors touted to explain the nature or conduct of the U.S., the historic events highlighted, and the explicit and implicit linkages to Mexico. It is important to note that the analysis here pays minimal attention to differences based on course subject, class level, primary versus secondary source, or even year of publication. Instead, discussion centers around five broad themes or areas that structure the treatment of the U.S. in the texts.

Portrayals of the U.S.

The texts present five primary themes or narratives involving the U.S. Each theme appears heavily, though not exclusively, in a particular historical period. The themes include: (1) the origins of the U.S.; (2) U.S. expansionism, Texas, and the subsequent war with Mexico; (3) U.S. economic power; (4) the U.S. and the Mexican Revolution; and (5) the U.S. as a global superpower in the twentieth century. These serve to organize the analysis and discussion. While the U.S., as historic agent, enjoys discussion and direct focus in all, the narratives differ in a variety of ways.

U.S. Origins and Independence

The student's first literary encounter with the U.S. centers on the English colonies in North America. Though the extent of the treatment varies from multiple pages to one page, the narrative tends to focus on key domestic traits of the colonies, with emphasis on their democratic and liberal values. The sixth-grade 1974 text stresses the colonists' escape from religious persecution and their inherent belief in religious freedom: traits the author links to the colonists' ability to "live together in peace" and self-government.[10] The text, which offers the most extensive discussion of the origins of the U.S., also quotes the Declaration of Independence's passages about man's natural equality and briefly discusses the Constitution, the purposes of the newly established government, the federal system, and the separation of powers.[11] Calling the Constitution "the first written constitution of our times," the text concludes with this prodemocratic statement: "The North Americans now had a government that they themselves had elected."[12] The fifth-grade 1964 text also highlights the principle of self-government and individual freedoms. In fact, it labels the colonies in the map as "self-governing colonies" rather than "possessions," the term used to refer to other areas of the continent. This emphasis on democratic values is particularly noteworthy in the secondary school texts. Raul Bolaños underscores the democratic aspect of the colonies, including a reference to the "Meeting House" where all citizens had access to elected representatives. He describes the struggle for independence, the contributions of the Declaration of Independence, and, ever so briefly, how the Constitution established separate powers.[13] Concepción Jiménez also stresses freedom, referring to the theme of religious persecution, the idea of freedom of thought, self-government (learned through assemblies), and equality. She too recites Jefferson's "All men are created equal" verse and hoists U.S. independence up as an example of the achievement of political freedom.[14] The other text by Jiménez also stresses the liberal origins of the U.S. In this text, she credits the Constitution with fostering equality and characterizes the young U.S. as "free and sovereign": an embodiment of the ideas of the age of enlightenment.[15] Carlos Alvear similarly emphasizes democratic principles to describe the formation of the U.S., noting the role of self-government and the ability of the Constitution to create a democratic form of government.[16]

Though such democratic and liberal accolades are clearly the most prominent themes used to describe the English colony of North America and the young, independent U.S., most texts do highlight to some degree at least the limited scope of these principles by pointing to the situation facing Indians, blacks, or others, or by referring to the economic principles that lay behind the democratic edifice. Though mentioning religious reasons as a cause for the establishment of the colonies, the fifth-grade 1964 text cautions readers that religious tolerance did have its limits. In an implicit reference to U.S. perceptions of Mexicans, such religious intolerance applied particularly to the Catholics: "Catholics were tolerated in very few colonies and even in these areas their social and political condition was strongly inferior."[17] This text also expresses the limits of U.S. liberalism by noting the tendency to "strip them [Indians] of their lands, keep them as far away as possible, and exterminate them mercilessly and systematically."[18] And yet, despite this seeming condemnation, the same text nonetheless cushions slavery rather softly within the statement that whites were "insufficient to work the lands and other businesses [and thus] had to bring black Africans to serve them as slaves."[19] Jiménez similarly conditions his statement on equality by including the statement "except for the black slaves"; but this is a minor reference that takes away little from the broader liberal message.[20] Of all the texts, Sergio Gómez et al. is perhaps the strongest in highlighting the taking of lands from the Indians and the brutality of slavery, thereby circumscribing any democratic and liberal image of the U.S.[21]

At the other extreme, many texts fail to qualify the scope of the democratic principles when describing the period. In Bolaños's extensive discussion of the English colonies and U.S. independence, there is scant mention of the mistreatment of Indians. In fact, he even disguises it somewhat by saying the Saxons remained on the land "through the negotiation of peace with the natural groups of redskins, or through war against them."[22] The ambiguity here allows the reader perhaps to ponder whether the treatment was pacific or not. The Jiménez and Alvear texts similarly provide virtually no reference to the treatment of the indigenous or the slaves. Indeed, both play down this side of U.S. history.[23]

The Gómez et al. text and to a lesser extent the fifth-grade 1964 text offer the only deviation from placing full and central emphasis on the democratic and liberal principles of the U.S.[24] Adopting an economic determinist point of view, Gómez et al. attribute U.S. independence to the growing economic autonomy of the colonies, placing freedom of private property alongside freedom of thought in their discussion of the Constitution. It is also within this economic-centered context that the authors highlight the Indians, slavery, and even Calvinism. The fifth-grade 1964 text, though in a minor and subsequent reference, also clarifies the relative weight of these causal factors, noting that the colonies existed primarily for economic and secondarily for religious reasons.[25]

The linkage to Mexico within the narrative here is generally favorable though quite limited: the U.S. serves as a source of inspiration or example for New Spain and Mexico. The fifth-grade 1964 text refers to U.S. independence as a source of inspiration for Latin America and France,[26] while the fourth-grade 1960 text lists U.S. independence as the first of three factors that stirred up the *criollos* and showed the Spanish American elite that freedom, equality, and human rights could be put into practice.²⁷ Gómez and Alvear also explicitly refer to the U.S. (along with France) as an inspiration for Mexico's independence movement.²⁸ Ma. de la Luz Vázquez and Meyra Egremy also refer to U.S. independence as an example, particularly for the *criollos*, since the U.S. movement provided them with revolutionary propaganda. Still, these authors seem to contend that the French Revolution was more influential than the American. Continuing with this theme of influence, the authors later refer to the U.S. Constitution as one of three influences on the Mexican constitution of 1824.²⁹

U.S. Expansionism, Texas, and the War

Arguably, the more pervasive and penetrating images of the U.S. in the texts arise from their treatment of U.S. expansionism. The "next chapter" following U.S. independence, this narrative encompasses U.S. treatment of the indigenous, Texas independence and annexation, the war with Mexico and Mexico's loss of territory, and in a less direct way even the country's treatment of Latin America during the nineteenth and twentieth centuries. All the texts pay close attention to U.S. expansionism, either from a global or a specifically Mexican perspective. Most highlight how the U.S. expanded its territory through a variety of means. Bolaños, for example, refers to "purchase, annexations and violence," while Gómez et al. cite "purchases, interventionism and war" as the instruments of U.S. expansion.³⁰ But irrespective of mode, the bottom line in all cases is that there was really no limit to the lengths to which the U.S. would go to acquire land or spread its influence.

The Monroe Doctrine and, to a lesser degree, Manifest Destiny reside prominently within the U.S. expansionist narrative. The two factors serve both to demonstrate and to explain the expansionist tendencies of the U.S. All the texts interpret the Monroe Doctrine not as an anticolonial policy (even though this purpose may be mentioned in a straw man–like fashion only to be dismissed), but as an undisputable policy of hegemony. Bolaños, for instance, describes the Monroe Doctrine as a policy designed to "maintain them [American territories] solely and exclusively under the influence of the United States [and wherein] this new American state presented itself as the sole arbiter of continental destiny."³¹ To reinforce its importance, the text includes a picture of James Monroe with the caption stating how his Doctrine attempts to "maintain all the people of the American continent under the power of the United States."³² Following a discussion of the dream of Bolivarian Pan-Americanism, the fifth-grade 1964 text provides a similar paragraph on *La Doctrina Monroe* whereby the U.S. "hoped to ensure . . . its own supremacy over the New World."³³ It too offers a picture of the U.S.

president. The sixth-grade 1974 text clarifies the Monroe Doctrine in terms of "according to which they were called to dominate all of America."[34] And though Vázquez and Egremy acknowledge that in theory the Monroe Doctrine sought to keep out colonial powers, they point out that "nonetheless, the subsequent expansionist U.S. policy demonstrated that the Monroe Doctrine defined its will to keep the American Continent under its hegemony."[35] In a special text box, Gómez et al., in turn, tout the Monroe Doctrine as justifying U.S. expansionism, which they go on to describe as "America for the 'Americans,' that is for the North Americans."[36] Jiménez also begins an explanation of U.S. expansion by mentioning the Monroe Doctrine, and though she refers to the purpose of the doctrine as preventing European intervention, the next paragraph notes that the U.S. intention "was for these [Latin American countries] to remain under their influence, that is, under their political and economic dominance so as to obtain primary materials and markets."[37]

At this point, the texts proceed to highlight the pernicious effects U.S expansionism has had on others, particularly the Indians and, most importantly, the Mexicans. Gómez et al., for example, portray U.S. expansionism as leading to the forced removal and the extermination of the indigenous groups, offering a list of the names of Indian nations to further dramatize this dreadful historical reality.[38] Jiménez notes that if the indigenous refused to leave their lands, they were exterminated and the survivors forced to live in zones reserved just for them. All this was due, the text notes, to "the ambition of these [North Americans] for their territories and their natural wealth."[39]

The most prominent effect of U.S. expansionism, of course, is on Mexico and the Mexicans. From Texas independence and the war to the Mesilla purchase, the texts couch their discussion of these events within the context of U.S. expansionism. Even the universal history texts, which offer very limited treatment of the U.S. war with Mexico, anchor the event in the waters of U.S. expansionism. Gómez et al., for example, who like Bolaños provide minimal treatment of the war, mention the war with Mexico briefly and then in the next two paragraphs describe the U.S. war with Spain and its acquisition of colonies, thus placing them all within a common framework of U.S. imperialism.[40] Some texts present the U.S. takeover of Texas and subsequent territories as premeditated and, as such, almost inevitable: a conclusion Josefina Vázquez found in the official liberal texts of the nineteenth century.[41] Alvear, for example, contends that the U.S. wanted to make Texas a state from the outset. Hence President Jackson favored the rebellion and sought any pretext to go to war and take Mexican territory.[42] Jiménez, who offers the most extensive and detailed treatment of the period, claims that Texan opposition to centralism served merely as the "pretext" to launch a movement that included Mexican federalists, U.S. agents, and U.S. colonists.[43]

Within this format, the texts make it clear who was right and who was wrong. Vázquez and Egremy point to the error of the U.S.'s claim that the Texas border extended to the Rio Bravo by referring to the Rio Nueces border as the one "shown in official documents" to be the true border.[44] "According to incontrovertible documents," the fourth-grade 1960 text makes clear, the border of Texas had never extended to the Rio Bravo, leaving little doubt as to who was in the right.[45] Indeed, the subsequent paragraph begins, "Although Mexico was right." Vázquez and Egremy make the point even more emphatically. Using a special text box, they reproduce *"Cartas sobre la provincia de Texas"* [Letters on the province of Texas], written in 1829 by Manuel Mier y Terán. The letter states that "the North Americans . . . have successively taken everything that has touched them. . . . There is no power like that of the North, that through silent paths has made the most important conquests in the world. . . . They begin by faking rights like in Texas that are impossible to support in a serious discussion, they present ridiculous pretexts founded on historical facts that no one admits to."[46]

Though most texts adopt this harsh and critical posture, not all do. Still, even the most benign view of U.S. expansionism is less than friendly. Alvear clarifies that many U.S. statesmen believed that the U.S. should extend its territories. He cites Jefferson and his acquisition of Louisiana, U.S. efforts to capture Canada and its purchase of Florida, and then describes the 1823 Monroe Doctrine in these terms: "The United States wanted to take for itself the role of protector and in a certain way of the political guide for the American continent."[47] He gives this a somewhat positive spin by noting that the U.S., based on the Monroe Doctrine, took a stand against European incursion and even opposed the French in Mexico. Even so, he concludes, "It was not rare that their agents worked to have U.S. institutions be considered the model, while working also to augment U.S. influence over the new nations of Hispanoamerica."[48]

Before exploring the significance of U.S. actions during this period and the nationalist lessons the texts stress, it is important first to assess the reasons dished up to account for U.S. behavior and the unfolding of historic events. Such explanations are important in setting the stage to discuss historic lessons and their relevance today. Two broad categories of reasons exist: U.S.-based and Mexican-based factors.

Among the U.S.-based factors that receive mention, perhaps the most neutral—and obviously applicable only to Texas independence—is that the U.S. simply held different interests than the Mexicans. The sixth-grade 1992 text, for example, explains the movement in Texas in part by noting the different interests that separated the Protestants and the Catholics. Others, like the fourth-grade 1960 text, refer simply to the Texans' lack of willingness to accept centralized control. Another factor offered to account for U.S. behavior is race. Though most depict the Monroe Doctrine and Manifest Destiny as pro-U.S. and anti-other, Jiménez also highlights its racial dimension; she refers to Manifest Destiny as "in reality having racist roots."[49] Another U.S.-based factor relates to power asymmetries and a U.S. predisposition to take advantage of weaker countries like Mexico. The sixth-grade 1992 text, for instance, notes that despite initially recognizing the new republic, the U.S. (and France) "observed the weakness of the country and sought the opportunity to benefit from it."[50] The fourth-grade 1992 text similarly contends that the U.S. took advantage of Mexico's weaknesses to take control of Texas, California, and New Mexico. In a subsequent section, the author builds on this theme, noting that the U.S. declared war based not only on a "pretext" but "sure of their capacity for an armed invasion."[51] In a similar manner, the sixth-grade 1974 text notes how France, England, and the U.S. all "tried to take advantage of the Latin American countries," that "Latin America was a victim of the rich countries," and that within this context "the United States invaded us in 1847 and took half our territory."[52]

Nevertheless, the most prominent U.S.-based reason given for U.S. expansionism is the nation's ambition for land. The sixth-grade 1974 text is straightforward: "the ambition for Mexican lands was so great that in 1846 the United States declared war on our country."[53] Mier y Terán's 1829 letter included in Vázquez and Egremy, as noted above, refers to the U.S. as "the greediest country for land."[54] The sixth-grade 1992 text also notes that the U.S. wanted the land from the beginning, and that despite Mexican laws or efforts to prevent the influx of Americans and the rejection of U.S. offers, Polk's moves exposed the "expansionist ambitions" of the U.S.[55] Jiménez also touts "their ambition for these territories and natural riches" as the reason for the treatment of the Indians, while Gómez et al. refer to "the fever for gold and the possession of new lands."[56]

Normally U.S. ambition prevails over all other possible reasons, now reduced to nothing more than "pretexts." The fourth-grade 1960 text, for example, which interestingly does not refer to U.S. ambition *per se*, but rather to the ambition of the southern cotton states, declares Texans' opposition to Mexico's centralist constitution as merely a pretext for the war. It further minimizes this factor by stating that "much propaganda was made against the new Mexican laws; they said that under such laws the conditions of the Texans would get worse."[57] The Jiménez text also claims that centralism served as a mere "pretext" to launch the Texas independence movement.[58] Indeed, U.S. ambition was so strong, it seems, that the war is portrayed as almost inevitable despite Mexico being right or despite its goodwill attempts to defuse the situation. Jiménez stresses, for instance, how President Herrera tried everything to prevent the annexation of Texas, even promising to recognize the independence of Texas, but to no avail.[59]

While most indict U.S. ambition, few try to account for it. This fosters the impression that the U.S. is naturally and uncontrollably ambitious. Jiménez does go one step further, however, by offering an economic rationale for U.S. expansionist tendencies. First, she refers to the (conquered) land as rich in resources, indicating that the objective of U.S. expansion was economic. In the next paragraph, she then explains in detail how the southern states needed more land to produce cotton and the northern states needed more land because of their growing population. She then goes on to posit the question: "And where do you think these territories were that the U.S. needed? Well in the hands of Mexico."[60]

In addition to these U.S.-based ingredients, the texts also highlight a variety of Mexico-based factors to explain U.S. expansionism at the nation's expense. To begin with, most diminish the importance of Texas to Mexico seemingly as a means to account for the ease by which Texas achieved its independence. The sixth-grade 1992 text highlights the fact that in 1832 Texas had a population of 24,700 of which only 3,400 was Mexican, a point that comes across as almost a rationale for the defeat.[61] The fourth-grade 1992 text, the Vázquez and Egremy text, and the fourth-grade 1960 text also mention a similar demographic mismatch, with the latter adding that many Mexicans in Texas felt abandoned by the central government as a result.[62] Gómez et al. partially explain the U.S. victory in Texas as a result of the fact that the territories were "little known and studied by the Mexicans."[63] Sarah Corona similarly cites one text during the modernization period (post-WWII) that goes so far as to call Texas a "distant colony" that was "really Yankee,"[64] while according to Vázquez the official liberal text of the nineteenth century by Alfonso Toro referred to Texas as just "nominally" belonging to Mexico.[65]

Other factors explaining Mexico's loss include bad luck, the ineptitude of General Santa Anna, Mexico's goodwill, the country's foreign debt, and, above all, domestic political disputes. The fourth-grade 1960 text, for example, makes the U.S. victory sound almost fortuitous by noting that Santa Anna, who at "various times was able to defeat the Texans," was "*surprised* and taken prisoner by the small army of Texans that remained." Still, like other texts, the narrative blames the affair, in whole or in part, on the failures of Santa Anna or, as it states, the "unskillfullness of Santa Anna." It continues pointing out that with Santa Anna prisoner, "the war could have continued on and certainly with success," but that to gain his release, he had to sign the pact granting Texas independence.[66]

Though most portray the U.S. in negative terms, as noted earlier, Jiménez crystallizes this point further by underscoring Mexican goodwill as one of the many factors hastening the disastrous outcome. Specifically, the author touts the policy of allowing foreigners into the northern province provided they profess Catholicism and loyalty to the central government as naive and destined to failure.[67] Further underscoring Mexican goodwill, the author later mentions that Mexico began negotiations to avoid the annexation of Texas and that at one moment war did not seem possible.[68] Such references to Mexican goodwill, of course, contrast (and help define) U.S. ambition and ill will. Still, few texts depict this clear binariness as does one passage in the 1970s text *La Patria Mexicana*. It describes and personalizes what may have been a fictional event in the war: "In one of many encounters, a Mexican official was about to thrust his sword into a Yankee, but the Yankee on his knees, begged for a pardon; the Mexican turned his sword away and continued on, but the Yankee stood up and killed the official with his rifle firing at his back."[69]

Foreign debt also stands out in many texts as one of the factors contributing to the historic event. Jiménez, for example, notes how Mexico stood on the edge of bankruptcy, deep in debt to foreigners, mainly to the U.S. This situation triggered foreign pressures on Mexico and foreign efforts to capitalize on the situation. The author mentions specifically how U.S. Ambassador Butler used "dirty" methods to pressure Mexico to cede Texas in payment for the debt.[70] Vázquez and Egremy also refer to the debt as a major factor igniting war: "Since Mexico had not paid [the U.S.] the costs for the indemnization for the conflict in Texas, President James Polk had a declaration of war ready against our country, which he sent forward on May 13, 1846, for invading their territory!"[71]

But despite all these, by far the most important factor in the texts to account for Mexico's loss at the hands of the U.S. revolves around Mexico's internal political disputes. The sixth-grade 1992 text indicts the "chaos" that reigned in Mexico.[72] The fourth-grade 1960 text calls the fact that "there was no peace or unity among Mexicans" as "the worst of all."[73] Alvear, in turn, refers to "the impotency of the Mexican government" to explain why "Texas would become independent."[74] Through word association, the chapter in the fourth-grade 1992 text covering the war actually sports the title "*Del desorden al desastre*" [from disorder to disaster].[75] And in perhaps the most extensive treatment of the war, one text suggests that the U.S. exploited the governmental instability during the period. The author notes factional struggles at various points in the discussion, including the rebellion in 1841 by Paredes

Arrillaga against Bustamante and the (multiple) return(s) of Santa Ana to power. In one depiction of this problem, the author asks the reader rhetorically, "What do you think happened when Mexican troops that should have contested the U.S. turned and rebelled against Herrera in 1845?" The author then goes on to cast the explicit association: "While the internal struggles became more intense, the whole country was victim to a foreign invasion that within a few months threatened to arrive at the center of the country."[76]

In contrast to the tendency to play down the importance of Texas as a way to account for Mexico's failure to keep the northern province, the texts stress the importance of the war and the loss of territory that occurred a decade later, enshrining these as critical historical watersheds for the nation.[77] All the texts make clear to the student the extent of the loss and the humiliation. They do this through a variety of mechanisms. First, they all note the extensiveness of the lost territory, usually by referring to it as "more than half the nation's territory." In a typical passage, the fourth-grade 1960 text states that Mexico lost Texas, New Mexico, Arizona, and Alta California "or two million, two hundred and forty thousand square kilometers, an area greater than half the territory."[78] Though Bolaños provides the shortest and most neutral treatment of the war, he nonetheless personalizes the loss by employing the first person plural: "They detached Texas from *our* country," . . . "the war with *our* country," and "*we* lost more than two million square kilometers" (emphasis added).[79] Second, the authors crystallize the significance of the defeat for the nation. Jiménez, for example, refers to it as "a hard strike against the honor and dignity of our country" and later as "one of the worst humiliations of your history."[80] The sixth-grade 1992 text, after calling "the military humiliation" the "greatest disgrace," dramatically and ironically notes how on September 16 in 1847 (Mexican independence day), the U.S. flag flew over the National Palace as "the nation suffered its worst military and moral defeat in its history."[81] Taking a somewhat different tack, the sixth-grade 1992 text underscores the war's significance by drawing a historic parallel, equating the U.S. war with the conquest. It does this by noting how the U.S. took "the route followed by Hernán Cortez."[82] For some, the significance of the defeat extends beyond Mexico. As the text by Aguirre Cinta sums it up: "History does not record an act more vile than the robbery the Americans committed against us, taking by force that considerable portion of our territory."[83]

Besides referring to the loss of land and the humiliation, some texts further drive home the loss by noting the opportunity costs involved or the subsequent and timeless discriminatory treatment Mexicans living in the area have suffered: two images that further shape national consciousness. The opportunity costs are made clear by noting that part of the land that was lost (California) would subsequently be the site of the *"fiebre del oro"* [gold fever].[84] Such references, of course, feed the myth of the lost treasure of California and Texas: a neat mechanism to blame Mexican failures on the U.S. (in other words, we would be rich if we still had California or we would not be poor had the U.S. not taken California from us).[85] Another text emphasizes the discrimination that Mexicans would subsequently suffer in the lost territories. As Jiménez points out, Mexicans became the "objects of mistreatment and expulsions, despite the fact that the treaty prohibited it." The author then links this group of historic Mexicans to current-day Hispanics by referring to them as the "origin of the Chicano community in the United States." He then adds that "they constitute one of the most important ethnic minorities in that country."[86] Jiménez reiterates this point in a separate "Activities" section at the end of the chapter. After presenting Article VIII of the Treaty of Guadalupe Hidalgo setting out the rights Mexicans were supposed to retain, the author asks the student reader a series of questions such as: "What do you think happened to the Mexican population in the territories?" "Have you ever been in the U.S.?" "How are Mexicans treated in the U.S.?" "Are their rights respected?" "Do they have equal pay?"[87] In the end, the pedagogical exercise drives home not only the message relating to the consequences of the loss of territory, but U.S. discrimination against Mexicans and its failure to comply with an international treaty.[88]

The significance of the event, in turn, translates easily into critical lessons for the nation, defining aspects of patriotism and the "needs" of the nation. Statements vary, but common themes are easily located. One theme is patriotism. The fourth-grade 1960 text stresses the heroism: "Although our army had no military triumphs, they demonstrated, during the battles they fought, a great heroism . . . and they merit our recognition and our respect—an example of love for the Fatherland."[89] Most texts illustrate patriotism by mentioning the *niños héroes* and, in some cases, providing the names of the seven fallen cadets. In terms of highlighting the "needs" of the nation, the texts' basic message centers on the need for unity to protect the country against the U.S. The fourth-grade 1992 text highlights, for instance, the imperative to "end the mistakes of Santa Anna and the political disorder."[90] Jiménez puts it in the following terms: "This defeat, due more to the disunity of the country than U.S. power, would be one of the most terrible lessons that we Mexicans have lived, and we must assimilate it so that it never happens again."[91] Still, none is clearer than the fourth-grade 1960 text, which, under the subheading of *"Reflexiones"* and shadowed by a picture of the flag, notes that the defeat taught a lesson that "we must never forget: the unity of all Mexicans is indispensable, since with internal peace there is progress, and with progress, the force to enable us to cover ourselves against traps and injustices." A forceful paragraph stressing the importance of being ready to defend the *patria* follows. "We must," it states, "unite so as to give greater strength daily to our Fatherland: let the example and the sacrifices of the heroes of 1847 help you achieve your greatest desires and help you see the need to understand well the history of Mexico."[92] The extent of the lesson is drawn perhaps to its ultimate extreme in the conclusion to Manuel Mier y Teran's letter: "anyone that agrees to giving up the land," it contends, "should be considered a traitor and punished with death."[93]

One clear and final lesson sketched nicely by the description and analysis of this period is "don't trust the U.S." This message nestles behind the image of U.S. ambition unchecked by reason and Mexico's goodwill. It fastens to Jiménez's discussion of the U.S.'s failures to abide by the Treaty of Guadalupe Hidalgo.[94] Interestingly, the U.S.'s lack of compliance with international agreements is a point made in the discussion of other historic periods as well. Vázquez and Egremy, for instance, note that the U.S. frequently violated the border with Mexico despite the existence of treaties. They note specifically the Otis-Adams treaty and other treaties in 1821 and 1844 in which the "U.S. promised to respect the border with Mexico"; but, "Despite these agreements, the North Americans continued their incursions into Mexican territory."[95] In a similar vein, the sixth-grade 1992 text notes that the arrangements in the Bucareli accord in 1923 were never applied.

Indeed, it is in this context—as a historic lesson duly learned—that this national tragedy and injustice receive something approaching a "positive spin."[96] One sixth-grade text, for example, credits the war with an increase in the search for national identity, with artists, intellectuals, and writers all seeking to create a national culture that was liberal and romantic, that glorified freedom, the *patria*, love, the family, loyalty, and heroism.[97] Indeed, this echoes a conclusion drawn by Vázquez, who also attributes the rise of Mexican nationalism, and particularly its pessimistic and introverted nationalism, to the war with the U.S.[98] More specifically to the purposes here, the war crystallized a particular type of nationalism characterized by an unmistakable anti-U.S. stripe, or as one text notes: "Since the plunder of 1847, Mexico's enmity toward the United States has been as great as it has been sincere and just."[99]

The U.S. as an Economic Power

The third major context in which the reader encounters the U.S. relates to economic matters. Regardless of whether the text covers universal or Mexican history, they all depict the U.S. as a developed or advanced country and a powerful economic player. This theme covers a broad historical expanse, though in the Mexican history texts, as we will see momentarily, it concentrates in and around the period of the *Porfiriato*.

In the universal history texts, discussions of global changes marking the nineteenth century include references to the economic growth and development of the U.S., though usually these are couched within a broader context that includes many European countries as well. Bolaños, for instance, highlights the U.S. in his discussion of the great economic changes of the period. He refers to the use of steamships in the U.S., important inventions such as Edison's lightbulb, and even the creation of the American Federation of Labor. Later, the text refers to the U.S. when describing the Depression, noting that by 1925 the U.S. had become a world economic power. It notes that Germany depended on the U.S. for loans, that the U.S. was the most affected by the Depression, and that FDR's New Deal saved the U.S. economy.[100] Gómez et al. mention the U.S. as one of a handful of developed countries benefiting from the great economic and social transformations of the nineteenth century.[101] In a similar manner, the sixth-grade 1974 text hoists the U.S. up as an example of economic development. With clear reference to consumer abundance, the text features a drawing of a Sears catalog and another drawing of a woman who appears modern, if not North American, with the caption "consumer society."[102]

Alvear takes a somewhat different approach, emphasizing private property and individual initiative to describe U.S. capitalism. Despite providing a positive image of the U.S. as an example of economic development, Alvear nevertheless associates U.S. capitalism with inequality, pointing out how at times property has remained in the hands of the few. He even goes so far as to note that Jews have held much of the financial power in the U.S. Still, he seems to pull his punches somewhat by suggesting that things in the U.S. are not as bad as in Europe, and that U.S. capitalism increases standards of living: "But it is important to note that while capitalism in Europe has been of a markedly reactionary type, with a limited tendency to recognize the rights of workers, U.S. capitalism has been concerned with elevating the standard of living of the majority of its people."[103] And yet, in a contrasting message, Jiménez describes the U.S. origins of May Day, careful to note that the day is not celebrated in U.S. This helps depict the U.S. as harboring perhaps an antilabor form of capitalism.[104]

Besides casting the U.S. as an example or a model of economic strength, the texts also anchor U.S. hegemony and influence, particularly over Latin America, the world, and Mexico (to be described later), in economic currents. The texts tend to describe such economic relationships as exploitative and particularly beneficial to the U.S. This is a slight variation on the ambitious and expansionist image of the U.S. crafted in the discussion of the war with Mexico, but with descriptions of U.S. behavior taking on an increasingly economically imperialist tone. Now rather than conquering territory, U.S. expansionism takes the form of controlling markets, while intervention involves protecting those markets. Describing the broadening of U.S. markets and communications abroad, the fifth-grade 1964 text refers to the U.S.'s need to sell its manufactured goods abroad and buy primary materials. In a similar discussion of commercial expansion in the latter half of the nineteenth century, the sixth-grade 1992 text refers to the U.S.'s need to expand its commercial ties to Latin America and even acquire colonies.[105] In one passage, it stresses the fact that "their greatest interest was to trade with the nations of Latin America" to obtain raw materials, despite the fact that this "impeded the development of industry in each of these countries." And after pointing to the existence of U.S. trade with China, the text then reminds its readers that yet again "the principal zone of commercial influence for the U.S. was Latin America, the region where it obtained concessions and privileged treatment for its merchants, and if a country . . . opposed them, in defense of their interests, the U.S. promised to intervene to get favorable governments."[106] The sixth-grade 1974 text similarly describes how Latin America became dependent on England, France, and the U.S., which exploited the region's resources. As such, Latin America became the producer and exporter of the raw materials needed by the industrialized countries: a situation whereby the rich countries controlled the process. And the outcome, according to the text, was hardly positive: "While they got rich, the producing countries were always in worse conditions."[107]

Some texts link U.S. economic strength and its economic influence abroad explicitly, reminiscent of classic imperialist thought. Jiménez, for example, posits that the U.S. placed "itself at the head of the countries of America, even to the point of controlling the main part of the Latin American markets" because of the need for raw materials. The text goes on to describe the Spanish-American war, the emergence of the U.S. as a colonial power, and its subsequent interventionist tendencies within this imperialist, almost mercantalist, context: "Since the second third of the nineteenth century, the United States intervened in the affairs of the Latin American countries and . . . has exercised a policy of economic expansion that has resulted in the conquest of markets and sources of raw materials, first in Latin America and later in the whole world, until it became a world power."[108] The sixth-grade 1974 text offers a similar economic rationale. After noting the role of European money in the U.S., it too alludes to the need for cheap raw materials as leading the U.S. to dominate Latin American markets. This economic logic also lay behind the U.S. desire for colonies and hegemony over the Caribbean. Consequently, the explosion of a boat in Havana harbor in 1898 served merely as a "pretext" to declare war on Spain. By noting that the situation of Cuba was sad because the country simply changed *metropoli*, the text paints the U.S. with the same brush as other imperial powers.[109]

The prominence of this economic role—economic reductionism, perhaps—can even be seen in descriptions of more contemporary events. For example, the sixth-grade 1974 text highlights the U.S. role in World War II before entering the conflict as one based on its control over resources, particularly its control over "the primary materials of Latin America," and its industry, which it describes as the most important in the world. It further underscores the U.S. as a base of huge military production and then fastens the importance of the U.S.'s subsequent involvement in the war to economics: "Since the U.S. had great resources and enormous production . . . the North Americans satisfied their own needs and helped the Russians and the English."[110] The text seems, then, to leave the reader with the impression that the primary contribution of the U.S. to World War II was economic rather than military. The same text, under the subheading *"Surgen las superpotencias"* [the emergence of the superpowers], also points to the economic consequences of the war on the U.S., noting that the U.S. enjoyed economic growth because it was not touched by the war, thereby allowing the U.S. to increase its investments in poor countries in industry, hotels, and so on.[111]

Texts focusing on Mexican history also portray the U.S. as a powerful economic agent. They offer a more refined image of the impact of the U.S. economically on Mexico and provide less emphasis on the negative consequences of the relationship. In some contrast to the depiction with regard to Latin America or the world, the major image here is of the U.S. as the source of foreign investment in Mexico or as a major economic partner. Such treatments concentrate on the period of Porfirio Díaz. Without exception, the texts highlight the overwhelming presence of foreign investment in narrating the period, usually with specific references to the U.S. Vázquez and Egremy, for instance, include the U.S., along with England, France, and Germany, as the source of huge foreign investments, referring specifically to the U.S. in terms of its control over mining and petroleum.[112] The sixth-grade 1992 text similarly stresses the role of U.S. capital in the construction of Mexico's rail lines in this period.[113]

All of the texts depict the consequences of the nation's economic ties to the U.S. during the *Porfiriato* in both negative terms—the U.S. as the recipient of concessions and often greater benefits that those enjoyed by Mexico or Mexicans—and positive terms—as a factor contributing to Mexican growth and development. On the one hand, the texts cast the U.S. as enjoying special treatment vis-à-vis locals or, at worst, as exploiting Mexico: a view supported by the broader treatment toward Latin America highlighted above. In referring to the *Porfiriato,* Vázquez and Egremy, for instance, stipulate that national capital could not compete against foreign capital and therefore concentrated attention on the countryside.[114] And yet, as they argue, the North Americans possessed the most important agricultural enterprises in the country.[115] The authors also highlight how just giving foreign enterprises equal treatment led to the elimination of national industry or their being bought out because of the technological superiority of foreign firms.[116] In one passage, Jiménez clearly depicts foreign investments as exploitative, pointing out that the investments "benefited from the exploitation of our resources. The country received certain profits, but this was not comparable to what the foreigners took . . . [who were only concerned with] exploiting resources at the lowest cost."[117] The author even contends that government officials realized this pernicious situation and tried to limit it, but were unable to because concessions had already been granted. Later, the author explicitly links the foreigners' wealth to Mexico's poverty: "The great concessions to the foreign capitalists had enriched them; however, the peasant class did not enjoy the benefits of Porfirian progress."[118]

Encompassed within this depiction are the economic underpinnings of U.S. intervention, though again the point is not nearly as strong as it is in relation to Latin America. U.S. involvement in the Cananea labor strike in Chihuahua in 1906 fits within this profile. The sixth-grade 1992 text contends the U.S. intervened to protect its economic interests, noting that the strike was put down by the army and "los *rangers estadounidense.*"[119] An even more important economic-based U.S. intervention in Mexico centers on the oil expropriation: a theme explored in the subsequent section looking at the Revolutionary period.

On the other hand, despite these negative connotations, most texts also highlight the gains to Mexico from its economic ties to the U.S. Vázquez and Egremy, for example, credit foreign investment with spawning Mexico's first economic transformation. After noting the lack of sufficient Mexican capital to provide progress, the authors then offer a clear lesson for the nation: "For Mexico to progress, it was necessary to acquire loans from abroad that contributed to Mexican economic development."[120] Dennis Gilbert finds that the school texts during the Echeverria period made a similar claim.[121]

The texts further establish this point by spotlighting the economic advances and progress in the northern states—advances clearly due to the region's proximity and ties to the U.S. The sixth-grade 1992 text refers to the new rail lines as uniting the center with the north of Mexico and with the U.S.[122] Later, the author notes that the good relations during World War II brought economic growth (in bold) because Mexico became a provider of workers and products to the U.S. war economy.[123] The implication here is rather clear. In a similar manner, Jiménez cites the need to connect the nation's industrial and mining centers with the U.S. as the main impetus for constructing rail lines in the north.[124] After noting the U.S. role in constructing the rail lines in Mexico and that by the end of the nineteenth century Mexican commerce with the U.S. had become more important than with Europe, the sixth-grade 1992 text highlights the linkage of northern Mexican industry to the U.S. and attributes its growth to the "flourishing economies of the south and southeastern U.S." As a result, "The population went north in search of jobs and opportunities."[125] Again, the image created is not only that the U.S. is the pole of development, but that bilateral and even personal economic ties translate into progress for Mexico and Mexicans.

It is clearly within this rather positive context that the relationship comes off as mutually beneficial: a statement spanning different historic moments. Vázquez and Egremy, for instance, note how commercial relations with the U.S. during the late nineteenth century "were among the most cordial and thought was given to making a Commercial Treaty. Later, the possibility of adopting a common currency for all the nations of America was studied."[126] Presumably students would draw historic parallels to NAFTA and the present.

These dual, conflicting images of the U.S. as an economic agent are rather clear and important. Jiménez offers perhaps the best example of this duality. She recognizes the importance of foreign investment for economic development and alludes to its role during the *Porfiriato* in promoting Mexico's progress; and yet, simultaneously, she characterizes it as exploitative.[127] A similar contradictory message emerges in discussions of the impact of the U.S. economy on Mexican development during and after World War II. Vázquez and Egremy, on the one hand, attribute Mexico's industrial development during the war to the fact that Mexico was cut off from acquiring industrial goods from the U.S. and other developed economies. This view tends to support the extreme dependency position insofar as it envisions U.S.-Mexican economic relations as an obstacle to Mexican development. On the other hand, the author also notes positively how the U.S.'s need for Mexican raw materials fed Mexican development.[128] This crafts a distinct lesson: that the relationship in fact facilitates rather than blocks development. But while this text depicts U.S. inattention to Mexico during the war as good for the Mexican economy, the sixth-grade 1992 text refers to the favorable situation that Mexico enjoyed following the war as a result of the U.S. becoming a world power, suggesting that the economic ties are good, not bad, for Mexico. As the author concisely states: "Mexico benefited from this situation."[129] And to help defy any notions of exploitation, the author actually refers to foreign companies at this point as *"socios"* [partners]. The

fourth-grade 1992 text similarly contends that the war "increased the economic opportunities for Mexico."[130]

Building on the image of foreign investments and other economic ties to
the U.S. as being something good for Mexico, one text goes a step further
and links such benefits to political stability. This echoes the main historic
lesson drawn from the war with the U.S., noted earlier: the imperative of
national unity. The fourth-grade 1992 text credits the political stability of the
Porfiriato with bringing in foreign investments and facilitating exports,
though it still adds the disclaimer that the peasants did not progress from
this arrangement.[131] If we attach this to the earlier historic lesson, the reader
is left with the conclusion that political stability is not only necessary to prevent the U.S. from taking advantage of a weak and divided Mexico (the war
period lesson), but also necessary for Mexico to enjoy the benefits of its economic relationship with its northern neighbor.

The U.S. and the Mexican Revolution

Discussions of the Mexican Revolution rarely mention the U.S., though the
few references are important in contributing to national perceptions precisely
because of the saliency of the Revolution itself to the nation's history. Generally, the U.S. surfaces in two contexts: as a neutral or safe haven where Mexican exiles reside and as an interventionist agent shaping events for selfish
political and economic reasons at Mexico's expense. Jiménez, for example,
refers to the U.S. when he notes that Francisco Madero went into exile in the
U.S., from whence he proclaimed the Plan de San Luis Potosí.[132] The sixth-
grade 1992 text similarly notes that General Orozco sought refuge in the
U.S.[133]

Beyond these references, interventionism stands out as the main theme
when it comes to the U.S. and the Revolution. Treatments of the U.S. during
this phase of the patriotic story echo earlier depictions of the U.S. as expansionist and economically hegemonic. Jiménez is clear in arguing that the U.S.
sought to, and did, influence Revolutionary Mexico: "The country that most
influenced the Mexican Revolution was the U.S.A."[134] Such intervention
encompassed U.S. support—specifically Henry Lane Wilson's support—for
the counterrevolution of Victoriano Huerta, the U.S. invasion of Veracruz in
1914, the U.S. policy of nonrecognition of the Carranza government, and
U.S. actions revolving around the oil nationalization in 1938.

All texts not only mention U.S. involvement in the Huerta counterrevolution, but generally cast it as second only to the war in terms of its pernicious
effects on the country. The depiction is reminiscent of U.S. behavior in the
mid-nineteenth century and its economic conduct afterwards, though the

degree of blame on the U.S. varies somewhat. At one extreme, Vázquez and Egremy stress Henry Lane Wilson's hostility toward Francisco Madero and contend that the counterrevolutionary pact was "celebrated" in the U.S. embassy. Driving home the importance of the U.S. role, the authors include a text box containing a letter written by Luís Manuel Rójas (the legislator who presided over the Constitutional convention) entitled "*Yo acuso a* Henry Lane Wilson" [I accuse Henry Lane Wilson]. The letter poetically recites the opening line at every stanza. It accuses Wilson of threatening U.S. armed intervention, of profiting from capital invested in Mexico, and of being responsible for the political assassinations of Francisco Madero and Pino Súarez.[135] By contrast, Jiménez describes the role of the U.S. in slightly more ambiguous terms, noting merely that the agreement between Huerta and Felix Díaz was signed at the U.S. embassy with the approval of Henry Lane Wilson. There is no implication here that the U.S. actually orchestrated the plan.[136]

While U.S. intervention in the counterrevolution invites easy condemnation because it helped destroy patriots (Madero and Pino Suarez) and reward a major villain (Huerta), the texts equally denounce U.S. intervention in Veracruz in 1914—even though it arguably did the opposite. But this time the texts attack U.S. intervention on a more universal level, thereby allowing the authors to privilege national unity in the face of U.S. intervention. The sixth-grade 1992 text, for example, stresses how the U.S. capture of Veracruz triggered protests from revolutionaries like Carranza himself (the targeted beneficiary) who felt that the problems of the nation should be resolved by Mexicans and not foreigners.[137] Jiménez similarly calls the U.S. occupation of Veracruz "unjustified."[138] The bottom-line message here seems clear: even U.S. "help" through intervention is considered illegitimate.

The texts also pose the U.S.'s nonrecognition policy, its refusal to obey the nation's laws or Supreme Court mandates, its boycotts, and its many threats as distinct forms of intervention, clear signs of the country's antirevolutionary posture. The sixth-grade 1992 text, for instance, highlights the U.S.'s refusal to recognize Mexico's new government out of fear over the application of Article 27 to its petroleum companies, though it notes that the true legal battle prompting expropriation was whether Mexico had the right to make its laws applicable to foreign companies.[139] Generally, the texts justify and laud the oil expropriation as a supreme act of national sovereignty, of defiance and resistance. Not only do they portray the U.S. as the culprit that justified the expropriation, but they also cast the U.S. response to it as overly harsh. Vázquez and Egremy, for example, highlight how the U.S. refused to buy Mexican silver and denied Mexico credit because of the expropriation, despite the fact that Mexico was already paying compensation for the expropriation of petroleum and agricultural lands and making payments on its foreign debt.[140] Jiménez also points out that the foreign companies paid meager wages, did not provide safe working conditions, and got the U.S. government to pressure Mexico by, among other measures, boycotting Mexican silver.[141] By now sensitive to U.S. intervention, the reader could implicitly understand how the sheer likelihood of U.S. intervention during the Revolution could fundamentally shape events in the country—its chilling effect. Still, Jiménez makes this point explicit: "Besides, the Revolutionary governments feared that the U.S.A. would decide to intervene directly in Mexico, just as occurred in the end [referring to Veracruz]."[142]

Interestingly, just one text cites the Pershing expedition. It states simply that Pancho Villa "penetrated the city of Columbus" while supplying no mention of the nature of his acts. Moreover, it notes that instead of capturing Villa, the expedition increased the rebel's popularity. Indeed, General Pershing, who would later become famous in World War I, "failed with Villa, who always eluded him with skill."[143] The treatment thus casts Villa as a hero in part because of his ability to outfox and frustrate not only the U.S., but also a general whose skill was demonstrated subsequently in Europe.

Of particular interest here are the reasons the texts give for U.S. intervention in the Revolution, a point that helps the reader forge a deeper understanding of the U.S. and, in turn, a clearer sense of why Mexico should be concerned about its northern neighbor. A mildly generic reason entails U.S. interests. The fourth-grade 1992 text, for example, simply states that President Wilson felt that Madero was opposed to U.S. interests and therefore conspired to eliminate him.[144] At one point, Jiménez makes a similar blanket statement to account for U.S. policy: "Throughout the revolutionary period, the U.S. government maintained a policy of not recognizing any faction, but of offering support to anyone that would guarantee its interests."[145] At a subsequent point, however, the author refines those interests by noting how the U.S. supported "the faction that guaranteed political stability to protect its investments."[146] She also presents this economic-based motivation as anchoring the U.S. policy of nonrecognition in the postrevolutionary years and during the oil industry expropriation. Drawing historic parallels to demonstrate the truly ahistoric nature of the problem, the sixth-grade 1992 text notes how President Calles collided "like his predecessors" with U.S. and English petroleum companies over the application of Article 27 and, furthermore, how the conflict almost prompted another military invasion of Mexico.[147]

Some texts provide other reasons besides U.S. interests (economic or otherwise) to account for U.S. conduct during the period. The sixth-grade 1992 text, for instance, argues that Mexican democracy threatened the U.S.: "Wilson considered that a democratic Mexico could be too independent and threaten the properties and interests of U.S. companies in the country."[148]

The U.S. as a Global Power

The final (and in some ways residual) narrative on the U.S. relates to the U.S. as a power in a more global context in the twentieth century. This narrative is important in terms of crystallizing the superpower status of the U.S., highlighting the country's involvement in shaping global events, and depicting U.S. values and priorities.

In many ways, despite the U.S. role in the two world wars, U.S. global power does not become a central theme in the texts until the Cold War. Indeed, the discussions of both World War I and II are far from U.S.-centric (especially compared to U.S. texts) and even seem to downplay or at times disguise the U.S. role. For example, the U.S. gets little treatment in Bolaños's description of World War I. Though he mentions the U.S. entrance into the war following the sinking of the Lusitania, there is little mention of the U.S.'s effect on the war's outcome. Similarly, in the author's discussion of the subsequent period of a new world order (League of Nations), he portrays the U.S. as just one of a group of actors.[149] Gómez et al. also refer to the sinking of the Lusitania as prompting U.S. involvement and mention that with the incorporation of the U.S., which provided war materials, soldiers, primary materials, and economic support, the Entente won. This almost seems to characterize the role of the U.S. as a sponsor of the war effort rather than an agent. The authors do go on to note the leadership of Woodrow Wilson in creating the League of Nations as well as the fact that the U.S. did not join it, though they offer no explanation to resolve what must strike the reader as a rather odd contradiction.[150] The sixth-grade 1966 text also offers very limited treatment or emphasis on the U.S. in its discussion of World War I. It too portrays the U.S. as just one of many countries that entered the war and provided help. The sixth-grade 1974 text does note that the entrance of the U.S. decided the victory of the allied forces, but not necessarily in military terms, since it too spotlights how giant U.S. industries provided supplies and arms.[151]

Some texts note the U.S. in discussing the interwar years, highlighting the nation's growing economic and political power. One section in Gómez et al. titled "*El periodo entre guerras*," for instance, prominently features three pictures (icons) of the U.S. (the Statue of Liberty, a coin with the U.S. flag as background, and the Capitol building) with a narrative touting the U.S. as "the country enjoying the greatest benefits of the war" because it did not suffer damages. In this text, the authors go on to describe the global economic strength of the U.S., noting that during the 1920s it had become the main creditor to Europe, and enjoyed extensive economic and financial expansion. The section then highlights the decline in purchasing power in Europe as the main cause for the Depression, which in turn led to a crisis of "overproduction" in the U.S. The text consequently credits the Depression for the rise of European fascism.[152] In a similar manner, a text box in the Jiménez book stresses the importance of the U.S. in helping Europe economically after the war. The author also refers here to *"diplomacia del dólar"* as guaranteeing U.S. markets in the American continent.[153]

Even more interestingly, the U.S. does not dominate the coverage of World War II either. Most texts, of course, discuss European events preceding U.S. involvement, noting the country's initial neutrality and its subsequent entrance into the war following the bombing of Pearl Harbor. Playing on the interventionist notion, Bolaños even titles the section "U.S. intervenes in the war."[154] But even from that point on, most treatments generally refer to the Allies rather than specifically the U.S., except with regard to the war in the Pacific where the U.S., rather than the Allies, is credited with defeating Japan. What the Allies represent, however, differs even within the same text. At one point, Gómez et al. refer to the Allies as the "western capitalist countries" that hoped that Hitler would attack the Soviet Union to destroy socialism. Yet later, they quote Roosevelt's reference to the Allies as the "arsenal of democracy."[155] The texts also differ in terms of the U.S. role and responsibility for ending or winning the war. Again following the anti-Soviet theme just noted, the authors characterize the U.S. nuclear attack on Japan as being "just a show of force and intimidation against the Soviet Union."[156] This contrasts with an earlier passage in Alvear which depicts the U.S.'s Good Neighbor policy as hostile toward Fascist regimes, but not Russian communism.[157] Interestingly, the sixth-grade 1966 text does not even mention the U.S. when it notes the atomic bombs in 1945, while the sixth-grade 1974 text, following its description of the atomic attacks, shields the U.S. from blame by suggesting that "all the world felt responsible for the genocide committed at Hiroshima and Nagasaki."[158] It further offers a somewhat positive spin on this historic event by crediting it for giving birth to the United Nations and efforts to fashion world peace.

As noted, it is during the Cold War that the U.S. becomes a far more central agent in the texts. Here, the texts tend to characterize or label the U.S. (and the West) as capitalist and to portray the U.S. as not only the vanguard of the capitalist camp, but as expansionist, hegemonic, and the main beneficiary of the global policies of the period. This is noteworthy since one alternative to characterizing the U.S. and the West as "capitalist powers" would be to refer to them as the democratic powers or as representatives, to borrow a commonly used U.S. label, of the "free world." Such characterizations, however, are absent in the Mexican texts. The sixth-grade 1974 text, for example, labels the U.S. as the head of the group of capitalist countries that did everything it could to isolate the Soviet Union and other socialist countries.[159] This builds on an earlier statement in the text anchoring U.S. fear following the Russian Revolution in the fact that "the majority of its population [U.S.] is closely tied to private property and feared for the loss of their possessions if socialism were to win."[160] Bolaños, Gómez et al., and Jiménez also label the Western bloc as a "capitalist" bloc, thereby essentially defining the Cold War in economic as opposed to political terms.[161] Gómez et al. allude not only to U.S. leadership of the bloc, but to its hegemony: "The U.S. sought to extend its system of private enterprise, to flood the world with the increased introduction of products in order for them to be market driven and to ensure its political and military influence."[162] Jiménez paints this picture of U.S. influence and expansionism during the Cold War in the following terms: "The United States took advantage of the economic and military weakness of Western Europe to dominate and exercise its influence by way of establishing military bases and investments and economic 'help' like the Marshall Plan. . . . This influence guaranteed the U.S. political regimes unsympathetic to communism."[163] Even U.S. help to others, as reflected in this quote, is qualified or downplayed. Bolaños, for instance, highlights the Truman Doctrine and the Marshall Plan as helping the U.S. as well as Europe, while Jiménez characterizes the Marshall Plan and U.S. investment in Europe as promoting U.S. commercial and military interests.[164] Indeed, the economic reach of the U.S., according to the text, extended throughout the world: "In the poor countries, the U.S. (like other colonial powers) purchased raw materials at low prices, to later sell manufactured products at higher prices": a situation the author refers to as "neocolonialism."[165]

Some texts also seem to either blame the Cold War on the West or the U.S. or portray the Soviet Union in slightly more favorable terms: a point facilitated by characterizing the ideological split along economic as opposed to political lines. Gómez et al., for example, blame the Cold War on the West, attributing the problem to its "failure to comply with the Potsdam treaties."[166] The authors then portray the Soviet Union as subject and victim rather than agent, as reacting to the Truman Doctrine and the Marshall Plan. The following page similarly notes that all the missiles made by the Soviet Union were in response to the encirclement established by the U.S. and its allies around the Soviet Union. Jiménez also seems to portray the U.S. and the West in less than sympathetic terms compared to the Soviet Union. After describing the U.S. as taking advantage of "the economic and military weakness of Western Europe to dominate" (see quote above), Jiménez notes that "the Soviet Union, for its part, formed an alliance of countries set on the constitution of a new society based on the Soviet socialist model. First they established provisional government with communist participation [and later established] 'people's democracies.'"[167] Such terms as "dominate" and "exercise influence," and the qualifying "help" in quotations, used to refer to the U.S., differ fundamentally from those—like "formed," "constitution of a society," and "democracy"—used to refer to the Soviet Union. This posture can also be gleaned from a subsequent note where the author emphasizes that Truman believed that his country had the right and duty to intervene militarily and expand its economy to "help" countries under the "communist threat" while (in the same sentence separated by a semicolon) the author posits that "for his part," Stalin "defended the struggle for world peace as well as the struggle of peoples against imperialist capitalism."[168] And yet, at another point in the text, the author seems to equate the two: The U.S. and the Soviet Union "became enemies due to their efforts to impose their economic, political and military influence on many countries."[169]

The sixth-grade 1974 text also illustrates this differential treatment. It posits that the U.S. sought to isolate the socialist countries by suspending commercial relations, orchestrated the "Red Scare," and greatly increased its military power. While it admits that the socialist countries used propaganda, it does not say that they armed or sought to isolate the capitalist countries.[170] Gómez et al. also craft a different image of the two superpowers. While the "U.S. sought to extend its influence of free enterprise" (noted above), the authors explain the power of the Soviet Union by pointing to how the Red Army "*liberated* Europe from fascism" (my emphasis). The authors subsequently use the term "*democracias populares*" to refer to the socialist governments.[171]

This narrative on U.S. power and hegemony extends throughout the Cold War era, providing the context to briefly mention the U.S. in relation to events ranging from Cuba and Vietnam to the Gulf War or more general global trends. Somewhat surprisingly, the treatment of the U.S. is limited and generally soft-spoken. In references to U.S. policy toward Latin America during the contemporary period, the fifth-grade 1964 text briefly mentions the U.S. in reference to the Organization of American States, but provides no analysis or criticism of U.S. posture toward the organization. Alvear mentions the Alliance for Progress in generally favorable terms as "*una tarea de ayuda*" [a task of help] put in place by Kennedy.[172] Even in reference to the Chilean coup of 1973, the only text that mentions this event notes that large foreign enterprises were not in agreement with the reforms (consistent with the economic deterministic narrative); it does not, however, specifically implicate the U.S. in the overthrow.[173] Somewhat more direct criticism is given to U.S. policy toward Cuba. After noting that the countries of the Third World were forced to choose between the U.S. and the Soviet Union, the sixth-grade 1974 text refers to Cuba in the following terms: "The U.S. orchestrated an intense anti-Castro propaganda campaign, blocked external trade with Cuba, and succeeded in getting all the Latin American countries except Mexico to break relations with the new government."[174]

References to Vietnam, in turn, tend to characterize U.S. actions as interventionist:[175] as backing a government that tried to maintain the privileges of the powerful sector,[176] a dictatorial regime because it was unable to accept the independence of Indochina,[177] or simply an "unpopular government."[178] Gómez et al. refer to the U.S. bombing North Vietnam on a "pretext;"[179] Jiménez points out that the war was unpopular;[180] Bolaños states that the U.S. was eventually obligated to negotiate peace;[181] and the sixth-grade 1974 text states simply that in 1972 the U.S. withdrew its troops.[182] None seem to stress the defeat, morally criticize U.S. involvement, or draw parallels to other historic events.

The treatment is somewhat harsher when it comes to the Third World in general, however, but the authors often couch the U.S. here within broader references to the superpowers or powerful or rich nations. In a lengthy section on the needs of the Third World, for instance, the sixth-grade 1974 text notes that the superpowers "perfected their arms and increased their arsenals to maintain their dominance" and that part of the difficulty for Third World countries is "that the powerful nations do not always keep the promises they make." The author then links the situation facing the Third World directly to Mexico by briefly describing Mexico's proposal for a New International Economic Order in highly favorable terms.[183]

In exploring changes in the twentieth century, Gómez et al. similarly highlight the extent of global inequality: "For a minority, life has been comfortable or at a middle standard; while for the majority existence has been full of poverty and hunger."[184] By mentioning the Apollo 11 lunar landing on the same page (complete with a picture of a U.S. astronaut standing on the moon), the author crafts an image that stresses not only U.S. economic opulence, but its priorities (going to the moon as opposed to dealing with the "poverty and hunger" of the majority; focusing on the moon rather than attending to the needs of people on the earth).

Referring to the 1980s, the U.S. receives minimal attention once again. The sixth-grade 1992 text notes friction between Mexico and the U.S. resulting from their differing attitudes toward the Central American conflicts. These differences, it contends, made it difficult for Mexico to better negotiate its economic problems with the U.S.[185] Meanwhile, Bolaños mentions the U.S. in a brief discussion of the problems of the Middle East. He refers to the U.S.

role in crafting the Camp David Accords (including a drawing of the three leaders) and later offers a one-page description of the Persian Gulf War. Both sections merely describe the events and the U.S. role without offering much in the way of value judgments or evaluations of the events.[186]

The final contemporary context where the U.S. receives mention is in relation to the neoliberal economic reforms sweeping the globe and Mexico since the 1980s. Vázquez and Egremy provide a brief paragraph on such changes, referring to commercial opening favorably in terms of pressuring national firms to modernize and become more productive, thereby increasing living standards. As part of a list of recent reforms, the authors simply refer to "easier access to transnational capital" with no real explanation or discussion of any potential negative consequences. The next paragraph mentions that as part of this economic strategy Mexico "has sought to better its commercial relations with the U.S. (Mexico's biggest trading partner) and Canada, through a trade agreement." Interestingly, the text makes no specific mention of NAFTA.[187] The sixth-grade 1992 text does briefly mention a possible free trade agreement with the U.S. and Canada, labeling it "a fundamental change." It couches this change, however, in the context of broader global trends (Mexico as subject) and suggests that the economic bloc is comparable to the European Union (seemingly raising the status of Mexico in the bloc).[188]

Comparison and Discussion

Departing now from the historic and thematic organization, three additional areas merit attention. The first centers on the pattern of references to the U.S. in the text, with particular notice of those areas where the authors do not mention the U.S. The second area relates to the factors identified in the text to explain the U.S. and, by extrapolation, Mexico. The third area returns us to the issue of whether Mexican perceptions of the U.S., as presented in the text, are different today than in the past, suggesting a process of ideological revisionism and nationalist reconstruction.

The Pattern of References to the U.S.

So far the analysis has looked only at the presence of the U.S. in the texts, and not its absence. It is important to consider the absence of the U.S. because it too influences perceptions of self and other. Posed differently, the question here centers on an evaluation of the nature of the treatment of the U.S. in the texts.

First, none of the texts are especially U.S.-centric. The national history texts are Mexicocentric while the universal history texts tend to be more Eurocentric than Mexicocentric. Though perhaps unsurprising, this is an important point given that most U.S. history or Western civilization texts in the U.S. tend to be U.S.-centric.[189] The universal history texts by Bolaños, Gómez et al., and Jiménez, for example, all devote substantial attention to the age of absolutism, examining major European ideas and thinkers of the period, with absolutely no mention of the U.S. Even later when the U.S. enters the historical drama, the continuing coverage of Europe helps balance and offset the treatment of the U.S. Bolaños, for example, gives more space to the French Revolution (13 pages, plus 6 on the Napoleonic period) than the U.S. independence movement (9 pages). The limited emphasis on the U.S. in descriptions of the world wars, noted earlier, also exemplifies this point. Also, though most of the texts deal with political, diplomatic, and economic history, the one text that includes a social and cultural concern totally excludes the U.S. in the discussion of "high culture" (arts, music). Here, all the attention centers on the Europeans.[190] And the one text that even mentions the U.S. in cultural terms refers to its "consumer society," mentions the U.S. as the source of movies and jazz in a paragraph on pop art, and even includes a picture of Superman: an icon representing both U.S. power and consumer culture. This text also presents the reader with Walt Whitman's poem "*Canto a mi mismo.*"[191]

This basic point also applies to the Mexican history texts. Though the U.S. occupies a central role in certain historical periods (like the Mexican-U.S. war), it remains invisible during much of the history. Vázquez, for instance, offers extensive treatment (57 pages) of pre-Colombian Mexico with obviously no mention whatsoever of the U.S. In fact, it is not until page 134 that the reader first encounters the U.S. Even when the U.S. becomes influential, the texts cover broad expanses of Mexican history without a trace of the U.S. Strikingly, even the fourth-grade 1960 text's coverage of the stabilizing development period (1940–1970) offers no mention of the U.S., despite the importance of the relationship to Mexican development. One of the Jiménez texts, which covers the 1940–1990 period in the book's last unit, likewise hardly mentions the U.S., as if its role in influencing Mexico during the period were negligible. The author does cast Mexico's import substitution policy as a reaction to the war effort of the developed countries—a policy that gave Mexico the opportunity to modernize its industrial plant—and the "crisis" of 1982 as a reaction to the global crisis in the mid-1970s, but neither discussion targets or mentions the U.S. specifically.[192] Overall, the extensive coverage of Mexico's economic development during the Mexican Miracle period and beyond seems to omit the external sector and the role of the U.S., even to the point of failing to mention or dwell on NAFTA or trade in the most recent era. The discussion above on the U.S. as a global power in the Cold War era also highlights this lack of attention to the U.S. as an agent shaping Mexican developments. Even Vázquez, who uses an entire chapter to describe the distinct regions of Mexico, does not distinguish or discuss the border region. In some ways, the absence of the U.S. in the extensive discussions of the PRI-government Mexican Miracle period helps to construct the image of a strong and positive Mexican government. At a broader level perhaps, the spotty overall attention to the U.S. helps illuminate those moments where the U.S. is treated, sharpening the broader image of the country and its lessons for Mexico.[193]

Finally, it is important to note that none of the texts reviewed here do much in the way of contrasting U.S. and Mexican culture directly—a discursive device common in the writings of the intellectuals as shown in chapter 5. References to U.S. cultural traits surface from time to time— industriousness, sense of equality, ambition—but rarely do these serve as a backdrop to depict in some binary or oppositional context the nature of the Mexicans or Mexican culture. Still, certain important contrasts between the two are sketched more or less directly, including Mexico's inclusive treatment of its indigenous versus the exclusionary treatment by the U.S. during the colonial era, Mexico's weakness versus U.S. strength, or Mexicans' goodwill versus the ill will of the U.S. during the nineteenth-century war. Certainly, the authors do not hoist the U.S. up as a benchmark to gauge Mexican democracy or economic development, probably since such a posture would undermine the positive interpretations of the PRI government. This device, to be sure, is best left to the regime's critics.

Corona uncovers more of this device in her review of texts. She highlights the classic Anglo-Latin approach in certain texts from the 1970s that stereotypically characterize the Anglo as individualistic and pragmatic and the Latin as communist with an emphasis on the community. For example, she cites one text that contrasts the Anglo, who is "colder, less sensitive and, consequently less apt at the fine arts" with the Latin, who has a capacity "for the fine arts, for the ideal, which have made of them men who know how to color . . . life and make the world more beautiful."[194] Corona interprets this as saying that the Americans have the defect of being perfect, and the Mexicans of being infantile: differences the text attributes to the different intentions of the colonizers.[195]

Defining and Explaining Success and Failure

Even absent the more explicit comparisons, the texts nonetheless do fashion implicit comparisons that operate to define Mexican "failures" by reference to U.S. "successes," thus prompting students to question the underlying reasons for both. Describing the U.S. as "a great economic power," as "one of the principal democracies of the world"[196] or as having a government that was "the dream of all the nineteenth-century liberals,"[197] the texts not only draw attention to the fact that Mexico has none of these, but beg questions as to why the U.S. should be so blessed (and, by extrapolation, Mexico not). Jiménez makes this point forcefully in the beginning of the chapter titled "Development of New Powers" by posing the following question: "Do you know which country is the most powerful in the world and how it came to have such power and territorial extension?" The answer comes equally directly: "The U.S.A. is a world power and the most powerful nation on earth."[198]

Exploring specifically what the texts portray as Mexico's shortcomings or how they account for such failings is beyond the scope of this study. Yet, through extrapolation, students can answer this question based on the factors offered to account for U.S. success. Three sets of factors can be identified. One set relates to colonial influences. In the midst of describing U.S. self-governance, the sixth-grade 1974 text argues that England paid little attention to the colonies, thus offering this as a causal factor behind their subsequent development (the implication: Mexico's importance to Spain was a disadvantage in terms of self-governance).[199] Bolaños more explicitly compares English colonization to that of Spain, underscoring that rather than extensive lands, the Saxons created small landholdings, which, in turn, facilitated development.[200] The fifth-grade 1964 text also draws a distinction between the two colonial experiences. It notes how the U.S. colonists "gave great impulse to industry utilizing some of the advances achieved by England."[201] It also differentiates the colonies on the map, as noted earlier, labeling the English colonies as "colonies" (of English, Dutch, and Swiss origin) and the rest of America as "possessions." Alvear too emphasizes a critical colonial difference, the exclusion of the indigenous: "Different from Spain, the British colonial effort completely excluded the Indian [and thus] there was no *mestisaje* as in Latin America." The author then lays out for the reader the advantages of this exclusionary policy. He refers first to the fact that the U.S. colonists "did not confront the complex national problems of the contact of two cultures, as happened in the Spanish colonies," and later, notes how the resulting homogeneity and equality (with brief mention that the blacks were slaves) created a society that developed because everyone had to work hard to survive.[202] Explanations rooted in timing also relate to differences in the colonial experience. The sixth-grade 1966 text makes clear this factor: "The U.S. obtained their independence before the countries of Latin America, which gave them time to organize themselves when the Industrial

Revolution began and not suffer, as happened in the other countries of America, continuing turmoil and internal war. They were thus able . . . to develop their industry and become a great industrial power."²⁰³

A second factor offered to account for U.S. "success" relates to internal qualities specific to U.S. society, both political and cultural. For example, the sixth-grade 1974 text, which calls U.S. democracy the dream of nineteenth-century liberals, explains U.S. success at becoming a *"potencia mundial"* by referring to freedom of expression, association, and religion.²⁰⁴ Other texts serve up U.S. cultural traits to explain the country's economic (development) and political (democracy) success. The fifth-grade 1964 text points to "hard work and industriousness" to explain U.S. economic power. It then reiterates and qualifies the point, stressing that it was not the government that accomplished this feat, but rather the people.²⁰⁵ Gómez et al. similarly refer to "their hard-working character, influenced by Calvinist religion."²⁰⁶ Such cultural factors can even be implied in the Alvear text where, by noting the obscure fact that George Washington refused to accept a third term—he even quotes Washington's "first in war, first in peace" speech—he links U.S. democracy to the wisdom of its political leader(s).²⁰⁷ Vázquez and Egremy also implicitly refer to cultural factors underpinning U.S. development by noting that the Mexican government permitted North Americans in Texas under the assumption that *diligent foreigners* would help develop the country (emphasis mine).²⁰⁸

Finally, the texts account for U.S. "success," particularly in terms of its economic development and emergence as a world power, as owing to the natural abundance of the land. The fifth-grade 1964 text, for example, explains that the U.S. colonists "knew from the beginning how to take advantage of the riches the land had to offer." To be sure, this factor grows as the nation's boundaries grow through U.S. expansionism. Under the subheading of "U.S. begins to grow," the sixth-grade 1974 text notes that despite the dangers, many in the U.S. took advantage of the "available" lands, which enabled them to enjoy the rights granted by the Constitution.²⁰⁹ The fifth-grade 1964 text, in turn, touts the purchase of Louisiana as giving the U.S. "one of the richest regions on earth."²¹⁰ References to the gold rush following the U.S. conquest of California also point to natural resources as the foundation of U.S. economic abundance. The sixth-grade 1974 text, after noting the victory over Mexico, for example, stresses that the U.S. had thus became "an enormous country, with abundant natural resources."²¹¹ Gómez et al. also highlight the abundance of the land to explain U.S. development: "The region was rich in wood, deposits of carbon and iron . . . which permitted the English colonists to dedicate themselves to agriculture and, with time, to develop a flourishing commerce."²¹² In a similar approach, Bolaños attributes the U.S.'s emergence as a world power to U.S. expansionism, while Jiménez touts the acquisition of territory abundant in natural resources as the key to U.S. development.[213] Indeed, she states that with such an extensive territory, the U.S. set out to take advantage of all the natural resources available, which, in turn, would allow it to industrialize. Two pages earlier, Jiménez answers the question regarding "which is the most powerful country and how did it get that way" by referring to U.S. expansion. This in turn sets the stage for her discussion of the Monroe Doctrine.[214]

While references to U.S. industriousness, ability to take advantage of natural resources, or small landholdings all come across as relatively benign and neutral, explanations based on U.S. expansion, which as noted earlier is generally portrayed as ruthless, anti-indigenous, and anti-Mexican, tend to morally weaken the meaning of U.S. "success" in the texts. Gómez et al. condition success by expressing the reason for U.S. economic development during the early period in purely exploitative terms or, as they state, "owing principally to the expulsion of Indians from the lands [and] the use of black slaves." Adding to this image, the authors refer in the subsequent paragraph to the slave-based aristocracy on the Southern plantations.[215] This narrative, of course, is all in addition to references to "their hard-working character shaped by Calvinism."

Recent Changes in the Treatment?

The final question centers on whether the more recent texts exhibit any fundamental changes in their narrative on the U.S., perhaps reflecting the changing policy environment in Mexico. First, the critical posture toward the U.S., particularly in reference to its treatment of Mexico, and the incumbent nationalist lessons for Mexico, seem to be common themes throughout the years with only minimal variation. In differentiating two brands of nationalism during the post-Revolutionary period—"one traditionalist, defensive, conservative, Yankeephobic, Hispanic and pessimistic" and the "other, the official [line], revolutionary, xenophobic, indigenous, optimistic and populist"—Vázquez shows that their only point of convergence may have been perceptions of the U.S.[216] Indeed, continuity rather than change seems to characterize the depiction of the U.S. during the Mexican-U.S. war. Corona and Gilbert uncover the tendency for the early texts to blame the war on Mexico's defects, the 1950s texts on "nascent U.S. imperialism," the 1960s texts on "U.S. expansionism," the 1970s texts on the "ambitions of the North Americans," and the Salinas-Zedillo texts on "manifest destiny" and the U.S. "drive to dominate."[217] Though the reasons vary somewhat, they all seem to paint a remarkably similar picture of U.S. behavior before, during, and after the war. There also seems to be minimal deviation from pinpointing the war as a watershed event shaping Mexican nationalism, or from the ultimate nationalist demand emerging from it: the need for unity.[218] Indeed, the 1960 passage, "We must never forget: unity of all Mexicans is indispensable" seems equal to that of a 1994 text: "The war with the U.S. offers a moral: the need to be united."[219] And though both Vasquez and Gilbert contend that the pre–World War II elementary texts exhibited intense distrust of American power, it is hard to conclude that the post–World War II texts do not.

In sum, while I fail to see any substantial change over the years under review, others, looking at just the primary-level texts, do highlight changes over time. Corona, for instance, argues that the texts during the Socialist Education period (1930s) portrayed the U.S. in its worst light, while those of the postwar, Modernization era actually promoted a more pragmatic, Good Neighborly image of the U.S.[220] Vázquez tends to agree, noting that during the postwar period the texts sought to instill a sense of Pan-Americanism, including the biographies of American heroes, mentions of American songs and dances, and a greater focus on the relations that brought the two countries together rather than dividing them. She also finds that during this period, 1958–1964, the "nationalism that emerged was less xenophobic and introverted than the prior period and of course more popular."[221]

Gilbert also argues that the texts have changed their tune in recent times, particularly in their treatments of U.S. investments. He contends that the distinguishing feature of the Salinas-Zedillo texts is their more sanguine view of U.S. investments (not the U.S. itself) and their tendency to associate U.S. investment and integration with Mexican progress and modernization. According to Gilbert, the new texts celebrate and praise foreign investment and growing integration with the American economy: "What separates the Salinas-Zedillo histories from free texts is their relentless enthusiasm for U.S. and other foreign investment, and for integration with the American economy. Foreign investment, seen as damaging in the Lopez Mateos texts, a (perhaps necessary) evil in the Echeverria texts, becomes a limitless good in the Salinas-Zedillo histories. Dependency on the United States is likewise transformed from a danger to an opportunity."[222] In conclusion, he touts this as a possible "shift in ideological perspective on the part of the Mexican regime."[223] And yet, Gilbert himself recognizes not only that the changes are limited to the economic ties, but that the shift is one of subtle degree and not kind. As shown here, most texts before the 1990s also stress the importance of U.S. investment in Mexican development, particularly during the *Porfiriato*. Even the text from the Echeverria period highlights how the accomplishments of the *Porfiriato* "depended in large measure on the United States and European countries because it [Mexico] needed capital and technology."[224]

That texts from earlier periods associate Mexican economic progress with U.S. investment and that the secondary texts from the 1990s remain critical of U.S. economic ties both tend, in my view, to soften the conclusion that a marked ideological revisionism has occurred. The big difference, to be sure, is that earlier texts did not have to grapple with the Mexican economic crisis of the 1980s or tout the reforms in a light favorable to the current regime.[225]

Conclusion

Exploring the narrative of the U.S. in a sample of primary and secondary school texts, the foregoing suggests certain traits that seem to help map a complex Mexican image of the U.S. and, in turn, to influence perceptions of self and nation. At one level, the texts clearly portray the U.S. as a democratic, rich, and powerful country blessed with certain unique features that allowed it to become so. Though the greatest praise seems to attend U.S. democracy, and all three themes—democratic, rich, and powerful—make the U.S. stand out as a model of "success," the virtuousness of these is nonetheless limited somewhat by the nation's treatment of "others." At another level, however, the texts construct a clear and uncompromising image of an unchecked, ambitious, expansionist, and exploitative power that rarely accepts any challenge to its hegemony. The historic lesson, as the sixth-grade 1992 text drives home, is that the U.S. is "always disposed to intervene in Mexico."[226] This narrative also encompasses the notion that the U.S. is anti-Mexican and anti–Third World (anti-"other"), both internally and externally and, consequently, cannot be trusted. The two levels differ in that the former level, highlighting the U.S. as a model, tends to relate to the domestic features and behavior of the U.S., while the latter relates primarily to external U.S. behavior. This parallels a finding regarding the intellectual elite in chapter 5.

On the other side of the equation, the texts contribute much to the nationalist image of Mexico, fathering important lessons for the nation. At one level, the democratic, developmental, and powerful "success" of the U.S. serves, through opposition, to define Mexico's political and economic "failures." U.S. "power" contrasts with and defines Mexico's "weakness." Moreover, the developmental success of the U.S. creates an opportunity structure in which Mexican economic growth, development, and progress center unmistakably on strengthening the country's economic ties to the U.S. The lesson is, in a sense, that "like it or not" Mexico has to deal with the U.S. economically in order to progress, even though it may have some negative consequences—like the impact on the peasants during the *Porfiriato*. And yet, at another level, despite this unrelenting need to engage the U.S. in the name of progress, the *sine que non* of guarding the *patria* against the ambitious, exploitative tendencies of the U.S. is patriotism, loyalty, and national unity. But the texts do not seem to stop there. Taking it one step further, they then draw the critically important political implication that the State (at the time the PRI government) has not only provided national unity and stability, but also has been able to negotiate the difficult path of checking the power of the U.S. while at the same time engaging the U.S. for the country's economic progress.

Finally, though these are preliminary, there seem to be only minimal changes in the treatment of the U.S. in the texts over the years. If anything, it seems that continuity outpaces change as it relates to the textbook image of the U.S. and the U.S.'s role in shaping national identity. If anything, by spotlighting economic opening and integration, texts today heighten the relevance of the U.S. to the nation, sharpening the importance of these images and the application of the nation's historic lessons to today's problems. Once again, however, school texts provide merely one dimension of the Mexican image of the U.S., possibly influential during one's youth. Attention turns now to political caricature, providing glimpses, often humorous, of the Mexican views of the U.S.

Notes

1. Given the political and ideological stakes, battles over the content of school texts have often been intense. Mexican history features many such political struggles, ranging from the liberal-conservative clash over school texts in the nineteenth century, the 1891 debate leading to the emphasis on "national unity," the struggle in 1919 culminating in the removal of U.S. texts from the classroom, the recentralization of education under José Vasconcelos, Cárdenas's move to a socialist-based education over the objections of the Church and the right, and the 1959 creation of a program of free national primary school texts—which triggered massive public protests in Monterrey—to the public controversy following the proposal of new texts in 1992. For a review, see Gilbert, "Rewriting History"; Peter H. Neumann and Maureen A. Cunningham, *Mexico's Free Textbooks: Nationalism and the Urgency to Educate.* World Bank Staff Working Papers, Number 541. (Washington, D.C.: World Bank, 1982); and Vázquez, *Nacionalismo y Educacion en Mexico.* As Dennis Gilbert, in "Rewriting History," concludes, "the politics of national history reflect the politics of the nation" (274).

2. Hobsbawm, *Nations and Nationalism since 1780,* 12.

3. Concepción Barron de Moran, *Mi libro de Cuarto Año: Historia y Civismo* (Mexico City: Secretaria de Educación Público, Comisión Nacional de los Libros de Textos Gratuitos, 1960), 1.

4. Neumann and Cunningham, *Mexico's Free Textbooks,* 55.

5. Sarah Corona Berkin, "EUA Para Niños: La imagen de EUA en los libros de texto de las primarias Mexicanas de este siglo," paper presented at the XIX Congress of the Latin American Studies Association, Washington, D.C., September 28–30, 1995, 4.

6. While this and past studies focus on social science texts, even natural science texts contain political messages regarding the U.S. Lilian Alvarez de Testa (*Mexicanidad y libro de texto gratuito* [Mexico City: UNAM, 1992], 48) cites a sixth-grade natural science text that points out that most scientific research is conducted in developed countries, which determine what problems should be resolved through science. The text then notes that 75% of the money in scientific research goes to the search to create better arms and "the possession of these arms enable them to maintain their dominance over our countries."

7. Vázquez (*Nacionalismo y Educacion en Mexico*), who coordinated the free textbook program in the 1970s, examines a large sample of primary school texts stretching from the mid-nineteenth century to the 1960s, pinpointing major ideological divisions in the texts' discussions of the conquest, the indigenous, the U.S., and class. Though limited to primary school texts, Vázquez is the only analyst to focus on texts prior to and following the development of the free text program in 1959. None has tried to duplicate the scope of Vázquez's classic study. Alvarez de Testa, in *Mexicanidad y libro de texto gratuito,* provides a more focused analysis exploring the narrative on the indigenous in the free texts. She highlights, above all, the misrepresentation of the indigenous and the anti-indigenismo contained in the texts. Dennis Gilbert, in "Rewriting History," in turn analyzes the new texts proposed in 1992 amid significant controversy to spotlight the ideological revisionism attempted by the Salinas-Zedillo team. Finally, Corona, in "EUA Para Niños," compares treatments of the U.S. in a series of texts from each of six time periods: State formation (to 1929); socialist education (1930s); modernity (1940s); welfare State (1950–1960s); neopopulist (1970s–1980s); and neoliberal (1990).

8. Barron de Moran, *Mi libro de Cuarto Año;* Amelia Monroy Gutiérrez, *Mi libro de Quinto Año: Historia y Civismo* (Mexico City: Secretaria de Educación Público, Comisión Nacional de los Libros de Textos Gratuitos, 1964); Eduardo Blanquel and Jorge Alberto Manrique, *Mi libro de Sexto Año: Historia y Civismo* (Mexico City: Secretaria de Educación Público, Comisión Nacional de los Libros de Textos Gratuitos, 1966); Josefina Vázquez, *Ciencias Sociales: Sexto Grado* (Mexico City: Secretaria de Educación Público, Comisión Nacional de los Libros de Textos Gratuitos, 1974); *Mi libro de Historia de Mexico Cuarto Grado* (Mexico City: Secretaria de Educación Público, Comisión Nacional de los Libros de Textos Gratuitos, 1992); and *Mi libro de Historia de Mexico Sexto grado* (Mexico City: Secretaria de Educación Público, Comisión Nacional de los Libros de Textos Gratuitos, 1992).

9. Carlos Alvear Acevedo, *Historia Universal Contemporánea* (Mexico City: Editorial Jus, 1999); Raul Bolaños Martinez, *Historia de la Humanidad: De las Épocas Moderna y Contemporánea. Segundo Curso* (Mexico City: Ediciones Pedagógicas, 1994); Sergio Orlando Gómez Méndez, Silvia Ramírez Campos, Rosa Ortiz Paz, and José Rodríguez Arrvizu, *Historia 2: Edad Moderna y Contemporánea. Segunda Edición* (Mexico City: Prentice Hall, 1998); Concepción Jiménez Alarcón, *Historia del Hombre 2. Curso de Historia Universal para Segundo Grado* (Mexico City: Fernández Edi-

tores, 1998), and *Historia del Hombre en México. Curso de Historia de México para Tercer grado* (Mexico City: Fernández Editores, 1998); and Ma. de la Luz Vázquez Segura and Meyra Egremy Pinto, *Historia de Mexico* (Mexico City: Limusa Noriega Editores, 1996).

10. Sixth-grade 1974 text, 32.
11. Sixth-grade 1974 text, 33.
12. Sixth-grade 1974 text, 34.
13. Bolaños Martinez, *Historia de la Humanidad*, 44.
14. Jiménez Alarcón, *Historia del Hombre 2*, 57.
15. Jiménez Alarcón, *Historia del Hombre en México.*
16. Alvear Acevedo, *Historia Universal Contemporánea*, 100.
17. Fifth-grade 1964 text, 117.
18. Fifth-grade 1964 text, 114.
19. Fifth-grade 1964 text, 114.
20. Jiménez Alarcón, *Historia del Hombre en México*, 57.
21. Gómez et al. *Historia 2*, 37–40.
22. Bolaños Martinez, *Historia de la Humanidad*, 39.
23. Jiménez Alarcón, *Historia del Hombre 2* and Alvear Acevedo, *Historia Universal Contemporánea.*
24. Gómez et al. *Historia 2: Edad Moderna y Contemporánea*, 38–40.
25. Fifth-grade 1964 text, 117. While this period enjoys the bulk of the discussion on the internal politics of the U.S., Gómez et al. *(Historia 2)* and Jiménez Alarcón *(Historia del Hombre 2)* do go on to discuss the civil war period. In keeping with the economic theme, Gómez et al. (66) attribute the war to the fact that the North-South division prevented the consolidation of U.S. expansionist capitalism. The authors also downplay the freeing of the slaves by noting, first, that "one of his [Lincoln's] purposes" was to provoke desertions among the South's forces (a reason that undermines or at least dampens any notion that they were freed for humanitarian reasons) and later pointing out that the granting of rights to the blacks was not easily accepted—reference is made to the Klan—and that in practice slavery continued until the end of the century. Jiménez (89) also discusses the civil war, highlighting the issue of slavery. He makes Lincoln out as a more sympathetic figure not only by noting his freeing of the slaves, but by mentioning his humble origins and his opposition to the French invasion of Mexico. This is consistent with Corona's ("EUA Para Niños," 11) finding that the texts treat Lincoln as the "Saint of American democracy." Still, Jiménez does note that racial discrimination continues today, broadening the point to include women, Latins, and, of course, Mexicans who work in the U.S. to better their standard of living "even through illegal means."
26. Fifth-grade 1964 text, 131.
27. Fourth-grade 1960 text, 48.
28. Gómez et al., *Historia 2;* and Alvear Acevedo, *Historia Universal Contemporánea.*
29. Vázquez and Egremy, *Historia de Mexico*, 134, 164.
30. Bolaños Martinez, *Historia de la Humanidad*, 84; Gómez et al. *Historia 2*, 65.
31. Bolaños Martinez, *Historia de la Humanidad*, 84.
32. Bolaños Martinez, *Historia de la Humanidad*, 86.

33. Fifth-grade 1964 text, 153.
34. Sixth-grade 1974 text, 90.
35. Vázquez and Egremy, *Historia de Mexico*, 176.
36. Gómez et al. *Historia 2*, 65.
37. Jiménez Alarcón, *Historia del Hombre 2*, 84.
38. Gómez et al. *Historia 2*, 65.
39. Jiménez Alarcón, *Historia del Hombre 2*, 85.
40. Gómez et al. *Historia 2*, 65.
41. Vázquez de Knauth, *Nacionalismo y Educacion en Mexico*, 204.
42. Alvear Acevedo, *Historia Universal Contemporánea*, 209.
43. Jiménez Alarcón, *Historia del Hombre en México*, 138.
44. Vázquez and Egremy, *Historia de Mexico*, 178.
45. Fourth-grade 1960 text, 95.
46. Vázquez and Egremy, *Historia de Mexico*, 181–82.
47. Alvear Acevedo, *Historia Universal Contemporánea*, 208.
48. This same pattern—U.S. violent expansionism and lack of reason—characterizes the Mesilla sale. Jiménez Alarcón (*Historia del Hombre en México*, 146) refers to the fact that the New Mexico governor invaded the territory—an invasion that seemed likely to cause another war—and the U.S. used as a pretext the inhabitants losing their protection against Indian attacks for making the sale. Vasquez and Egremy (*Historia de Mexico*,180), under the subheading, "The Sale of la Mesilla," note how the U.S. "demanded from Mexico the sale of the Mesilla, threatening to declare war and occupy that region if it did not cede to the pressure."
49. Jiménez Alarcón, *Historia del Hombre en México*, 140.
50. Sixth-grade 1992 text, 78.
51. Fourth-grade 1992 text, 48.
52. Sixth-grade 1974 text, 64.
53. Sixth-grade 1974 text, 90.
54. Vázquez and Egremy, *Historia de Mexico*, 181–82.
55. Sixth-grade 1992 text, 82.
56. Jiménez Alarcón, *Historia del Hombre 2*; and Gómez et al. *Historia 2*, 86.
57. Fourth-grade 1960 text, 91.
58. Jiménez Alarcón, *Historia del Hombre en México*, 138.
59. Jiménez Alarcón, *Historia del Hombre en México*, 143.
60. Jiménez Alarcón, *Historia del Hombre en México*, 139–40.
61. Sixth-grade 1992 text, 80.
62. Fourth-grade 1992 text; Vázquez and Egremy, *Historia de Mexico*, 175; and fourth-grade 1960 text.
63. Gómez et al. *Historia 2*, 65.
64. Corona, "EUA Para Niños," 15.
65. Vázquez de Knauth, *Nacionalismo y Educacion en Mexico*, 204.
66. Fourth-grade 1960 text, 92.
67. Jiménez Alarcón, *Historia del Hombre en México*, 138.
68. Jiménez Alarcón, *Historia del Hombre en México*, 142.
69. Cited in Corona, "EUA Para Niños," 13.
70. Jiménez Alarcón, *Historia del Hombre en México*, 138–39.

71. Vázquez and Egremy, *Historia de Mexico,* 178.

72. Sixth-grade 1992 text, 81.

73. Fourth-grade 1960 text, 94.

74. Alvear Acevedo, *Historia Universal Contemporánea,* 209.

75. Fourth-grade 1992 text, 48.

76. Jiménez Alarcón, *Historia del Hombre en México,* 138, 143–44. Of course, despite the different factors, none suggest that there was one sole factor behind Mexico's defeat and most mention a combination of factors that taken together refer to Mexico's weakness defined in terms of U.S. strength.

77. One indication of this difference is that while the reader is usually told that Texas was sparsely populated, the size of the Mexican population in the other lost territories is never mentioned. That a larger number (and probably percentage) of Mexicans now live in those (now U.S.) areas than did in 1847 may be an interesting point, but contrary to the prevailing nationalist discourse.

78. Fourth-grade 1960 text, 97.

79. Bolaños Martinez, *Historia de la Humanidad,* 84.

80. Jiménez Alarcón, *Historia del Hombre en México,* 143, 145.

81. Sixth-grade 1992 text, 79, 83.

82. Sixth-grade 1992 text, 83.

83. Cited in Vázquez de Knauth, *Nacionalismo y Educacion en Mexico,* 137.

84. Sixth-grade 1992 text, 82; Jiménez Alarcón, *Historia del Hombre en México,* 146.

85. Turner, *Dynamics of Mexican Nationalism,* 37.

86. Jiménez Alarcón, *Historia del Hombre en México.*

87. Jiménez Alarcón, *Historia del Hombre en México,* 147.

88. The sixth-grade 1992 text (78) notes another consequence of the U.S. tendency to take advantage of weaker countries and intervene: to separate Mexico from other Latin American countries. "Mexico became separated from Hispanic-American countries and very close to the influence of the United States, which began its territorial expansion." This point is important since it tends to blame the U.S. for cutting Mexico off from its heritage and a presumably "natural" relationship with certain other countries.

89. Fourth-grade 1960 text, 95–96.

90. Fourth-grade 1992 text, 50.

91. Jiménez Alarcón, *Historia del Hombre en México,* 145.

92. Fourth-grade 1960 text, 98.

93. Cited in Vázquez and Egremy, *Historia de Mexico,* 181–82.

94. Jiménez Alarcón, *Historia del Hombre en México.*

95. Vázquez and Egremy, *Historia de Mexico,* 175.

96. The only text to mention U.S. compensation (15 million pesos)—a potentially positive spin, I suppose—qualifies it by noting that the better part of that money was never paid to the Mexican government because it was used to pay the claims by U.S. citizens against Mexico (Jiménez Alarcón, *Historia del Hombre en México,* 145).

97. Sixth-grade 1992 text, 95.

98. Vázquez de Knauth, *Nacionalismo y Educacion en Mexico,* 40.

99. Cited in Vázquez de Knauth, *Nacionalismo y Educacion en Mexico,* 199.

100. Bolaños Martinez, *Historia de la Humanidad.*

101. Gómez et al. *Historia 2*, 83.

102. Sixth-grade 1974 text, 144–45.

103. Alvear Acevedo, *Historia Universal Contemporánea*, 212.

104. Jiménez Alarcón, *Historia del Hombre 2*, 90.

105. Sixth-grade 1992 text, 186.

106. Sixth-grade 1992 text, 189.

107. Sixth-grade 1974 text, 129, 130.

108. Jiménez Alarcón, *Historia del Hombre 2*, 90, 92.

109. Sixth-grade 1974 text, 93.

110. Sixth-grade 1974 text, 138, 139.

111. Sixth-grade 1974 text, 163.

112. Vázquez and Egremy, *Historia de Mexico*, 234, 232.

113. Sixth-grade 1992 text, 101.

114. Vázquez and Egremy, *Historia de Mexico*, 195.

115. Vázquez and Egremy, *Historia de Mexico*, 235.

116. Vázquez and Egremy, *Historia de Mexico*, 316.

117. Jiménez Alarcón, *Historia del Hombre en México*, 196.

118. Jiménez Alarcón, *Historia del Hombre en México*, 208.

119. Sixth-grade 1992 text, 107.

120. Vázquez and Egremy, *Historia de Mexico*, 195.

121. Gilbert, "Rewriting History," 285.

122. Sixth-grade 1992 text, 101–2.

123. Sixth-grade 1992 text, 137.

124. Jiménez Alarcón, *Historia del Hombre en México*, 196.

125. Sixth-grade 1992 text, 103.

126. Vázquez and Egremy, *Historia de Mexico*, 234.

127. Jiménez Alarcón, *Historia del Hombre en México*, 195.

128. Vázquez and Egremy, *Historia de Mexico.*

129. Sixth-grade 1992 text, 138.

130. Fourth-grade 1992 text, 73.

131. Fourth-grade 1992 text, 58.

132. Jiménez Alarcón, *Historia del Hombre en México*, 217.

133. Sixth-grade 1992 text, 110; Vázquez and Egremy's (*Historia de Mexico*, 140) discussion of Hidalgo offers a similar portrayal of the U.S. Here, the authors note how the father of independence sent an emissary to the U.S. to get the U.S. to recognize the independence struggle, but the emissary was captured and never arrived (What message does that portray?). The next page also notes that Hidalgo and various collaborators traveled to the U.S. to acquire arms.

134. Jiménez Alarcón, *Historia del Hombre en México*, 229.

135. Vázquez and Egremy, *Historia de Mexico*, 295–96.

136. Jiménez Alarcón, *Historia del Hombre en México*, 225.

137. Sixth-grade 1992 text, 112.

138. Jiménez Alarcón, *Historia del Hombre en México*, 229.

139. Sixth-grade 1992 text, 125.

140. Vázquez and Egremy, *Historia de Mexico*, 290–91.

141. Jiménez Alarcón, *Historia del Hombre en México*, 244.
142. Jiménez Alarcón, *Historia del Hombre en México*, 234.
143. Jiménez Alarcón, *Historia del Hombre en México*, 233.
144. Fourth-grade 1992 text, 62.
145. Jiménez Alarcón, *Historia del Hombre en México*, 229.
146. Jiménez Alarcón, *Historia del Hombre en México*, 234.
147. Sixth-grade 1992 text, 129.
148. Sixth-grade 1992 text, 111.
149. Bolaños Martinez, *Historia de la Humanidad*, 139.
150. Gómez et al., *Historia 2*, 115.
151. Sixth-grade 1974 text, 111.
152. Gómez et al., *Historia 2*, 130.
153. Jiménez Alarcón, *Historia del Hombre 2*, 173.
154. Bolaños Martinez, *Historia de la Humanidad*, 181.
155. Gómez et al., *Historia 2*, 147, 151.
156. Gómez et al., *Historia 2*, 174.
157. Alvear Acevedo, *Historia Universal Contemporánea*, 213.
158. Sixth-grade 1966 text, 202; and sixth-grade 1974 text, 142.
159. Sixth-grade 1974 text, 163.
160. Sixth-grade 1974 text, 129.
161. Bolaños Martinez, *Historia de la Humanidad*, 202; Gómez et al., *Historia 2*, 157; and Jiménez Alarcón, *Historia del Hombre 2*, 219.
162. Gómez et al., *Historia 2*, 157.
163. Jiménez Alarcón, *Historia del Hombre 2*, 208.
164. Bolaños Martinez, *Historia de la Humanidad*, 202; and Jiménez Alarcón, *Historia del Hombre 2*, 219.
165. Jiménez Alarcón, *Historia del Hombre 2*, 219.
166. Gómez et al., *Historia 2*, 173.
167. Jiménez Alarcón, *Historia del Hombre 2*, 220.
168. Jiménez Alarcón, *Historia del Hombre 2*, 222.
169. Jiménez Alarcón, *Historia del Hombre 2*, 220.
170. Sixth-grade 1974 text, 163.
171. Gómez et al., *Historia 2*, 157.
172. Alvear Acevedo, *Historia Universal Contemporánea*, 213.
173. Sixth-grade 1974 text, 175.
174. Sixth-grade 1974 text, 175.
175. Jiménez Alarcón, *Historia del Hombre 2*, 213.
176. Bolaños Martinez, *Historia de la Humanidad*, 212–14.
177. Gómez et al., *Historia 2*, 176–77.
178. Sixth-grade 1974 text: 167.
179. Gómez et al., *Historia 2*, 176–77.
180. Jiménez Alarcón, *Historia del Hombre 2*, 223–24.
181. Bolaños Martinez, *Historia de la Humanidad*, 208–14.
182. Sixth-grade 1974 text, 167.
183. Sixth-grade 1974 text, 179.
184. Gomez et al., *Historia 2*, 213.

185. Sixth-grade 1992 text, 149.
186. Bolaños Martinez, *Historia de la Humanidad,* 219, 229–31.
187. Vázquez and Egremy, *Historia de México,* 319.
188. Sixth-grade 1992 text, 151.
189. Of course, in contrast to U.S. texts, Mexican texts do not need to provide the "illusion of benevolence" that is incumbent upon the imperial powers (Said, *Orientalism,* xvii).
190. Gómez et al., *Historia 2,* 95–100.
191. Sixth-grade 1974 text, 159. The poem is presented on page 94.
192. Jiménez Alarcón, *Historia del Hombre en México,* 266, 267.
193. One exception to this is found in Alvear Acevedo's (*Historia Universal Contemporánea,* 218) reference to López Mateos receiving President Kennedy from the U.S. While the Kennedy visit was the first in many years, signifying perhaps a new era in the relationship, the text does not make that point. Really, it provides no reason as to why this event would be editorially significant. This leads one to speculate that perhaps Kennedy's Catholicism and hence his popularity among Mexican people could be the motive.
194. Corona, "EUA Para Niños," 7.
195. Corona ("EUA Para Niños," 18) also interprets treatments of the war as setting up a contrast between the two countries. Specifically, she contends that references to Santa Anna and the *Niños Héroes* are "equivalent to presenting, before an adult country, a childish and immature country." She goes on to argue that the image portrays the U.S. as protector and friend to an immature Mexico with Mexico locked into a situation of dependence.
196. Fifth-grade 1964 text, 66.
197. Sixth-grade 1974 text, 89.
198. Jiménez Alarcón, *Historia del Hombre 2,* 84.
199. Sixth-grade 1974 text, 32.
200. Bolaños Martinez, *Historia de la Humanidad,* 39.
201. Fifth-grade 1964 text, 65.
202. Alvear Acevedo, *Historia Universal Contemporánea,* 33.
203. Sixth-grade 1966 text, 188.
204. Sixth-grade 1974 text, 89.
205. Fifth-grade 1964 text, 81.
206. Gómez et al., *Historia 2,* 37.
207. Alvear Acevedo, *Historia Universal Contemporánea,* 208.
208. Vázquez and Egremy, *Historia de México,* 177.
209. Sixth-grade 1974 text.
210. Fifth-grade 1964 text, 162.
211. Sixth-grade 1974 text, 90.
212. Gómez et al., *Historia 2,* 37.
213. Bolaños Martinez, *Historia de la Humanidad,* 84; and Jiménez Alarcón, *Historia del Hombre 2,* 86.
214. Jiménez Alarcón, *Historia del Hombre 2,* 84.
215. Gómez et al., *Historia 2,* 37. Of course, most texts combine the reasons, providing a more complete rationale to account for the U.S. successes. To capture the

total flavor, the fifth-grade 1964 text provides a good example (162). It notes that economic and political development in the U.S. were different (from what is only implied) and proceeds to offer a list of reasons why: "They knew from the beginning how to take advantage of the riches of the land for their own colonies. . . . In addition, soon they gave a great impulse to industry utilizing some of the advances achieved by England. . . . For all these reasons, the great abundance of natural resources and the will and industriousness of the colonists would later result in the United States becoming an economic power." The next line then notes that politically the U.S. also had certain advantages over Latin American countries "since upon establishing themselves, the English immigrants strove to conserve in America the political intervention that customs and laws of England gave the community." Later, in the discussion of U.S. expansion, the text notes how the purchase of Louisiana gave it "one of the richest regions on earth."

216. Vázquez de Knauth, *Nacionalismo y Educacion en Mexico,* 190.

217. Corona, "EUA Para Niños"; and Gilbert, "Rewriting History."

218. Corona, "EUA Para Niños," 4; Gilbert, "Rewriting History," 285; and Vázquez de Knauth, *Nacionalismo y Educacion en Mexico,* 40.

219. Fourth-grade 1960 text, 98; *Historia cuarto grado* (México: Secretaria de Educación Públicao, 1994), 116, cited in Corona, "EUA Para Niños," 19.

220. Corona, "EUA Para Niños," 13–15.

221. Vázquez de Knauth, *Nacionalismo y Educacion en Mexico,* 251.

222. Gilbert, "Rewriting History," 286.

223. Gilbert, "Rewriting History," 294.

224. Cited in Gilbert, "Rewriting History," 285.

225. Here it is important to reiterate the fact that the current study includes secondary as well as primary school texts. This is critical, first, in helping to account for my inability to find strong support for the changes noted by Gilbert in "Rewriting History." He, after all, focuses only on the free texts from the primary schools.

226. Sixth-grade 1992 text, 120.

4

Gringolandia in Political Caricature

POLITICAL CARTOONS OFFER a nice break from the "official" images soberly offered by the school texts. Mexican political caricaturists have long incorporated the theme of the U.S. into their work, though rarely have they toed any "official" line. Forever contesting the limits of censorship, political cartoonists have a reputation for their leftist orientations and staunch criticism of the government and government policy.[1] Sporting a unique medium that both reflects and influences political culture, political cartoonists provide a dose of humor as they crystallize critical themes and images through exaggeration.

This chapter explores images of the U.S. contained in Mexican political cartoons. It examines the cartoons' political messages, their underlying meanings, and the graphic presentations of the U.S. and Mexico. The chapter starts with a brief discussion of the theoretical and methodological setting, moves to a discussion of a series of reoccurring themes in cartoons plucked from the contemporary period, and concludes by addressing the issue of change by comparing these images to those found in a wide sample of caricatures dating back into the late nineteenth century.

Theoretical and Methodological Note

To the enjoyment and edification of many, Latin American studies have a relatively well-established tradition of analyzing political caricature. Among the many works contributing to our understanding of the region are Ariel Dorfman and Armand Mattelart's exposé on U.S. imperialism, David Foster's analysis of popular culture, John Johnson's interpretation of U.S. policy, and *The Americas Review* special issue edited by Rosáura Sánchez and

Beatrice Pita, among others.[2] Such analyses are premised on the notion that political caricature, in order to be understood and "funny," must be anchored in popular culture while at the same time shaping perceptions and popular narratives.[3] As Sánchez and Pita point out, political cartoons represent "potent social and ideological texts" that "synthesize a longer narrative" and, as such, participate "in the construction of identities."[4] Coupled with the fact that cartoons are able to convey ideas swiftly to a passive viewer, caricature is thought to be particularly influential: "Most people . . . are probably more influenced and swayed by a pithy editorial cartoon than by a weighty, albeit more cogently reasoned, newspaper editorial or socio-political essay."[5]

Two approaches were used to locate and identify Mexican political caricatures focusing on the U.S. One approach involved a review of major newspapers during key moments in contemporary Mexico-U.S. relations. "Major newspapers" here refers to *Excelsior* and *La Jornada* from Mexico City, *El Informador*, *Siglo 21*, and *Ocho Columnas* from Guadalajara, and *El Norte* of Monterrey as well as the national news weekly *Proceso*. These periodicals feature many if not most of Mexico's more prominent contemporary political caricaturists, including Oswaldo Sagastegui and Marino (*Excelsior*), Curry (*Ocho Columnas*), El Fisgón (*Siglo 21, La Jornada*), and Fran (*El Norte)*, and span the ideological spectrum.[6] "Key moments," in turn, refers here to the debate in the U.S. over Clinton's proposed financial bailout of Mexico in January 1995;[7] the passage of a new immigration law in the U.S., and the drug certification process in March 1997; the execution of a Mexican national, Ireneo Tristan Montoya, in Texas on June 18, 1997;[8] and President Bill Clinton's first official visit to Mexico, May 5–7, 1997. Though the first four events did not take place in Mexico *per se*, they all focused on Mexico, triggering multiple reactions in the country. These events were selected because it is during such times—when the U.S. is "in the news"—that perceptions and images of the U.S. surface publicly, and become reinforced and reified. All caricatures referring to the U.S. during these periods were collected and analyzed.[9] The second approach involved a much more comprehensive search of political cartoons in Mexico. But rather than an examination of the newspapers, this approach rested primarily on the extensive review of edited volumes, collections, books, and articles on Mexican political cartoons in general.[10] These works reproduce drawings from the nation's main dailies. This endeavor provided a good crop of cartoons covering a wide range of time periods and "moments" in the bilateral relationship, and featuring the nation's most prominent artists and authors, including El Fisgón, Helioflores, Naranjo, Calderon, Helguera, Rius and many others.

Combined, the two approaches yielded from 150 to 200 panels, though certainly only a small, representative sample can be reproduced here.

Images of the U.S. and Nation in the Contemporary Period

Caricatures portraying the U.S. present a number of interwoven messages. In most cases, an individual cartoon illustrates a variety of themes. For analytical purposes, however, the discussion proceeds thematically, setting out four major themes found in the cartoons: (1) U.S. power, its use and abuse; (2) U.S. hypocrisy; (3) U.S. anti-Mexicanism; and (4) related perceptions of the nation. I follow an exploration of these with a brief discussion of the meanings found within the artistic dimensions of the caricatures.

Theme 1: U.S. Power, Its Use and Abuse

The first, and clearly the most prominent, theme in the political cartons centers on the sheer presence and power of the U.S. in and over Mexico, and, most importantly, the abuses of that power. Figure 4.1 by Curry clearly depicts this theme, pointing to the overwhelming presence of U.S.-owned companies on the Mexican landscape and in the Mexican consciousness. It equates the presence of these companies with a national invasion. Many other drawings depict the U.S. asserting its power over Mexico in a more direct fashion, usually to obtain something from Mexico. The drawing by Naranjo in figure 4.2, for example, shows the U.S. cashing in on the Mexican debt to gain control of Mexican oil, while in figure 4.3 Nerilicón depicts the U.S. trying to use NAFTA and the ending of the tuna embargo to gain control of Mexican oil. Arredondo and Rius describe this drawing: "NAFTA would serve to . . . help us forget U.S. arbitrariness in commercial questions. . . . But the tuna boycott, which represented a huge loss of money annually for Mexico, told us that the *gringos* had never thought about forgetting these things."[11]

Many of the cartoons from the financial bailout of 1995 play on this theme. Figure 4.4, for example, shows Uncle Sam waving the "bailout money," while riding the back of the Mexican (like a *burro* chasing grass). Figure 4.5 similarly illustrates an active U.S. using its power to "capitalize" on Mexico's misfortune. It carries the message that the U.S. not only wants Mexico's oil, but it is more concerned about conditions and oil than providing aid.

Besides feeding an abuse of power, the preponderance of U.S. power is

Figure 4.1

"The gringos are going to invade us in 2003!"
"Going to?"

Source: Ocho Columnas (Guadalajara), November 14, 1996.

Figure 4.2

Servicing the debt—Interest payments
Uncle Sam: "In barrels of ten thousands, please."

Source: Naranjo, "Uso Racional" (1984).

Figure 4.3

Tuna Embargo
Source: Nerilicón, "Abrelatas," *El Economista,* 1993.

Figure 4.4

Figure 4.5

Source: *El Norte* (Monterrey), January 27, 1995.

If there is no petroleum . . .
"And the money?"

Source: *Excelsior* (Mexico City), January 26, 1995.

also shown as contributing to U.S. neglect of or lack of concern for Mexico. Indeed, this may be the prerogative of power. Figure 4.6, also from the bailout period, shows not only the image of a powerful U.S., fully capable of helping Mexico, but of a U.S. totally detached, unconcerned, and seemingly unaffected by Mexico's fate. Reflecting Mexico's frustration over the protracted debate in the U.S. on whether to help Mexico, it shows Uncle Sam pondering the bailout while Mexico literally drowns. As with the depictions of an activist U.S. seeking Mexico's oil, the drawing does not portray the U.S. as acting in a friendly or neighborly way; hence the sarcasm in the title. Interestingly, figure 4.7 provides a slightly different spin on this theme. In contrast to the earlier drawings showing an apathetic U.S., this panel shows the U.S. bound to Mexico because of NAFTA and thus having no choice but to help its "partner." That an instrument of punishment symbolizes NAFTA, and that neither figure seems too happy about the situation, suggest that the U.S. is not only reluctant to provide aid, but does so only because of its own situation.

In some ways, the drawings on the bailout suggest that Mexico needs the

Figure 4.6

Figure 4.7

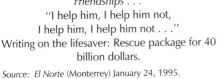

Friendships . . .
"I help him, I help him not,
I help him, I help him not . . ."
Writing on the lifesaver: Rescue package for 40
billion dollars.
Source: El Norte (Monterrey) January 24, 1995.

Partners
Source: Excelsior (Mexico City), January
30, 1995.

U.S. and therefore benefits from U.S. assistance. Other cartoons, however, highlight the opposite position, that U.S. power and the bilateral relationship actually hurt Mexico. Many of the depictions drawn during the NAFTA debate illustrate this theme, particularly those found in cartoon-based works like El Fisgón and Helguera's *El Sexenio me da risa* and Fisgón's *Como sobrevivir el neoliberalismo sin dejar de ser mexicano.*[12] Figures 4.8 by Perujo and 4.9 by Naranjo provide just two examples. Rather than casting NAFTA as an opportunity, they show Mexico getting screwed and losing its language and identity as a result of the trade agreement.

The drawings focusing on this theme of power suggest a relationship that can hardly be considered warm, friendly or, as we will see in subsequent panels, even honest. The vision of the U.S. as powerful translates first into the perception that the U.S. is self-serving and second into the notion that the U.S. is incapable of having a deep, meaningful relationship with Mexico. In other words, because the U.S. is constantly pursuing power to its own benefit,

Figure 4.8   **Figure 4.9**

Source: Perujo, "Souvenir," *El Economista,* 1990.

IMF's Mr. Camdessus: "I don't think that
NAFTA will distance you from
Latin America."
Mexican: "I'm not so sure,
Mr. Camdessus."
Source: Naranjo, "Fuera de cuadro," 1992.

it is unable to act in a friendly or neighborly manner. This view then seems to link friendship or neighborly behavior, on the one hand, with equality of power, on the other. And given the asymmetries of power between the two countries, it tends to preclude the possibility of a "good" relationship between the two. The relationship between the two countries thus necessarily remains shallow and forced: a point depicted in some of the subsequent panels.

Theme 2: U.S. Hypocrisy

A second broad theme closely interwoven into this view of U.S. power involves U.S. hypocrisy. This theme embraces a range of subthemes, including a questioning of the ostensible purpose of U.S. involvement in Mexico, particularly what the U.S. presents as altruistic behavior (a.k.a. exposing the true reasons), the inability of the U.S. to understand others, and, most prominently, the contradictions between U.S. conduct internally and abroad.

Like earlier panels showing the U.S. seeking concessions from Mexico, taking advantage of its strength and Mexico's weakness, figure 4.10 by Fran, published during the drug certification process, transmits the hypocrisy theme by attacking directly the notion that the U.S. did Mexico a favor by certifying its antidrug efforts. Instead, it shows (the) certification (flower) as actually a dressing-up of U.S. power: a means to garner concessions from Mexico. In a somewhat similar manner, figure 4.11 by El Fisgón shows the true manner by which the U.S. "lent Mexico a hand" during the bailout.

Similar cartoons also highlight the contradictory posture of the U.S. toward Mexico. In figure 4.12, drawn during Clinton's visit, Sagastegui's reference to "injured" refers not to Clinton—who had knee surgery prior to his trip to Mexico—but to the Mexican immigrants hammered by the recent immigration reform. It reminds the reader that despite the appearance of kindness surrounding Clinton's visit, one should not forget his role in passing the anti-Mexican immigration reform. The image is that Clinton's

Figure 4.10

Flower: *Certification*
Thorns: *Threats, armed DEA, capturing drug traffickers,
extraditions, control, pressures.*

Source: *El Norte* (Monterrey), March 1, 1997.

Figure 4.11

Uncle Sam: "Not so fast, I have got you good."

Source: El Fisgon, "El rescate," *La Jornada,* 1995.

Figure 4.12

Figure 4.13

Injured

Source: Excelsior (Mexico City), May 6, 1997.

"No. We are not interested in all of PEMEX; we will keep the *petroleo* and you keep the Mexicans."

Source: El Fisgon, "Paquete de ayuda," 1992.

"friendly" appearance hides the distinct reality of his anti-Mexicanism. In a similar way, El Fisgón in figure 4.13 mocks the distinction between the U.S.'s (long-felt) desire for Mexican oil and its anti-Mexican posture. It suggests that "they don't like us, just our oil." Naranjo also depicts this perception of the U.S. as double-faced in figure 4.14, welcoming and yet at the same time distancing itself from Mexico.

Some cartoons highlight the view that the U.S. fails to understand others, to recognize its own problems, or to see the gap between what it says and what it does, or what it demands of others and what it delivers itself. Figure 4.15 by Naranjo, for instance, contrasts the U.S.'s "supposed" concern for human rights with its treatment of Mexican migrants. Figure 4.6 presented above echoes this theme by showing the U.S. so unconcerned about Mexico's drowning as to leave its decision on whether to help entirely to fate, thereby effectively stripping the veil of "friendship" that so often adorns Mexican-U.S. relations. As noted, the title provides the sarcasm since clearly friends do not behave in this manner.

Figure 4.14

On wall: *Mexico is dangerous; Don't visit Mexico; Lookout for the Mexic . . .*

Source: Naranjo, "Sincero," 1985.

Figure 4.15

Source: Naranjo, "Habito de leer," 1992.

The drug war, and particularly the controversial issue of certification, have often evoked this image of U.S. hypocrisy (see figure 4.12). The drawing by Sagastegui in figure 4.16, for example, underscores the wide split between the internal situation and external posture of the U.S. It contrasts U.S. pressures on others in the drug war with the nation's insatiable demand for drugs. "Farol de la Calle," the title of this drawing, provides the first part of the Mexican saying, *"Farol de la calle; obscurdidad de su casa,"* which refers to someone who attempts to project a pure image outside the home, but is something entirely different inside the home. In this case, the artist draws a distinction between the posture of the U.S. abroad—with its process of certification in hand—and its behavior internally—its seemingly insatiable desire for a fix. Projecting a poignant image of U.S. society, the artist links Uncle Sam's habit to the "American way of life." Figure 4.17 by Magú similarly contrasts the dual demands of the U.S. in the drug equation: the demand for drugs and the demand for action.

While the prior theme focused on U.S. power, the theme of hypocrisy

Figure 4.16

Farol de la Calle...

Street Light

Source: *Excelsior* (Mexico City), May 8, 1997.

attacks the foundations of the use of U.S. power by questioning the U.S.'s authority to criticize Mexico or to offer (or dictate) solutions. This, in turn, feeds a tendency in Mexico to react more to the messenger than the message when it comes to the U.S. Given that Mexicans are fully aware of the problems associated with the debt, illegal immigration, and drug trafficking, reaction seems to center not so much on the problems or even the truth or veracity of U.S. claims, but on the moral authority of the U.S. to sit in judgment of Mexico. The resulting tendency is to respond by stressing the U.S.'s vices—its insatiable demand for drugs—or simply to censure the underlying conceit and paternalism that allow it to "sit in judgment" of others. This stance also echoes within the Mexican desire to resist U.S. pressures and to turn the tables and mockingly "sit in judgment" of the powerful U.S.: a theme displayed in a subsequent panel referring to the nation.

Theme 3: U.S. as Anti-Mexican and Racist

A third image of the U.S. exhibited by the caricatures entails a prime component of this hypocritical view just noted: the idea of the U.S. as anti-Mexican

Figure 4.17

Uncle Sam to Attorney General: "Listen, you're not exaggerating?
Later who will supply us with marijuana?"

Source: Magú, "Batalla antidrogas," *La Jornada,* 1985.

and even racist. Many, if not most of the panels presented thus far, depict a U.S. that is at best unconcerned about Mexico (neglect) or, at worst, decidedly anti-Mexican. Either way, all tend to portray the U.S. as something less than a "friend."

Many panels make this point of U.S. anti-Mexicanism, some in rather graphic terms. Figure 4.18 by El Fisgón illustrates a key component of this discourse. In addition to drawing attention to the relative size and power of the U.S. and Mexico, it puts to rest the question why Mexicans entering the U.S. are often referred to as "wetbacks." More blistering attacks see the U.S. as not only anti-Mexican, particularly in the context of the treatment of Mexican migrants in the U.S., but also as racist. Figure 4.19 from Guadalajara's *Ocho Columnas* casts the new immigration law as part of a U.S.-based process of "ethnic cleansing." It portrays the U.S. as xenophobic, racist, and anti-Mexican. A similar theme can be found in El Fisgón's drawing in response to the execution of Tristán Montoya in figure 4.20. It shows Mexicans excluded from a system of justice reserved for others and suggests that the execution was a product of U.S. racism. By placing Mexicans into a category alongside African-Americans (and using the most racist of terms), the artist

Figure 4.18

Source: El Fisgon, "¡Esos mojados!" *La Jornada,* 1995.

Figure 4.19

On broom: *New U.S. Immigration Law*
On dustpan: *Ethnic Cleansing*

Source: Ocho Columnas (Guadalajara), 1997.

Figure 4.20

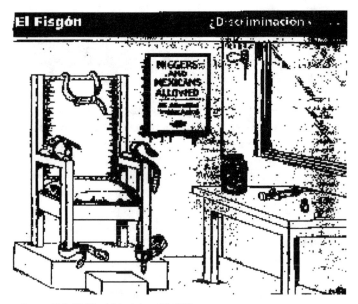

Source: Siglo 21 (Guadalajara), June 19, 1997.

seems to suggest that the exclusion of the Mexicans relates more to race than to nationality.

While the two themes discussed earlier revealed the U.S. wielding power at Mexico's expense, despite trying to give the appearance of a good neighbor, the anti-Mexican and racist theme seems to provide the underlying rationale to account for U.S. behavior. When the U.S. pursues an anti-Mexican position, in short, it is seen as owing fundamentally to the fact that the U.S. does not like Mexico, perhaps because of racism and the accompanying sense of superiority. This view, importantly, is not contradicted by any policy that might presumably help Mexico since such a policy (e.g., the financial bailout) can still be dismissed—in accordance to the first theme—as an example of the U.S.'s self-serving behavior. In sum, the U.S. only helps Mexico when it stands to gain something in return, not because it really wants to help Mexico or because it is a friend. Again, none (all) of these themes portrays (betray) the image of friend or neighbor.

Theme 4: Perceptions of the Nation

Besides providing images of the U.S., the caricatures focusing on the U.S. also offer a distinct discourse on the nation. In many ways these interwoven themes just discussed on the U.S. serve to define Mexico. Four subthemes related to perceptions of the nation can be teased from the drawings. First, the power of the U.S. contrasts with and thus defines Mexico's weakness, while the abuse of that power expresses the nation's dependency and vulnerability. Figures 4.4 and 4.5 shown earlier, for instance, graphically exhibit the nation's weakness, with the latter showing Mexico naked save for is petroleum. The title goes a step further by pondering what would happen if Mexico did not have the petroleum.

A second prominent theme related to the nation centers on portrayals of the government as an accomplice to the U.S. Figure 4.21 by Calderón shows the reliance of then-Mexican president Salinas on U.S. President George Bush. The message is direct: without Bush, Salinas has no leg to stand on. In figure 4.22, Naranjo shows an even broader alliance linking the U.S. and the IMF with the PRI. The cracking egg refers to the change of policies within the PRI government that is, clearly, to the pleasure of the U.S. government and the IMF. Figure 4.23 from *El Norte* also demonstrates the power differential and this subtheme of the Mexican government as an accomplice. The power versus weakness theme is shown not only by Clinton towering over his Mexican "counterpart," but by the fact that Clinton is shown as merely temporarily handicapped (owing to the surgery), while President Zedillo (Mexico) is permanently handicapped and thus in need of help. In that the

Figure 4.21

Source: Calderón, ''TLC'' *Reforma*, 1992.

Figure 4.22

Source: Naranjo, ''Ay, qué ternura,'' 1987.

Figure 4.23

Source: *El Norte* (Monterrey), May 6, 1997.

handout here is not so much for Mexico as for the ruling PRI, as indicated by the wheels on Zedillo's cart, however, the panel also shows the U.S. helping the PRI government and not the nation itself.

The asymmetry of power, the hypocrisy, and the anti-Mexicanism of the U.S. discussed earlier all combine to make resistance in the face of U.S. pressures a virtue: a third subtheme relating to perceptions of the nation. As shown with the panels relating to NAFTA, Mexico is often depicted as threatened with the loss of its rights and identities owing to the new relationship with the U.S. Resistance therefore becomes the only noble solution. Highlighting the humility and animosity evoked by the U.S. captures one expression of this urge to resist. Figures 4.24 and 4.25, both by Marino, offer examples of these sentiments by hinting at the injustices occasioned by the asymmetry of power, and hence expressing the desire to "turn the tables"

Figure 4.24   **Figure 4.25**

Pending Accounts
Source: *Excelsior* (Mexico City), May 6, 1997.

Suspicion
"Clinton is in Mexico . . ."
"I wonder if he has his papers in order?"
Source: *Excelsior* (Mexico City), May 7, 1997.

and assume the "moral authority" against a powerful "other." In "Pending Accounts" (figure 4.24), though many in the audience seem content listening to Clinton, the speaker ponders the impact of "decertifying" Clinton. In "Suspicion" (figure 4.25), by questioning whether Clinton has his papers in order, Marino reverses the humiliating position of Mexicans in the U.S. of being "automatically suspect."

A final subtheme regarding perceptions of the nation relates to broader images of the relationship. While many of the drawings examined thus far have shown the U.S. harboring anti-Mexican attitudes despite trying to give the appearance of being pro-Mexican, some depict a similar Mexican perception of the U.S. and the relationship. Figure 4.26 by Sagastegui and figure 4.27 from *El Bravo* express the broad message that despite living together as

Figure 4.26   **Figure 4.27**

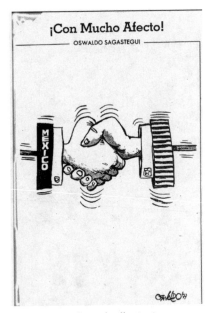

With much affection!

Source: *Excelsior* (Mexico City), May 7, 1997.

U.S.: [in thought] "Mexican pig, loafer, incurably corrupt, apathetic and accommodating, trafficker" Mexican: [in thought] "gringo trickster, rat wants more Mexican land, seditious and drug addict, barbarian invader, violator of international rights"

Source: *El Bravo* (Matamoros), May 30, 1991.

neighbors, the friendship, though present, explicit, and, owing to NAFTA, maybe even necessary, remains superficial and forced, struggling to repress the weight of strong cultural, racial, ideological, and nationalist animosities. The sarcastic title *"Con Mucho Afecto!"* in figure 4.26 nicely captures the view that under the surface and below the rhetoric, the two countries remain "distant neighbors."[13]

The image of a weak and vulnerable country vis-à-vis the U.S. is readily apparent in the cartoons. On the one hand, this seems to make U.S. assistance necessary. But when coupled with the perception that the U.S. is really anti-Mexican, that it always tries to take the moral high ground, and yet helps only when it is in its own interests to do so, feeds a sentiment of animosity and humiliation on the other hand. This, as noted, fuels the desire to turn the tables and pass judgment on the U.S. This position supports the ideas of social liberation informing Latin American thought and cultural identity.[14] But the perception of the nation illustrated here also suggests the view that Mexico may behave in a manner similar to the U.S. Both, in other words, seem to hide their true sentiments behind a series of pleasantries. This suggests that the relationship can occur and grow, but that the two camouflage rather than overcome the mutual animosity. Both, of course, repress their sentiments to further their own interests, to be sure: a theme fully consistent within the nationalistic narrative. But the asymmetry of power suggests a fundamental difference: as the subaltern, Mexican hypocrisy (the hiding of its feelings) arises out of a need that is externally imposed, while U.S. hypocrisy is an extension of U.S. power and the U.S. character. Mexico, in other words, *must* deal with the U.S. and therefore carefully channel the expression of any anti-U.S. sentiments; the U.S., by contrast, is free not only to determine its own policies, but to express its own character. In other words, Mexico has no choice (dependent—subject), while the U.S. does (independent—agent).

The Artistic Dimension

Besides the more explicit message or "joke" contained within the caricatures, the graphic images themselves are also relevant in terms of understanding the overall narrative, and thus they merit some attention. In some ways, the images reinforce the themes stressed earlier, while in other cases they add new dimensions or even points of contrast. First, as seen throughout our review, the artists prefer to use Uncle Sam or President Clinton to represent the U.S. The fact that the symbols tend to refer to the U.S. government as opposed to the American people lends some support to the conclusions of

Knight and Turner that the Mexican is not necessarily xenophobic or negative toward the U.S. people, but rather targets his or her anger or frustration
toward the U.S. government.[15] Chapter 8 on public opinion explores this
question further. Second, the caricatures depend heavily on male images. The
use of a male figure to represent the U.S. speaks perhaps to a gendered view
of power, though Mexico (the weaker party) is rarely drawn as a woman or
as representing feminine qualities. Doing so would clearly question Mexico's
sense of machismo. Third, the U.S. figure is normally taller than the Mexican,
indicative of the relative power of the U.S. Still, it is interesting that Uncle
Sam rarely appears particularly strong or decisive, or portrays the evil caricature of, say, Hernán Cortes in the famous Diego Rivera mural.

In drawing Mexico, again except for the occasional use of the president to
represent the Mexican government, most of the caricatures rely on a male
figure, usually distinguished by the *sombrero* or a moustache, or other such
cultural markers. In contrast to the portrayal of the U.S., many of the depictions of Mexico seem to refer to the population rather than the government.
Though sometimes dressed poorly, some representations—like figures 4.4
and 4.7—combine middle-class and popular class symbols like the sombrero
with a tie and sandals. The multiclass nature of the Mexican in both these
drawings dealing with the economic crisis suggests that all classes in Mexico
have been affected by the crisis and, perhaps, that nationalism and nationalist
differences take precedence over class divisions. Again the gendered view
expressed through the depictions is clear and the absence of females in the
graphics is striking.

Equally striking perhaps is that the drawings fail to incorporate any racial
features and thus offer no racial distinctions between the North American
(Uncle Sam) and the Mexicans. The Mexicans depicted in the drawings seem
just as white as Uncle Sam or Clinton. This is particularly interesting given
the theme of race within the discourse as referred to earlier. While it might
suggest a narrative in which the "other" is portrayed as racist, while "self"
recognizes no such racial differences or hierarchies—a view consistent with
the national self-image—it could also reflect the tendency for subaltern subjects to internalize the racial images and hierarchies of the West.[16]

The Historical Question

Do these contemporary images differ from those of the past? Turning attention to the issue of change in the discourse, a review of scores of cartoons
from the past suggests that there has been little if any change. In fact, the
historic parallels among the drawings are rather striking. Again, it is impor-

tant to reiterate that only a small sample of the drawings from years past that were reviewed can be presented here, though they illustrate the major themes and images uncovered during the research.

First, past images strongly echo the perception of U.S. presence, power, and abuse of power at Mexico's expense. Figure 4.28 by Rius from the fifties, highlighting the presence of multinationals (mainly U.S.) in Mexico to sarcastically question Mexico's independence, neatly parallels Curry's image from figure 4.1. Similarly, figure 4.29, published in 1903, showing Porfirio Díaz, José Ives Limantour, and others groveling for the U.S. to intervene to save the Mexican currency, waxes reminiscent of the U.S. financial bailout in 1995. Figure 4.30 also depicts U.S. power, showing President Wilson "pushing and directing" Carranza and the Revolution "to seed death in the national territory by way of the U.S. stimulus."[17] Figure 4.31, meanwhile, from the seventies, echoes an earlier theme: the U.S. desire for Mexican oil.

Historical cartoons also highlight the theme of U.S. hypocrisy in its various guises. Drawn during the chaotic period of the Mexican Revolution, figure

Figure 4.28   **Figure 4.29**

"What did he say?"
"Long live independence."
Source: Rpt in Rius 1984, 97.

Saving the devalued currency.
Source: El Hijo del Ahuizote, February 8, 1902.

Figure 4.30

Source: La Guacamaya, February 15, 1914.

Figure 4.31

Source: Oswaldo, "En la mira," *Excelsior,* May 20, 1976, p. 7A, redrawn by Janet Griffing.

4.32 notes that in its strong preoccupation with Mexican (in)stability, the U.S. failed to recall its own tumultuous civil war. Playing on a Mexican saying, González notes in his analysis of this panel, "Our revolutionary anarchy was the 'straw in the other's eye,' and the beam in their own eye was the southern revolution in the U.S."[18] In a similar manner, figure 4.33 points to the tendency for the U.S. to disguise its use of power. In this case, the U.S. Alliance for Progress, touted by the U.S. as evidence of its goodwill, is portrayed as a ploy hiding its real pursuit of dollars: the gleam in the wolf's eyes. Finally, the drawing by Covarrubias in 1928 shown in figure 4.34 provides a striking parallel to figure 4.16. Though separated by almost half a century, both underscore the U.S. hypocrisy. One refers to Prohibition, the other to drugs.

The views of the nation contained in the cartoons from the past also are strikingly similar to those found in drawings from the more contemporary period. As noted, contemporary panels tend to portray Mexico as small, weak, dependent, and vulnerable compared to the large, powerful, and independent U.S. At a time when "Yankee capitalism was well established in Mexico due to mining concessions and concessions of enormous extensions of 'vacant lands,'" figure 4.35 from the influential *El Hijo de Ahuizote* in 1898

Figure 4.32

Figure 4.33

Illustrated sentence
Source: *Revista de Revistas*, August 29, 1915, p. 18.

President Diaz Ordaz as Red Riding Hood: "Why do you have such lovely eyes, grandmother?"
Wolf = Alliance for Progress

Source: Rius, "Alianza para el progreso," 1965.

Figure 4.34

Source: Miguel Covarribias, "Ley del Estado Seco," 1928.

Figure 4.35

O PATONES O PATANES

Calzado para escoger, que propone *El Hijo del Ahuizote.*

Source: Danuel Cabrera, "O patones o patanes," *El Hijo del Ahuizote,* May 1898.

presents Mexicans with the stark choice of either U.S. or Spanish (Gachupin) imperialism.[19] In figure 4.36, famed muralist José Clemente Orozco nicely captures U.S. power and Mexican weakness. In this case, however, U.S. imperialism is simply benefiting from the failed policies of the Mexican government.

Historical panels also emphasize the role of the U.S. as an accomplice to the government, usually to the detriment of the people. Figure 4.37, for example, shows Porfirio Díaz (the great Mexican villain) seeking U.S. support to maintain his hold on power, while figure 4.38 attacks U.S. collusion in repressing Mexican workers in Cananea in Chihuahua. Figure 4.39 displays a similar theme. It refers to an opinion held by many that Uncle Sam plays a predominant role in the designation of Mexican presidents.

Figure 4.36

Uncle Sam in mangled Spanish: "Oh, Mr. Sota amd Gama and Caloca, accept my congratulations, you are very good agents for me, the more land you distribute, the less corn, lard and eggs does Mexico produce, and that I can sell more and more. Hurrah for the agrarianist!"

Source: Jose Clemente Orrozco, *L'ABC*, 1925.

Figure 4.37   **Figure 4.38**

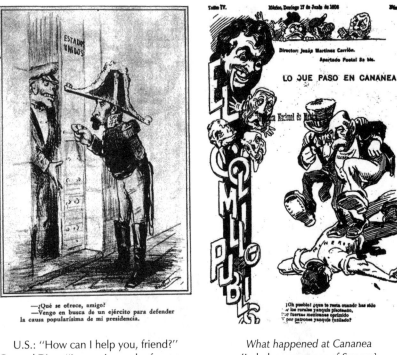

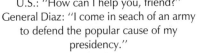

—¿Qué se ofrece, amigo?
—Vengo en busca de un ejército para defender
la causa popularísima de mi presidencia.

U.S.: "How can I help you, friend?"
General Diaz: "I come in seach of an army
to defend the popular cause of my
presidency."

Source: "Moctezuma," *La Carabina de Am-brosio,* December 1875.

What happened at Cananea
[Isabel = governor of Sonora]

Source: El Colmillo Publico, June 24, 1906, p. 384.

Finally, history shows the importance of Mexican resistance to U.S. pressures. While many drawings during the Revolution criticize U.S. support of Huerta, figure 4.40 shows not only U.S. meddling in Mexican affairs, but the domestic adversaries stopping their fight long enough to agree that such intervention is improper. The cartoon in figure 4.41, our last panel, perhaps best dramatizes the virtue of resistance against the U.S. Drawing on the biblical David and Goliath struggle between the weak and the strong (represented here by Woodrow Wilson), it points to the need to "exalt the justice of our country before imperialist ambition."[20] Such a narrative echoes throughout many of the contemporary cartoons.

Figure 4.39

Uncle Sam: "Careful with the paint, little
man; I painted it for someone else."

Source: La Satira, September 17, 1911.

Figure 4.40

The two Mexicans to Uncle Sam: "You, don't get involved."

Source: Revista de Revistas April 6, 1913.

Figure 4.41

Female onlooker: *Patria*
David's club: *Justice*
David's pants: *The People*
Goliath's [Woodrow Wilson] shield: *United States of America.*
Goliath's sword: *Ambition*

Source: *La Guacamaya,* May 17, 1914.

Conclusion

In summary, political caricatures from the contemporary period tend to portray the U.S. as powerful, self-serving, and anti-Mexican. They depict a U.S.
that disguises its self-serving moves as being beneficial to Mexico, of hiding
a reality of caring little about or not even liking Mexico or the Mexicans.
They show a U.S. that is hypocritical, often assuming a position of moral
superiority and applying one set of standards to others while failing to recognize its own shortcomings. Such postures seem to attend in particular to the
more controversial issues of drugs, migration, and the U.S. desire to possess
Mexican oil, and they feed a tendency in Mexico to attack the messenger.
Moreover, they suggest a relationship that, while perhaps beneficial to the
Mexican government, is hardly considered beneficial to the nation. The car-

toons, indeed, turn resistance into a national value, though recognizing that the power differential makes this difficult to do in reality. This "reality," in turn, forces Mexico to also hide its true sentiments toward its northern neighbor. Finally, the cartoons show that despite indications that Mexico may have nurtured a new relationship with the U.S. in recent years, the same themes found in the contemporary cartoons marked cartoons from years past. Continuity, rather than change, seems to dominate. Many of these same themes—the U.S. as power-hungry, hypocritical, and even anti-Mexican—we see in the writings of Mexico's intellectuals: the subject to which we now turn.

Notes

1. According to Carlos Monsiváis ("Las caricaturas me hacen llorar," *Proceso* 1198 (October 17, 1999) (electronic version), the self-censorship that once restrained the cartoonists and other journalists has eased considerably in recent years.

2. Ariel Dorfman and Armand Mattelart, *Para leer el Pato Donald* (México: Siglo XXI, 1971); David William Foster, *From Mafalda to Los Supermachos: Latin American Graphic Humor as Popular Culture* (Boulder, CO.: Lynne Rienner, 1995); John Johnson, *Latin America in Caricature* (Austin: University of Texas Press, 1993); *The Americas Review* special issue 23 (1–2) (1995) edited by Rosáura Sánchez and Beatrice Pita; and Rius (Rio, Eduardo del), *Un siglo de caricatura en México* (Mexico City: Grijalbo, 1984). See also Estela Arredondo and Rius, *Los críticos del imperio: La historia de los últimos sexenios a través de la caricatura* (Mexico City: Grijalbo, 1998); Rafael Carrasco Puente, *La caricatura en México* (Mexico City: Imprenta Universitaria, 1953); Salvador Pruneda, *La caricatura como arma política* (Mexico City: Instituto Nacional de Estudios Históricos de la Revolución, 1958); and Manuel Toussaint, "The Political Caricature in Mexico," *Mexican Art and Life*, October 4, 1938.

3. Naomi Lindstrom, "The Single-Panel Cartoon," in *Handbook of Latin American Popular Culture*, edited by Harold E. Hinds Jr. and Charles M. Tatum (Westport, CT: Greenwood Press, 1985), 207–27.

4. Rosáura Sánchez and Beatrice Pita, "Cartooning and Other Graphic Arts: An Introduction," *The Americas Review* 23 (1–2) (1995): 7–27.

5. Foster, *From Mafalda to Los Supermachos*, 65.

6. The newspapers used here represent a wide range of circulation levels and coverage as well as ideological shadings. *Excelsior* leads the way, enjoying one of the largest circulations in the country (reported at 200,000 but considered to be about 90,000), and, like *La Jornada* (actual circulation of about 40,000) and *Proceso*, it is sold throughout the nation. The dailies from Guadalajara and Monterrey, by contrast, have smaller circulations and a more regional orientation. Given certain direct and indirect controls over the media in Mexico, it could be argued that all the newspapers are basically mainstream or moderate in tone. With the exception of *La Jornada, Proceso,* and perhaps *Siglo 21* in Guadalajara, none of the other papers in the study could be considered particularly left-leaning. *Excelsior* is generally considered a

solid, middle-of-the-road paper representing elite opinion: a status to which Monterrey's *El Norte* also aspires. See Raymundo Riva Palacio, "A Culture of Collusion:
The Ties that Bind the Press and the PRI," in *A Culture of Collusion: An Inside Look
at the Mexican Press,* edited by William A. Orme (Miami, FL: North-South Center
Press, 1997), 21–32.

7. Most know the story of the economic crisis. The steep drop in the value of the
peso in late December 1994 unleashed a severe financial pinch, threatening moneyed
interests both at home and abroad. Promptly recognizing its direct and indirect
impact on the U.S. and U.S. investors, President Clinton initially proposed that the
U.S. cover half of an $18 billion international package of loan guarantees to Mexico.
Though garnering early support from congressional leaders, the proposal met stiff
resistance from the American public and congressional rank and file, triggering an
intense and divisive debate in the U.S. In the end, opposition prompted Clinton to
withdraw the initial proposal from Congress, alter it to a $47 billion loan guarantee
drawing on the Treasury Department's Exchange Stabilization Fund and commit-
ments from the IMF and the Bank for International Settlement (BIS), justify it as a
matter of "national security," and then authorize it without Congressional approval.
The internal debate, which emphasized a host of Mexican ills from immigration to
corruption to NAFTA, rested primarily on the viability of the loans and the question
of "guarantees" or "conditions."

8. Ireneo Tristan Montoya was convicted in 1986 for the murder of an American motorist.

9. Portions of this chapter appear in Stephen D. Morris, "Exploring Mexican
Images of the U.S.," *Mexican Studies/Estudios Mexicanos* 16 (1) (2000): 105–39.

10. Arredondo and Rius, *Críticos del imperio;* Carrasco, *Caricatura en México;*
Manuel González Ramírez, *Caricatura política* (Mexico City: Fondo de Cultura Económica, 1955); Pruneda, *Caricatura como arma política;* Rius, *Un siglo de caricatura
en México;* Toussaint, "Political Caricature in Mexico"; and Jose Guadalupe Zuño,
Historia de la Caricatura en México (Mexico City, 1967).

11. Arredondo and Rius, *Críticos del imperio,* 275.

12. El Fisgón and Helguera, *El Sexenio me da risa La historieta no oficial* (Mexico
City: Grijalbo, 1994); El Fisgón, *Como sobrevivir el neoliberalismo sin dejar de ser mexicano* (Mexico City: Grijalbo, 1996)

13. Obvious reference is made to Alan Riding, *Distant Neighbors: A Portrait of
the Mexicans* (New York: Vintage Books, 1986).

14. Ofelia Schutte, *Cultural Identity and Social Liberation in Latin American
Thought* (New York: State University of New York Press, 1993).

15. Knight, "Popular Culture and the Revolutionary State"; and Turner, *Dynamics of Mexican Nationalism.*

16. See Pieterse and Parekh, "Shifting Imaginaries."

17. González, *Caricatura política.*

18. González, *Caricatura política,* 418. This refers to a popular Mexican saying,
"no puedes ver la paja en el ojo ajeno."

19. Pruneda, *Caricatura como arma política,* 200.

20. González, *Caricatura política,* 412.

5

Gringolandia in the Writings of the Intellectual Elite

BRANDISHING A RANGE OF MEDIA—from essays and novels to op-ed pieces—Mexican intellectuals have long dominated the debate over national identity. Their ideas have influenced many.[1] And as in the political cartoons, the U.S. theme resides conspicuously within their writings. Mexican thinkers have not only crafted a particular image of the U.S., as we will see, but have often portrayed and defined the Mexican through a contrast with his or her U.S. counterpart. As Carlos Fuentes posits, Mexican nationalism is defined "by the proximity of another nationalism: North American."[2]

This exploration of the themes and images of the U.S. and the nation in the writings of the Mexican intellectual elite draws primarily on selected writings of Agustín Basave, Roger Bartra, Jorge Castañeda, Carlos Fuentes, Carlos Monsiváis, Octavio Paz, Samuel Ramos, and José Vasconcelos. Though this list is hardly exhaustive, these authors are among the most influential Mexican thinkers of the twentieth century. Combined, their writings offer different approaches, span many decades, and focus extensively on the questions at hand. Basave's philosophical tome on the nature of the Mexican, *Vocación y estilo de México,* for instance, devotes an entire chapter just to *malinchismo* and another to comparing the U.S. and Mexico.[3] Bartra's anthropological classic, *La jaula de melancolia,* and his journal discussions on culture and power likewise invoke the U.S. to describe the nature of Mexican culture.[4] Through *Limits to Friendship, The Estados Unidos Affair,* and *Utopia Unarmed,* Castañeda—the foreign minister under the Fox government—provides a straightforward political science approach, stressing the country's differences with the U.S., U.S. domestic and foreign policy, and the Latin American left's vision of the U.S.[5] In such works as *Laberinto de Soledad, El ogro filantrópico, Tiempo nublado,* and *One Earth, Four or Five Worlds,* Nobel laureate Octavio Paz develops a nuanced philosophical analysis of the U.S. people, its history, and its institutions, usually in juxtaposition to Mexico.[6] In like manner, novelist and critic Carlos Fuentes offers the reader a specific narrative about Mexico's northern neighbor in such essays as *Tiempo Mexicano* and *Nuevo tiempo mexicano* and in the highly acclaimed novels *La región más transparente, Gringo viejo,* and *Cristóbal nonato* [Christopher Unborn].[7] In *La región más transparente,* for instance, Fuentes adorns every character with a particular relationship and opinion of the U.S., while *Cristobal nonato* offers a futuristic vision of what might happen to Mexico if it develops too close a relationship with the U.S. Carlos Monsiváis, in turn, explores everyday life and culture in contemporary Mexico through a series of essays collected in *Los rituales del caos* and *Mexican Postcards.*[8] His work stresses U.S. cultural influence and its role in forging Mexico's hybrid culture. Samuel Ramos, by contrast, provides a psychoanalytical view of the Mexican *Profile of Man and Culture in Mexico.* Highly influential, the work highlights the Mexican desire to imitate mainly European societies but also the U.S., linking this in turn to the Mexican's sense of inferiority.[9] Finally, through such works as *Ulises criollo* and *La raza cósmica,* José Vasconcelos goes to great lengths to describe the nature of the U.S. and particularly the dangers associated with its influence over Mexico.[10]

In contrast to earlier chapters that address images of the U.S. and the nation separately, this chapter explores both *a la vez.* It proceeds by examining four major themes relating to variable images of the U.S. and their effects on Mexico. Each theme elaborates and builds on the characteristics associated with the U.S. identified in the writings. Following a review of these themes, the latter section of the chapter draws the various strands of the exposition together to explore the contested and contradictory nature of Mexico's views of the U.S., linkages between the perceptions of the U.S. and views of self, and the impact of recent changes.

The U.S. in the Discourse of Mexican Intellectuals

Discussion of the U.S. by Mexican intellectuals is rarely intended as an end in itself, but rather as a discursive means to explain and create a narrative on Mexico. Two notable exceptions are Paz's exploration of the U.S. in *One Earth, Four or Five Worlds* and Castañeda's *The Estados Unidos Affair.* Though separated by a decade, both interestingly explore the "contemporary" crisis facing the U.S. In a chapter entitled "The Imperial Democracy," Paz concentrates on what he sees as the decadence of U.S. society marked by the rise of doubt, pleasure, melancholy, despair, remembrance, and nostalgia.[11] Castañeda, in a chapter titled "Desafíos de la democracia en Estados Unidos [challenges to U.S. democracy]," highlights declining accountability, growing exclusionism, and lack of dynamic political debate as forging an ongoing political crisis in the U.S.[12]

But beyond these exceptions, most writings on the U.S. deploy the U.S. as a device to help describe and create Mexico. Since it is this context that makes perceptions or images of the U.S. important, the discussion adopts this approach. Stated somewhat differently, the exploration here looks not so much at the question of how Mexican thinkers characterize the U.S. *per se*, but at how their portrayals of the U.S. help define and construct Mexico. The answer to this question can be broken down into four subfoci, each rooted in the varying perceptions of the U.S., that provide the organization for this discussion: (1) as Mexico's predominant "other," the U.S. helps define Mexico and Mexicanness through contrast; (2) as Mexico's primary model of "success" or "modernity," the U.S. serves as the archetype that Mexico aspires to; (3) as a dominant, imperialist power, the U.S. is seen as a force (agent) shaping Mexico through direct and indirect influence; and (4) as an anti-Mexican power and the nation's predominant "other," the U.S. is perceived as a "threat" to Mexican identity and interests, thus serving as a force to be resisted or a countermodel to be contested.

Theme 1: The U.S. as a Backdrop to Define and Describe Mexico

At a broad level, Mexican thinkers frequently describe the U.S. in contrast to Mexico and vice versa.[13] Perhaps Paz best captures the general nature of this approach: "Mexicans view that country [the U.S.] as 'the other' inseparable from ourselves and . . . at the same time . . . radically and essentially extraneous or foreign . . . the other side is geographic: the border; cultural: an other civilization; linguistic: an other language; historical: an other [relationships to] time (the United States runs to the future while we are bound still to our past); metaphoric: [the United States] is the image of all that the [Mexicans] are not; they are strangeness [(otherness)] itself."[14]

Typical of this approach, analysts employ an incredibly wide range of oppositional or Manichaean categories to depict the U.S. and Mexico, prompting the notion that the U.S. represents the opposite of the Mexican, or, as Castañeda contends, as "radically, substantially and fiercely distinct from the U.S."[15] In *Labyrinth of Solitude*, for example, Paz contrasts the North American trust and optimism with the Mexican suspiciousness and "willingness to contemplate horror"; the North American's wish to perfect the world with the Mexican's desire to redeem it.[16] In "Espejo indiscreto" he contends that the U.S. is tied to the future and sports a tradition of change, while Mexico is tied to the past and supports a tradition of resistance; that while equality and individualism in the U.S. historically fomented the role of society, in Mexico and Latin America "precisely the opposite occurred."[17] Indeed, in *Tiempo nublado*, Paz portrays the two as not only representing "distinct versions of Western civilization"—one in which the Reformation triumphed and the other in which the Counterreformation triumphed—but as modern expressions of an ancient, primordial opposition predating both countries.[18]

Basave employs this analytical approach more extensively than does Paz, providing a laundry list of differences to define the two peoples. He characterizes the Mexican as courteous and proud and the North American as rude and simple; the Mexican as having an extensive imagination and the North American as being simple; the Mexican as lacking perseverance and the North American as being well disciplined; the Mexican as having spiritual curiosity and being cultural and artistic and the North American as emphasizing statistical analysis and sociological systemization; the Mexican humor as more complicated and profound than the simple and jovial humor of the U.S.; Mexican society as vertical (hierarchical, traditional) and U.S. society as horizontal (no traditionalist complex, not rigid, egalitarian); that the Mexican is obsessed with spiritual matters, while the U.S. is obsessed with progress measured in terms of economic prosperity. The binary list goes on, containing over 50 such descriptions.[19]

Fuentes also uses the U.S. to describe through contrast the Mexican and vice versa. In *Gringo viejo*, for instance, he points to a wide range of oppositional differences, including the manner of walk ("the step of the *gringo* [is] long and quiet, not clicking and rapid and short as in the world of the children of Spain"); the cuisine (the bland, simple, and quick of the U.S. compared to the long and exotic of Mexico); the perception of Christ (the Mexican Crucifix with a bleeding and suffering Christ compared to the sanitized Calvinistic Christ); and perspectives on death (for Arroyo, the Mexican protagonist, death is an integral part of life, while Harriet sees the opposite: that life and death are separate things, thereby equating sin, death, and the devil.)[20]

Table 5.1 provides a glimpse at many of these contrasts. It shows Mexico as generally manifesting qualities opposite to the ones associated with the U.S. From this perspective, Mexico represents, as Paz suggests, a negation of the U.S. such that being Mexican means, in certain ways, not being *gringo*.[21]

Though many of these traits are wielded for descriptive purposes, three characteristics enjoy much more detailed analysis by the authors, highlighting much of the prevailing intellectual image of the U.S. as well as this oppo-

TABLE 5.1
U.S. (Other) and Mexico (Self) as Opposites

U.S. ("other": different)	Mexico ("self": defined through difference)
• triumph of the Reformation and Enlightenment—true to its roots	• triumph of the Counterreformation —has tried to break with the past (Paz)
• reformist, trusting, optimistic	• contemplates horror, nihilistic, suspicious (Paz)
• no past due to its treatment of the indigenous: future-oriented (Paz)	• "Mexico is Mexico thanks to the Indian presence" —history and tradition are the "center of our existence" (Paz)
• no historical memory	• a country with memory (Fuentes) "for Mexico [history] is the essence of the present" (Castañeda)
• ability to avoid any disagreeable subject	• the Mexican confronts death face to face (Paz)
• wishes to avoid contact with foreigner for fear of contamination	• believes in contact and communion (Paz)
• pragmatic	• image of Mexican as spineless and idle (Bartra)
• critical thought	• no critical thought (Basave)
• quantitative	• qualitative (Basave)
• individualistic	• family- and group-oriented (Basave)
• powerful—independent	• weak—dependent
• success	• failure
• progress and modernity	• lack of progress and modernity
• democratic	• not democratic—authoritarian

sitional approach. First, most stress differences related to time, referring to the U.S. as clearly future-oriented and hence having virtually no history, and Mexico as a country shackled to its past. Paz, for example, calls the U.S. "the kingdom of the future" while for Mexico "history [is the] center of our existence."[22] Fuentes, similarly, sees the U.S. as suffering a form of amnesia, lacking any sense of tradition, whereas Mexico is a country with memory.[23] Castañeda makes a similar point: "For the United States, history is folklore plus the recent past; for Mexico, it is the essence of the present."[24]

Despite such agreement, the reasons behind this fundamental difference and the implications vary. Paz, for example, attributes the U.S.'s historic vacuum to its treatment of the indigenous population and to the fact that from the beginning the country agreed on the basic ideals guiding the nation.[25] Such ideals, moreover, rooted in Puritan Protestantism, allowed individuals and not public institutions to determine society's "ultimate ends."[26] This, he concludes, freed the U.S. "of the weight of history and meta-historical ends."[27] For Castañeda, by contrast, the U.S.'s lack of history stems more from the nation's immigrant roots and the homogeneity occasioned by social equality. According to Castañeda, the U.S. had no shared history, nor was history important. For Mexico, however, a divided and less unified country than the U.S., history becomes the only source of unity: "If in the United States the cohesive element is 'the American dream,' historic memory is what unifies Mexico. Without it the country as we know it might not exist."[28]

A second prominent oppositional trait featured in the literature pits the two cultures generally, characterizing U.S. culture as materialistic, individualistic, and pragmatic, basically cultureless, and Mexico's as deeply spiritual and culturally rich. Again all the authors seem to express this view in some guise or another. Typical of the romantic authors of the time—the early part of the twentieth century—Vasconcelos in *La raza cósmica* emphasizes the moral and cultural decadence of the U.S. He alludes to the mediocrity of U.S. culture, its crass materialism, and lack of spirituality, reserving special attack for its Protestant beliefs. This, of course, sets the stage for Vasconcelos to highlight the Mexican love for culture, the arts, philosophy, and the virtues of Catholicism.[29] Ramos similarly characterizes U.S. culture as instrumentalist and lacking a humanist tradition: again, the opposite of Mexico.[30] Paz expresses the view that the U.S. has tended to overemphasize the role of the individual, resulting in a "passive indifference to values" and a neglect of its public responsibility.[31] It is on this level that Paz unearths the root of U.S. decadence, and the nature of its moral crisis.[32] Fuentes is perhaps even more critical of predominant U.S. culture, labeling it as *Pepsicoatl*: a type of mythical, fetishist, and consumerist pop culture with the linguistic tie to the prehispanic legend of Quetzalcoatl. Fuentes links this loss of culture in the U.S. to the nation's material development.[33]

Finally, most authors tend to highlight the different historical foundations of the two societies, again offering these in binary form. In *Mexico and the U.S.*, Paz provides an extensive contrast, seeing the two societies as representing an ancient opposition predating both countries with two "distinct versions of Western civilization" subsequently grafted on top. In one, the Reformation triumphed, and in the other, the Counterreformation.[34] Years later in the *Philanthropic Ogre*, Paz reaffirms this view of two distinct versions of Western civilization by claiming that Latin America represents a combination of civilizations of the West (Counterreformation and liberalism together). And yet, offering a somewhat different view, in his Washington Address in 1978, he contends that the major difference between the two is that "Mexico is Mexico thanks to the Indian presence, [whereas] in the United States the Indian dimension does not appear." Castañeda also emphasizes the different historical foundations of the two nations, but in a sociological rather than a cultural sense. As noted earlier, he stresses the immigrant origins and egalitarianism of the U.S. as opposed to the lack of equality and integration in Mexico.

In sum, the writers envision the U.S. as historyless and cultureless, materialistic and pragmatic, individualistic and alone, loose in morals and a product of the Reformation. These serve through opposition to help construct the Mexican identity of self and nation. But in returning to the broader pattern, it is important to note that not all the juxtapositions listed in table 5.1 refer to simple Manichaean categories (e.g., history versus no history; culture versus cultureless; Reformation versus Counterreformation, etc.). The last few entries move beyond this simple device to suggest several closely related hierarchical schemes. These all tend to cast the U.S. as not just different or opposite from Mexico, but in a sense "better" or "superior" to Mexico. The first envisions the U.S. as strong and independent, thereby defining Mexico's weakness and dependence. Couched within the imperialist theme to be discussed later, this strength includes political and economic power, as well as the weight, though not the content, of U.S. culture. Though critical of the nature of U.S. culture as noted, most nonetheless recognize its pull or influence. As Monsiváis points out, "Americanization is the only culture with global pretensions whose weight exceeds even the brutal fact of colonialism."[35] It is within this context then that the culture of the "cultureless" penetrates and contests the culture of the nation: a concern or threat that will be explored more fully later.

A second hierarchical opposition centers on definitions of success and failure with the U.S. serving to define success and, hence, by contrast, Mexico's failures. Fuentes captures this dichotomy nicely: "The United States has had success in all the lines in which Mexicans have failed. We live a national failure side by side with the maximum success story of modernity."[36] Again the oppositional dimension is quite clear. Basave makes a similar point: "The North Americans have achieved their mission faster than us. They already have realized their epic when we are still suffering our tragedy."[37]

The third hierarchical construct, modern versus traditional, reflects a linear view of modernity in which the U.S. essentially defines modernity while, in turn, it reveals Mexico's lack of modernity or lack of progress. This hierarchical device echoes the success versus failure distinction noted earlier. Though perhaps critical of U.S. materialism and culture (or lack thereof), many thinkers have praised U.S. economic prosperity and development, usually to decry Mexico's lack of development. Monsiváis, for instance, calls U.S. culture *"el totem de la modernidad,"*[38] while Paz describes the U.S. as the "archetype of modernity."[39] At times, this notion of modernity goes beyond material development or progress to encompass political democracy as well: the fourth and final juxtaposition in the table. Mexican intellectuals have often praised U.S. democracy, again, usually in the context of exposing and decrying Mexico's lack thereof. Paz, for instance, extols U.S. democracy, particularly its ability to engage in criticism: "One of the great achievements of the American people has been to preserve democracy."[40] Monsiváis also provides a dose of praise, pointing to the U.S. as an example of an open society with a strong civic tradition.[41] Even Fuentes, though strongly critical of U.S. democracy in his earlier works, extends a measure of admiration for U.S. democracy. In referring to the Mexican perceptions of the U.S. as Jekyll and Hyde, he acknowledges a "better" half (Jekyll), which includes the U.S. successes in the areas of domestic democracy and development.[42]

Three nuances cascade from the use of these binary schemes—both the nonhierarchical and the hierarchical ones—further informing Mexican images of the U.S. and self. First, the use of oppositional categories to define self (Mexico) and other (the U.S.), as is characteristic of such styles of thought, tends to exaggerate difference and suggest a virtual zero-sum perception: you are either one or the other. This tendency makes it difficult to come to grips with any midpoints or to plant the notion of hybrid cultures in firm soil. Basave in particular is quite explicit in rejecting the idea of combinations: "To want to fuse together or unify . . . is to want confusion or destruction. The differences are maintained, they cannot be fused or suppressed."[43] Perceiving the traits of self and other as opposites, moreover, implies that any embrace of U.S. traits will be seen (or touted) as a rejection of national traits, as threatening. This seems to make anti-Americanism synonymous with Mexicanness: a position perhaps best captured by the intellectual Zamacona in Fuentes's novel *La región más transparente*: "Perhaps I am sick with hate for the United States. I am Mexican for something."[44]

Castañeda seems to approach this issue somewhat differently. On the one hand, he notes the importance of difference and its permanence: "Inequality, time and history are not soluble in water or free trade. The real test for the future of both countries resides in their acceptance of their differences, without pretending that they are secondary or temporary."[45] And yet, on the other hand, he recognizes the possible combinations, suggesting a more nuanced (postmodernist?) mixing of U.S. and Mexican traits: a combination where U.S. influence does not necessarily mean a rejection of Mexicanness or a complete embrace of the U.S. He states, for instance, that urban, literate Mexicans "do not see their nationalism endangered by the food they eat, the clothes they wear, or where they keep their money" just as such actions do not mean a complete acceptance and glorification of everything the U.S. does. "Even the modern Mexican middle classes continue to harbor deep feelings of resentment and even anger at the United States. Their penchant for American lifestyles and products should not be mistaken for an ebbing of traditional suspicion and hostility toward the United States."[46]

Combinations, such as these noted by Castañeda, imply the rejection of dichotomous thinking and a more nuanced and complex view of identity. A Mexican, in other words, can remain "Mexican" even if he or she walks and talks like a *gringo*. But such a notion still seems to beg the question about what defines the essence of the "Mexican." How much or what kinds of U.S. influence are considered to be acceptable and what kinds truly detract from one's national self? Is the essence, as Castañeda seems to suggest here, "the traditional suspicion and hostility toward the United States?"

A second nuance regarding the prominent use of such binary categories centers on the tendency for analysts to link the various traits together in such a way as to account for the distinct outcomes enjoyed by the two societies: that is, to use the binary categories to explain the hierarchical differences. Paz, for instance, draws on a range of historical opposites to explain to the reader why the U.S. became democratic and Mexico did not. This includes the presence or absence of a historical rupture and the establishment or nonestablishment of autonomous communities.[47] In his 1978 Washington Address, for instance, he points out "harmony, not contradiction, existed between the North Americans' religious convictions and their democratic institutions, whereas in Mexico Catholicism was identified with the viceregal regime and was its orthodoxy." As a result, Paz concludes, republican democracy in Mexico meant a radical break with the past and thus fathered conflict, while in the U.S. republican democracy did not.[48] Castañeda points similarly to past oppositions to account for the distinct hierarchical outcomes. As noted earlier, he stresses the different social foundations of the two societies—one marked by equality, the other by hierarchy—to account for the different perceptions of the nation as well as the greater material progress of one over the other.

Finally, there is the tendency in the literature to refer to these polar differences to account for the troubled nature of the relationship between the two countries. Paz contends that the historical and cultural differences are the foundation of the two countries' poor relations. Even if asymmetry in economic and political power disappeared, he argues, the tensions and differences between the two countries would not disappear, but would become more acute.[49] Fuentes seems to agree with this view. Profiling the troubled relationship between the two countries, the novel *Gringo viejo* underlines how the distinct ethics of the two prompt individuals to misread and misinterpret one another.[50] Castañeda also echoes this view, attributing the fact that the U.S. is often surprised when crisis erupts in Mexico to the misunder-

standings bred by the two countries' multiple historical, cultural, and sociological differences.[51] Basave goes so far as to suggest that Mexico's feeling of
cultural authority combined with the U.S. feeling of industrial superiority
make the two countries basically incompatible.[52]

Theme 2: The U.S. as a Model to Imitate

The use of hierarchical categories, especially the treatment of the U.S. as the
embodiment and definer of the modern and the successful, feeds a tendency
to want to imitate the U.S. So besides being employed as a model to define
Mexico through opposition, paradoxically the U.S. also shapes Mexico by
serving as an example, a model to emulate. According to Monsiváis, Mexicans see in the U.S. a type of utopia: "Mexicans now have a new City of
God where one can be modern, where one can be rich, where one can be
successful."[53] Fuentes concurs, asking: "How can we not see in this neighboring power a new center of identity which will protect us and heal, once and
for all, the national wound?"[54] At one level, Monsiváis seems to define the
process of modernization in just such "American" terms: "To modernize is
to liquidate the inefficiencies . . . to imitate the way North American society
assimilates technology." He even attributes Mexicans' faith in NAFTA to a
desire to imitate the U.S. or what he calls "reverence before the triumphant
mentality, the idea to exist through imitation."[55]

This perception of the U.S., it should be noted, includes the U.S. not only
as an economic and political model, but also as the key ingredient ensuring
personal success (personal modernity). If the U.S. represents prosperity and
modernity, then embracing the U.S. in some manner becomes a step toward
partaking in those riches and appropriating into one's own identity the
markers of the modern. This point can be seen in Monsiváis's description of
the thinking of the individual Mexican: "Just give me a chance anywhere,
that is all I ask. That is why I study English, the language of the present and
the future, really, cross my heart, I'll go to the States, learn something about
computers, come back, finish my degree in tourism, get a job in my friend's
hotel, work hard, pay attention to the details and always present myself well
. . . and that's it!"[56] Consequently, English expressions, clothes sporting U.S.
icons, and even dreams of working in the U.S. and participating in the consumer society, all become personal manifestations of imitation and a basic
part of Mexican popular nationalism.[57]

But in addition to prodding imitation, such hierarchical conceptualizations also nurture a negative image of self. The view of the U.S. as the land
of opportunity highlights and provides context to the describing or denouncing of the lack of opportunities in Mexico. Indeed, the two go hand in hand.

Parodi even suggests that the two are inversely and proportionally related such that the degree of imitation or acceptance of U.S. influence is determined by the degree of Mexico's perceived failure.[58] This paradoxical tendency is perhaps best manifested in the uniquely Mexican notion of *malinchismo*. Popularly used to refer to someone preferring the foreign over the local, Basave defines *malinchismo* as "the social complex of fondness for the foreign, with an undervaluing and disdain for your own."[59] Such a vision goes well beyond products, cultural or otherwise, of the two societies, however. At one level, glorifying the qualities of the "other" implicitly denigrates those of self. "The image of Mexican as spineless and idle is created," according to Bartra, "in contrast to the pragmatic image of Anglo-Saxons."[60]

At a broader level, this tendency to associate the U.S. with success while also linking U.S. traits to its success (noted earlier) has prompted many Mexican thinkers throughout the nation's history to identify traits of the Mexicans—from the indigenous culture to the legacies of Spain—as obstacles to progress and development, setting the stage for a full embrace of foreign ideas and models. This tendency for the Mexican to disown his or her past because of the pursuit of progress, moreover, lies at the root of the inferiority complex noted by Ramos and the solitude identified by Paz, though both were critical of these outcomes. Ramos attributes the nation's sentiments of inferiority to the tendency for people to compare themselves and their nation with others. And though he concentrated on Europe, Maccoby extends this to the U.S.: "Mexican authors underestimate the effects that living in the United States' shadow has on their feelings of inferiority."[61] In a similar fashion, Mexicans hide behind masks, according to Paz, because they are basically orphans who have denied their origins.[62] By attributing the weakening of traditional Mexican culture to the conviction among the young that the traditions are inefficient and that Americanization is the key to an international mentality, Monsiváis seems to suggest that this pattern remains alive and well today.[63]

But while many cast the U.S. as the "totem of modernity" and all thinkers point to the common tendency in Mexico to imitate the U.S., most condemn this tendency in their discussions of Mexican history. Ramos and Paz, as just mentioned, blame imitation as Mexico's main historical error, dating back to the liberals prior to and during the *Porfiriato*.[64] For most, the criticism rests on two pillars. The first is the inapplicability of the U.S. model for the specific circumstances of Mexico. According to this view, imitating the U.S. fails to take into account the unique features of the nation. Exporting models in lockstep, so the basic argument goes, never works. Conditions differ and these differences alter the functioning of the model. Second, this tendency to embrace the U.S. model is criticized for the implied rejection of Mexico's own values. Because of these two ideas, Paz and others argue strongly for a uniquely Mexican road to development.

Within this context, it is important to note how many thinkers seem to associate imitation with a particular group in society, usually characterizing these actors as antinational. Fuentes sees the Mexican bourgeoisie and middle class as being the most inclined to imitate the U.S.[65] Monsiváis seems to share this view, arguing that this imitative tendency is strongest among the upper and middle classes who "are obsessed daily with being less Mexican . . . [while] the dominated are interested in re- appropriating the national, since this is all they can feel, their Mexicanness."[66]

Perhaps a shade short of explicit imitation but nonetheless a consequence of the hierarchical view is the notion that the U.S., as the epitome of modernity, represents an image of Mexico's future, the nation's inevitable *porvenir*. From this perspective, U.S. influence, assimilation, or even the disappearance of "Mexican" cultural values are touted as simply products of modernity and, even if not embraced explicitly, must be accepted as somewhat "inevitable." Monsiváis, for example, touts U.S. influence as part of a broader process that "is global, irreversible and should be examined from perspectives that see everything as 'cultural penetration,' or imagine societies as perennially virginal."[67] This tendency is particularly true when thinkers tie U.S. cultural values to U.S. economic development, thereby implying that if (or when) Mexico attains such economic heights, its values will have to undergo fundamental change. By linking the U.S.'s material (economic) development to its loss of culture, for instance, Fuentes implies that such economic development in Mexico would come at the expense of the nation's culture.[68] This thus leaves Mexicans with a difficult choice: economic development at the price of losing the cultural traits that proudly distinguish them from the *gringo*, or remaining "behind" the U.S. in terms of modernity though maintaining cultural "superiority."

Theme 3: The U.S. as an Imperialist Power Influencing Mexico

A third narrative on the U.S. expressed by these thinkers relates to U.S. political and economic influence over Mexico. Given the sheer weight of the U.S. vis-à-vis Mexico, most authors explored here emphasize the agency of the U.S. in forging Mexican reality. Labeling it at one point a relationship of domination, for instance, Paz criticizes the U.S. for maintaining and protecting the liberal regimes of the nineteenth century, for confiscating and diverting the course of the Mexican Revolution, and for fomenting internal divisions.[69] Fuentes's versions of Mexican history similarly emphasize a host of ills begotten by U.S. intervention, just as his novels tend to depict North

Americans as exploitative and as *metiches* [meddlers]. In *Tiempo mexicano*, for instance, U.S. influence over Mexico reaches from imposing its linear perception of time to turning Mexico into a dumping ground.[70] Monsiváis's discourse also recognizes the importance of direct U.S. involvement as a key ingredient in shaping Mexican history and everyday culture. This includes the country's passion for soccer and even the tone of a Julio César Chávez boxing match with a U.S. challenger, as cited in the introductory chapter. Summing up the popular view regarding the dramatic impact of the U.S. on the nation, Monsiváis notes: "In 1847 the largest half of the national territory was lost, and since then the historical traumas have gotten worse, we once were a nation and now we are the spoils of the franchises."[71]

Such U.S. influence is especially pronounced at the cultural level, according to Monsiváis, bolstering the pluralism and hybridization of Mexican culture. What he calls at one point the "rampant North Americanization of the country" had already transformed Mexico by the 1950s, ruining the previous concept of nationhood and crafting a new mentality that is "still linked to very deep national ideas, but indifferent to tradition and unable to fabricate a coherent version of the national past and future."[72] U.S. influence extends well beyond the realm of culture, to be sure. Castañeda, for example, attributes many of the post-eighties economic and political reforms in Mexico to U.S.-led pressures on the political elite.[73]

It is within this context of direct U.S. influence that many of the thinkers spend a great deal of attention exploring and attacking U.S. foreign policy. Though almost all agree that the U.S. has been influential in shaping Mexican history, a range of views emerge regarding the underlying features of U.S. conduct toward Mexico. Three non-mutually exclusive approaches can be discerned. First, for some, U.S. influence is a mere outgrowth of the asymmetries of power and the U.S., like any other country, simply pursues its own national interests. Castañeda, for instance, stresses that Mexico sees everything the U.S. does as interventionist in part because of the sheer asymmetries of power between the two,[74] while Fuentes, downplaying U.S. actions in support of democracy, sees the motive as simply protection of its own interests.[75] But while asymmetries play a role, most highlight specific characteristics of U.S. policy, pointing to traits deeply embedded in the nation's culture and history to explain its foreign policy behavior. The consensus view among Mexican intellectuals seems to stress the Calvinistic sense of mission in the U.S. that, coupled with the nation's lack of historical roots, informs a foreign policy characterized by naiveté, a lack of understanding of others, and a schizophrenic desire to remain isolationist and yet be internationalist.[76] Paz, for instance, describes the U.S. as an empire that not only transfers its inequalities into the international arena, but also harbors a "reluctance to con-

front the outside world, [an] inability to understand it, and [a] lack of skill
in manipulating it."[77] When combined with its puritanical ethic, "instead of
understanding, they [U.S.] pass judgment" so that ultimately "what the U.S.
has lacked is not power but wisdom."[78] Part of this is due to what Paz in
Tiempo nublado refers to as the U.S.'s cultural blindness or its tendency to
ignore the "other" both domestically and in foreign relations.[79] Fuentes, who
vehemently attacks U.S. imperialism whenever he can, also sees the U.S. as
being guided by a puritanical vision that manifests itself in a "superiority
complex," blinding it to the realities of Latin America, and leading it, among
other things, to grossly exaggerate external threats.[80] Indeed, in an interview
with journalist Bill Moyers, Fuentes states rather categorically, "The most
detestable aspect of the United States is its self-righteous, holier-than-thou
aspect."[81]

While such attributes of U.S. foreign policy clearly imply a perception of
policies not favorable to Mexico, a third characteristic of this view of the U.S.
as imperialistic sees the U.S. as decidedly anti-Mexican. Fuentes, for instance,
describes the anti-Mexican xenophobia in the U.S., the country's irrational
tendency to blame Mexico for its problems, and the belief that Mexico is not
only part of its "backyard," but a country long ruled by a race that, in the
words of Pancho Villa, is "*el mero diablo en persona*" (the devil incarnate).[82]
It is this underlying premise that blends with U.S. power, its lack of culture,
and its ignorance of others to facilitate the rejection of U.S. influence by most
thinkers: a fourth subtheme in the exploration of intellectual images of the
U.S. and nation.

Theme 4: Shaping Mexico through Resistance

Images of the U.S. as imperialist and anti-Mexican, shouldering values
opposed to the nation's identity, all inform a final aspect within the discourse: one that sees the U.S. as shaping Mexico not directly through its
influence, but through Mexican resistance. This line of reasoning can be seen
in a number of areas as analysts often cite national and popular resistance to
the U.S. as a key factor to explain Mexican history and the nature of Mexican
society, or as a prescription for the nation. Paz, for instance, attributes the
French intervention in the mid-nineteenth century to the conservatives' concern over the "ideological contagion" from the U.S.[83] Citing John Mason
Hart, Fuentes views the Mexican Revolution in similar terms, going so far as
to describe it as "a war of national liberation against the U.S."[84] Even in the
subsequent period, according to Fuentes, after relying on official U.S. help to
eliminate rivals Villa and Zapata (direct U.S. involvement), Carranza forged
an alliance with workers and peasants precisely "to counter U.S. pressures."[85]

Monsiváis similarly describes the policies of cultural nationalism of the 1920s—policies largely championed by Vasconcelos—as a reaction or resistance to U.S. influence.[86] Moreover, such a posture of resistance, according to Castañeda, has been assumed over the years not just by the left, congenitally critical of U.S. imperialism, but also by the right as well who "contemplate[s] U.S. influence as a mortal threat to the customs and morals of the nation."[87]

Fundamental to this image of the U.S. as an agent shaping Mexico via resistance has been the role of the U.S. in crafting the contours of Mexican nationalism and, by extension, a range of Mexican public policies.[88] As Fuentes contends, Mexican nationalism arises from the loss of the falsely independent nation that was undermined by the war with the U.S.; it "is defined . . . to a great extent by the proximity of another nationalism: North American"; and it is "besieged by the forces that move the U.S. toward integration and by proximity with a nationalism more powerful than ours."[89] Indeed, the U.S. stands at the center of Mexico's historic lesson, usually associated with Justo Sierra, and enshrined in the school texts as shown in chapter 3: that internal division inevitably invites U.S. intervention. Castañeda reiterates the point: "Mexicans are taught from early on that the United States has always had designs on our country, either through direct territorial ambition or by seeking to influence our affairs to make Mexico more amenable to American interests and wishes."[90]

Politically, anti-Americanism has been crucial in mobilizing support for one's cause or demobilizing one's opponents.[91] By crystallizing the need for national unity and a strong, unified state, this perception of the U.S. (as a threat) supports a host of policy outcomes, ranging from Mexico's struggle to maintain an independent and at times anti-imperialist foreign policy, to its post-Revolutionary policy casting the State as the supreme arbiter and sole embodiment of the national interest.[92] The creation of the *Partido Nacional Revolucionario* (PNR)—the forerunner to the PRI—by President Calles in the late twenties, the incorporation of mass corporate organizations under President Cárdenas in the thirties, and the electoral and political reforms solidifying a one-party system in the fifties, as well as the fraud and repression in subsequent years, cannot be fully understood but for the forced unity derived from or justified by the perception of an external (U.S.) threat. Indeed, alluding to this link between culture and political power, Bartra sees Mexicans as imprisoned in the "sphere of national unity . . . so that whoever wishes to break the rules imposed by authoritarianism will be immediately accused of wishing to renounce (or worse, betray) the national culture."[93]

Though Bartra, among others, sees this nationalist response as an ideological tool of control wielded by the ruling elite (a superstructural pretext)—the instrumentalist view of nationalism cited in chapter 1—many nonetheless agree that Mexico should resist U.S. pressures and the temptation to imitate it since, as history shows, whenever the U.S. has gotten involved, it has been with the support of some domestic group.[94] But this is nothing new. Ramos issued just such a warning more than half a century ago: "Mexico at present is vulnerable to the threat of the white man, who, if we are not careful, may overcome the country by the pacific means of financing and technology. We refer, clearly enough, to the Yankee."[95]

So just as the U.S. represents a model to be imitated, it also paradoxically serves as a countermodel or force to be resisted. Arguably the most poignant critique offered by Ramos and Paz, cited earlier, centers on the problems inherent in employing foreign models of development. The villainization of the Díaz regime rests heavily on the dictator's adoption of a foreign model, particularly a U.S.-inspired economic model, and the denial of Mexico's traditional values and its past, all, so the narrative goes, to the detriment of the "people." Such a strategy as that employed by Díaz resulted not only in Mexico's failure to modernize, but in an irreparable fracturing of its identity that has complicated its development ever since.[96] It is firmly within this context that Paz rejects entirely the possibility of fostering progress by way of embracing the democratic and legal principles of the U.S. Because it is not possible to change the past or traditions, he contends, Mexico must resist the temptation to imitate, and erect a truly Mexican road to modernity.[97] Vasconcelos and Basave similarly support a policy of resisting both the U.S. and the compulsion to imitate it. Vasconcelos, for instance, rejects imitation because it means denying Mexico its Hispanic past, while according to Basave, "To attempt to become North Americans is to lose our own style and to open the doors to the Anglo-Saxon invasion."[98]

Fuentes seems even more outspoken in his rejection of imitating the U.S. and hence the need to resist U.S. pressures and the internal temptation to imitate. Arguing that the problem for Mexico and the rest of Latin America is precisely that it has opted for the ideology of its exploiters[99] and calling such imitation "*la Democracia Nescafé,*"[100] Fuentes goes to great lengths to reject the *Pepsicoatl* culture of the U.S.: the epitome of modernity.[101] Like Paz, Fuentes feels that imitation means a loss of that which makes Mexico distinct. Though admitting that adopting the U.S. model (*Pepsicoatl*) may be the easiest path, he nonetheless maintains that it means losing culture, which is simply too high a price to pay for progress and development.[102] Thus, like Paz, he proposes a model for Mexico that is rooted in large part on a rejection of the U.S. model: "Democracy *with* memory, progress *with* culture, the future *with* the past" (emphasis added).[103]

The idea of resistance raises the question of what precisely to protect.

Fuentes seems to provide part of the answer in this quote: memory, culture, and the past. Though most respond to (or duck) this question by noting the need to protect simply the "national interest" or "national identity," there is little precision or agreement as to what these terms mean or even their authenticity. Monsiváis, above all, rejects the idea of protecting national identity precisely because it would make it necessary to define what to defend.[104] In some ways, the "identity" to be protected entails some idealized image of an autonomous nation and culture, free from U.S. influence: something that has never existed except within the mythical discourse. In his classic work, Bartra refers to a paradise subverted or lost—primitivism—rooted in a stereotypical image of the Mexican and created by the elite as part of a system of political legitimization.[105] This vision of the ideal Mexican or national character, I would contend, is also an outgrowth of the Manichaean pattern noted earlier wherein Mexicans not only identify with certain values determined by the intellectual elite as defining the Mexican—even though in reality they may embrace a complex combination of traits associated with the nation and those associated with the U.S.—but, according to Bartra, are taught to feel guilty by the perceived destruction of the ideal past.[106]

And yet, there is also a sense not just that resistance to U.S. influence is difficult because of the problems in defining what to protect, but that such resistance is inherently costly and in the end maybe even futile. Though conscious of the issue, Monsiváis, for instance, takes the position that guarding against U.S. influence would require censorship, which would be a greater evil than U.S. influence itself.[107] Indeed, many thinkers have criticized the "forced unity" implicit in resistance to the U.S. because it has historically come at the cost of liberty and democracy, as if national sovereignty in the shadow of the giant means the absence of freedom and diversity.[108] Indeed, Bartra, who tends to see anti-Americanism as an ideological device of the Mexican political elite to ensure its hold on power, directly attributes the country's lack of democracy amid stability to the country's nationalist myth.[109] Of course, such resistance is particularly deemed ineffective to the degree that one sees the U.S. as the epitome of modernity: in such a case, resistance becomes both futile and folly.

Paradoxes, Parallels and Recent Changes

In bringing the various strands of the discussion together, three points merit attention: (a) the nature of Mexico's paradoxical vision of the U.S.; (b) parallels between this image of the U.S. and images of self and nation; and (c) the impact of recent changes as explored by some of the thinkers under review.

Paradoxical Images of the U.S.

It is common, both in the literature and in popular discourse, to refer to the contradictions inherent within the Mexican narrative of the U.S.: what many refer to as a "love-hate" view of the U.S. More philosophical, Paz calls it "a mythic image" that is "contradictory, emotional, and impervious to criticism."[110] As highlighted here, this contradictory image entails both forces of attraction and their antithesis: the forces of resistance. Two basic foundations for this mythical "love-hate" vision of the U.S. can be identified in the writings of the intellectuals. First, the use of oppositional categories to define self (Mexico) and other (the U.S.) lends itself to the impression that the opposing values, since they define one another, "threaten" the values of self and nation. Bolstered by the view that the U.S. is imperialistic and anti-Mexican, this pattern of thinking tends therefore to enshrine "anti-Americanism" as a Mexican trait. As noted, this feeds a tendency not only to define the Mexican as *not being gringo*, but also to define anti-Americanism as the flip side of Mexicanness. And yet, the simultaneous use of hierarchical oppositional categories whereby the U.S. represents "success" and "modern," coupled with the view linking (explaining) Mexico's "failures" to the specific traits that distinguish it from the U.S., lends itself to a countertendency: to emulate and imitate the U.S., accepting and perhaps even welcoming its influence in the name of progress, while nurturing a devalued view of those qualities associated with self. Combined, these conflicting strands suggest that the much-desired modernity based on imitation of the U.S. implies a negation of self and the loss of identity.[111] As Bartra puts it, "the nationalist spirit speaks in the name of a race that reacts against modern life."[112] This, thus, supports a paradoxical view wherein, as Paz notes, the U.S. becomes "the enemy of our identity and the unconfessed model of what we want to be."[113]

The second pillar of this paradoxical image of the U.S. centers on a more nuanced view of the U.S. that draws two fundamental distinctions. One centers on a neat distinction between the U.S.'s internal operations (democracy, open society, self-critical, pragmatic, rich) and its external policies (imperialist, self-righteous, anti-Mexican) or as Paz notes, "its [U.S.] national virtues and international acts."[114] Mexican intellectuals have often praised U.S. democracy and prosperity, as noted earlier, even pointing to the U.S. as an example for Mexico in these areas. And yet they are quick to condemn U.S. policy abroad, particularly toward people they feel the U.S. views as racially inferior. These paradoxical strands inform a close distinction between the desire to want to imitate the U.S. and yet the tendency to reject U.S. intervention. They also underlie the Mexican tendency to condemn U.S. hypocrisy as Mexicans recognize the fissure separating the U.S.'s posture abroad and its internal values or policies. These views, it can be argued, refer distinctively to U.S. perceptions of itself (internal values and policies) and its views of others (external values and policies).

The other distinction separates the material and even institutional from the cultural. Generally, praise of the U.S. privileges the material dimension, the technological progress, or the democratic procedures, and these inform the model for emulation. Imitating the U.S. or embracing the U.S. in these areas is considered okay and not a threat to identity. By contrast, the cultural component, the *pepsicoatl* culture, is what invites condemnation, feeding rejection and resistance. Imitation in this realm is thus construed as a denial of identity and antinational. Of course, the deeper debate centers on the relationship between these two and hence the idealized possibility of embracing one (progress) without the other (culture). Is it possible to enjoy the development of the U.S., even through closer relations, without inadvertently having the national culture altered?

Paralleling Images of Self and Other

Fundamental to the overall approach employed here is that perceptions of "other" are intimately linked to views of "self." In several ways, the Mexican view of its predominant "other" (U.S.) in the literature reviewed here parallels the views of "self." First, both views are highly contested and enjoy considerable attention in the literature. Mexico's intense concern with national identity, in short, parallels and reflects its historic preoccupation with the U.S. Second, both images feature substantial ambiguity and contradiction. Stated differently, the mythical "love-hate" vision of the U.S. parallels the myths, mysticism, and contradictions inherent within Mexico's image of itself.[115] So just as Mexicans harbor a contradictory image of the U.S., they also exhibit a certain paradoxical view of the nation, of self, as represented within the idea of *malinchismo*. Many thinkers make this point, though some indirectly. Monsiváis, for instance, makes this point from a historical angle. Highlighting the importance of "other" in the creation of Mexican identity, he stresses the ambiguity surrounding Mexicans' view of *Malinche,* whose attraction to the foreigner betrayed her people and yet whose rape made her the mother of a new, mestizo race.[116] Ultimately, it is precisely the difficulties of coming to grips with the nation's violent and hybrid origins, this paradoxical view of self, which informs Ramos's oft-noted reference to Mexicans' inferiority complex and the Mexicans' solitude described by Paz. In other words, the historic ambiguity concerning the nation's origins—particularly the perception of its previous "other" (Spain)—overlays a similar ambiguity toward its more contemporary "other" (the U.S.). Perhaps Bartra captures this paradoxical image of self best by noting that the Mexican expression *Hijos de la Chingada* during the independence movement, an expression intermixed with affection and aggression, refers not to foreigners, but to the Mexicans themselves.[117]

Finally, these two tendencies—the view of self and other—play off on one another. Both the preoccupation with and the ambiguity informing its image of the U.S. make it difficult for the Mexican to understand or construct him- or herself or the nation. According to Paz, despite the extensive debate and struggle, it remains difficult for the Mexican to locate his own image precisely because of the image of the U.S.[118] Fuentes would seem to agree: "The North American world blinds us with its energy . . . we cannot see ourselves, we must see you."[119] In this context as well, Castañeda warns that Mexico is obsessed with the U.S. He recommends that it pay less attention to its northern neighbor.[120]

The contradictory image of the U.S.—the attraction and the resistance—and the contradictory image of self together underscore the contested nature of Mexican nationalism. In a sense, Mexico is neither the "idealized" version that "would exist" if it were not for the U.S. nor the "ideal" that must be protected and shielded from U.S. pressures; instead, Mexico is the negotiated product of these opposing forces: one in a sense defining Mexico and pulling Mexico apart and away from its roots; the other, the counterforce, the resistance, struggling toward integration. This process of constructing the nation and identity is the result of what Monsiváis refers to as a process of "negotiation" between nationalism and cosmopolitanism[121] or what Paz has in mind when he concludes that Mexico entails the unity emerging from the clash of contradictory forces.[122] Or as only Monsiváis can phrase it: "The Mexican is no longer an existential and cultural problem and despite the abundant discussions, national identity is not at risk. It is a changing identity, continually enriched with the talk of the poor, the contributions of the mass media, the academic renovations, the ideological discussions, Americanization, and resistance to the widening of misery."[123]

The Impact of Recent Changes

As set out in the introduction, one of the reasons to explore the question of Mexican images of the U.S. and nation resides with recent political and economic changes. This question will be approached here in two ways: firstly, by looking directly at the discussion of the recent (post-eighties) changes by the thinkers themselves; and, secondly, by assessing the degree to which perceptions of the U.S. and the nation have changed in recent years.

Though these are beyond the temporal horizon of many of the intellectuals discussed here—like Vasconcelos, Ramos, and perhaps even Paz—others, particularly Bartra, Castañeda, and Monsiváis, devote serious attention to recent political and economic changes. They highlight the confluence of domestic political change and global changes, the weakness of the nationalist myth and nationalist policies, and an increasing polarization in the country over perceptions of the U.S. and nation. Monsiváis, for instance, who not only emphasizes that Americanization has increased since the 1950s, but incorporates notions of Americanization and hybridity into his visions of a plural Mexican culture, as noted above, clearly sees globalization as hastening the spread of U.S. influence. He sees the young and middle class in particular, who see Americanization as the key to development, as particularly prone to this imitative tendency.[124] In many ways, this is a result of the failures of past nationalist policies to provide a solution.[125] The result, according to Monsiváis, as quoted earlier, is a growing gap between the elite and the masses over the value and the defense of national identity and culture.[126] Bartra, like Monsiváis, also sees the current period as one of significant cultural transition. He attributes this not to globalization *per se*, but to the destruction of the link between the State and culture and the withering of the nationalist myth triggered by the political crisis of 1988. According to Bartra, the crisis showed the need to cast the old nationalism aside in order to pursue democracy. The vacuum created by the loss of the nationalist myth is filled in part, he suggests, by the increasing desire to be a part of the U.S.[127]

Castañeda also focuses on the issue of changing perceptions growing out of the end of the Cold War and (like Bartra) Mexico's domestic political changes. He highlights three important changes. The first involves a change in Mexico's political posture toward the U.S. According to Castañeda, Mexican political groups had pretty much respected the "unwritten rule" to not seek American involvement in domestic matters up until the late 1980s, but Salinas violated and erased this rule. Not only did the PRI government enlist the U.S. as an ally (NAFTA), but the opposition followed suit and began to reject the nationalistic posture of resisting all contact with the U.S., forming strategic alliances with groups in the U.S. Fundamental to this shift, Mexicans, according to Castañeda, moved beyond their coherent, monolithic view of the U.S., enabling them to differentiate among various U.S. actors and interests: a point illustrated in the political discourse discussed in chapter 2.[128] Second, Castañeda highlights the impact of the end of the Cold War on Mexico's perceptions of the U.S. While not altering the U.S. propensity to intervene in Latin America, the end of the Cold War did, according to Castañenda, result in the outpouring of more favorable sentiments toward the U.S.—now the sole remaining superpower—while depriving the left of its principal enemy.[129] As a result, opposition to integration with the U.S. is strong, but "increasingly hollow," since few see many alternatives: "The question for Mexico is thus changing from 'Is integration desirable?' to 'Is it reversible, and if not, what are the consequences for Mexico; can it be successfully administered and can Mexico get the most out of it?' "[130] And yet Castañeda, like Monsiváis, also sees heightened polarization in Mexico. But rather than a distinction between the "cosmopolitan" elite and the "nationalistic" masses, he characterizes it more accurately as a division between those tied in some way to the U.S. and those who are not: a division extending beyond class lines (chapter 8 provides some empirical support for this hypothesis). For Castañeda, perceptions of the U.S. and the nation are clearly at the crux of this potentially volatile political and cultural division.

A second approach to the issue of change centers on a comparison of the more recent writings with those of the past. Though alluded to already in some cases, some basic differences can be identified. First, the more recent writings seem more likely to recognize certain virtues of the U.S. internally and, perhaps because of the end of the Cold War, even play down U.S. imperialism. The edges of the rightist (Vasconcelos: pro-Catholic, anti-Protestant) critique and the leftist (Fuentes: anticapitalist and anti-imperialist) critique of the U.S. have seemingly worn away somewhat. Fuentes, as noted, even seems to acknowledge U.S. democracy as more real than fraudulent in more recent writings, while Castañeda praises the left's newfound ability to differentiate the U.S. politically and economically and to cure itself of its historical knee-jerk opposition to anything that smells of the *gringos*.

The more recent writings also tend to emphasize, within this post–Cold War globalist vision, a Mexico far more open to the world and the U.S.: to view the U.S. as an opportunity, to borrow from the political model presented in chapter 2. Even Fuentes contends that if democratic, Mexico could actually benefit from NAFTA: "We have the advantage over any other developing country of sharing a border with the largest market in the world."[131] Indeed, opposition to integration with the U.S., as Castañeda, cited earlier, contends, is "increasingly hollow." Attached to this view is a rejection of the old anti-Americanism as a pretext used by the elite to justify its authoritarian practices. A more open Mexico thus not only means economic opportunity, but it also removes one of the biggest obstacles to democratization. To paraphrase Paz , if forced unity made necessary by resistance to the U.S. was achieved at the cost of liberty and democracy, then it seems that few are willing to pay this price any longer.[132]

Finally, recent views of the U.S. and nation seem to offer a more nuanced image of the U.S. and U.S. influence, while offering a more positive assessment of hybrid cultures and playing down the threat of Americanization.

Abandoning a monolithic image of the U.S. enables certain interests in Mexico to side with like-minded interests in the U.S. for political or social reasons; it enables one to reject the simplistic notion that "eating at McDonald's" is a cultural threat or sign of loss of culture; and it facilitates a narrative wherein Mexico can become modern without necessarily losing its identity. Monsiváis, in particular, sees American influence as a fundamental part of the growing pluralism of Mexican culture in the contemporary period and thus not putting it "at risk."[133] This more differentiated view means that accepting attributes of the U.S. does not mean a complete acceptance and glorification of everything the U.S. does. It also facilitates the idea that in the contemporary period Mexico is actually influencing and shaping the U.S., thus contesting the historic view that saw influence as a one-way street from North to South. Indeed, in response to the question of whether there will be Mexican cultural influence over the U.S. more than vice versa, by the nineties Fuentes was arguing that it is the U.S. that should be more worried than Mexico.[134] This narrative also harbors the notion that Mexicans tend to take something foreign (or U.S.) and alter it to make it uniquely their own. Citing the Aztec tactic that "if you repeat a word enough you nationalize it," Monsiváis even notes parenthetically how "in exchange for Texas and California we have been stripping the *gringos* of their vocabulary."[135] This poststructuralist perspective is interesting since at one level it seems to envision imitation as giving way to hybridization and maybe eventually "ownership" or "authenticity." And it seems to offer, at another level, a more benign view of imitation, making it palatable and not anti-Mexican. Again, Monsiváis best exemplifies this globalist and postmodernist view as partially cited earlier: "The process is global, irreversible and should be examined from perspectives that do not see everything as 'cultural penetration,' or imagine societies as perennially virginal. If Americanization affects the culture, social vitality promotes resistances and 'Mexicanizes' in some way the Americanization."[136]

And yet, despite these many and important differences, the writings spanning the years also offer a large dose of continuity. Indeed, the early writings hardly strike the reader as extremely anachronistic. They all seem to emphasize fundamental differences separating the *gringo* and the Mexican, despite even the development of more hybrid cultures in recent times (Monsiváis) or the greater level of integration. Indeed, the differences between the two peoples as mapped out by Vasconcelos, Ramos, and Paz many years back echo the differences that Castañeda cites to explain the failures of the two countries to understand one another during the recent economic crisis. Moreover, such differences, they all tend to agree, not only explain the distinct outcomes of the two societies and complicate the relationship, but should be acknowledged and embraced, not denied. The differences, in short, cannot be painted over or suppressed by those who wish to emulate the U.S. or deny the nation's past, as the earlier passage from Castañeda made clear. Again most tend to agree that when the country forgets itself or loses itself in the glaring image of the U.S. other, it loses its way, only to find failure and frustration. The country therefore, these thinkers seem to argue, needs to construct its own path to development and modernity, a path that includes what are perceived as the values and excludes the vices attached to both the national culture and the U.S.: a selective synthesis of the two.

All authors also continue to view with suspicion and care the political, economic, and cultural influence of the U.S. and the U.S. government. This includes the tendency to criticize those who imitate or embrace the U.S. as a model. Through various mechanisms, both Fuentes and Castañeda, in particular, opposed NAFTA and the neoliberalism of the Salinas era. Though acknowledging four U.S. financial bailouts of Mexico, Castañeda, for instance, contends that the price for Mexico has been high in terms of conditionality, humiliation, and the continuance in power of the PRI regime: "They have atrophied the emergence and development of new leadership."[137] With some exceptions, the writers also all seem to express a common concern over U.S. cultural influence, whether depicted as the spread of the evils of "Protestantism" (Vasconcelos, Ramos), *pepsicoatl* culture (Fuentes), or "Americanization" (Monsiváis). And yet there is neither agreement about nor any answer to what precisely constitutes Americanization, or at least which brand of it is considered negative. As Castañeda points out, and Monsiváis and others would surely agree, merely eating at McDonald's is not a substantial cultural threat and it does not mean that tacos or national identity will disappear from the streets. Nonetheless, given the sheer weight of U.S. cultural industries and consumer habits, this concern remains valid. Indeed, the futuristic vision of the nation expressed by Fuentes in *Cristóbal nonato*— where parts of the nation come under the direct cultural, political, or economic control of the U.S.—manifests the fears Mexicans have had with respect to the U.S. for many years. And, of course, all the intellectuals examined here seem to continue to recognize the importance of the U.S. to the nation and national identity, highlighting the people's paradoxical attraction and resistance to the U.S. as something fundamental to the nature of being Mexican. The many references to the U.S. and their play on the paradoxes makes this final point quite clear. John Kraniauskas nicely captures the paradoxes, the change and continuity, in his introduction to the collection of Monsiváis essays: "In the last twenty years, Mexican society has contracted new habits . . . renounced many of its more nationalistic expressions, is 'Americanized' and simultaneously 'de-Americanized' . . . it wants to be modern and fails, wants to hang on to tradition but is unstable."[138]

Conclusion

This exploration of the views of some of Mexico's most influential, admired, and brilliant intellectuals reveals a particular image of the U.S. and, most importantly, its linkage to perceptions of the nation, the national interest, and public policy. Future-oriented, historyless, cultureless, materialistic, obsessed with progress, individualistic, having no sense of public responsibility, simple, egalitarian, developed, modern, democratic, imperialistic, unable to understand others, naïve, puritanical, self-righteous, arrogant, having a superiority complex, and so on, *ad nauseam,* are among the many qualities used to depict the U.S. More importantly though, these images have been used over the years not only to define through contrast the meaning of Mexico and the Mexican, but to shape and define what they aspire to be and not to be. In addition, the analysis shows a variety of changes in certain views in recent years. More contemporary views are much more nuanced and complex, embracing images of culture and identity as evolving. These more recent views also recognize that embracing certain cultural aspects of the U.S. or even engaging the U.S. do not necessarily mean someone is less Mexican or that Mexican identity is at risk. And yet, certain images of the U.S. have survived the years. National cinema—our next focus—brings to life many of the traits of the *gringo* and the Mexican, and the paradoxes, described here.

Notes

1. Fernanda Eberstadt, "Montezuma's Literary Revenge," *Commentary,* May (1986): 35. On the role of intellectuals in Mexico see Roderic A. Camp, *Intellectuals and the State in Twentieth Century Mexico* (Austin: University of Texas Press, 1985).

2. Fuentes, "Decay of Nations," 12.

3. Agustín Basave Fernandez del Valle, *Vocación y Estilo de México: Fundamentos de la Mexicanidad* (Mexico City: Limusa, 1990).

4. Bartra, *Cage of Melancholy;* "Culture and Political Power in Mexico"; and "La venganza de la Malinche: hacia una identidad postnacional," *Este País,* Abril (1991): 17–19.

5. Pastor and Castañeda, *Limits to Friendship;* Jorge Castañeda, *Utopia Unarmed,* and *The Estados Unidos Affair: Cinco ensayos sobre un "amor" oblicuo* (Mexico City: Aguilar, Nuevo Siglo, 1996).

6. Octavio Paz, *Labyrinth of Solitude* (1961), reprinted in *Labyrinth of Solitude and Other Essays;* "El Espejo Indiscreto," in *El ogro filantropico, 1971–1978* (Barcelona: Seix Barral, 1979), 53, originally published in *Plural* 58, July 1976, reprinted in *Labyrinth of Solitude and Other Essays; Tiempo nublado* (1983), reprinted as "Mexico and the United States" in *Labyrinth of Solitude and Other Essays;* and *One Earth, Four or Five Worlds: Reflections on Contemporary History* (San Diego: Harcourt, Brace

Jovanovich, 1986). Analysis of the writings of Paz also comes from Abel A. Alves, "History, Mexico, the United States and Humanity in the Writings of Octavio Paz," *CLIO* 20 (1) (1990): 53–63; Willard Gingerich, "The Poetics of History: A Defense of the Washington Address of Octavio Paz," *The New Scholar* 9 (1–2) (1984): 13–37; and Gorka, *Images of the United States*.

7. Carlos Fuentes, *La región mas transparente* (Mexico City: Planeta, 1958); *Tiempo mexicano* (Mexico City: Planeta, 1971); *Gringo viejo* (Mexico City: Fondo de Cultura Económica, 1985); *Christopher Unborn*. Translated by Alfred MacAdam (New York: Vintage, 1989); *Nuevo Tiempo mexicano* (Mexico City: Aguilar, 1994). Analysis of the writings of Fuentes also comes from Francisco Javier Ordiz Vazquez, "Carlos Fuentes y la Identidad de México," *Revista Iberoamericana* 58 (1992): 159, 527–38.

8. Carlos Monsiváis, "Notas sobre la cultural mexicana en el siglo XX" in *Historia general de México*. Tomo 2 (Mexico City: El Colegio de México, 1976), 1375–548; "Muerte y resurrección"; "Para un cuadro de costumbres. De cultura y vida cotidiana en los ochentas," *Cuadernos Políticos* 57 (1989); "Heart of the Mexican Dream," *New Perspectives Quarterly* 8 (1) (1991): 51–52; "De la Cultura Mexicana"; "Interrelación Cultural entre México y Estados Unidos," in *Mitos en Las Relaciones México-Estados Unidos*, edited by Ma. Esther Schumacher (Mexico City: SRE y Fondo de Cultura Económica, 1994), 435–59; "La Malinche y el Primer Mundo," in *La Malinche, sus padres y sus hijos*, edited by Margo Glantz (Mexico City: UNAM), 139–47; *Los rituales del caos* (Mexico City: Procuradura Federal del Consumidor y Ediciones Era, 1995); and "Will Nationalism Be Bilingual?"; *Mexican Postcards*, translated and with an introduction by John Kraniauskas (London: Verso, 1997).

9. Samuel Ramos, *Profile of Man and Culture in Mexico*. Translated by Peter G. Earle. Introduction by Thomas B. Irving (Austin: University of Texas, 1962).

10. José Vasconcelos, *La raza cósmica: Misión de la raza iberoamericana*, ninth edition (Mexico City: Espasa-Calpe Mexicana 1948); and *Obras completas* (Mexico City: Libreros Mexicanos Unidos, 1957).

11. Paz, *One Earth, Four or Five Worlds*.

12. Castañeda, *Estados Unidos Affair*.

13. Ordiz, "Carlos Fuentes y la Identidad de México," 527.

14. Paz, "Espejo Indiscreto."

15. Castañeda, *Estados Unidos Affair*, 89.

16. Paz, *Labyrinth of Solitude*, 33.

17. Paz, "Espejo indiscreto," 60.

18. Paz, *Tiempo nublado*, reprinted as "Mexico and the United States" in *Labyrinth of Solitude and Other Essays*, 357, 360.

19. Fernandez del Valle, *Vocación y Estilo de México*, 760–64.

20. Fuentes, *Gringo viejo*, 134, 92, and 103, cited in Frederic W. Murray, "The Dynamics of Inter-cultural Dissonance in *Gringo viejo*," *Chasque: Revista de Literatura Latinoamericana* 19 (1) (1990): 21.

21. Paz, "Espejo Indiscreto," 53.

22. Paz, *One Earth, Four or Five Worlds;* and "Espejo Indiscreto," 36.

23. Fuentes, *Nuevo Tiempo mexicano*, 10.

24. Castañeda, *Estados Unidos Affair*, 100.

25. Paz, *Labyrinth of Solitude.*
26. Paz, "Espejo Indiscreto," 59.
27. Paz, *One Earth, Four or Five Worlds,* 31.
28. Castañeda, *Estados Unidos Affair,* 101–2.
29. Rick Langhorst, "Los Estados Unidos vistos por José Vasconcelos," *Los Ensayistas,* March (1982): 117–22.
30. Ramos, *Profile of Man and Culture in Mexico,* 99.
31. Octavio Paz, "The Border of Time," *New Perspectives Quarterly* 5 (1) (1988): 46–52.
32. Paz, *One Earth, Four or Five Worlds,* 21–22.
33. Fuentes, *Tiempo mexicano,* 37.
34. Paz, *Labyrinth of Solitude and Other Essays,* 357–60.
35. Monsiváis, *Mexican Postcards,* 193.
36. Fuentes, *Nuevo Tiempo mexicano,* 86.
37. Fernandez del Valle, *Vocación y Estilo de México,* 765.
38. Monsiváis, "De la Cultura Mexicana," 185.
39. Paz, *One Earth, Four or Five Worlds,* 46.
40. Paz, *One Earth, Four or Five Worlds,* 60.
41. Monsiváis, "Heart of the Mexican Dream."
42. Fuentes, "Decay of Nations," 12.
43. Fernandez del Valle, *Vocación y Estilo de México,* 764.
44. Fuentes, *La región mas transparente,* 394, cited in Gorka, *Images of the United States,* 87.
45. Castañeda, *Estados Unidos Affair,* 103.
46. Pastor and Castañeda, *Limits to Friendship,* 15–16.
47. Paz, "Espejo Indiscreto," 57–60; and Paz, *Labyrinth of Solitude,* 372–73.
48. Cited in Gingerich, "Poetics of History," 17.
49. Cited in Gingerich, "Poetics of History," 23.
50. Murray, "Dynamics of Inter-cultural Dissonance," 22.
51. Castañeda, *Estados Unidos Affair.*
52. Fernandez del Valle, *Vocación y Estilo de México,* 786.
53. Monsiváis, "Heart of the Mexican Dream," 51.
54. Fuentes, "Decay of Nations,"12.
55. Monsiváis, "De la Cultura Mexicana," 195, 209.
56. Monsiváis, *Rituales del caos,* 215.
57. Monsiváis, "Muerte y resurrección," 19.
58. Parodi, "Nationalism and Globalization."
59. Fernandez del Valle, *Vocación y Estilo de México,* 746.
60. Bartra, *Cage of Melancholy,* 32.
61. Cited in Bartra, *Cage of Melancholy,* 80.
62. Paz, *Labyrinth of Solitude.*
63. Monsiváis, "De la Cultura Mexicana."
64. Ramos, *Profile of Man and Culture in Mexico;* Paz, "Espejo Indiscreto," and *Labyrinth of Solitude.*
65. Fuentes, *Nuevo Tiempo mexicano,* 61.
66. Monsiváis, "Muerte y resurrección," 21.

67. Monsiváis, "De la Cultura Mexicana," 200.

68. Fuentes, *Tiempo mexicano*, 37.

69. Paz, *Labyrinth of Solitude*, 385; Paz, "Espejo Indiscreto,"63; and Paz cited in William Anthony Nericcio, "¿Nobel Paz?: A Pre- and Post-Nobel Survey of Mexican Writers: Evolving Views of Mexico, the United States and Other Na[rra]tions," *Siglo XXI* 10 (1–2) (1992): 183.

70. Cited in Gorka, *Images of the United States*, 63.

71. Monsiváis, *Rituales del caos*, 33–34.

72. Monsiváis, *Mexican Postcards*, 20.

73. Castañeda, *Estados Unidos Affair*, 122.

74. Castañeda, *Estados Unidos Affair*, 122.

75. Cited in Gorka, *Images of the United States*, 122.

76. Pastor and Castañeda, *Limits to Friendship*, 34.

77. Paz, *One Earth, Four or Five Worlds*, 32, 36.

78. Paz, *One Earth, Four or Five Worlds*, 50, 39.

79. Cited in Nericcio, "¿Nobel Paz?," 174.

80. See his 1983 Harvard address, cited in Gorka, *Images of the United States*, 69.

81. Cited in Gorka, *Images of the United States*, 70.

82. Fuentes, *Nuevo Tiempo mexicano*, 110; and material cited in Murray, "Dynamics of Inter-cultural Dissonance," 22.

83. Paz, "Espejo Indiscreto," 63.

84. Fuentes, *Nuevo Tiempo mexicano*, 47.

85. Fuentes, *Nuevo Tiempo mexicano*, 52.

86. Monsiváis, "Notas sobre la cultural mexicana," 1379, 1420.

87. Castañeda, *Estados Unidos Affair*, 114.

88. According to Castañeda, *Utopia Unarmed* (273), nationalism throughout Latin America has tended to feature a strong anti-American component and, given the tendency to see the elite or the upper and middle classes as particularly prone to imitate the U.S., to associate the nation with the "people" while perceiving the elite as foreign.

89. Fuentes, "Decay of Nations," 11, 16.

90. Pastor and Castañeda, *Limits to Friendship*, 56–57.

91. Castañeda, *Utopia Unarmed*, 290.

92. Segovia, "Nacionalismo mexicano," 48.

93. Bartra, *Cage of Melancholy*, 165.

94. Pastor and Castañeda, *Limits to Friendship*, 57.

95. Ramos, *Profile of Man and Culture in Mexico*, 123.

96. Nericcio, "¿Nobel Paz?," 175.

97. Paz, *Labyrinth of Solitude*, 372.

98. Fernandez del Valle, *Vocación y Estilo de México*, 753.

99. Fuentes, *Tiempo mexicano*, 31.

100. Fuentes, *Nuevo Tiempo mexicano*, 61.

101. Ordiz, in "Carlos Fuentes y la Identidad de México," seems to agree with this interpretation of Fuentes.

102. Fuentes, *Tiempo mexicano*, 37.

103. Fuentes, *Nuevo Tiempo mexicano*, 11.

104. Monsiváis, "De la Cultura Mexicana," 208.

105. Bartra, *Cage of Melancholy*.

106. Bartra, *Cage of Melancholy*, 20.

107. Monsiváis, "De la Cultura Mexicana," 208.

108. Paz, "Espejo Indiscreto."

109. Bartra, *Cage of Melancholy*, 3.

110. Paz, *Labyrinth of Solitude*, 358.

111. Paz, "Espejo Indiscreto," 57.

112. Bartra, *The Cage of Melancholy*, 104.

113. Paz, "Espejo Indiscreto," 61.

114. Paz, *One Earth, Four or Five Worlds*, 39.

115. See Fuentes, *Nuevo Tiempo mexicano*, 201.

116. Monsiváis, "La Malinche y el Primer Mundo," 146.

117. Bartra, *Cage of Melancholy*, 160n. On pages 152–54 he also points to this contradictory and mythical image of self. Here he discusses the *Malinche* and the Virgin of Guadalupe as two incarnations of the same original myth, combining treachery, rape, salvation, and motherhood.

118. Paz, *One Earth, Four or Five Worlds*, 61.

119. Cited in Gorka, *Images of the United States*, 67.

120. Pastor and Castañeda, *Limits to Friendship*, 21.

121. Cited in Gutierrez and Gutierrez, "En torno a la redefinición," 93.

122. Cited in Lajous Vargas, "Mexico: Culture and Identity in the Information Age," 110.

123. Monsiváis, "De la Cultura Mexicana," 192.

124. Monsiváis, "De la Cultura Mexicana," 209.

125. This view is nicely expressed by Parodi in "Nationalism and Globalization."

126. Monsiváis, "Muerte y resurrección," 21.

127. Bartra, "Venganza de la Malinche."

128. Castañeda, *Estados Unidos Affair*.

129. Castañeda, *Utopia Unarmed*, 1, 253.

130. Pastor and Castañeda, *Limits to Friendship*, 241.

131. Fuentes, *Nuevo Tiempo mexicano*, 89.

132. Paz, "Espejo Indiscreto."

133. Monsiváis, "De la Cultura Mexicana," 192.

134. Fuentes, *Nuevo Tiempo mexicano*, 200.

135. Monsiváis, *Los rituales del caos*, 213.

136. Monsiváis, "De la Cultura Mexicana," 200.

137. Castañeda, *Estados Unidos Affair*, 125.

138. Monsiváis, *Mexican Postcards*, xvi–xvii.

6

Gringolandia in the National Cinema

FOR YEARS, MEXICAN CINEMA has made significant artistic and cultural contributions to the nation and the world. From the highly acclaimed movies, directors, and actors during the "*Época Dorada*" (1940–1954) (i.e., *María Candelaria*, 1946; *Los Olvidados*, 1950; *Los Tres García*, 1946; Emilio Fernández, Luis Buñuel, Ismael Rodríguez; Cantinflas, María Félix, Dolores del Río, Pedro Infante, Jorge Negrete) to recent, award-winning productions (i.e., *Como agua para chocolate*, 1992; *La invención de Cronos*, 1993; *La Ley de Herodes*, 2000; *Amores Perros*, 2000), Mexican cinema offers a "window on the complexities of Mexico itself."[1] As Joanne Hershfield and David Maciel advise in the introduction to their edited collection on Mexican cinema, "For anyone interested in Mexico, the cinema is a marvelous source that reveals its traditions, folklore, musical heritage, regional diversity, archetypes, ethnic makeup, symbols, myths, and national character."[2]

Like the writings of the intellectuals and the drawings of the cartoonists, the U.S. appears prevalently on and behind the motion picture screen in Mexico. This chapter explores *gringolandia* in the Mexican national cinema at two distinct, though somewhat related, levels. The first—and perhaps the less obvious of the two—centers on the role of the U.S. (or, more appropriately, Mexican perceptions of the U.S.) in shaping the industry itself. Cinema has always been an important area of policy concern, given its impact on culture and identity. The first segment of the chapter thus focuses on the nature of State policy and explanations of the industry grounded in particular perceptions of the U.S. and the nation. The second section of the chapter looks at the content of Mexican cinema, the images and messages within the stories. Premised on the notion that Mexican films "have been instrumental in reflecting, if not forming, cultural attitudes,"[3] attention centers on the way the U.S. and the nation in relation to the U.S. have been portrayed in Mexican films. The concluding section then focuses on the issue of change during recent years. Generally, the chapter draws on secondary materials, though the personal viewing of scores of movies complements this approach.

The U.S. and the Mexican Cinematographic Industry

From the beginning, the Mexican cinematographic industry emerged in response or resistance to the U.S., and it has developed ever since in the shadow of Hollywood. Early U.S. movies offended many Mexicans. If it was not Hollywood's portrayal of the Mexican—usually the evil villain in Westerns—then it was the moral values depicted in the Hollywood productions that upset the Mexicans and triggered criticism. During the silent era, for example, the moral themes (or lack thereof) depicted in U.S. films provoked hostility from the Church and other Catholic groups.[4] Many saw such values as a threat to the national culture. Typical of this view, one observer saw Hollywood as feeding "the development of a great sexual appetite not appropriate to our character and Latin sensibilities, the creation of a spirit of imitation of habits and attitudes, with the resulting abandonment of Mexican customs and the annulment of our spirit of recreation, the birth of a macho and gun-slinging instinct that is improper for our violent temperament and whose consequences have devalued human life."[5] Indeed, Mexicans have accused the U.S. cinema over the years of causing alcoholism, promoting promiscuity, altering demand by encouraging the desire for luxury commodities, and threatening the national economic order.[6]

Historically, concerns such as these have prodded the government to become involved in the industry, developing a range of defensive and offensive measures.[7] One early weapon to counter the perceived threat from U.S. cinema was to restrict foreign movies considered offensive. In 1915, the city council of Mazatlán banned all foreign movies depicting Mexicans as villains.[8] By 1919, the federal government had decreed prior censorship so as to avoid the exhibition of "immoral" movies, including those offensive to Mexico. A few years later, President Obregón ordered Mexican consuls in the U.S. to inform the government of movies that were offensive so that these could be banned even before reaching Mexico. In April of that same year, he went so far as to prohibit the importation of all Paramount movies until they suspended the world showing of *Her Husband's Trademark* (1922) because of its unfair depiction of Mexicans. Altogether, the policy blocked the showing of some 28 movies and pushed the Association of Motion Pictures Producers and Distributors of America to agree not to produce movies offensive to the Mexicans.[9] President Cárdenas, a few years later, also ordered the censoring of U.S. movies that ridiculed the image of the Mexicans, this time seeking support among other Latin countries for a continentwide ban.[10] According to Moisés González Navarro, "the Mexican government tried to convince the North American people that, from an ethnological standpoint, Mexicans belonged to the white race and that they therefore had the same rights as Caucasian North Americans."[11]

In addition to defensive measures, the government at times has also taken on the role of supporting the national industry, thereby helping national artists craft an alternative to the Hollywood images. Such measures have included everything from State financing or ownership of production and distribution companies (structural and industrial support) to the promotion of certain themes or narratives (cultural and ideological support). In many cases, these two have gone hand in hand. According to Aurelio de los Reyes, for instance, President Carranza promoted the production of film early on as a way to deal with the denigrating movies of the U.S.[12] Years later, with the creation of the *Banco Nacional Cinematográfico* and State-run production and distribution companies, and the exemption of the industry from income taxes, the government institutionalized and deepened its role in support of the industry.[13] Noting that by the 1950s the bank financed over half the movies produced in the country (a figure that would increase to 70% between 1965 and 1970), Paranaguá concluded, "cinema had become a State industry."[14] Yet following a brief period of decline and neglect, President Echeverría restructured the industry and repositioned the State even more directly in the industry, providing generous financing, relaxing censorship, and creating three State-run production companies.[15] According to Monsiváis, Echeverría virtually nationalized the industry.[16] State assistance peaked in 1976, however, and began to fall, pushing production back into the hands of independent producers.[17] After producing 26.5% of national movies between 1971 and 1976, the share of State production fell to just 7% roughly a decade later.[18] This decline in State support, most would agree, paralleled a general decline in the quality and quantity of Mexican films.

In addition to providing support, the government has also periodically tried to use its power to carve out a market niche for national cinema, again with the idea of curbing the influence of Hollywood. President Cárdenas, for instance, decreed that theaters show at least one national movie per month,[19] though distributors often found ways around it.[20] A 1952 decree went further, mandating that 50% of screen time in each movie theater be used to show national films; but, again, the law was unenforceable due to pressures from the monopoly that controlled most theaters and that preferred Hollywood movies.[21] Though rarely enforced, this screen time requirement remained on the books until the 1990s. (Chapter 7 on marketing offers data comparing market shares of U.S. and Mexican motion pictures.)

The State has also sought to influence the content of Mexican movies so as to counter Hollywood's influence. Official censorship of scripts began in 1941, under the control of *Gobernación*; but the political use of cinema dates back to the very beginning of the industry.[22] Porfirio Díaz gave the first national cinema its strong propagandistic character, using cinema politically to summarize history through a select group of heroes and *caudillos*.[23] The Cárdenas government similarly promoted national production of cinema that contained themes "consistent with the ideological program of the state." As Dávalos points out, these included important images of the U.S.: "The vigor of revolutionary nationalism with all of its populist and authoritarian contradictions generated a reactionary response with characteristics of Catholicism and anti-United States thoughts."[24]

Golden Age films also engaged in a political and cultural re-visioning of national identity, crafting an "idealized, romanticized, and imaginary Mexico."[25] These films—as we will see, usually using the *gringo* in juxtaposition—stressed the integrity of family, showed how capitalism unleashes greed, exalted *machismo* and patriarchy, and associated class with nation: "the lower the station, the more genuine the Mexicanness."[26] According to Monsiváis, during this period cinema "refashioned the idea of the nation by transforming nationalism into a big spectacle."[27]

Though in some cases State control and content went hand in hand as noted above, this was not always true. Paranaguá argues that State promotion of film was designed "to save what was there, rather than to shape production culturally or socially."[28] Even at the height of State control under Echeverría, the level of State censorship declined, thus freeing moviemakers to determine content. This relaxation of censorship set the stage for the period of the highly critical Nuevo Cine during the 1970s, replete with political and social themes.

It is important to stress that it is not just the State that has reacted to the U.S. and Hollywood. Mexican filmmakers have done so as well. According to Hershfield, Golden Age films were designed to free the cinema from the dominance of European and U.S. models.[29] In describing the works of the eminent director of the period, Emilio Fernández (*María Candelaria*, 1943; *Flor Silvestre*, 1943; *La Perla*, 1945; *Enamorada*, 1946; *Maclovia*, 1948; and *Río Escondido*, 1948), Hershfield posits that the director's purpose was in part to "neutralize Hollywood's influence."[30] Still, "one cannot underestimate the significance of the State on Mexican cinematic production."[31] To borrow from Hayes, the Mexican State often engaged in paternalism as a means to counter or arrest (U.S.) media imperialism.[32]

Certainly the U.S. has shaped the industry in more ways than simply providing a force to be resisted or contested. The U.S., particularly Hollywood, has also influenced the Mexican industry more directly by serving as a model to be imitated or embraced, and by providing or removing opportunities for the development of the industry. So while U.S. cinema triggered a nationalist reaction on the one hand, it also became the "inevitable model" from the very beginning for the national industry on the other. Mexican cinema learned from Hollywood, and adopted its techniques and genres, even as it sought to "nationalize" it and give it a distinctive Mexican flavor.[33] Hence, since the early development of the national cinema, "nationalism and imitation are inextricably woven together."[34]

One critical way the U.S. has shaped the industry has been to define the meaning of success, thereby shaping the career patterns of Mexican filmmakers and actors. Mexicans are quick to point with pride to the Hollywood "success" of Mexican actors from Cantinflas and Anthony Quinn to Salma Hayek, or the international awards of films like *La Invención de Cronos* (Cannes, 1993) or *Como agua para chocolate* (Academy Award, 1993). The fact that such actors are rarely accused of *malinchismo* or that the national awards, *los Arieles*, seem to be given less play suggests a U.S. validation of quality: that is, one truly "succeeds" in the "Hollywood" (cinema) game when *gringos* or other foreigners say so! This same point can also be seen in the luring to Hollywood of Mexican directors enjoying U.S. box-office success. As Noriega notes, the directors of successful films like *Like Water for Chocolate* and *El Mariachi* "headed to Hollywood, not Mexico City, in the wake of their critical and popular success in the United States."[35]

The U.S. has shaped the industry in other ways as well. The Golden Age, for example, owed much of its existence to the lack of competition from Hollywood and the extensive financial and technical support offered by the U.S. government to the Mexican film industry during the period. This policy of support was part of the U.S. government's war strategy to bolster its image abroad and solidify alliances. Seth Fein credits this alliance for making the Mexican film industry the third largest in the country by 1947, and for making Mexican movies more widely available at the national and the international level.[36] In the late 1940s, in fact, Mexican movies enjoyed better than 40% of national screen time, while over 300 movie theaters in the U.S. exclusively showed Mexican movies.[37]

Just as it had flourished, the Golden Age also ended in large part as a result of U.S. actions. After the global war, Hollywood production and competition reemerged and the U.S. government suspended its program of direct assistance. Concerned now about the ideological impact of Mexican films in the U.S. and intent on using Hollywood to further its own ideological and cul-

tural agenda (Cold War era), the U.S. government, along with U.S. distributors, engaged in a series of tactics designed to thwart Mexican policies
supporting the national industry. In response to Mexican-imposed limits on
foreign investment in movie studios, for instance, the U.S. used its power to
limit the distribution of virgin film, thereby crippling the Mexican industry.[38]
Combined, such factors led to both a decline in the production of Mexican
movies and a significant dip in quality.[39] As Fein notes in reference to this
period, "The Mexican state chose to support its national film industry in a
framework that did not directly challenge U.S. hegemony. The result was
films of declining quality."[40]

Film scholar Charles Berg agrees. He attributes the breakdown of the paradigm created during the Golden Era to, among other factors, the industry's
increasing dependence on Hollywood.[41] But even in the nineties, the Mexican
industry is described in the context of its subordinate relationship to the U.S.
Noting the increasing use of Mexican facilities to produce U.S. movies in the
contemporary period (i.e., *Titanic, Total Recall, Romancing the Stone, Clear
and Present Danger*), one observer labels the Mexican cinema industry as
simply a "*maquiladora*."[42]

Two key points emerge from this brief review of the Mexican film industry.
First, it exemplifies the importance of the U.S. (mediated as perceptions of
the U.S.) in shaping Mexican policy and, more specifically, the nature of the
Mexican film industry. The perception has long existed that through its cinema the U.S. offends the sensibilities of the Mexican and, more critically, that
it presents and "sells" a set of values undermining national cultural values.
This perception, in turn, has led the State at different times and in different
guises to insert itself into the industry and ally with Mexican moviemakers
to help define and protect national identity. Second, the brief profile highlights the role of the State in contributing, *but only contributing,* to the content of Mexican cinema. As Saragoza and Berkovich note, there is a clear
connection "between Mexican cinema, the State and national identity."[43] But
it would be a gross exaggeration to present the themes portrayed in Mexican
cinema as merely another representation of the State's ideological interests, a
view somewhat typical of the Frankfurt School of cultural analysis. The Mexican State has never had complete control over the message, nor is there
abundant evidence to suggest that the views of the State, particularly when it
comes to the U.S., have differed dramatically from those within the artistic
community. In other words, Mexican movies represent much more than the
State's "hegemonic discourse." Consistent with the Birmingham or Cultural
Studies School, which characterizes movies as a means of exploring "the
many points of view present in a given society," Mexican films are treated
here as representing the ideas, passions, and creative talent of scores of

filmmakers as well as the culture from which they emerge and with which they communicate.[44] It is within this context that we now turn to an analysis of the content of Mexican cinema.

Gringos and Gringolandia in Mexican Cinema

As alluded to at the outset, exploring film content is important for what it reveals about a culture and society. According to film scholar George Gerbner, "Media content indicators . . . will tell us about the shared representations of life, the issues, and the prevailing points of view that capture public attention, occupy people's time, and animate their imagination."[45] Siegfried Kracauer echoes this fundamental theoretical point: "The films of a nation reflect its mentality in a more direct way than other artistic media for two reasons: first, films are never the product of an individual . . . second, films address themselves, and appeal to, the anonymous multitude. . . . What films reflect are not so much explicit codes as psychological dispositions—those deep layers of collective mentality which extend more or less below the dimension of consciousness."[46] Of course, most analysts of Mexican cinema concur with these views, stressing the link between the national self-image and the cinematic self-representation, with causality moving in both directions.[47] "Mexican cinema reveals how an industry, closely aligned with the state, has represented Mexico to itself, to the Spanish-speaking world, and to international 'art film' audiences."[48] Cinema, in short, both reflects culture and contributes to its construction.

Mexican cinema has enjoyed substantial analysis over the years, with a handful of works focusing specifically on the images of the U.S.[49] John Mraz looks at images of the U.S. in Mexican cinema during the period of Miguel Alemán; Ricardo Pérez explores the images contained in the *charro* movies from 1920 to 1946; Julia Tuñón examines the presentation of the U.S. in the movies of the Golden Era; and David Maciel and Norma Iglesias focus attention on the cinematographic representations of the Mexico-U.S. border.[50] David Wilt's dissertation stands out, however, as providing the most comprehensive study to date, analyzing a range of images of U.S. citizens in over 600 Mexican films from 1930 to 1990.[51]

The extent of the presence and significance of the U.S. in Mexican film is a matter of some debate, however. Tuñón calls the presence of the U.S. in Mexican movies scarce;[52] and yet, Wilt uncovered U.S. characters in more than 10% of all Mexican films. More significantly perhaps, Wilt found that all such characters were deliberately inserted, meaning that their nationality was critical to the story line. At least in terms of the "foreigner" in the Mexican movie the *gringo* certainly has been prominent. As Pérez notes, "Among the stereotypes of the foreigner that were most often used as a counterpoint to the nationalistic images, the North American or *gringo* was perhaps one of the oldest and most recurring."[53]

In his extensive review, Wilt identifies four basic stereotypes of the U.S. in Mexican cinema: the tourist, the blonde, the exploiter, and the racist. Following a brief elaboration of each based almost entirely on Wilt, attention then turns to the role such images have played in shaping or defining perceptions of self and nation.

The Tourist Stereotype

The first basic image of the U.S. found in Mexican film centers on the U.S. as personified in the tourist. Such characterizations have been particularly common since the 1940s. The *gringo* tourist is usually a male, marked by his clothing (either Yankee garb or wearing inappropriate attire), affinity for large cigars, pipes, or chewing tobacco, inability to speak or understand Spanish properly, usually a general disrespect for or disinterest in Mexico, and an air of presumed superiority. Poor language skills, an easy marker of a *gringo,* are used to indicate incompetence and lack of respect for Mexico (insofar as the *gringo* expects the Mexican to speak English).[54] This device also allows the Mexicans a framework to mock the *gringo.* The North American tourist is also "pushy, belligerent and crude, but these are [presented] as false demonstrations of his masculinity," according to Wilt, because the tourist is also shown as "sexually inept, a coward, a fool, cannot fight or hold his liquor, is henpecked, a cuckold."[55] Indeed, in any direct physical confrontation in the cinema, the Mexican character wins. The *gringo* tourist's sexual inferiority is further demonstrated by the loss of his U.S. girlfriend to the Mexican, his futile pursuit of Mexican women, his effeminate, perverse, or homosexual nature, or by his being henpecked. In the end, the tourist image reveals U.S. life as morally decadent despite being materially wealthy: "In speech, dress, manners, moral and spiritual attitudes, the Mexican film image of the United States is that of an alien, even decadent culture—the United States is seen as the home of hippies, drug dealers and drug users, homosexuals, and rapists . . . [that] U.S. citizens have paid a stiff price to obtain material wealth."[56]

Examples of the *gringo* tourist in Mexican movies are many. In the movie *Tropicana* (1956), after the North American does not understand the Mexican's reference to him as a "*rico ganadero*" [rich cattleman], the Mexican makes the sign of the horns to which the North American replies "Oh yes, me *tener muchos.*" The Mexican thus mocks the *gringo* not only by making the cuckold sign, but by getting the tourist to agree that he is indeed one. In *Tlayucan* (1961), the lack of respect for Mexico by U.S. tourists is shown when a group of female U.S. tourists wearing slacks leave a church sporting a sign saying "Women in Pants Forbidden." *El redescubrimiento de México* (1978) makes a similar point when a Mexican museum tour guide says he simply invents stories for U.S. tourists because they are really not interested in the artifacts, just in taking pictures. This same message can also be seen in *El Campeón ciclista* (1956) when the North American claims the mariachis are not Mexican because they are not dressed like Mexicans in U.S. films. *Gitana tenías que ser* (1953) also highlights the *gringo* tourist stereotype. It shows a group of drunken North American tourists in a bar (unable to hold their liquor) who are quick to start a fight and easily defeated by the Mexicans. *Conexión México* (1987) and *La Camioneta gris* (1989), in turn, use drugged *gringo* tourists to show the absence of values and to fix the blame of the world's drug problem on the U.S. *El Charro y la dama* (1949), in turn, depicts a North American fiancé who pays more attention to business than to his girl and who proves unable to get his girl back from her Mexican kidnapper. He not only gets the wrong man, but also ends up getting beaten up by a group of women, exposing him "for the inadequate creature he is."[57] Finally, in *Un Extraño en la casa* (1966), a U.S. tourist is portrayed as sexually perverted, killing one woman and trying to kill another, only to be foiled by a young Mexican girl and a comic. As we will see, such images play an important function in demonstrating the superiority of Mexican values, including *machismo*.

The Blonde Stereotype

A second stereotypical image prominent in the Mexican movie is the blonde. Also a tourist but a female, the blonde is characterized as outspoken, independent, aggressive, and forward, and at times avaricious, dangerous, and even evil. She is portrayed as sexually permissive and even sexually aggressive: a woman of loose morals, usually as a result of her assertiveness. She is known for henpecking her husband or divorcing him with ease. The stereotypical blonde in Mexican cinema is not simply a translation of the "dumb blonde" stereotype in U.S. cinema, however, because she is portrayed as perhaps more intelligent and cunning than the Mexican women. The blonde is also depicted as being attracted to Mexico and particularly Mexican men because of the inferiority of the U.S. male as illustrated by the tourist stereotype.[58]

In *24 horas de vida* (1968), for example, the U.S. blonde orders her U.S. companion around, mocks him in Spanish, and seduces him into planning a murder. Demonstrating what Wilt refers to as the "predatory Blonde," *Aca-pulco a go-go* (1965) finds a U.S. blonde making a beachboy an accomplice to the murder of her stepmother.[59] In *El Pecado de Laura* (1948) the U.S. female leaves her U.S. boyfriend to work as a dancer in Mexico. She is then seduced, impregnated, and abused, all because of her sin of ambition. In some films, like *Triunfo sucio* (1979), the blonde is a prostitute who is married, even enjoying the façade of being high-class: an allegory of the hypocrisy of U.S. life. In those cases where the U.S. female is portrayed as a suitable mate, she either has some Latin blood as in *Los Tres García* or comes to accept Mexican culture.[60] As we see later, it is precisely through her acceptance of Mexico and the Mexican male that the *gringa* serves as the site of the reconciliation of the two cultures and societies.

The Exploiter Stereotype

Drawing from historical and political bases, Mexican movies referring to the U.S. as exploitative or with U.S. characters personifying such conduct are many, dating back to the earliest films. An ad for the documentary film *La invasión norteamericana* (1914) showing the U.S. takeover of Veracruz, for example, not only refers to the U.S. as "our eternal enemy," but also describes the film as revealing "the iniquitous deed committed by the *yanqui* invader."[61] When personified in film, the exploiter is depicted as strong and ruthless. He is obsessed with money, often to the exclusion of family and love, and is callous in his pursuit of money and power, but his actions usually lead to misery, poverty, unhappiness, and even death. In this quest, the exploiter sees Mexico as a country rich in natural resources underutilized because of what he sees as the natural inferiority of the Mexicans (lazy) and their culture. He thus presents himself and particularly the U.S., U.S. capitalism, and U.S. culture as the keys to Mexico's progress and development. In *En defensa propia* (1977), for instance, the U.S. character states categorically: "This is a backward region and I am progress. Nobody and nothing can stop progress."[62]

The exploiter stereotype encompasses a wide range of conduct, from U.S. annexation of Mexican territory, the exploitation of Mexican natural resources, the treatment of Mexicans in the U.S., and drug trafficking (*El Mundo de los drogas*, 1963; *Guerra de las drogas*, 1990; *La Revancha*, 1985) to the trafficking of newborns (*La Secta de la muerte*, 1990; and *Traficantes de niños*, 1990). Despite little attention to the 1847 war, many films refer to the loss of Mexican territory to the U.S. *El Ultimo Mexicano* (1959), for example, opens with a voice-over referring to the year 1850 in Texas, in what was once Mexican territory, but where the U.S. flag now rules.[63] In *¿Nos traiciona el*

Presidente? (1987) a U.S. military officer tries to bribe a Mexican general to overthrow the Mexican government, while President Obregón is pressured to name a successor sympathetic to U.S. goals in the region. According to Wilt, this movie "contains a virtual litany of Mexican grievances against the United States: historical military aggression, territorial acquisition, economic domination, attempts to influence Mexican internal and external politics, an unfair and politically motivated policy on undocumented workers."[64]

In a similar manner, in *El Mexicano* (1965) and *Alma grande en el desierto* (1966), the *gringo* villain tries to gain control of gold mines, while in Luis Buñuel's first film in Mexico, *Gran casino* (1946), the *gringos* seek to exploit Mexican oil, only to have the oil field blow up in the end rather than fall into foreign hands. The movie *Rosa Blanca* (1961; released 1972) also deals with foreign exploitation of Mexican oil, as does *La Perla* (Emilio Fernández, 1945).[65] In this latter classic, "the foreigner, perverse and greedy, exploits the kind, innocent and unarmed Indian," killing in order to acquire pearls that the Mexican owner refuses to sell.[66]

A common setting for the exploiter is in the U.S. "One of the most popular themes in Mexican cinema is the story of Mexican workers in the United States."[67] Though some early movies, like *Quiero ser artista* (1958) or *Ustedes los ricos* (1948), did make favorable reference to working in the U.S., most films show the negative side. *Adiós mi Chaparrita* (1938), for example, opens showing U.S. border guards firing on Mexicans crossing the Rio Grande. A similar scene opens *Espaldas mojadas* (1953, 1977). In *Pito Pérez se va de bracero* (1948) the main character points not only to Mexico's nature, but to that of the U.S.: "I don't think it should be illegal to enter a friendly country. In my country, *gueritos* like you are found everywhere."[68] Films like *Raíces de sangre* (1976), *Atacan las karatecas* (1977), *Wetbacks* (1977), and *Ley fuga* (1984), among others, also show how "the abuses in the *mojado* films are caused by the greed and ruthlessness of the Exploiter."[69]

Wetbacks (*Los mojados*) (1977) is a tragic story, chock-full of images of the U.S. It opens with the voice-over referring to the "hallucination" and the "*fábula* of the dollar" as luring Mexicans north. The opening scene then shows what awaits the Mexican when a group of entrants are rounded up and shot in cold blood by U.S. border agents. The agents then plant drugs on the dead Mexicans to make them appear to be part of a drug-trafficking ring. The balance of the film focuses on the pursuit of the lone escapee of the group—the potential witness who can expose the truth, played by Jorge Rivero—and the conspiracy behind the brutal murders. The conspiracy is composed of U.S. politicians and business interests, with some support from the Mexican-American community, all seeking to maintain the flow of cheap labor. The avaricious nature of the U.S. and its denigrating view of the Mexicans are stunningly clear throughout the film. So too is the lesson for the Mexicans: going to the U.S. brings only suffering. At one point, the female friend of the lone survivor of the massacre chastises herself for having come to the U.S. She once believed in becoming rich, but now lives in misery and longs to return to Mexico. In the end, state police arrest the U.S. "bad guys" based on the testimony of the courageous Mexican witness. In some ways, the climax demonstrates an underlying faith in the U.S. judicial system, despite the corruption of the local politicians. And yet in the end, though truth wins out and virtue prevails, the main protagonist dies, gunned down by snipers, unable to return to his two true loves: the woman and their country.

The Racist Stereotype

The final image identified by Wilt, and the least numerous of the four, entails the U.S. character as a racist. The most negative of the four images, the racist stereotype appears often in films set in the U.S., with many dealing with black-white relations. The U.S. character is often depicted as mentally unbalanced, usually as part of an extremist group like the KKK as in the movie *Las Braceras* (1979). The actions of the racist range from name-calling and discrimination to harassment and murder, though some films, like *El Mexicano* (1965), try to balance things out by showing other *gringos* rejecting the racist *gringo*.[70]

For example, in *El Preso numero 9* (1979), after a minor auto accident in the U.S., the *gringos* call the protagonist a "Mexican son of a bitch" and then proceed to beat him up. Adding insult to injury, the Mexican then gets jailed for the episode. In *El Muro de la tortilla* (1979) a lawyer advises his client not to hire Mexicans because they are bad people. Later when it is revealed that he is a member of the Klan, he states, "I have real American blood, [I belong to] the white race. A race that you and the worthless blacks try to degrade."[71] According to Wilt, such treatments "reinforce the general image of the United States as a Racist nation,"[72] and, as we see momentarily, help depict Mexico as nonracist.

Reflections on Self and Nation

Such stereotypes as set out by Wilt, of course, tell us little about the *gringo*, but much about the Mexican. In fact, the *gringo* is used in Mexican movies as a way to highlight, construct, and praise the values of Mexico and the Mexican. In most cases, films tend to present the U.S. and Mexico as virtual opposites, with the U.S. characters serving less as characters and more like functions.[73] In the words of Mraz, "the *gringo* in Mexican cinema is, basically, a form of the non-Mexican . . . its function is to serve as the antipode of the Mexican in the definition of the Mexican."[74] "By referring to the United States, Mexican cinema cannot avoid looking at its own country and highlighting its characteristics through contrast: if they are individualistic, we are solidarity; if they are cold, we are warm and even volcanic; if they are alone, we have extended and solid family institutions; if they are rich, we are poor and with much honor."[75]

Certain articulations tying images of the U.S. to images of the nation are not too difficult to discern. The U.S. tourist, who is *"despistado y bobalición"* [absent-minded, silly], for instance, functions to show the ingenuity, agility, and *machismo* of the Mexicans.[76] Offering a reverse image of the idealized Mexican male, the *gringo* tourist reinforces Mexicans' sense of self-esteem.[77] Showing the *gringo* as less than *macho* provides an arena wherein Mexicans can feel superior to the U.S., "countering what they perceive as years of intervention and exploitation in which Mexico has generally been the loser."[78] In a similar manner, the blonde stereotype represents the reverse image of the idealized Mexican female. On the one hand, the inevitable suffering of the aggressive and promiscuous U.S. female demonstrates the evils of her lifestyle and hence the glory of the values—submissive, chaste, family-oriented— associated with the female Mexican characters. Though an object of sexual desire and hot for the Mexican male (a sign of his superiority), the blonde is rarely worthy of marriage. As with the tourist stereotype, then, Wilt interprets this as a means of "striking back at the dominance of the U.S."[79]

Just as the cinematographic image of the *gringo* helps depict the superiority of the Mexican male and female, it also helps demonstrate the superiority of Mexican culture and values, and hence the dangers posed by the U.S. In *Carne de presidio* (1951), for example, a *gringo* prisoner, after noting how U.S. prisons give inmates medicine to control their physical desires whereas Mexican prisons allow for conjugal visits, concludes that "there [in the U.S.] one is not a man. Here one is imprisoned, but free."[80] *Rosa Blanca* (1961; released 1972) also juxtaposes the two cultures, contrasting competing images of the "good life." Depicting efforts of a U.S. oil company to buy land from a Mexican family that refuses to sell because ancestors are buried on it (symbolizing the value of family and the past), the U.S. character argues that with the money the Mexican can buy a new truck that will allow him to make it to Tuxpan in half an hour (symbolic of U.S. materialism and efficiency). The Mexican protagonist, Jacinto, however, responds by noting that he actually enjoys traveling early, seeing the sun come up and the corn growing: values he would lose by having a truck. This same theme plays out in a subsequent scene where the director of the Los Angeles company, who ends up acquiring the Mexican land by using false documents, is shown constantly giving money to his wife, daughter, and lover. According to Tuñón, the scene demonstrates clearly "the coldness and absence of human values" of the U.S. people.[81]

One mechanism to demonstrate the value of the national culture over the foreign culture is to have the *gringos* themselves praise and embrace the Mexican culture, thus implicitly at least denying or rejecting their own. The father of the U.S. female in *Los Tres García* (1946), for example, in many ways represents the "good *gringo*," not just because he does not intervene with moral judgments or try to exploit Mexico, or because he accepts his daughter's marriage to a Mexican, but because he acknowledges the value of Mexican culture.[82] At one point, in fact, he laments not having been born in Mexico. The U.S. character in *Ave Charro* (1921) similarly ends up praising the "beauty of the Mexican women, the dignity of the men, and the happiness of the Mexican *fiestas*."[83]

The exploitation and racial themes also bolster a strong sense of nationalism, demonstrating the direct dangers to Mexico posed by the U.S. *Una gringuita en México* (1951), for example, criticizes U.S. influence inside the country. It opens with scenes of Mexico City as a voice-over notes how Mexico is changing: how its *palacios* look poor, and how one now finds this . . . (a scene of a modern restaurant with signs, in English, of 'waffles,' and 'hot cakes'). This contrast prompts the voice-over to then warn: "Little by little the physiognomy of a magical, customary, romantic Mexico is being lost."[84] *Campeón sin corona* (1945) offers a unique twist to this theme, focusing on the inferiority complex of the Mexican that stems from the nation's proximity to the U.S. Casting English as embodying the "power and impenetrable center from which Mexicans have been cast out," it depicts a Mexican boxer who finds himself unable to defeat his Chicano rival because the latter speaks English.[85] The extent of U.S. power is shown even more pointedly in *El Chacharas*. Here the U.S. tourist is depicted as a sex maniac who molests young girls, but in one case the father of one of the girls actually refuses to denounce him because the North American has threatened to stop buying Mexican oil and make the dollar go up.[86]

This image of the northern threat rings particularly true with respect to the Mexicans going north or those returning south. Both *Espaldas mojadas* (1953) and its remake *Mojados* (1977) provide a "catalogue of migrant suffering" in the U.S. *Espaldas mojadas* (1953) begins with a voice-over stating explicitly that the intention of the movie is "to warn citizens of the inconvenience of abandoning the country illegally at the risk of suffering bothersome and painful situations."[87] Later in the film, the main character delivers the essential message once again: "Once they exploit you and make you work from sunup to sundown, you'll return to Mexico worse than you came."[88] Exploitation in the U.S. is not the sole reserve of *gringos*, of course. In *La ilegal* (1979) it is the Mexicans, not the North Americans, who exploit the migrant. As such, it shows how the U.S. contaminates the Mexicans to the point of actually turning them against their own people: "Mexicans are not compromised by the failure of their own system but by *el norte*, which contaminates all who come into contact with it. . . . Only those—like the consul [the hero in this film]—who maintain their loyalty to Mexico will remain impervious to the evils of the United States."[89]

This same theme can also be found in the context of Mexicans returning home after extensive periods in the U.S. Indeed, many films cast the cultural conflict between the two societies within a single Mexican character: a conflict that is resolved by the triumph of the superior Mexican values. *Primero soy mexicano* (1950), for example, depicts a Mexican youth returning home after studying in the U.S. for 10 years. He reflects cultural differences through his beliefs ("free thinker"), his preference for U.S. food, and his treatment of others (calls his father "daddy," greets with a handshake rather than a firm embrace). His refusal to eat during the *gran fiesta* given on his behalf because he had already eaten "lunch," moreover, exhibits the incompatibility of the two cultures. In the end, of course, the young man (once under the intoxicating influence of the U.S.) returns to his national senses. "The story of *Primero soy mexicano* is," as Mraz describes it, "the elimination of the contradictions that Rafael embodies of wanting to be *gringo*; his salvation is his reincorporation of an exclusive and essential Mexicanness. . . . The reincorporation of Rafael into the great family demonstrates that homogeneity is more important than individual characteristics in defining Mexicanness . . . the only solution is the unconditional acceptance of the doctrines of the Fatherland."[90]

Other movies have also used this device, adopting similar story lines. In *La devoradora* (1946) the Mexican protagonist returns, missing Mexico after studying medicine in the U.S. In the end of the picture, he too returns to his cultural and nationalist senses. In *Acá las tortas* (1951) the children go to study in the U.S. and return calling themselves by their American names and using *spanglish*: something "*embarassamente*" to the parents. They no longer even like Mexican food, with one stating that "my tastes are accustomed to more refined food." Only after the death of their brother, however, do they return to their senses, working in the end in the family business making *tortas*. *Sin Fortuna* (1979), similarly, depicts returning Mexicans critical of the U.S. treatment of Mexicans and extolling the virtues of staying in Mexico.[91]

The many films of famed comic Tin Tán fit loosely within this context, though with a twist. As the *pocho* archetype, Tin Tán uses a mixed, deformed language that invites condemnation linguistically and socially. Monsiváis defines the *pocho* as "someone without a race who has forgotten his roots and who has exchanged the vitality of idiosyncrasy for the superficiality of Americanization."[92] As Mraz points out, "Tin Tán took on the character of other cultures to ridicule them and ended up affirming reigning Mexicanness."[93] Tin Tán also, moreover, embodied resistance to the U.S.: a challenge to the racial discrimination and hence a symbol of cultural resistance.[94] In the end, such movies demonstrate that "losing the customs results in something worse and more dangerous than the North Americans themselves."[95]

Underlying this danger of the U.S. is the notion that the two cultures and societies are basically incompatible. Many films drive home this point. In *Los Tres García* (1946), for example, one of the cousins, in reference to his blonde cousin (Lupita Smith Garcia) whose father is from the U.S., comments that "it is absurd and unpatriotic to have blond hair and be called Lupe." And despite John's (the father's) niceness and even his accolades for the Mexican culture, he never truly incorporates into society, similar to the fate of John in *Like water for chocolate,* explored below. This incompatibility theme also lies at the heart of *Rosa Blanca*. According to Tuñón, this classic tale "deals with opposite universes, without any possibility of mutual understanding and even contact."[96]

It is also within this context that the U.S. is often depicted as not only representing modernity, but a modernity that comes at the cost of tradition, often pitting generations against one another. In *El Diablo . . . No es tan Diablo* (1949), an older man criticizes the youth who speak English, and play loud jazz music and American football, for adopting "exotic and ridiculous [foreign] customs."[97] In the movie *A Donde van nuestros hijos* (1956), similarly, the daughter cries in opposition to her tyrannical father: "Look, Dad, one can't live like in the Middle Ages; see how Americans have changed everything?"[98] Though such "modern" qualities are sometimes touted as a threat, they are also in some ways portrayed as inevitable, forging a difficult choice for the Mexican. For this reason, Monsiváis concludes that Mexican cinema "praises the customs that are disappearing and it criticizes the modernity that is being promoted."[99]

The treatment of migration certainly pivots on this paradoxical theme as well. "Most Mexican films about migration to the United States recognize the lure of the north, yet accentuate the negative side of crossing over the border."[100] Indeed, *Espaldas Mojadas* (1953, 1977), as noted earlier, shows this difficult, almost impossible choice, depicting the U.S. as invitingly modern and yet the modern as inherently costly: "Over there, on the other side, the skyscrapers are an architectural symbol of the most powerful country on earth where all its inhabitants have cars, radio and television." And yet, for those who go without the proper documents, the country offers nothing more than suffering. Instead of showing the skyscrapers, the movie shows the U.S. as a place where one feels alone: "Enclosed within yourself, alone, in a wheel of solitude, you in the center, and you do not receive a sound or a look: nobody sees you, nobody hears you, you do not exist!"[101] Just as having a truck in *Rosa Blanca* implies a loss of the ability to enjoy the beauty of life, solitude represents the existential price of modernity.

At times, however, the screen offers more positive images of hybridity. The stereotypical blonde, in fact, is often the site where the two cultures can effectively come together, though only under certain conditions. As Pérez notes, a Mexican can only fall in love and accept the *gringa* when she has become more Mexicanized.[102] Tuñón concurs, noting that "the possible relation between the two cultures can only be based in terms of feminine subordination"; that the *gringa* can have a relationship, but she must accept Mexico, remain in Mexico, and become part of a Mexican family.[103] Indeed, Pedro Infante's glorious statement in *Los tres García*—"Long live Panamericanism—and the closeness of the American women"—stems from his amorous desire for the *gringa*.

In many ways, Tin Tán, as in *El Rey del barrio* (1949), also represents a sort of synthesis of the traits of both societies.[104] Monsiváis especially promotes this alternative view of the famous actor: that Tin Tán accepts hybridity and embodies the compatibility of the two cultures. Taking it one step further, Monsiváis contends that Tin Tán plays an important role in helping Mexico overcome the traditional notion that "Americanized" was the object of jest and scorn: "Tin Tán, without pretending to be aware of it, does away with the rejection and the incomprehension. His dress and his manner decree for the first time popular modernity and anticipates its overflow of style. . . . [As such he] interprets the syncretism that will mark the second half of the century."[105] Mraz would probably agree with this interpretation, noting how Tin Tán represented alternative possibilities to the nationalist model of the time, thereby violating the rules of the Alemán ideology.[106]

In some ways, the critically acclaimed *Like Water for Chocolate* exemplifies both these tendencies: incompatibility and syncretism. On the one hand, the U.S. doctor, John, remains excluded and alone throughout the picture, despite the noble nature of his character (much of the noble nature of his character is made palatable and believable by giving him an indigenous grandmother. More importantly, this allows him—in contrast to the materialism of the *gringo*—to recount the mystical key to life and love, thereby foreshadowing the magical realist conclusion of the film). John fails to gain Tita's hand in marriage, or even sleep with her, even though, as she states, she feels comfortable and protected when she is with him. In the end, John remains alone and dejected, unable to partake in the elaborate meal or share in the toast at his own son's wedding. The exclusion and incompatibility are clear. And yet, on the other hand, the story itself—a story of the struggle to over-come tradition set in the northern border region—is recounted by a Mexi-can-American: the daughter (Tita's grandniece) of the union of a Mexican female (Tita's niece and Pedro's daughter) and a North American male (John's son). Moreover, she recounts this story while sitting in a clearly "modern" kitchen, perhaps in the U.S., perhaps in Mexico. This ambiguity itself shows just how the Mexican-American can live in the world of the modern and continue to honor and respect those from the past regardless of which side of the border they are on.[107] The temporal distinction is also criti-cal here since it suggests that the incompatibility of the two societies—like the tradition whereby the youngest daughter can never marry—has, with time, eroded.

Such postures and images as discussed thus far have clear political over-tones and functions. The cinematographic images of the U.S., for example, provide a mechanism to channel criticism and opposition: to redirect blame for societal ills. As Wilt holds, "the real resentment many Mexicans still feel about historical 'exploitation' by the United States is used to deflect criticism of the Mexican government."[108] The treatment of the U.S. as racist serves not only to portray the Mexican as nonracist, but also as a substitute to deflect attention away from the country's racial problems, a theme rarely explored by cinema. At the same time, images of the U.S. provide a backdrop to help mold a national culture and offer a particular and unified image of self, using difference vis-à-vis the U.S. other to overcome regional and ethnic differ-ences. According to Hershfield, the purpose of director Emilio Fernández was not only to neutralize the influence of Hollywood, but also "to dramatize Mexico's past and present in order to portray what he believed was an authentic national identity."[109] This task dovetailed nicely with the interests of the authoritarian State since the dominant images and messages helped cast the State as the main defender of the nation against the powerful and prominent threat embodied by the U.S. Golden Age cinema, above all, offered a distinct and clear image of the nation, identified and located Mexi-canness among the poor, and placed *cardenismo* and the State as central, patriarchical symbols. As Saragoza and Berkovich contend: "The state estab-lished itself as both the logical end point for and guardian of the historical patrimony of the past for the nation . . . [and] Mexican cinema played a significant role in these efforts, lending crucial support to the legitimation of the state."[110]

The Issue of Change

Over the years, Mexican cinema has clearly undergone many changes. As described previously, the State's treatment of cinema and its role in the industry, as well as the fortunes of the industry itself, have all changed periodically. Though still present in some limited form as seen in the temporary blocking of *Ley de Herodes* (2000) during the election year of 2000, formal State censorship, State financing, and market protection have all greatly declined in recent years. Consistent with the policies of neoliberalism, the State has abandoned its efforts to restrict U.S. movies, while privatizing many State production and distribution companies. Such changes, on the one hand, have weakened the State's ability to shape the content of Mexican pictures or to use cinema for its own political and ideological purposes. On the other hand, such moves have expanded the ability of filmmakers to delve deeper into political and critical themes. And like State policy, the fortunes of the industry have ebbed and flowed during the years, almost in cyclical fashion as a consequence of trends inside and outside the country. The success of the Golden Age, for instance, contrasts with the decline of the postwar years, just as the 1990s renewal of the industry counters the prospects of the late 1980s as described by Berg in the following terms: "Today Mexico faces nothing less than the obliteration of Mexican filmmaking altogether."[111]

In many ways, these changes mirror shifts in cinema's image of the nation. Berg highlights a marked change in the content of Mexican cinema beginning in the 1960s. In contrast to the nationalist images projected during the Golden Era, he sees contemporary cinema as depicting solitude, offering a communal redefinition of *mexicanidad: la nueva comunidad.*[112] García Riera similarly notes a reduction in the "national unification" role so prominent in the Golden Era. He attributes this shift to a variety of factors, including the reduction of State support for the industry, the closing of the Cuban market, the difficulty of exploiting markets in other countries, the rise of TV, and competition from U.S. cinema.[113] Saragoza and Berkovich also draw a sharp distinction between the 1934–1968 and the post-1970 periods. The former coincided with the construction of the authoritarian State, and featured a basic consensus regarding Mexican identity, while the latter presents a lack of consensus: the absence of a national image. They draw particular importance to how recent changes have undermined cinema's ability or desire to serve the interests of the State as it had done for nearly three decades. Indeed, just as the relaxation of censorship under Echeverría gave rise to the critical films of the 1970s, the policies of the Salinas era have triggered a creative renewal of critical filmmakers, eager to tackle controversial issues and experiment with new images of a re-visioned and reconstructed nation.[114] This renewed energy has raised the level of film production in the 1990s (and most would agree, the quality) to a point equal to the Golden Age.[115]

And yet despite such industry changes, the degree of change in the treatment of the nation is not easy to discern. Monsiváis, for example, seems to privilege continuity over change, contending that "the old myths continue to exercise their power." As he notes: "The repertory of three decades of Mexican cinema exhibited central myths and adjacent legends and sketched a portrait of a people: generous, prejudiced, and more emotional than rational; pious and fanatic; an enemy of bigotry and more liberal than it seemed; inhibited by the Lord and Master and all Lords in general; candid, as rebellious as possible, an enthusiast of the memorized joke, and always looking for amusement wherever it could be found."[116]

Like the broader issue, assessments of the degree of change in cinematographic treatments of the U.S. in recent years vary. In general, Wilt sees a high degree of continuity, positing that contemporary films continue to play on the four basic stereotypes of the U.S., though the mix has shifted somewhat.[117] Images of the U.S. described by the tourist and blonde stereotypes were common throughout all periods, while the exploitation and racial images have been around just since the 1970s.[118] Even historical "good periods" in the relationship did not seem to alter the depiction of the U.S., according to film critic García Riera. In characterizing movies during the war years, the so-called Era of Good Feelings, for example, he notes that "the references to the North American in the national cinema were no more benevolent than usual." In fact, in the movie *Como Mexico no hay dos!* (1944), García Riera stresses that the *pocho* was made ridiculous, "a frequent thing in the Mexican movies of the period."[119]

But despite the continued prevalence of these stereotypical images of the U.S. and the nation, Wilt does stress a number of more specific changes reflecting the context of social, political, and other external factors affecting the film industry and changes in general attitudes toward the U.S. The inclusion of the American as tourist in film has varied, for instance, with fewer examples of this image since the 1970s. Since the 1960s, the stereotypical blonde has lost her friendly image, becoming more avaricious, dangerous, and evil. It has become rare now for the blonde to form a lasting relationship, being defined more and more as a disposable sex object. Even direct comparisons with the Mexican female have changed in more recent years, given the changing role of the female in Mexican society. In contrast to the tourist, the exploitation stereotype has appeared with greater frequency with time, with the most examples appearing in the 1980s (76 appearances in the 1970s and 1980s compared to just 44 in the four prior decades). Though the existence of these images in pre-film novels shows historical continuity, Wilt nonetheless acknowledges a trend in more recent years toward "depictions of exploitation, discrimination and physical danger, with fewer portrayals of the 'good life' to be found in the *otro lado*." He attributes the greater prominence of these themes precisely to the greater willingness of filmmakers to treat political themes and the lessening of political censorship. The least numerous of the four stereotypes and yet the most completely negative, the racist stereotype, hardly appeared until the 1970s and 1980s (33 appearances in the 1970s and 1980s compared to 5 in the prior years). Wilt highlights the importance of the Spanish-speaking audience in the U.S. and its concern over racial discrimination for prompting the industry to address this theme.[120]

Conclusion

In sum, as imagined through Mexican cinema, the U.S. functions as a device to help define national culture. It serves to help engender loyalty and love for the culture and a willingness to protect and defend it. And it contributes to a narrative that casts the Mexican State as an ally in this all-critical endeavor. U.S. characters embody and represent not only the values considered inappropriate for the Mexicans, but also traits that metaphorically represent the interests and values that threaten those of the nation. This threat can take place either through the actions of U.S. citizens on either side of the border, or through the contamination of the U.S. on Mexicans living and working there. The *gringo*, moreover, provides a backdrop to show the superiority of Mexican culture, the *machismo* and agility of the males, and the morals and virtues of the Mexican female. And while some changes have occurred in these images over the years, such changes hardly suggest that the Mexican cinema image of the U.S. has "improved" strikingly in recent years, despite the growing level of contact, NAFTA, or political changes. Indeed, the *gringo* in *Like Water for Chocolate*, as noted, still does not get the girl and ends up dejected. And though the *gringo* in *Ley de Herodes* (2000) gets both the Mexican girl and the money, his desire to exploit whom he calls a Mexican "greaser" is abundantly clear.

Notes

1. Chon A. Noriega, "Mexican Cinema in the United States: Introduction to the Essays," in *The Mexican Cinema Project*, edited by Chon A. Noriega and Steven Ricci (Los Angeles, CA: UCLA Film and Television Archive, 1994), 3.

2. Joanne Hershfield and David R. Maciel, eds. *Mexico's Cinema: A Century of Film and Filmmakers* (Wilmington, DE: Scholarly Resources, 1999), xi.

3. Carl J. Mora, *Mexican Cinema: Reflections of a Society* (Berkeley: University of California Press, 1989), 2.

4. Gustavo A. García, "In Quest of a National Cinema: The Silent Era," in *Mexico's Cinema: A Century of Film and Filmmakers,* edited by Hershfield and Maciel, 7.

5. Statement is by Juan León, cited in Tuñón, "Mirada al vecino," 108–9.

6. Tuñón, "Mirada al vecino," 109.

7. The political concern over cinema fits within a broader narrative that casts cinema as distinct from other exports or commodities. Under the "cultural exception" argument, a motion picture is seen as a "powerful instrument and self-affirmation of the language and culture" (García Canclini, *Consumidores y Ciudadanos,* 118–19). This, in turn, justifies policies to limit the presence of foreign (U.S.) films and to encourage national production. France, Spain, and Italy are among the countries that still maintain quotas to limit U.S. movies. Understandably, given the market possibilities, the U.S. attacks such policies as anti-free trade. For more on this view, see McAnay and Wilkinson, eds. *Mass Media and Free Trade: NAFTA and the Cultural Industries.*

8. Moisés González Navarro, "Racism and *Mestizaje,*" in *Common Border, Uncommon Paths,* edited by Rodríguez and Vincent, 65.

9. Aurelio de los Reyes, "El gobierno mexicano y las películas denigrantes, 1920–1931," *México Estados Unidos: Encuentros y desencuentros en el cine,* edited by Ignacio Duran, Iván Trujillo, and Monica Verea (Mexico City: Imcine, 1996), 28.

10. de los Reyes, "Gobierno mexicano y las películas denigrantes," 25.

11. González Navarro, "Racism and *Mestizaje,*" 65.

12. de los Reyes, "Gobierno mexicano y las películas denigrantes," 26.

13. Charles Ramírez Berg, "The Cinematic Invention of Mexico: The Poetics and Politics of the Fernandez-Figueroa Style," in *Mexican Cinema Project,* edited by Noriega and Ricci, 13–24; Olga Nájera-Ramírez, "Engendering Nationalism: Identity, Discourse, and the Mexican *Charro,*" *Anthropological Quarterly* 67 (1) (1994): 7.

14. Paulo Antonio Paranaguá, "Ten Reasons to Love or Hate Mexican Cinema," in *Mexican Cinema* (London: British Film Institute, 1995), edited by Paulo Antonio Paranaguá, 9.

15. Charles Ramírez Berg, *Cinema of Solitude: A Critical Study of Mexican Film, 1967–1983* (Austin: University of Texas Press, 1992), 6.

16. Monsiváis, "Notas sobre la cultural mexicana."

17. Berg, *Cinema of Solitude,* 7.

18. Valenzuela, "Identidades culturales frente al TLC," 123.

19. Monsiváis, "Notas sobre la cultural mexicana," 1520.

20. Wilt, *Stereotype Images,* 120.

21. Wilt, *Stereotype Images,* 137.

22. Paranaguá, "Ten Reasons," 9.

23. Andres de Luna, "Labyrinths of History," in *Mexican Cinema,* edited by Paranaguá, 171–72.

24. Federico Dávalos Orozco, "The Birth of the Film Industry and the Emergence of Sound," in *Mexico's Cinema,* edited by Hershfield and Maciel, 32.

25. Berg, *Cinema of Solitude,* 15.

26. Berg, *Cinema of Solitude,* 22, 25.

27. Carlos Monsiváis, "Mythologies," in *Mexican Cinema*, edited by Paranaguá, 127. I am in no way suggesting that censorship was targeted solely or primarily at countering the U.S. The guiding principle of censorship has always been to protect and promote the interests of the state and the ruling party, the PRI. The government delayed the release date and withdrew public funds from the production of the 2000 hit *Ley de Herodes*, for instance, because of its direct political assault on the PRI. While at times protecting the political interests of the regime coincided with projecting a negative image of the U.S., that has not always been the case. Under the 1949 law, which warned that certain themes would not be permitted, the government considered films that "injure friendly nations" to be an "attack on the order and public peace" (Wilt, *Stereotype Images*, 290). Under this law, the government banned *Espaldas Mojadas* (1953) for a number of years because of its anti-U.S. sentiments.

28. Paranaguá, "Ten Reasons," 9.

29. Joanne Hershfield, "Race and Ethnicity in the Classical Cinema," in *Mexico's Cinema*, edited by Hershfield and Maciel, 81.

30. Hershfield, "Race and Ethnicity," 87.

31. Alex M. Saragoza and Graciela Berkovich, "Intimate Connections: Cinematic Allegories of Gender, the State and National Identity," in *The Mexican Cinema Project*, edited by Noriega and Ricci, 25.

32. Joy Elizabeth Hayes, "Early American Radio Broadcasting: Media Imperialism, State Paternalism, or Mexican Nationalism?" *Studies in Latin American Popular Culture* 12 (1993): 31–56. This was true in other media as well. In radio, for example, Hayes (32) highlights how through regulation the state created a nationalistic framework and "disseminated one possible version of a national culture . . . by giving the national language, music, and popular cultural forms a privileged position in both commercial and state broadcasts."

33. Monsiváis, "Mythologies," 117.

34. Paranaguá, "Ten Reasons," 8.

35. Noriega, "Mexican Cinema in the United States," 4. An argument can even be made that the appeal of the U.S. cinema may have even influenced in some minor way the course of the Revolution. According to de Luna, "Labyrinths of History" (173), Pancho Villa signed a contract with Mutual, a U.S. company, to film his battles. Historical rumor has it that Villa agreed to conduct his battles during certain periods of the day to ensure proper lighting.

36. Seth Fein, "From Collaboration to Containment: Hollywood and the International Political Economy of Mexican Cinema after the Second World War," in *Mexico's Cinema*, edited by Hershfield and Maciel, 123–64.

37. Fein, "From Collaboration to Containment," 128.

38. Fein, "From Collaboration to Containment."

39. Eduardo de la Vega Alfaro, "The Decline of the Golden Age and the Making of the Crisis," in *Mexico's Cinema*, edited by Hershfield and Maciel, 165.

40. Fein, "From Collaboration to Containment," 155.

41. Berg, *Cinema of Solitude*, 37.

42. Cited in Berg, *Cinema of Solitude*, 215.

43. Saragoza and Berkovich, "Intimate Connections," 25.

44. Wilt, *Stereotype Images*, 3.

45. George Gerbner, cited in Wilt, *Stereotype Images*, 7.
46. Cited in Mora, *Mexican Cinema*, 3.
47. Berg, *Cinema of Solitude*, 5.
48. Noriega, "Mexican Cinema in the United States," 1.
49. See, for example, Berg, *Cinema of Solitude;* Duran et al., eds., *México Estados Unidos;* Emilio García Riera, *Breve Historia del Cine Mexicano, Primer Siglo 1897–1997* (Mexico City: Instituto Mexicano de Cinematografía, 1998); Hershfield and Maciel, *Mexico's Cinema;* Monsiváis, "Notas sobre la cultural mexicana"; Mora, *Mexican Cinema;* Paranaguá, "Ten Reasons."
50. John Mraz, "Lo gringo en el cine mexicano y la ideologia alemanista," in *México Estados Unidos,* edited by Duran et al., 83–92; Ricardo Pérez Montfort, "En contrapunto de la imagen nacionalista. El estereotipo norteamericano en el cine de charros 1920–1946," in *México Estados Unidos,* edited by Duran et al., 93–103; Tuñón, "Mirada al vecino"; and David Maciel and Norma Iglesias, *El Norte: The US-Mexican Border in Contemporary Cinema* (San Diego: Institute for Regional Studies of the Californias, San Diego State University, 1990).
51. Wilt, *Stereotype Images.*
52. Tuñón, "Mirada al vecino," 110.
53. Perez Montfort, "En contrapunto de la imagen nacionalista," 98.
54. Wilt, *Stereotype Images*, 202.
55. Wilt, *Stereotype Images*, 207.
56. Wilt, *Stereotype Images*, 227.
57. All these examples come from Wilt, *Stereotype Images*, 203–20.
58. Wilt, *Stereotype Images*, 255.
59. Wilt, *Stereotype Images*, 269.
60. Wilt, *Stereotype Images*, 248, 257.
61. Cited in Mora, *Mexican Cinema*, 17–18.
62. Cited in Wilt, *Stereotype Images*, 299.
63. Wilt, *Stereotype Images*, 305.
64. Wilt, *Stereotype Images*, 308.
65. Wilt, *Stereotype Images*, 313–14.
66. Tuñón, "Mirada al vecino," 113.
67. Wilt, *Stereotype Images*, 325.
68. Wilt, *Stereotype Images*, 331.
69. Wilt, *Stereotype Images*, 339.
70. Wilt, *Stereotype Images*, 339, 374.
71. Wilt, *Stereotype Images*, 378–79.
72. Wilt, *Stereotype Images*, 375.
73. Tuñón, "Mirada al vecino," 111.
74. Mraz, "Gringo en el cine mexicano," 84.
75. Tuñón, "Mirada al vecino," 128.
76. Tuñón, "Mirada al vecino," 111.
77. Wilt, *Stereotype Images*, 228.
78. Wilt, *Stereotype Images*, 225–26.
79. Wilt, *Stereotype Images*, 282.
80. Cited in Mraz, "Gringo en el cine mexicano," 83.

81. Tuñón, "Mirada al vecino," 118.

82. Tuñón, "Mirada al vecino," 112–13.

83. Cited in Pérez Montfort, "En contrapunto de la imagen nacionalista," 98–99.

84. Tuñón, "Mirada al vecino," 122.

85. Rafael Hernández Rodríguez, "Melodrama and Social Comedy in Cinema of the Golden Age," in *Mexico's Cinema*, edited by Hershfield and Maciel, 115.

86. Wilt, *Stereotype Images*, 222.

87. Cited in Tuñón, "Mirada al vecino," 115.

88. Cited in Berg, *Cinema of Solitude*, 197.

89. Berg, *Cinema of Solitude*, 200.

90. Mraz, "Gringo en el cine mexicano," 86–87.

91. Wilt, *Stereotype*, 163.

92. Carlos Monsiváis, "Cantinflas and Tin Tán: Mexico's Greatest Comedians," in *Mexico's Cinema*, edited by Hershfield and Maciel, 70.

93. Mraz, "Gringo en el cine mexicano," 89.

94. Monsiváis, "Cantinflas and Tin Tán," 68–69.

95. Tuñón, "Una Mirada al vecino," 126.

96. Tuñón, "Una Mirada al vecino," 118.

97. Wilt, *Stereotype Images*, 227.

98. Cited in Hernández Rodríguez, "Melodrama and Social Comedy," 119–20.

99. Carlos Monsiváis, "All the People Came and Did Not Fit onto the Screen: Notes on the Cinema Audience in Mexico," in *Mexican Cinema*, edited by Paranaguá, 150.

100. Berg, *Cinema of Solitude*, 197.

101. Tuñón, "Mirada al vecino," 116.

102. Pérez Montfort, "En contrapunto de la imagen nacionalista," 103.

103. Tuñón, "Mirada al vecino," 121–22.

104. Tuñón, "Mirada al vecino," 114.

105. Monsiváis, "Cantinflas and Tin Tán," 70–71.

106. Mraz, "Gringo en el cine mexicano," 89.

107. Interestingly, despite the setting in northern Mexico, "the narrative overlooks (in both senses of the word) the forced annexation of what is now the Southwestern United States" (Victor Zamudio-Taylor and Imma Guiu, "Criss-Crossing Texts: Reading Images in *Like Water for Chocolate*," in *The Mexican Cinema Project*, edited by Noriega and Ricci, 51).

108. Wilt, *Stereotype Images*, 356.

109. Hershfield, "Race and Ethnicity in the Classical Cinema," 87.

110. Saragoza and Berkovich, "Intimate Connections," 27.

111. Berg, *Cinema of Solitude*, 217.

112. Berg, *Cinema of Solitude*, 212.

113. García Riera, *Breve Historia del Cine Mexicano*, 136.

114. Saragoza and Berkovich, "Intimate Connections," 27–28.

115. David R. Maciel, "El Imperio de la Fortuna: Mexico's Contemporary Cinema, 1985–1992," in *The Mexican Cinema Project*, edited by Noreiga and Ricci, 33.

116. Monsiváis, "Mythologies," 126–27.

117. This conclusion is based on a personal conversation with David Wilt years after his study.

118. Wilt, *Stereotype Images.*

119. García Riera, *Breve Historia del Cine Mexicano,* 129.

120. Wilt, *Stereotype Images,* 170, 263, 395, 326, 395, 383.

7

Gringolandia in the Consumer Market

M EXICANS' GREATEST CONTACT with the U.S. takes place through the
consumer market. Political cartoons displayed in chapter 4 mocked the
omnipresence of U.S. products and U.S. companies as an "invasion," undermining the nation's "independence." Indeed, perceptions of the U.S. as a
model of progress and modernity, as efficient and pragmatic, as individualistic and materialistic, and as a potential partner in development—important
themes discussed in earlier chapters—all coalesce on the consumer market.

Attention to the Mexican consumer is important for three reasons. First,
consumption is not a neutral act, but a social act with political meaning. As
Sut Jhally notes: "Goods always mean something within a social context
where different interests are being played out. . . . Consumers derive utility
from goods both from their embodied characteristics and from the 'environmental conditions' of their use."[1] Consumption, in short, is a "means by
which the values of a particular social class can be expressed."[2] Goods often
translate into values of prestige, reputation, and status, and are used in a
social way for "competitive display" or as sources of envy.[3] Consumption of
a product may indicate an acceptance of the cultural traditions attached to
the product's use. And a part of the "meaning of a product" (what Marx and
others often refer to as the fetishism of commodities) relates to who produces
and uses them.[4]

Second, consumption is important because as a social act it both reflects
and constructs personal identity. As Nestor García Canclini notes, "when we
select products and we appropriate them, we define what we publicly consider valuable, the ways in which we integrate and which distinguish us in
society, in which we combine the pragmatic and the enjoyable."[5] Indeed,
many of the questions asked by citizens today (What do I belong to? What

— 215 —

rights do I have? Who represents me? etc.) are answered by mass media and private consumption.[6]

Finally, consumption is important because more than any other realm examined thus far, it cuts to the heart of globalization and the issue of Americanization. Through the expansion of multinational corporations during the latter half of the twentieth century, with their capacity to homogenize and eliminate local competitors, integrate production, provide uniform goods, and engage in global marketing schemes, a truly global consumer market has begun to emerge, touching the lives of virtually every citizen. For many, this process has enhanced the ability of international actors to shape identity, thereby limiting the influence of the State and the idea of the nation in the process. "Identity," as García Canclini avers, "is now, for millions of people, an international co-production."[7] For Mexico, of course, international "actors" generally means the U.S., and the cultural impact is often seen in a nationalized context: "For the rulers of Latin America who concentrate commercial trade with the United States, globalization is almost synonymous with 'Americanization.'"[8]

Building on these essential points—that consumption is a major point of contact, and that it is rooted in and influences perceptions of the U.S. and the nation—this chapter explores consumption patterns, marketing and advertising studies, and a sample of ads to explore Mexican images of the U.S. and the nation. It builds on the assumption that information used to develop strategies to improve sales for a company provides insight into the Mexican consumer's perceptions of national and U.S. products. The discussion briefly reviews consumption patterns and then proceeds to explore studies of the Country-of-Origin (COO) effects in Mexico. Analysis then turns to advertising, closing with a focus on recent changes and the intense debate over the cultural and nationalist impact of the consumer patterns, preferences, and trends.

Consumption Patterns

A cursory review of consumption patterns in contemporary Mexico shows that the availability and consumption of U.S. products in Mexico are widespread, though the pattern varies by sector. As any trip to a suburban mall (a U.S. import itself) or major retail store (including Wal-Mart) or a surf through the TV channels or radio stations reveals, U.S. products are widely accessible to a large portion of the Mexican population. According to one report in the mid-1990s, Mexican consumers spend more per capita on U.S. products than do the Japanese or the Europeans.[9] Though the level of imports of consumer goods is relatively small—just 9% of total imports in 1999—many U.S. goods are produced in Mexico by U.S. subsidiaries or under U.S. license (including, since 1991, franchises), thus penetrating and dominating key sectors of the consumer market. And most U.S. products— from TV programs sold to the Mexican-owned stations to Wal-Mart, 7-Eleven, Coca-Cola, McDonald's, or Domino's Pizza—are easily identifiable as originating in the U.S. (and, as we will see, ads rarely try to hide the fact).

The cinematographic industry is one site where U.S. (Hollywood) products enjoy clear market dominance. In 1993, Mexico ranked tenth in imports of U.S. movies with an investment of US$37 million.[10] Data show 20th Century Fox with a 24% market share, followed by Columbia-TriStar with 20% and Buena Vista with 17%.[11] Not only do U.S. companies control distribution and theaters, but most movies shown in theaters are Hollywood productions. Indeed, attendance at U.S. movies far outpaces that at Mexican movies, which has forced a dramatic drop in the production of Mexican cinema. As García Canclini notes, Mexicans are going to the movies in droves, but not to see Mexican movies: "As the manifested preferences point out, it is evident that there is not a public for the national cinema."[12] U.S. companies and products also dominate the "private" exhibition of movies: the video market. In 1998, Mexico ranked ninth as an overseas market for U.S. rental distributors with 84 million rentals and US$69.8 million in sales of films, videos, and other recordings.[13] Almost 80% of videos that circulate in Mexico are of U.S. origin.[14] These items are available, of course, at the market leader, U.S.-owned Blockbuster, where, interestingly, I once found Mexican films classified under the section "*Peliculas Extranjeras.*" It is hardly surprising then that the top-grossing films in Mexico in the late 1990s were all high-profile Hollywood productions like *Titanic* and *Star Wars: Episode I.*[15]

Some U.S. mass consumer products rival Hollywood's dominance in Mexico. Coca-Cola, for example, enjoys about a 68% share of the US$5 billion soft-drink market in Mexico, with Pepsi controlling most of the balance.[16] It is commonly asserted that Mexicans are in fact among the world's heaviest and most loyal Coke drinkers, and that the product can be found in the most remote villages of the countryside. U.S. manufacturers also dominate in such realms as processed foods, particularly snack foods, cigarettes, and cosmetics, among other areas.[17]

But such U.S. market presence and dominance does not extend throughout the economy. Availability of U.S. programming on television, for example, is great, but not dominant. The U.S. is clearly the major source of foreign programming, representing 75% of imports, and in early 1994, two national networks devoted almost 100% of prime time to U.S. imports. U.S. market share is even higher in cable and satellite services: an area where foreign ownership is not restricted by law. In 1996, for example, U.S. satellite services controlled 76.8% of the import market. But availability is not the same as consumption or consumer preference. According to Enrique Sánchez-Ruíz, imports represent only 30% of the total quantity of Mexican TV programming.[18] And U.S. satellite services garner only an 8.6% market share and despite recent gains, only 30% of households have cable TV.[19] More significantly, studies by Sánchez-Ruíz and Henry González focusing on the border and the Mayan population both found a clear consumer preference for Mexican television programs.[20] González confirmed a preference for such national programs as the *telenovela*, while Sánchez-Ruíz cites ratings to show that the national networks featuring Mexican programming have consistently enjoyed higher ratings than those showing U.S. programs. Even on cable, he notes, Mexican MTV and channels with Mexican movies do better than U.S. programs. Indeed, MTV Latin America in Mexico, an adaptation of the U.S. genre, discovered early on that "U.S. acts alone just won't cut it in Mexico's burgeoning youth market. In contrast to their older brothers and sisters, Mexican teen-agers today want to see Mexican acts." The network thus presents 40% of its music videos in Spanish compared to 60% in English.[21]

A similar pattern featuring availability of U.S. products but limited market share can be found in such culturally important areas as music, radio stations, franchising, and newspapers and magazines. In the world of music recording in 1997, for instance, "local repertoire" represented 65% of sales, compared to 30% for "Anglo repertoire," with Mexico's Luís Miguel the best-selling artist of the year.[22] These figures reflect recent booms in *ranchera* and *norteño* music and the increasing popularity of rock in Spanish.[23] Such music preferences are also reflected in the radio industry. Studies by Sánchez-Ruíz and González cited earlier both found a clear preference for Mexican radio stations and Mexican music.[24] In the early 1990s, the highest-rated music stations, like GRC's XHFO-FM (Sonidoz) and Radiopros XEQ-FM (La Ke Bunema), both featured *ranchera* or *norteño* music. Other major stations, like XHRCA-FM (Alfa 91.3), the top station in Mexico City, played 60% Eurodance, 30% U.S. pop, and 10% Spanish. XEDA-FM (Pulsar FM) plays mainly music in Spanish, and XHOF-FM (Orbita 195.7) plays 60% rock in Spanish and just 40% in English.[25] This is not to deny the presence or even popularity of U.S. music in Mexico, but merely to demonstrate its lack of solid market dominance. Indeed, the works of such artists as Michael Jackson, Madonna, Elton John, and U2, among others, have sold particularly well in Mexico; huge crowds have attended concerts by the Rolling Stones, Pink Floyd, Madonna, and others; and some radio stations, like Rock 101, feature music almost exclusively in English.[26]

U.S. franchises in Mexico have also grown rapidly in recent years due to the 1991 change in the Law on Technology Transfer. Today, many U.S. franchises dot the Mexican urban landscape. By the late 1990s, according to one report, Mexico had the ninth-largest franchise industry in the world, and it was the largest market for U.S. franchises.[27] U.S. franchises have become particularly dominant within the fast food sector, as might be expected. Though one report claims McDonald's, the largest U.S. franchise in Mexico with 126 stores, captures 39% of all franchise income, another report shows the Golden Arches with just a 24% share of the fast food market, compared to KFC with a 26% share and Domino's with a 22% share, with the three respectively dominating the chicken (37% market share), burger (32% market share), and pizza markets (29% market share).[28] And yet, of the 400 master franchises in Mexico, 60% are of Mexican, not U.S., origin. U.S. companies alone enjoy just 34% of the entire franchise market and 6% of the retail and restaurant sector.[29] Though many Mexicans are familiar with Big Macs and Domino's Pizza—the latter being sold at Mexican sporting events, including bullfights—with a 6% market share it is hard to see how these have replaced national products, as some have perhaps alarmingly claimed. After all, according to estimates by the government, there are about 180,000 taco stands in the country compared to just 235 McDonald's in the late 1990s.[30] Moreover, the success of, say, McDonald's hides the financial difficulties faced by other U.S. fast food chains in the country in recent years, including Arby's, Carl's Jr., Taco Bell, and Wendy's, which have lost money or pulled out entirely from the Mexican market.[31]

This mixed pattern regarding U.S. market penetration is also apparent in the area of newspapers and magazines. Due to legal restrictions, U.S. news companies cannot own newspapers. And though available—usually at a steep markup—U.S. newspapers like *USA Today*, the *Wall Street Journal*, and the *New York Times* have very limited circulations, usually only in Mexico City and among the elite. These periodicals, of course, can be picked up now off the Internet at a much lower cost, but their influence is still considered minimal except, again, in "official" channels. Thus Mexican-owned newspapers and news magazines, like *Proceso* and *Milenio*, clearly dominate the market, and though many of their stories may come from U.S. wire services, the emphasis remains on local and national news as presented and interpreted by Mexican journalists and editors. In magazines, of the top 10 magazines in terms of circulation in 1995, only two were clearly from the U.S.: *Reader's Digest* and *Playboy*. And *Readers Digest*, the leading magazine in 1995 with a circulation of 663,800, is not a mere translation, but a special Mexican edition.[32]

While cursory, such data nonetheless provide some insight into consumer preferences and perhaps a sense of the potential cultural influence of the U.S.

over Mexico. As shown above, while U.S. products dominate in certain markets that may be important culturally or economically, like cinema, their reign is not uniform throughout, and in many areas, despite availability, a clear consumer preference remains for Mexican as opposed to U.S. products. Marketing studies on Country-of-Origin (COO) effects, which delve further into consumer preferences and link these to perceptions of nation and others, support a somewhat similar conclusion.

Marketing Studies

It has long been accepted in the field of marketing that perceptions of the nation and of others influence consumers' views regarding specific products and their buying behavior. Research into Country-of-Origin effects (COO) is extensive.[33] While there is considerable debate over the meaning, the nature, and the role of COO effects as well as how marketers can utilize the information,[34] many, including Curtis Reierson, and Martin Roth and Jean Romeo, see COO effects as a manifestation of national stereotypes.[35] Perceptions of other countries, in short, influence more specific views regarding the products produced in those countries. In one study on Guatemala, Costa Rica, and El Salvador, for example, Robert Schooler linked negative product evaluations with negative attitudes toward the people from the countries where they were manufactured.[36] In addition to tapping views of others, COO effects also entail perceptions of the nation, specifically in terms of preferences for products made at home. According to one study, "one unique cue affecting prepurchase intentions may be nationalistic feelings which, as we have seen, may dominate other perceptions based on country of origin."[37] Studies conducted in the U.S., for example, have shown a preference for home country products, which is associated with nationalistic attitudes.[38]

On a broad level, COO studies show a variety of factors shaping perceptions of foreign products. First, there seems to be a generalized prejudice against products from developing countries.[39] In fact, COO effects are frequently explained in terms of the perceived level of economic development of the sourcing country.[40] This extends to people in developing countries as well, who tend to harbor a negative image of the workmanship, reliability, durability, and technical qualities of their own country's products.[41] Brenda Richey et al. explain this in terms of the perceived risks involved in buying such products.[42]

In addition to the impact of level of development, other studies have linked a positive evaluation of foreign products to age and education, both in a positive direction.[43] W. T. Anderson and William Cunningham even found an inverse linkage between preference for foreign goods and dogmatism.[44] Other studies, however, tend to draw distinctions across product lines rather than generalize across the board. Roth and Romeo, for instance, differentiate at both the country and product level, stressing the idea of product-country match: "If a country is perceived as having a positive image, and this image is important to a product category, the consumer will be more willing to buy the product from that country."[45] Most marketing-related studies involving Mexico tend to focus on U.S. consumer attitudes toward Mexican products or the Mexican-American and Hispanic consumers in the U.S.[46] Little research has been done on Mexican consumer behavior *per se.* Those studies that exist explore differences between the U.S. and Mexican markets in terms of attitudes, preferences, and tastes,[47] compulsive buying habits,[48] and the relative importance of country of design, country of production, and country of assembly in shaping consumer preferences.[49]

Still, evidence from the few marketing studies on Mexico shows, first, that consumption in Mexico is seen, as it is in the U.S., as a means of acquiring social status. According to James Roberts and Carlos Martinez, Roberts and Cesar Sepulveda, and Tim Triplett, there is a strong desire among Mexicans to join the ranks of the consumer culture.[50] According to Triplett, Mexicans, like those in the U.S., "attempt to signal their comparative degree of social power through consumption . . . [that] power is best demonstrated by one's material wealth."[51] Roberts and Martinez echo this finding, noting that young adult Mexicans in particular tend to associate social status with buying, and seek to acquire status through purchasing.[52]

In addition to evidence of an emerging consumer culture in Mexico perhaps mimicking that of the U.S., research points to a tendency for Mexicans to see U.S. products as superior to Mexican products, though the findings vary somewhat across the board. One of the earlier studies in the area looked at perceptions of the quality of a VCR, a TV, and a stereo made in Japan, Mexico, and the U.S. among a sample of respondents in Monterrey. The study found a clear perception of the U.S. product as being superior to the Mexican-made product: "Mexican consumers perceive household electronic products made in the United States to be more innovative, of higher quality, better than Mexican products, and are 'liked' better."[53] Consistent with this view, the study also found that "a person who buys a Mexican product is perceived as being less knowledgeable than a consumer purchasing an American product." Such a consumer is also perceived of as "being less satisfied with the product, less interested in quality," and yet as being more concerned about the domestic economy. The respondents, moreover, tend to see American products as "upper class"; and yet "owners of U.S.A-made products were less 'proud to show' them than non-owners." The authors conclude by highlighting the perception of superior quality of U.S. and Japanese products and suggesting that this holds "not only for variables that describe the quality of products (i.e., innovative, cheap), but for social-normative (e.g., proud to own) and affective influences (don't like) as well." Thus social pressure to consume foreign-made products, they conclude, is evident.[54]

Other studies have arrived at a similar conclusion: that Mexicans tend to perceive U.S. products as superior to national ones, and hence to prefer U.S. products. Richey et. al. looked at preferences among a sample of shoppers in malls in Mexico (Mexico City), Venezuela, and the U.S. for athletic shoes, garment bags, water heaters, and stoves produced in ten different countries. They found that in all areas, the Mexican respondents valued the products made in Mexico less than those manufactured in the U.S.[55] In a similar study that differentiated among products and perceptions regarding production and marketing strengths and weaknesses, Roth and Romeo found Mexicans to rank U.S. products higher than Mexican products in terms of quality (the U.S. averaged 5.965, behind Japan and Germany, and Mexico averaged 3.930, only above Hungary).[56] Similarly, in a survey asking respondents to rank the manufacturing and design quality of products from different countries (Germany, Japan, U.S., Mexico, Brazil, Thailand, and Chile), Gary Insch and J. Brad McBride found the Mexican sample consistently ranking the U.S. products higher (in the order listed above) than the Mexican products.[57]

Paul Herbig and Alain Genestre give some nuance to these views. They explore the quality of services associated with U.S. products, rather than the products *per se*. This encompasses issues of reliability, trust, and confidence in the employees providing the service, the physical facilities and equipment, the empathy provided to customers, and company responsiveness. Surveying businesses in interior and border cities in both countries rather than consumers, they found that the perceptions related not so much to U.S. products as to service quality: U.S. products, in other words, are perceived to be superior because of the perception of superior services.[58]

But despite such findings, these and other studies also show either no clear pattern or a more complex and muddled picture. William Bailey and Sheila Gutierrez de Pineres interviewed upper- and middle-income housewives in Monterrey and Guadalajara using a survey instrument developed to study American consumer ethnocentrism called the CETSCALE.[59] But rather than uncovering any clear and strong preference for U.S. or national products, they found that "respondents as a group were rather neutral about imported products," falling in the middle between preference for foreign and for national goods. The Roth and Romeo study just noted, though finding that the ranking for U.S. products was higher on average, also discovered that this was not true for all product lines. Mexican respondents (a sample of graduate students in their study) ranked the U.S. higher for autos, bicycles, and watches, but Mexico higher for shoes, crystal, and beer.[60] Insch and McBride make a similar discovery. Disaggregating the COO variable into country-of-design (COD), country-of-production (COP), and country-of-assembly (COA), they showed a sample of Mexican and U.S. students a series of ads for a TV, a bike, and tennis shoes while altering the information on COD, COP, and COA (Japan, U.S., and Mexico). They found that among the Mexican group COD affects perception of quality of shoes, but not the other two products; COA influences perceptions of the quality of the shoes and the bike, but not the TV; and knowledge of COP had no effect on perceptions of quality.[61]

One study looking at COO effects in Mexico tested Mexican preference for U.S. versus Mexican goods among consumers in Chihuahua.[62] The researchers conducted a series of taste tests of U.S.- and Mexican-made salsa and chips, altering the "Made in" labels. They also conducted a survey among the participants in the taste tests. Results from the two approaches differed. On the one hand, the taste tests found limited support for the notion of any preference based on COO. And of the six questions related to the tested products, COO bias was found in only two cases (*chile* salsa flavor and willingness-to-buy with preference for the "made in Mexico"). Contrary to the preference for U.S. products noted earlier, the authors conclude that *malinchismo* (the preference for foreign goods) "does not appear to significantly influence their preferences for the two food products examined."[63] And yet, the survey questions told a bit of a different story. Here, respondents indicated a degree of pride and interest in purchasing Mexican food products: a position, they contend, that may have been based on the notion that Mexican food products are less expensive, less contaminated with pesticides, and more nutritious than U.S. products. And yet at the same time, a majority felt that U.S. products are of better quality, have more attractive packaging, are cleaner, and are produced in cleaner plants, and two-thirds of the respondents said U.S. food products are more popular among their peers. As a result, the researchers aver that a combination of factors is at work: "Consumer responses to attitudinal questions identified both *malinchimo* and rather patriotic attitudes."

Moving beyond general statements regarding the population, it is possible to focus even closer on key socioeconomic and demographic differences in the area of consumption and COO effects. Despite differences overall, there seems to be a clear consensus in the literature associating preference for and perceptions of the superiority of U.S. products mainly with middle- and upper-income groups and the young. Raúl Cremoux found that junior high students in Mexico City preferred U.S. TV programs, that those in the upper-income groups were much more likely to listen to U.S. music or view U.S. movies at home or in the theater, and that lower-class students were more likely to prefer Mexican films.[64] David Maciel echoes the latter point, noting how during recent years only the lower classes (popular class) continued to attend Mexican cinema.[65] García-Calderon similarly argues that cable TV, enjoyed primarily by upper- and middle-class consumers, "promotes a cultural colonization which affects the middle and upper socio-economic sectors . . . that Cable TV has become a cultural dependency factor."[66] Nolan also sees preference for U.S. products as basically a middle-class phenomenon.[67]

The empirical COO studies provide some support for these class-based tendencies. Eugene Jaffe and Carlos Martinez, for example, found the lower-income group with a more favorable evaluation of Mexican-made products compared to the higher-income group, which tended to prefer U.S. and Japanese products.[68] Bailey and Gutierrez de Pineres also unearthed a tendency for respondents with a technical education, from the higher-income group, and within the ages of 31–35 to have the strongest preference for foreign goods (*malinchismo*), while those with only a primary education scored the lowest on the CETSCALE.[69] This fits well the finding noted earlier that Mexicans tend to see American products as "upper class."[70]

In summation, the findings from research on the COO effects in Mexico are generally consistent with other COO studies. The tendency for Mexicans to rank U.S. products superior to Mexican products echoes the findings linking consumer perceptions to level of development. Like others, Mexicans tend to perceive products and services from the more developed countries, including the U.S., as superior to and of higher quality than those from lesser-developed countries, including their own. This notion, of course, fits well within the tendency noted in chapter 5 to associate modernity, fashion, and technical progress with the U.S. Second, the studies also point to a more complex differentiation of perceptions regarding products, as shown by Roth and Romeo cross-nationally.[71] In other words, at a more discerning product-specific level, Mexicans prefer some U.S. products, but not all. Looking at the different preferences themselves, Mexicans seem generally to prefer U.S. products that are "higher-tech" and less "cultural," like TV sets as opposed to TV programming, formats like MTV, but with Mexican music, or bikes as opposed to something as traditional as salsa (cinema stands in some contrast to this pattern, though its high-tech features are appealing and movies with strong "special effects" content seem to do particularly well in Mexico). As with the consumption patterns profiled earlier, a mixed pattern emerges with regard to consumer preferences, combining, as one analyst put it, aspects of *malinchismo* with a strong sense of Mexican nationalism.

The findings linking class and age to perceptions of U.S. and national products also concur with the broader literature, though with some minor exceptions. As in Mexico, the general literature on consumer behavior has consistently found upper-income groups to favor foreign products and for lower classes to show a preference for the national brand.[72] Generally, this is consistent with the view that tends to associate a preference for U.S. things (*malinchismo*) with class standing. Both Carlos Fuentes and Carlos Monsiváis, as noted in chapter 5, note how the middle and upper classes are most likely to embrace and imitate U.S. culture. Fuentes, for example, sees the Mexican middle class as seeking to duplicate the U.S.'s *pepsicoatl* culture.[73] Monsiváis, meanwhile, notes how the middle or upper middle classes have produced a "progressive weakening of cultural nationalism."[74] He contends further that these groups have deserted "the practice of 'Mexicanness,'"[75] and that because of their preference for U.S. cable, they have come to see the U.S. as the new "City of God."[76] Indeed, the Jaffe and Martinez marketing study showed those preferring Mexican products—the lower classes—to be more concerned about the national economy; and yet, at the same time, they were perceived by others as being less knowledgeable.[77] This class division may reflect the fact that advertisers of U.S. products tend to target the upper- and middle-income groups: those with the purchasing power needed to participate in the global market.

The finding linking the Mexican youth with a preference for U.S. products, however, contrasts with the findings in the general COO literature. As noted above, Schooler and R. C. Tongberg both found older, not younger, persons to evaluate foreign products higher, though Chih-Kang Wang failed to confirm this finding in a cross-national study.[78] Nevertheless, the finding concurs with the view expressed by Monsiváis, who associates the weakening of traditional Mexican culture with the Mexican youth. Though they remain "closet Mexicans," he claims, the young see the nation's traditions as inefficient and Americanization as the key to an international mentality.[79]

Finally, the class and age differences seem to fit within general perceptions of globalization as affecting groups differently and thus producing different outcomes: that globalization excludes some and includes others.[80] This thesis echoes the views expressed by Cuauhtémoc Cárdenas in chapter 2 and Jorge Castañeda in chapter 5. Generally, the included are those with the purchasing power needed to participate in the global consumer society and/or the youth who easily learn and adapt to the new technologies supporting globalization. As García Canclini notes, "Globalization does not just homogenize and bring us closer together, but it multiples the differences and generates new inequalities."[81] Subsequent focus on public opinion allows further exploration of these differential images of the U.S.

Advertising

Central to the recognition of the symbolic meaning attached to consumption is advertising. While some tout advertising as being able to shape consumer values, others like Jhally hold that advertisers simply draw on "shared experiences, perceptions and attitudes of the segmented audience."[82] Like political cartoons, for an ad to create the desired effect, "it has to resonate with information the listener possesses."[83] As representations and abstractions of what they 'reflect,' "advertising absorbs and fuses a variety of symbolic practices and discourses."[84] Gary Gregory and James Munch illustrate the importance of this point in their study of family roles and norms in Mexican culture. They show that "attitudes and behavior toward ads are functions of the degree of consistency of cultural norms and roles depicted within the advertisements."[85]

At a broad level, ads sell not only products, but also a "way of life": a culture of consumerism. And as noted earlier, Mexicans clearly exhibit aspects of a consumer culture similar to that in the U.S., including a desire to use purchases of material goods to signal social status. Steven Bunker sees this tendency as dating back to the *Porfiriato*.[86] During this time, Bunker notes, U.S. products dominated the market, influenced consumer tastes, and "projected a vision of domesticity manufactured and sold in the United States, images that found enthusiastic acceptance among many northern Mexican consumers." Advertising, moreover, underscored consumerism as "part of the package that would help readers to succeed in love, business, and family life" (as a key to personal fulfillment).[87] Encouraged by Díaz's successors and couched within what Alan Knight calls a "developmentalist ideology," consumerism, promoted through advertising, became and remains a major vehicle that links the U.S. to ideas of material progress, modernity, and well-being. Historically, the U.S. has long cast itself and been perceived by the Mexican consumer as the creator of fashion and the definer of the "good life," thereby making imitation of the U.S. consumer a means to achieve the "good life" and erase the gap that "unjustly," in the eyes of the Mexicans, separates them from the *gringos*. Consumption of the latest fad, defined in the U.S., is thus seen as an embrace of modernity and all that it represents, despite competing views of the U.S. as anti-Mexican, devoid of family values, and lacking in culture. Yet underlying these images is the notion that the U.S. already enjoys that which the Mexican desires: the personal fulfillment promised by consumerism.

While generally ads sell modernity and progress, how do they deal specifically with these and nationalistic symbols? Given the general Mexican preference for U.S. products, particularly among the middle and upper classes,

Amit Ghosh suggests that companies emphasize country of origin, among other features, particularly to help reduce price sensitivity since U.S. products are generally more expensive.[88] Ads for U.S. products in Mexico do this in a certain way. They rarely make any attempt to fully hide their origins, though by the same token they rarely use any outward displays of the U.S. as a country, and often incorporate a Mexican theme to strike a sort of balance. On the one hand, Anglo brand names and models that "could be" from the U.S. tend to prevail in ads. This means that many people frequent Dairy Queen, Kentucky Fried Chicken, Pizza Hut, or Blockbuster conceivably without knowing exactly what those words mean. Product labels—though by law the important information must be in Spanish—continue to display English words in large print. A review of ads in a sample of two Mexican "women's" magazines indeed shows a range of products sporting English words: easy markers of the U.S. Examples in the first pages of an issue of the popular magazine *Vanidades de Mexico* include Clairol's *Daily Defense*, Calvin Klein's *Eternity for Men*, Cover Girl's *Super Thick Lash,* and Elizabeth Arden's *Matte Moisture Lotion: Visible Difference.*[89] In one issue of *Cosmopolitan de México,* one finds L'Oréal's *Kids* (shampoo), Ralph Lauren's *Polo Sport,* or Calvin Klein's *eyewear.*[90] Even feminine napkins in the drugstore carry the label *Feminine Hygiene* in English.

The sample of ads from both magazines also shows models with lighter skin tones and eye colors than most Mexicans. Of the 55 color ads in the issue of *Cosmopolitan* featuring female models, none of the young women could be considered *morena,* 28 had dark brown or black hair (thus arguably Mexican), 17 had brown or red hair (thus not clearly *gringa*), and only 10 had blond hair (thus clearly *gringa* or European, and not Mexican). Yet in the 39 cases where eye color could be detected, 26 had light eyes (thus probably not Mexican) compared to 13 with dark eyes (thus arguably Mexican).

Advertisements for *Mexican* products also bow to these popular perceptions and preferences at times. Rather than stressing their national origins, they often attempt to demonstrate quality by displaying the product's acceptance by U.S. consumers, thereby privileging U.S. preferences over Mexican preferences. Given the nature of the U.S. market, and the perception of quality of U.S. products, U.S. validation of value is considered important to the Mexican consumer. An old (1960s) TV ad for the Mexican cigarette *Delicados* provides a good example. It featured a *gringo* enjoying a smoke of the Mexican product, and offering his approval in bad Spanish: "Oh, Mexicanos, *Ovalados. Mucho bueno sabor.*" A popular Corona beer ad today provides a similar message. Though showing beautiful scenes of the Mexican landscape to draw the association of the value of the nation and the national product (beer), the voice-over touts the brand's exports to the U.S. as proof of the product's quality: "*de mayor ventas en los Estados Unidos.*" An ad for the Mexican beer *Superior* goes even further, perhaps, in playing on the perceptions of the public. As plastered on billboards throughout the country, it features a young, blond female in a swimsuit (clearly foreign and presumably *gringa*). The ad prompts consumers to draw the link between the quality of the beer, its title (*Superior*), and their previously existing cultural notion of the "quality" and perhaps the "looseness" of the blond female. The point is driven home by the fantasy-triggering caption: "*La rubia que todos quieren*" [the blond that everyone wants].

Yet, on the other hand, many ads for U.S. products try to embrace Mexico and use Mexican markers to help balance their "foreign" status. While they never totally disguise their origins, they do try to at least Mexicanize their product and approach. Julio Moreno, for instance, highlights the successful advertising strategy of Sears when it opened in Mexico back in 1947.[91] Bowing to Mexico's "anti-American nationalism," he contends, the ad illustrated the "American quality" of its merchandise, but presented Sears as a Mexican company. Also contrary to the pattern mentioned earlier, a focus-group study by Linda Ueltschy and John Ryans found a preference in Mexico for ads that are customized (in Mexican Spanish rather than English or neutral Spanish and with a Mexican setting).[92] It seems that many advertisers have taken this advice, at least in part. Coke, Pepsi, and McDonald's, for example, all run ads playing on the importance of the Mexican family or the love of soccer, or feature Mexican youth drinking their product in front of clearly identifiable Mexican urban locations. According to Ian M. Reider, president of Gallup Mexico, U.S. companies particularly increased their emphasis on Mexico during the economic crisis. His conclusion and advice: "Now it's smart to show you're with the people. In this context, Wal-Mart stores and Sam's began to advertise their products as 'proudly Mexican.'"[93] This may reflect the increasing reliance on domestic suppliers for a retailer like Wal-Mart, a tendency toward more nationalistic behavior during times of crisis, or the notion that under economic constraints, consumers will prefer national products because they are considered cheaper.

Recent Changes

Change, continuity, and historic patterns in the consumer market are not easy to discern, particularly since there are few historical COO marketing studies on Mexico. Popular wisdom and some evidence suggest an increasing presence and acceptance of U.S. products in the country. The percent of Mexican households with satellite and cable services, which tend to offer more U.S. programs than normal TV, for example, increased dramatically from 17.5% in 1990 to 30.7% in 2000.[94] U.S. satellite services alone grew from US$8.6 million in 1994 to US$99.9 million by 1996.[95] U.S. franchises have also grown tremendously in recent years, from virtually none in the 1980s to over 400 by the late 1990s. Though some pulled out as noted earlier, the overall pattern is strong and will probably continue. This means, as Ignacio Vazquez contends, that "Mexicans still eat tacos, but not quite as many now, mainly because of their ability to choose pizza from Domino's and Pizza Hut, hamburgers from Carl's Jr, McDonalds, Jack in the Box, and sandwiches from Subway. . . . One thing helping them is all the TV shows and movies that the U.S. has exported, which picture an American way of life that some consumers want."[96] In like manner, Circle Ks and 7-Elevens have sprung up on many street corners, often teaming up with PEMEX to convert the Mexican "service" station into something akin to the U.S. model. Their presence will surely alter the pattern of small neighborhood *tiendas* in the urban areas, though the Mexican franchise OXXO has become the market leader. Retailers like Wal-Mart—its largest store is in Mexico City—have also entered and rapidly gobbled up market share. Such trends suggest, in sum, that U.S. products and companies are more widely available and that Mexicans' acceptance of these products is greater than at any time in the past. Indeed, in commenting on the opening of Sears in 1947, Moreno notes that the favorable reaction by the public would have been impossible just a decade earlier due to anti-American sentiment.[97]

But while these tendencies suggest that the penetration of some U.S. products and their acceptance in the consumer market may have increased in recent years, this may not be true in other areas. It seems likely in some cases that the level of penetration remains relatively unchanged or even lower today than in the past (a point shown in chapter 1). Bunker, as noted, points to the dominance of U.S. consumer products as far back as the *Porfiriato*, suggesting that the current consumer culture and pattern are not all that new.[98] A generalized preference for U.S. motion pictures also spans the years, and the pattern is not linear. Berg dates the popular preference for U.S. movies to the late 1910s,[99] while Mora refers to how the "popularity of Hollywood films" undercut Mexican films as early as 1925.[100] Indeed, in 1930, 80.4% of the films exhibited in Mexico City were from the U.S. compared to just 1.6% from Mexico.[101] Though to a lesser degree, U.S. movies still dominated the market even during the war years and Mexico's Golden Age of cinema. From 1941 to 1945, 75% of the movies shown in Mexico City were U.S. productions, compared to just 13.5% from Mexico. Nonetheless, this figure of U.S. preference is higher than comparable figures during the 1950s (from 1953 to 1958, 58% U.S., 21% Mexican)[102] and even the 1980s (in 1983, 42.8% U.S.,

16.8% Mexican).[103] And though the mid-1980s brought record low box office revenues for Mexican movies and a brutal decline in production, some see the industry as rebounding in subsequent years.[104] In fact, under Salinas, a shift in policies fathered the emergence of a new generation of filmmakers and "provided the material and political conditions for a boom in Mexican film."[105] Daniel Moore echoes this point, noting how "Like Water for Chocolate," which earned US$20 million, triggered what many consider a revival in Mexican films comparable to the Golden Age.[106]

A similar nonlinear pattern may exist in the field of music. Rather than blanket coverage and broad acceptance of U.S. music to the detriment of the local culture, U.S. music may have been more popular in the past than it is today. Indeed some feel that Mexican music is witnessing a revival. According to Rita Herring of MTV Networks Latin America, Mexican teenagers today want to see Mexican acts "in contrast to their older brothers and sisters."[107] During the 1950s and 1960s, the Mexican youth listened often to Mexican bands sing U.S. (or British) songs in Spanish. Groups like *Los Hooligans, Los Teen Tops, Los Locos del Ritmo, Los Beltmonts,* and *Los Rebeldes del Rock,* and soloists like Cesar Costa, Enrique Guzmán, Julissa, Johnny Laboriel, Angelica Maria, Manolo Muñoz, and Alberto Vazquez all made their careers as types of mediums for U.S. (and British) music.[108] By contrast, Mexican artists today have nationalized U.S. genres or created unique Mexican pop music, capturing a large share of the domestic market. At the same time, these artists have begun to penetrate the U.S. and the global markets.

It remains unclear then whether U.S. products today are more dominant or more preferred by Mexicans than in the past. While preference or dominance may be true in certain product lines, that is not true in all areas, particularly when cultural tastes are involved. And it is important to bear in mind that neither availability nor market share is the same as preference. Still, one change in the consumer market is clear: the agents shaping identity. As García Canclini contends, identity is now shaped less by the state, nationalism, and national culture and more by consumption and the agents shaping consumption.[109] Indeed, policy changes since the mid-1980s in Mexico have greatly facilitated this. Consistent within the narrative offered by Carlos Salinas as discussed in chapter 2, the presence of U.S. products in Mexico and the subordination of culture to for-profit businesses are no longer considered a threat to the nation.[110] In a sense, as Javier Esteniou Madrid contends, the government abandoned its role in shaping national culture: "The government itself authorized that our cultural project be lost."[111] This suggests then a delinkage of the State from "national culture," molded more by the interplay of national and international market forces than politics. This tendency for a reduction in the role of national culture to shape identity also seems to be occurring outside of Mexico as well. Or as Ignacio Galceran and Jon Berry note, "In the 1990s, the Monroe Doctrine has been replaced by Wal-Mart, the Internet and MTV."[112]

Impact and Significance

Consumption of U.S. products, exposure to ads, preference for certain categories of U.S. products, and their trends may be one thing; but their significance and their impact are clearly another. To what extent does the diffusion of U.S. movies, programs, or products undermine national culture or feed that perception? Does eating at McDonald's or watching the Super Bowl make a Mexican any less Mexican in his or her own eyes or those of others? Or does the process create a growing divide within the once (more) homogenous culture, perhaps overlapping class divisions? The issue of such an impact is debatable from many angles, ranging from assimilation or how the messages are received[113] to the ramifications. And it is critical in terms of projecting the future of Mexican nationalism and perceptions of the U.S.

While attention to how the Mexican public views these patterns and tendencies awaits the subsequent chapter on public opinion, it is possible here to set out three distinct yet contested narratives regarding the impact of growing consumerism and U.S. products in Mexico. I label these the restricted (denationalistic), the unrestricted (nationalistic), and the globalist (postnationlist) perspectives. Certain aspects of this debate have already been highlighted in the analyses of the political and intellectual discourses in chapters 2 and 5.

The restricted (denationalistic) view holds that exposure to U.S. products, even cultural products, has limited effects on other areas of the culture and is therefore not to be considered a threat to Mexican nationalism or a cause to which the State, through policy, should respond. This perspective posits, for example, that eating at McDonald's occasionally does not make the Mexican any less Mexican. As Castañeda notes, Mexicans "do not see their nationalism endangered by the food they eat, the clothes they wear, or where they keep their money. . . . Their penchant for American lifestyles and products should not be mistaken for an ebbing of traditional suspicion and hostility toward the United States."[114] Indeed, mere exposure to U.S. products does not mean automatic acceptance of everything *gringo*. Providing some empirical support for this view, Jose Lozano found no significant differences in frequency of exposure to U.S. television programs between students who said they would want to be Mexican citizens if they were to be born again and those who would prefer to return as U.S. citizens. Those who said they would prefer to be U.S. citizens listened to U.S. music more, but he contends that the exposure related more to knowledge of English, such that the more English they knew the more they chose U.S. films and music.[115] In their study of Quebec, André Caron and Pierre Bélanger present a similar conclusion: "Getting to know more about the ways of life, values and norms of others through imported cultural artifacts does not correlate with an increased, unconditional admiration of these artifacts in detriment of one's own culture."[116] This view also echoes strongly within the official discourse. According to this view, as expressed by Jaime Serra Puche in August 1992, NAFTA leaves Mexicans "untouched" in culture: "We will not become North Americans: McDonald's and Domino's Pizza are here and for that we will not stop being Mexicans, and what is to be done is to strengthen our culture, cling to it so that it will survive."[117]

The unrestricted (nationalistic) view, by contrast, tends to conflate consumption of products with consumption of culture and to posit a zero-sum game in which the acceptance of the U.S. culture means the decline of Mexican national culture. Vázquez argues, for example, that when Mexicans buy imported food, "they are not only buying food, but cultural traditions as well."[118] Roberts and Martinez make a similar point: "The increasing presence of American companies, products, and culture in Mexico will undoubtedly affect the shopping behavior and attitudes of Mexicans."[119] Fernando Ortega Pizarro also refers to the fear of some that "with the franchises foreign traditions and customs are being imported."[120] Patrick Oster notes the impact of U.S. consumer culture on women in the country: "In real life in Mexico, it's great for Mexican women to look like an American. People who do look that way consider themselves lucky. . . . Companies that advertise . . . . a host of . . . products use blond models exclusively, as if the viewing public were all Scandinavians."[121]

This unrestricted (nationalistic) argument is most often heard in relation to cultural products. Alberto Montoya and María-Antonieta Rebeil, for example, hold that "commercial television has become in Mexico a vehicle for the transmission of North American culture, constantly eroding national identity and local cultures.[122] García-Calderon, as noted above, similarly argues that cable TV "promotes a cultural colonization," particularly among the middle and upper socioeconomic sectors.[123] García Canclini also highlights the view that the transformation of cinema, TV, and video in Mexico and beyond is restructuring cultural practices and preferences[124] and that a Hollywood movie or even a car does not just express U.S. culture, but is converted into a symbol of an imagined supranationalism.[125] Cinema may even affect people's basic perception of reality. As Deborah Holtz notes, "The videophiles relate with movies thinking that 'reality is somewhere else.'"[126]

Esteniou Madrid provides perhaps the best example of this unrestricted position. He accuses the electronic media of instilling a culture of consumption, an admiration for *"lo norteamericano"* and "the aspiration of the 'American dream' that seeks to achieve happiness by reaching an increasing economic level."[127] These are not just U.S. television programs, he argues, but also the national media, which imitate their U.S. counterparts. According to this view, the ramifications of this process are stunning: a "weakening of national identity," and the construction of a nation contrary to "the spirit of *nuestros raíces*": "Today we admire the status of North American life more than the national, the 'western truth' more than the contributions of the noble knowledge of the indigenous, the white over the bronze of our race, the stature of the conquerors over our smaller physical dimension, the Anglo-Saxon code over the rich universe of *náhuatl,* the dollar over the Mexican peso, our lustful dream is with the blond, light-skinned women rather than the dark-skinned."[128] This assimilation makes Mexicans believe that sexual satisfaction comes from the hunt for the blond and that personal success hinges on learning English and becoming more *gringo.*[129] "In less than a generation the roots of the North American transnational have been massively planted in our consciousness, to the degree that today we can say that in Mexican territory the first generation of North Americans have been born."[130] He then concludes by highlighting the ultimate paradox: that TV promotes a culture that exploits and views the Mexican as inferior, thereby fostering a sort of "national masochism": "Thus we profoundly desire to convert ourselves into that imaginary prototype that in real life denies our most elementary essence and which recognizes us as primary material and cheap labor for their benefit."[131]

While both the restricted (denationalistic) and unrestricted (nationalistic) narratives pivot on the importance of nation and national culture (in one it is not threatened and in the other it is), the third narrative, the globalist (postnationalistic) view, emphasizes a process ushering in either a universal culture or hybrid cultures somewhat immune from any nationalist context. Many believe that consumer cultures around the world are converging and becoming similar as a result of economic opening and transnationalization. According to García Canclini, this change has restructured cultural practices and preferences, with identity defined less in terms of belonging exclusively to a national community or difference than to hybridization and deterritorialized or transnationalized communities.[132] He thus speaks of a reelaboration of "lo propio" because of the nature of the goods and messages coming from a global culture: a redefinition of identity and sense of belonging.[133] He also describes how globalization, by transferring decisions away from the national to the economic transnational, has effectively reduced national authorities to administrators, while creating a symbolic and material vacuum at the national level and converting the citizen into a consumer. As such, equality becomes defined politically in terms of the right to be different, which, in turn, is defined largely through consumption.[134] This view appropriates the narrative used by the ruling elite that defines good economic policy (like NAFTA) in terms of access to higher-quality goods rather than to nationalistic objectives.

These views remain highly contested. Trying to clearly distinguish "universal culture" from "Americanization," or "hybridization" from "cultural distortion," or as simply a midway point in a process of assimilation, is not easy. In many ways, these terms hinge on the narratives used to describe the trends and processes. "Americanization," for instance, which has a clearly nationalist reference, suggests a threat to the national culture and hence the need for State action. The term "universal culture," by contrast, by conjuring an image of modernity and linear history (the move toward civilization) and by avoiding any nationalist terminology, suggests no direct threat to the nation or need for State action. At worst, the term actually posits the futility of opposing the "forces of history," "the market," or "globalization." Finally, the term "hybridity" also seems to assuage any nationalistic concern, casting "foreign" influence in a sense as both neutral and natural; but by suggesting a certain level of give-and-take, by hinting that cultural influences move in all directions and that all cultures are in some way hybrids, this terminology tends to create an image of underlying equality and personal freedom. Under hybridity, in short, each individual is free to construct his or her own identity, free from national, communal, or territorial biases or logics. As such the term suggests a postnationalist vision.

Conclusion

Focusing on the consumer market, this chapter offers a conclusion of diversity, paradox, and contestation. Though U.S. companies enjoy a clear and powerful presence in Mexico, even to the point of dominating certain sectors of the economy, and U.S. goods are generally perceived as being of higher quality and superior, in other areas Mexicans seem to see national products as better and at times to prefer them over the U.S. option. And despite the acceptance and positive assessment of U.S. companies and U.S. products, U.S. companies only subtly play on their U.S. origins in advertisements, often bowing to Mexican nationalism and adapting their products to local tastes rather than expecting local tastes to adapt to their product. Though the use of certain U.S. products seems to help define an individual as "rich" and "modern," it is also seen at other times and in other contexts as a rejection of the nation and a lack of concern for its well-being. Similarly, recent trends point to a dramatic increase in the levels of both U.S. penetration and the consumption of U.S. products as well as the limits to those increases and the resurgence of such culturally important Mexican industries as music, TV, and artistic cinema. The fact that Mexican culture—through music, food, and cinema—has simultaneously begun to enjoy an acceptance and penetration into the U.S. market further crystallizes and buttresses this countertrend or resistance. Just as many Mexicans decry the loss of identity resulting from the sale of U.S. products, Mexican products seem to be enjoying greater access to the U.S. market. And, of course, views differ over whether the growing presence of U.S. companies and products in the country, and a similar increase in the role of consumption in defining identity, should be matters of concern and, if so, what can or should be done about them. But the continuing and contested political debate over threats to the nation, as we saw in chapter 1, is nothing new, though certainly the "official discourse" has changed in recent years.

Since it is in the public realm where the competing discourses on the U.S. and the nation—discourses found in the political debates, the textbooks, the cartoons, the movies, the intellectual writings, and the market—battle to shape the views of the nation, focus turns now to public opinion. What images do Mexicans themselves have regarding the U.S. and the nation—particularly after being exposed continually to the politicians, the intellectuals, the school texts, the media, and the consumer market?

Notes

1. Sut Jhally, *The Codes of Advertising: Fetishism and the Political Economy of Meaning in the Consumer Society* (New York: St. Martin's Press, 1987), 6, 18.

2. Bruce D. Keillor, R. Stephen Parker, and Allen Schaefer, "Influences on Adolescent Brand Preferences in the US and Mexico," *Journal of Advertising Research* 36 (3) (1996): 49.

3. Jhally, *Codes of Advertising*, 7; M. Douglas and B. Isherwood, *The World of Goods* (New York: Basic Books, 1978), 59.

4. Jhally, *Codes of Advertising*, 25.

5. García Canclini, *Consumidores y Ciudadanos*, 19.

6. García Canclini, *Consumidores y Ciudadanos*, 13–14.

7. García Canclini, *Globalización Imaginada*, 124.

8. García Canclini, *Globalización Imaginada*, 12.

9. P. Nolan, "Making Your Mark in Mexico," *Potentials in Marketing*, September (1994): 34–35.

10. García Canclini, *Consumidores y Ciudadanos*, 118.

11. "Cinema: Mexico," *Screen Digest* 259 (October 1999).

12. García Canclini, *Consumidores y Ciudadanos,* 139.

13. "US film exports hit a record $5.7 B," *Hollywood Reporter,* August 26, 1999.

14. García Canclini, *Consumidores y Ciudadanos,* 136; "Reel Renaissance," *Business Mexico,* April 2000).

15. "Life comes back into Mexican Video Market," *Screen Digest* 284 (November 1999).

16. Cited in *Los Angeles Times,* October 28, 2000.

17. See J. Sinclair, *Images Incorporated* (New York: Croom Helm, 1987) on the substitution of local staples with processed foods.

18. Enrique Sánchez-Ruíz, "Notas sobre la globalización, el TLC y el espacio audiovisual mexicano," paper presented at the conference *La comunicación hoy: Escenarios y contraescenarios,* Universidad de las Américas-Puebla, México, November 23–25, 1993, cited in Lozano, "Media Reception on the Mexican Border with the US."

19. *The Industry Sector Analysis: Mexico* (Washington, D.C.: U.S. Department of State, 1995); *Consumer Mexico 1996* (London: Euromonitor PLC, 1996).

20. Sánchez-Ruíz, "Notas sobre la globalización"; and Henry Geddes Gonzales, "Mass media and cultural identity among the Yucatec Maya: The constitution of global, national and local subjects," *Studies in Latin American Popular Culture* 15 (1996): 131–54.

21. Thomas Catan, "I Want My MTV," *US/Mexico Business,* September (1998): 46–48.

22. Cristina Otalora, "Mexico shows signs of revival," *Music Business International* 8 (4) (1998): 45–46.

23. Ramiro Burr, "Mexican music market is booming due to diverse talent and a loyal immigrant audience," *Billboard* 110 (30) (1998): 49–51; Daniel S. Moore, "Latin Rockers seek Global Roll," *Variety* 384 (8) (March 28–April 3, 1994): 48, 64, 67.

24. See also Hayes, "Early American Radio Broadcasting."

25. Teresa Aguilera, "Mexican Radio." *Billboard* 108 (39) (1996): 39–41.

26. See John Lannert, "Gringos are Coming! Tours, Radio and TV Help Swell Sales of Foreign Acts," *Billboard* 106 (48) (1994): 73–75.

27. "Franchise Faena," *Business Mexico,* September 1999; "Comidas Rapidas," *US/Latin Trade,* October 1993.

28. "En 10 años McD's llegó a representar 39% del total ingreso pro franquisias" *Financiero,* February 26, 1994; "Mexican fast food market in infancy," *Market Latin America,* January 2000.

29. Thomas Catan, "Under the Golden Arches," *Mexico Business,* July/August 1997: 58–60; "Franchise Faena."

30. Wiebke Holleren, "Mexicans fear invasion by U.S. corn tortillas for health, economics," *DPA* (November 3, 2002), reprinted by Global Exchange (www.globalexchange.org).

31. "Big Company Watch," *Latin Trade,* July 1999.

32. *Consumer Mexico 1996.*

33. For a review of the literature see Khalid I. Al-Sulaiti and Michael J. Baker, "Country of origin effects: A literature review," *Marketing Intelligence and Planning*

16 (3) (1998): 150–99; W. J. Bilkey and E. Nes, "Country of Origin Effects on Product Evaluations," *Journal of International Business* Studies 8 (1) (1982): 89–99; N. Papadopoulos and L. A. Heslop, eds. *Product-Country Images* (New York: International Business Press, 1993); R. A. Peterson and A. J. P. Jolibert, "A Meta-Analysis of Country-of-Origin Effects," *Journal of International Business Studies* 26 (4) (1995): 883–900; and Jerome Witt and C. P. Rao, "The Impact of Global Sourcing on Consumer: Country-of-Origin Effects on Perceived Risk," *Journal of Global Marketing* 6 (3) (1992): 105–28.

34. Witt and Rao, "Impact of Global Sourcing."

35. Curtis Reierson, "Are Foreign Products Seen as National Stereotypes?" *Journal of Retailing,* Fall (1996): 33–40; and Martin S. Roth and Jean Romeo, "Matching Product Category and Country Image Perceptions: A Framework for Managing Country-of-Origin Effects," *Journal of International Business Studies* 23 (3) (1992): 477–97.

36. Robert D. Schooler, "Product Bias in the Central American Common Market," *Journal of Marketing Research* 2 (1965): 394–97. Such information is of obvious importance to marketers since they wish to create a desirable image for the product in the mind of the consumer (Jaishankar Ganesh and Gillian Oakenfull, "International Product Positioning: An Illustration Using Perceptual Mapping Techniques," *Journal of Global Marketing* 13 [2] [1999]: 85–111). Using country information may be beneficial in promotional efforts if consumers have a negative attitude toward the COO (Dana Nicoleta Lascu and Thomas Giese, "Exploring Country Bias in a Retailing Environment: Implications of Retailer Country of Origin," *Journal of Global Marketing* 9 [1–2] [1995]: 45). If nationalist sentiments in a particular market translate into a preference for domestic products, then ethnocentrism can be a source of competitive advantage. According to Papadopoulos ("What Product Country Images Are and Are Not," in *Product Country Images,* edited by N. Papadolous and L. Heslop, 24), "the challenge facing marketers is to ascertain the images foreign consumers hold about them and their origin countries, and, armed with this knowledge, decide whether any relevant action is indicated."

37. I. Levin, J. Jasper, J. Mittelstaedt, and G. Gaeth, "Attitudes towards 'buy American first' and preferences for American and Japanese cars: a different role for country-of-origin information," *Advances in Consumer Research* 20 (1993): 628, cited in Al-Sulaiti and Baker, "Country of origin effects."

38. H. Lee, C. Kim and J. Miller, "The Relative Effects of Price, Warranty and Country of Origin on Consumer Products Evaluations," *Journal of Global Marketing* 6 (1–2) (1992): 55–80; Levin et al., "Attitudes towards 'buy American first'"; and T. A. Shimp and S. Sharma, "Consumer Ethnocentrism: Constitution and Validation of the CETSCALE," *Journal of Marketing Research* 24 (3) (1987): 280–89.

39. D. K. Tse and G. J. Gorn, "An Experiment on the Salience of Country-of-Origin in the Era of Global Brands," *Journal of International Marketing* 1 (1) (1993): 57–76; Chih-Kang Wang and Charles W. Lamb, Jr., "The Impact of Selected Environmental Forces Upon Consumers' Willingness to Buy Foreign Products," *Journal of the Academy of Marketing Science* 11 (1983): 71–84; Witt and Rao, "Impact of Global Sourcing." It is important to stress that COO effects are not the only determinant of consumer evaluation of a product, thus raising questions as to COO's relative impact.

This too is an area of considerable debate and research. Sadrudin A. Ahmed and Alain d'Astous ("Comparison of Country-of-Origin Effects on Household and Organizational Buyers' Product Perceptions," *European Journal of Marketing* 29 [3] [1995]: 35–51), for example, contend that brand name is more important than country of origin, while Eugene D. Jaffe and Carlos R. Martinez ("Mexican Consumer Attitudes Towards Domestic and Foreign Made Products," *Journal of International Consumer Marketing* 7 [3] [1995]: 9) suggest that COO can be moderated by familiarity with and ownership of the product, the use of product information, gender, age, and income.

40. J. P. Bannister and J. A. Saunders, "UK Consumer Attitudes toward Imports: The Measurement of National Stereotype Image," *European Journal of Marketing* 12 (1978): 562–70; Victor V. Cordell, "Effects of Consumer Preferences for Foreign-Sourced Products," *Journal of International Business* 23 (2) (1992): 251–70; Gerald M. Hampton, "Perceived Risk in Buying Products Made Abroad by American Firms," *Baylor Business Studies*, October (1977): 53–64; Parameswar Krishnakumar, *An Exploratory Study of the Influence of Country of Origin on the Product Images of Persons from Selected Countries*, Ph.D. diss. (University of Florida, 1974); Schooler, "Product Bias"; R. C. Tongberg, *An Empirical Study of Relationships Between Dogmatism and Consumer Attitudes Toward Foreign Products*, Ph.D. diss. (The Pennsylvania State University, 1972); Chih-Kang Wang, *The Effect of Foreign Economic, Political and Cultural Environment on Consumers' Willingness to Buy Foreign Products*, Ph.D. diss. (Texas A&M University, 1978); Wang and Lamb, "Impact of Selected Environmental Forces."

41. Krishnakumar, *Exploratory Study*.

42. Brenda E. Richey, Patricia B. Rose, and Luis Dominguez, "Perceived Value of Mexican vs U.S. Products in Mexico, Venezuela, and the United States: Implications for Mexican Firms," *Journal of Global Marketing* 13 (2) (1999): 49–65.

43. Schooler ("Product Bias") and Tongberg *(Empirical Study)* also found this relationship, yet Wang *(Effect of Foreign Economic, Political and Cultural Environment)* was unable to support the finding. On the impact of education, see W. T. Anderson and William H. Cunningham, "Gauging Foreign Product Promotion," *Journal of Advertising Research*, February (1972): 29–34; Ronald J. Dornoff, Clint B. Tankersley, and Gregory P. White, "Consumers' Perceptions of Imports," *Akron Business and Economic Review* 5 (1974): 26–29; and Wang, *Effect of Foreign Economic, Political and Cultural Environment*.

44. Anderson and Cunningham, "Gauging Foreign Product Promotion."

45. Roth and Romeo, "Matching Product Category."

46. See Jose F. Medina, Joel Saegert, and Alicia Gresham, "Comparison of Mexican-American and Anglo-American Attitudes toward Money," *Journal of Consumer Affairs* 30 (1) (1996): 124–45; Ignacio Galceran and Jon Berry, "A New World of Consumers," *American Demographics* 17 (3) (1995): 26–33; and Madhav N. Segal and Lionel Sosa, "Marketing to the Hispanic Community," *California Management Review* 26 (1) (1983): 120–34.

47. Paul Herbig and Alain Genestre, "An examination of the cross-cultural differences in service quality: the example of Mexico and the USA," *Journal of Consumer Marketing* 13 (3) (1996): 43–53.

48. James A. Roberts and Carlos Ruy Martinez, "The Emerging Consumer Culture in Mexico: An Exploratory Investigation of Compulsive Buying in Mexican Young Adults," *Journal of International Consumer Marketing* 10 (1–2) (1997): 7–31.

49. Gary S. Insch and J. Brad McBride, "Decomposing the Country-of-Origin Construct: An Empirical Test of Country of Design, Country of Parts and Country of Assembly," *Journal of International Consumer Marketing* 10 (4) (1998): 69–91.

50. Roberts and Martinez, "Emerging Consumer Culture in Mexico"; James A. Roberts and Cesar J. Sepulveda M., "Money Attitudes and Compulsive Buying: An Exploratory Investigation of the Emerging Consumer Culture in Mexico," *Journal of International Consumer Marketing* 11 (4) (1999): 53–74; and Tim Triplett, "Middle-Class Mexicans Share Traits with Their US Counterparts," *Marketing News* 28 (1994): 8.

51. Cited in Roberts and Sepulveda, "Money Attitudes and Compulsive Buying," 54.

52. Roberts and Martinez, "Emerging Consumer Culture in Mexico."

53. Jaffe and Martinez, "Mexican Consumer Attitudes," 15.

54. Jaffe and Martinez, "Mexican Consumer Attitudes," 19–24.

55. Richey et al., "Perceived Value of Mexican vs U.S. Products."

56. Roth and Romeo, "Matching Product Category."

57. Insch and McBride, "Decomposing the Country-of-Origin Construct."

58. Herbig and Genestre, "Examination of the cross-cultural differences."

59. William Bailey and Sheila Amin Gutierrez de Pineres, "Country of origin attitudes in Mexico: The *malinchismo* effect," *Journal of International Consumer Marketing* 9 (3) (1997): 25–41.

60. Roth and Romeo, "Matching Product Category."

61. Insch and McBride, "Decomposing the Country-of-Origin Construct."

62. Jaime Almonte, Constance Falk, Rhonda Skaggs, and Manuel Cárdenas, "Country-of-Origin Bias Among High-Income Consumers in Mexico: An Empirical Study," *Journal of International Consumer Marketing* 8 (2) (1995): 27–44.

63. Almonte et al., "Country-of-Origin Bias," 41.

64. Raúl Cremoux, *La televisión y el alumno de secundaria del Distrito Federal* (Mexico City: Centro de Estudios Educativos, 1968).

65. Maciel, "Imperio de la Fortuna," 33.

66. C. García-Calderon, *Para conectarse a Cablevisión* (Mexico City: Ediciones El Caballito, 1987), 56, cited in Lozano, "Media Reception," 159.

67. Nolan, "Making Your Mark in Mexico."

68. Jaffe and Martinez, "Mexican Consumer Attitudes," 24.

69. Bailey and Gutierrez de Pineres, "Country of origin attitudes in Mexico."

70. Jaffe and Martinez, "Mexican Consumer Attitudes," 19.

71. Roth and Romeo, "Matching Product Category."

72. Anderson and Cunningham, "Gauging Foreign Product Promotion"; Dornoff et al., "Consumers' Perceptions of Imports"; and Wang, *Effect of Foreign Economic, Political and Cultural Environment.*

73. Fuentes, *Tiempo mexicano,* 129.

74. Monsiváis, "Notas sobre la cultural mexicana," 1486.

75. Monisváis, *Mexican Postcards,* 36.

76. Monisváis, "Heart of the Mexican Dream," 51.

77. Jaffe and Martinez, "Mexican Consumer Attitudes."

78. Schooler, "Product Bias"; Tongberg, *Empirical Study;* and Wang, *Effect of Foreign Economic, Political and Cultural Environment.*

79. Monsiváis, *Rituales del caos,* 187.

80. García Canclini, *Consumidores y Ciudadanos,* 26.

81. García Canclini, *Globalización Imaginada,* 50.

82. Jhally, *Codes of Advertising,* 128.

83. Jhally, *Codes of Advertising,* 129.

84. Jhally, *Codes of Advertising,* 142.

85. Gregory and Munch, "Consumers' Perceptions of Imports."

86. Steven B. Bunker, "'Consumers of Good Taste': Marketing Modernity in Northern Mexico, 1890–1910," *Mexican Studies/Estudios Mexicanos* 13 (2) (1997): 247.

87. Bunker, "Consumers of Good Taste," 248.

88. Amit K. Ghosh, "Brand management in post-NAFTA Mexico," *Journal of Product and Brand Management* 7 (2) (1998).

89. *Vanidades de Mexico,* Año 39 No. 13 (1999).

90. *Cosmopolitan de México,* Año 26 No. 12 (1998).

91. Julio Moreno, "Retail diplomacy in Mexico," *World Trade,* March (2000), 80.

92. Linda C. Ueltschy and John K. Ryans, Jr., "Employing Standardized Promotion Strategies in Mexico: The Impact of Language and Cultural Differences," *The International Executive* 39 (4) (1997): 479–95.

93. "Pitching to Peso-Pinchers," *Business Week,* May 15, 1995: 82.

94. *Consumer Mexico.*

95. *The Industry Sector Analysis.*

96. Ignacio Vázquez, "Mexicans are buying 'Made in USA' food," *Marketing News* 32 (18) (1998): 14.

97. Moreno, "Retail diplomacy in Mexico."

98. Bunker, "'Consumers of Good Taste.'"

99. Berg, *Cinema of Solitude: A Critical Study of Mexican Film, 1967–1983.*

100. Mora, *Mexican Cinema: Reflections of a Society,* 22.

101. Charles Ramírez Berg, "The Cinematic Invention of Mexico: The Poetics and Politics of the Fernandez-Figueroa Style," in *The Mexican Cinema Project,* edited by Noriega and Ricci, 13.

102. Mora, *Mexican Cinema,* 98.

103. Berg, *Cinema of Solitude,* 215.

104. Maciel, "Imperio de la Fortuna," 34; Berg, *Cinema of Solitude,* 214–15.

105. Maciel, "Imperio de la Fortuna," 34.

106. Daniel Moore, "Mexico Poised for a New Age," Variety 384 (8) (March 28–April 3, 1994): 37, 57–58.

107. Cited in Catan, "I Want My MTV."

108. See also Eric Zolov, *Refried Elvis: The Rise of the Mexican Counterculture* (Berkeley: University of California Press, 1999).

109. García Canclini, *Consumidores y Ciudadanos,* 14.

110. García Canclini, *Consumidores y Ciudadanos,* 25.

111. Javier Esteniou Madrid, "Crisis cultural y desnacionalización: la televisión mexicana y el debilitamiento de la identidad nacional," *Comunicación y Sociedad,* Mayo–Agosto (1999): 106.

112. According to Galceran and Berry ("A New World of Consumers," 28, cited in Roberts and Martinez, "Emerging Consumer Culture in Mexico," 8): "State policy continues to shape, in part, the pattern of ownership of U.S. companies in Mexico." Among the regulations limiting foreign investment, key strategic areas off limits to foreign investment and reserved to government include oil and other petrochemicals; basic petrochemicals; electricity; generation of nuclear energy; radioactive materials, postal service; telegraph; radiotelegraph; the issue of money; minting; and control, supervision, and surveillance of ports. Areas restricted to just national firms include domestic land transportation for passengers; tourism and freight except courier and messenger services; gasoline retail sales and distribution; radio and television broadcasting, not including cable; credit unions; and development banking. Foreign participation is limited to up to 25% in domestic air transportation, air taxis, and specialized air transportation; and to 49% in manufacturing and commercialization of firearms, publishing or printing newspapers for Mexican circulation, Series T-shares (issued in exchange for land use for agriculture, animal husbandry, and forestry), and fresh-water and coastal fishing within the 200-mile zone. Special permission is needed for investment beyond 49% in port services, shipping companies, education, legal services, credit information companies, insurance agencies, fixed-line communications cellular telephone services, drilling for oil and gas, construction of pipelines for oil and oil-related products, construction, operation and use of railways, and rail transportation services. The 49% limit on ownership of banks was lifted following the 1995 banking crisis, but it remains in effect for other financial activities like insurance and factoring companies (*Country Finance: Mexico* [London: Economist Intelligence Unit, 2000]).

113. Cremoux, *Televisión y el alumno.*

114. Pastor and Castañeda, *Limits to Friendship,* 15.

115. Lozano, "Media Reception."

116. André Caron and Pierre Bélanger, "A Reception Study of American Television in Quebec," in *Small Nations, big neighbor: Denmark and Quebec/Canada compare notes on American popular culture,* edited by Roger de la Garde, William Gilsdorf, and Ilja Wechs&elmann. Academic Research Monograph, no. 10 (London: John Libbey, 1993), cited in Lozano, "Media Reception," 183.

117. *La Jornada,* cited in Monsiváis, "Will Nationalism Be Bilingual?," 131.

118. Vázquez, "Mexicans are buying 'Made in USA' food."

119. Roberts and Martinez, "Emerging Consumer Culture," 8.

120. Fernando Ortega Pizarro, "Gracias a las franquicias, ya esta presente aqui el 'american way of life,'" *Proceso* 824 (August 17, 1992): 18–20.

121. Patrick Oster, *The Mexicans: A Personal Portrait of a People* (New York: Harper and Row, 1989), 248, 250.

122. Alberto Montoya and María-Antonieta Rebeil, "Communication television as an educational and political institution: A case study of its impact on the students of Telesecundaria," in *Communication and Latin American Society: Trends in Critical*

Research, 1960–1985, edited by R. Atwood and E. McAnany (Madison: University of Wisconsin Press, 1986), 147, cited in Lozano, "Media Reception," 158.

123. García-Calderon, *Para conectarse a Cablevisión,* 56, cited in Lozano, "Media Reception," 159.

124. García Canclini, *Consumidores y Ciudadanos,* 131.

125. García Canclini, *Globalización Imaginada,* 33.

126. Cited in García Canclini, *Consumidores y Ciudadanos,* 137.

127. Esteniou Madrid, "Crisis cultural y desnacionalización," 106–7.

128. Esteniou Madrid, "Crisis cultural y desnacionalización," 111.

129. Esteniou Madrid, "Crisis cultural y desnacionalización," 111.

130. Esteniou Madrid, "Crisis cultural y desnacionalización," 116.

131. Esteniou Madrid, "Crisis cultural y desnacionalización," 110–11.

132. García Canclini, *Consumidores y Ciudadanos,* 131.

133. García Canclini, *Consumidores y Ciudadanos,* 24.

134. García Canclini, *Globalización Imaginada,* 21; and García Canclini, *Consumidores y Ciudadanos,* 20.

8

Gringolandia in Public Opinion

N ARRATIVES BY POLITICIANS, school texts, cartoons, movies, and advertisements all mirror and mold popular opinion. Yet public opinion is
more than a mere by-product of these, since it too influences the politician's
spin, the artist's touch, and the advertiser's pitch. Advertisers, as noted in the
prior chapter, must draw on ideas shared by the public in order to "connect"
with the consumer. Similarly, public opinion frames the political debate,
defining the boundaries of policy.[1] The public outcry over the proposed
school textbooks in 1991, which prompted the government to backtrack, is
just one example of this influence.[2]

Seemingly the most direct means of exploring Mexican perceptions of the
U.S. and the nation is to ask the people, and for years polling firms and
researchers have done just that. This chapter analyzes Mexican perceptions
of the U.S. and the nation as expressed through public opinion polls. The
exploration strives to include much of the available data. It draws on secondary sources that cite or analyze polling data,[3] smaller focus group studies
exploring Mexican perceptions of the U.S.,[4] and the data from ten polls spanning the period, including one regional poll designed for this study. Though
survey questions and samples vary, the polls tap a range of attitudes relevant
to this study, including general opinion of the U.S., trust or confidence,
favorable and unfavorable attributes associated with the U.S., comparisons
of the two societies, evaluations of the bilateral relationship, support or
opposition to NAFTA, the likely impact of NAFTA, and level of contact with
the U.S. Table 8.1 lists the data sources used for this chapter.

The chapter divides into three sections. The first profiles Mexican opinions
toward the U.S. and the bilateral relationship, the level of contact, and policy
preferences related to the U.S. The second section then examines a series of
six hypotheses regarding possible linkages among these variables and likely

TABLE 8.1
Mexican Public Opinion Polls

- 1979 Mexico City Public Opinion Prior to the Presidential Visit (USIA)
  - Agency: Mexican affiliate of Gallup International
  - Dates: January 20–31, 1979.
  - Sample: N = 500. Residents of the Federal District, aged 18 or older.
  - Availability: Statistical results.
- 1986 New York Times Mexico Survey
  - Agency: New York Times
  - Dates: October 28–November 4, 1986.
  - Sample: N = 1,576. National sample of communities greater than 2,500 inhabitants; N = 299. Sample of communities with 1,000 to 2,500 inhabitants.
  - Availability: Data set
- 1991 Los Angeles Times Poll #258
  - Agency: Los Angeles Times
  - Dates: September 11–October 2, 1991
  - Sample: N = 1,546. National sample in 189 locations within 61 *municipios* (in homes).
  - Availability: Data set
- 1992 *Encuesta Sobre el Tratado de Libre Comercio*
  - Agency: CENII-IMES, Mexico.
  - Dates: November 1992.
  - Sample: N = 550. Residents of Mexico City.
  - Availability: Statistical results.
- 1993 Public Opinion in Mexico
  - Agency: Market and Opinion Research International (MORI de Mexico).
  - Dates: January–February 1993
  - Sample: N = 2,114. National sample plus oversample of N = 641 in cities in and around the Federal District.
  - Availability: Data set
- 1993 Citizen Opinion: Image of the United States
  - Agency: Gabinete de Estudios de Opinion [GEO] for *El Nacional*
  - Dates: January 14–18, 1993
  - Sample: N = 1,020. Adult residents of the Valley of Mexico.
  - Availability: Data set
- 1995 Survey of Political Culture in Jalisco
  - Agency: Centro de Estudios de Opinion [CEO], Universidad de Guadalajara.
  - Dates: June 15–17, 1995
  - Sample: N = 500. Metro Guadalajara. N = 250 Lagos de Moreno.
  - Availability: Statistical results.
- 1995 *Encuesta Omnibus*
  - Agency: MORI de Mexico
  - Dates: November 1995.
  - Sample: N = 500. Adult residents of Mexico City area.
  - Availability: Statistical Results
- World Values Survey, 1981, 1990, 1995–1996 (Inglehart et al., 1981–1984, 1990–1993, 1995–1997)
  - Agency: 1. IMOP (Gallup-Mexico); 2. and 3. MORI de Mexico
  - Dates: 1. 1981 2. May 1990; 3. Fall 1995, Spring 1996
  - Sample: 1. N = 1837; 2. N = 1531; 3. N = 1510. National samples
  - Availability: Data set
- 1998 USIA Polls
  - Agency: Gallup-Mexico for United States Information Agency
  - Dates: April and November 3–18, 1998.
  - Sample: N = 1,502. National in cities of 50,000 or more.
  - Availability: Statistical results.

determinants of these views. The third section then explores the likelihood that Mexican opinions of the U.S. have changed in recent years.

Data from opinion polls, and even focus groups, provide invaluable glimpses into the public's collective political mind, but they also sport a range of empirical problems and limitations.[5] First, polls assume that expressed opinions reflect underlying beliefs and values. Yet through the wording or the ordering of questions, or the structuring of the responses, polls may to some degree obtrusively fashion rather than simply identify opinion. Most polls, indeed, pigeonhole people's responses into structured categories, fail to gauge intensity of opinion, and overly rely on the respondent's self-definition of terms. Such problems, in turn, weaken comparability within a single poll and, of course, magnify it across multiple polls. Second, surveys provide merely a snapshot of public opinion, capturing the mood of the public at just one point in time. Results can thus be influenced by recent events, the news of the day, the scandal of the moment, or the economic climate, further complicating analysis over time, and rendering impossible the identification of any "authentic" view free of temporal or ephemeral factors. This also complicates any sort of analysis of change, since it is difficult to know if the benchmark measure is truly representative. Comparing results over time, as will be ventured here, is further complicated by the subtle differences between polls. Since no two polls nor samples are identical, it is difficult to know whether opinion has changed, or whether the measured difference is simply the result of differences in the structure of the polling instrument. Finally, many raise questions about the validity of polls carried out in an authoritarian setting such as Mexico's prior to 2000. Respondents in such environments are more likely to alter or disguise their opinion than respondents in more open societies.[6] Polls, in short, are not without their problems. This does not mean that the methodological device should be dismissed, however. Surveys can be quite helpful as a complementary methodological tool, helping to provide rough and somewhat crude indications of the public's perceptions and, through the use of statistical methods, helping to point to possible causal patterns.

Opinions about the U.S.

Data presented in table 8.2 show Mexicans generally have a favorable opinion of the U.S., the U.S. government, and the U.S. people. This assessment does not necessarily translate into widespread trust of the U.S., however, where opinion splits more evenly or where more respondents actually distrust than trust the U.S. Looking beyond these broad assessments, three of the polls

TABLE 8.2
General Perceptions of the U.S.

	Favorable	Unfavorable	
Opinion of the U.S.			
	72%	16%	(1991 Los Angeles Times)
	68%	22%	(1993 MORI)
	53%	39%	(1998 USIA—April)
	66%	33%	(1998 USIA—November)
Opinion of the U.S. Government			
	48%	27%	(1986 New York Times)
Opinion of U.S. People			
	47%	22%	(1986 New York Times)
	55%	29%	(1991 Los Angeles Times)
Confidence/Trust in the U.S.			
	20%	50%	(Inglehart et al., 1996: 9)
	45% [Trust in business]	48%	(1991 Los Angeles Times)

asked respondents to list what they liked and disliked about the U.S. On the positive side, respondents cited internal economic and political traits of the U.S., like "good economy/no inflation," "technology," "employment," and "democracy" (1986 New York Times); "economic opportunity," "rich country," "goods/products," "democracy and rights" (1991 Los Angeles Times); and "stable economy/high standard of living," "employment opportunities," and "quality of government" (1998 USIA). Equally consistently, the most frequently cited negative traits referred to social, cultural, and foreign policy aspects of the U.S., like "drug addiction," "racism," "treatment of illegal aliens," "armaments/nuclear weapons," "interventionism" (1986 New York Times); "racial discrimination," "superiority complex," "drugs and crime," "U.S. desire to dominate other countries," "warmongering" (1991 Los Angeles Times); and "abuse/unfair treatment of Mexicans," "discrimination/racism," "exploitative policies," and "degenerate quality of life/culture" (1998 USIA). This distinction, wherein positive assessments of the U.S. underscore domestic economic and political features and negative assessments tap domestic social and cultural aspects and U.S. treatment of others, is also illustrated in the 1998 poll's finding wherein 80% of respondents agreed that the statement "anyone can succeed if he works hard" adequately depicts the U.S., and 64% agreed that the statement "everyone thinks for him/herself" describes the country.

A key premise of the current study is that perceptions of the nation and "other" are inseparable, with perceptions of one playing an important part in defining the other. Unfortunately, surveys provide limited insights into the potential linkages between perceptions of the U.S. and the nation. Still, on the surface at least, it is clear that the favorable opinions of the U.S. do not translate directly into unfavorable views of the nation or vice versa. Data from the World Values Survey, for example, show Mexicans to have a strong sense of national pride, with over 90% of respondents answering "very proud" or "quite proud" of being Mexican. Moreover, Mexicans generally prefer Mexico to the U.S. In the 1993 GEO poll, 48% selected Mexico as the "best country," compared to just 12% tapping the U.S., and 80% said they would prefer to live in Mexico if given the choice. Data from the 1992 and 1995 polls also find Mexicans to be more likely to prefer national goods to foreign products. In the 1992 CENII poll, for instance, 39% preferred Mexican products compared to 24% opting for foreign goods; in the 1995 MORI poll, 31% versus 24% preferred domestic to foreign-made products. Such results raise doubts about the widespread presence of *malinchismo* (a preference for things foreign) found in some of the consumer marketing studies. More importantly, perhaps, the data suggest the coexistence of nationalistic, pro-Mexican views alongside relatively favorable views of the U.S. This finding seems to cripple the possibility of any simplistic notion of a pro-Mexican versus anti-U.S. dichotomy.

And yet if we look at more specific attributes of the two societies, there does appear to be some evidence of a deeper dichotomous pattern wherein the positive qualities of Mexico (the nation) contrast with (and define) the negative qualities associated with the U.S. (other) and vice versa. Here, the positive qualities of the U.S. (political and economic system) tend to be the areas most often condemned regarding Mexico, and vice versa. In a series of questions in the 1986 New York Times poll, for instance, a substantial majority of respondents indicated that North Americans have more political freedoms than Mexicans (79%) and more opportunities for becoming rich without working hard (80%), but that Mexicans are closer to their children (86%), have stronger values (80%), and are more religious (92%). Hence, while the positive traits associated with the U.S. tend to load heavily on the political and economic dimensions, as noted earlier, those spotlighting Mexico load more strongly on the cultural and spiritual facet.[7]

Pablo Vila's analysis of opinion along the border using focus groups taps further into the connection between views of the U.S. and views of self. Echoing the tendency to envision the U.S. in primarily economic terms, Vila identifies a narrative in which the (positive) economic factors associated with the U.S. are seen as undermining national culture.[8] Such a narrative parallels the views of Carlos Fuentes and his concern for *pepsicoatl* discussed in chapter 5.

Within this context, members of the focus groups believed that U.S. people actually work "too" much and, consequently, fail to enjoy leisure. This image, associated within the discourse to the strong cultural drive to acquire things (consumerist culture), forces the *gringo* into debt (which reduces his freedom) and a never-ending "rat race" lifestyle (which leads to a false sense of happiness). By contrast, Mexicans see themselves as being able to nurture an effective balance of work and leisure, thereby retaining control of their destiny and enjoying more freedoms and life. Couched within this narrative, living in the U.S. thus holds out the prospect of possible economic gains but at the expense of one's sense of freedom and control over his or her own destiny. As we see later, this narrative seems to parallel popular views on NAFTA.

Beyond mere perceptions of the U.S. and North Americans, survey data also reveal the level of personal contact Mexicans have with the U.S. The data show from 26% (1998 USIA) to 34% (1986 New York Times) of respondents having traveled to the U.S., 39% (1991 Los Angeles Times) to 61% (1998 USIA) of respondents having relatives in the U.S., and 25% in 1986 (1986 New York Times) and 45% in 1998 (1998 USIA) of respondents having met a *gringo*. The 1998 USIA poll and the regional 1995 Jalisco poll also measured indirect forms of contact. The 1998 national poll showed 40% of respondents had watched at least three to four U.S. television programs a week, and 55% had attended three to four U.S. movies within the past month. The regional poll found 46% of respondents followed a U.S. sport regularly, 16% had eaten at a U.S. fast food restaurant within the past month, and 35% listened to English-language music on the radio.

Table 8.3, in turn, presents the public's evaluations of various dimensions of the bilateral relationship. As shown, respondents generally see the U.S. as influential over Mexico and becoming more so in recent years. Opinion splits, however, over assessments of U.S. influence, with some polls pointing to the perception that the U.S. mistreats Mexico and other polls gauging the relationship more positively. Clearly though, views of the relationship are much more negative than general opinion of the U.S. Care should be taken here since a lot depends on question wording, and what appear as similar questions may be tapping different dimensions. Robert Pastor and Jorge Castañeda and Judith Hellman, for example, cite two 1986 polls conducted by the newspaper *Excelsior* showing 59% of respondents classifying the U.S. as an enemy country and 60% grading the U.S. as an unpleasant neighbor.[9] This is despite the favorable opinions toward the country. And yet, perhaps bowing to the reality of geography, data also show a strong desire on the part of the public for Mexico to deal cooperatively with the U.S. and improve the relationship. Ivan Zavala presents data showing a majority with a preference

TABLE 8.3
Evaluations of U.S. Influence and the Bilateral Relationship

1. Whose interests run the Mexican economy?
   67% US   33% Mexicans   (1986 New York Times)

2. How much influence does the US have over Mexico?
   55% too much   11% not enough   33% right amount   (1991 Los Angeles Times)
   45% a lot   15% limited   (1993 GEO)

3. Do you think the US will try to influence the presidential succession?
   53% yes   25% no   (1993 MORI)

4. Has US influence increased over the past ten years?
   81% yes   16% no   (1995 Jalisco)

5. Evaluation of

   a. US economic treatment of Mexico

	favorable	*unfavorable*	
	29%	26%	(1993 GEO)
		Agree	
• "unfair competition by US and Canada"		55%	(1995 MORI)
• "US does not comply with NAFTA"		45%	(1998 USIA—April)
		30%	(1998 USIA—November)

   b. US political treatment of Mexico

	favorable	*unfavorable*	
	24%	25%	(1993 GEO)
		Agree	
• "US does not evaluate Mexican and US counternarcotics equally"		68%	(1998 USIA)

   c. Mexican-US Relationship

	friendly/good	*unfriendly/poor*	
	66%	33%	(1986 New York Times)
	16%	32%	(1995 MORI)
	58%	38%	(1998 USIA—April)
	77%	19%	(1998 USIA—November)

   d. Increase in US influence

	good	*bad*	
	14%	66%	(1995 Jalisco)

	positive	*negative*	
e. Influence of US television			
	49%	47%	(1998 USIA)
f. Influence of US movies			
	44%	47%	(1998 USIA)

for improving relations with the U.S. for the sake of aiding the nation's economy (much more than with any other country),[10] while the 1998 USIA poll found a substantial majority agreeing with the view that Mexico should cooperate with the U.S. in order to resolve the nation's major problems. As many as 83% of respondents in the 1998 poll believed Mexico should cooperate with the U.S. more to resolve the problem of drugs, and 88% thought that cooperation is needed to resolve environmental problems. As we will see regarding expectations of NAFTA, there is a clear sense that many Mexicans envision the relationship and cooperation as economically important and beneficial to Mexico.

Few polls posed specific questions regarding the public's evaluations of the Mexican government's part in the bilateral relationship. Opponents of the PRI have often targeted blame for U.S. "misbehavior" on the Mexican government and not the U.S., as noted in chapter 2. Some evidence suggests that this pattern may hold for the public as well. In both the 1992 CENII poll and the 1995 MORI poll, large majorities graded the measures of the government in relations with the U.S. as either insufficient or inadequate. Only 32% in 1992 and 16% in 1995 rated the measures as "adequate." In the 1995 Jalisco poll, moreover, with an astounding 97% believing the government should protect national culture, only 54% thought the government was actually doing so.

One policy initiative prominently featured in most polls is a free trade agreement with the U.S. or what by 1991 became known as NAFTA. As shown in table 8.4, the public's support for NAFTA has been at times overwhelming, dipping to its lowest level only during the economic crisis of 1994–1995. Data cited by Daniel Lund also showed similarly high levels of support, 77% in favor in 1990, 62% in 1991, and 53% in 1992.[11] Such findings may indicate the success of the Salinas pro-NAFTA campaign or the sheer "reality" of having to live beside the powerful U.S.[12] Some of the policy preferences beyond NAFTA shown in the table, however, detract from this finding. Pointing in contradictory directions, data show support for free trade does not totally rule out the belief in the need for the government to limit imports or protect national culture.

Evaluations of the likely impact of NAFTA shown in table 8.5 provide some insight into the reasons for the public's support for free trade. Most respondents felt that NAFTA would provide significant economic benefits to the country; and yet, at the same time, they believed that the U.S. and the rich would benefit the most from NAFTA and that while the impact on economic and material areas would be positive, the impact on the culture and national control over petroleum would be negative.

Taken as a whole, the descriptive data reviewed here seem to show a public

TABLE 8.4
Policy Preferences

Position on Free Trade Agreement (NAFTA)		
Support	*Oppose*	
61%	15%	(1991 Los Angeles Times)
70%	26%	(1992 CENII)
47%	17%	(1993 MORI)
43%	40%	(1995 MORI)
Good for Mexico	*Bad for Mexico*	
47%	19%	(1991 Los Angeles Times)
47%	33%	(1993 GEO)

Should the government . . .
- *Encourage or discourage foreign investment*

Encourage	*Discourage*	
49%	33%	(1991 Los Angeles Times)

- Limit imports

Yes	*No*	
83%	16%	(World Value Survey 1995–1996)

- Protect national culture

Yes	*No*	
91%	1%	(1995 Jalisco)

with a generally favorable opinion of the U.S., but limited confidence in the U.S., particularly in its treatment of Mexico. It shows a public torn in a sense between acknowledging the necessity of opening the domestic economy to the U.S., because of the material benefits it brings, and recognizing that such dealings will probably be more beneficial to the U.S. and have some negative consequences for their country. The people seem to perceive a "Catch-22" situation wherein the country's relative political and economic weakness vis-à-vis the U.S. imposes less than optimal trade-offs. Ronald Inglehart et al. point to one of these trade-offs, confirming that people are more likely to support political integration (abolishing borders) if it means better quality of life, higher standard of living, and improvements in health care and the environment, but not if it implies a loss of cultural identity.[13]

Two key questions emerge from this conclusion: first, how far is the public willing to go in making such trade-offs? The 1995 Jalisco poll points to one limit at least: while 40% felt that PEMEX would be run more efficiently if owned by the U.S., only 5% recommended that it be sold to U.S. interests. In other words, efficiency, even for a business like PEMEX, was not the sole or determining value. The second key question is how do Mexicans reconcile these difficult trade-offs? Coming to grips with the trade-offs, either for the

TABLE 8.5
Perceived Likely Impact of NAFTA

NAFTA will most benefit

	The U.S.	Mexico		
	44%	21%		(1991 Los Angeles Times)
	51%	14%		(1993 MORI)

	The rich	All equally	The poor	No one	
	63%	29%	5%	0%	(1992 CENII)
	57%	16%	3%	15%	(1995 MORI)

Percentage saying NAFTA will . . .
- Increase industrial production
  - 77%   (1992 CENII)
  - 26%   (1995 MORI)
- Create jobs
  - 51%   (1993 MORI)
- Bring better services
  - 50%   (1993 MORI)
- Increase wages
  - 50%   (1992 CENII)
  - 7%   (1995 MORI)
- Change U.S. treatment of Mexico
  - 34% (44% said "no change")   (1993 GEO)
- Increase dependence
  - 58%   (1993 MORI)
- Threaten culture and tradition
  - 69%   (1995 MORI)
- Threaten control of petroleum
  - 55%   (1995 MORI)

country as a whole or for the individual, may entail some sort of conscious assertion of Mexican identity as proof that the real "costs" have gone unpaid or remain limited. Vila, for instance, concludes that Mexican-Americans engage in a constant imaginary dialogue with native Mexicans because they feel the need to prove that they remain loyal to Mexico and are not traitors, despite living in the U.S. for primarily economic reasons.[14] Even so, it is not clear to what extent this occurs in the interior, though certainly a similar pattern might exist. The fact that Mexicans continue to be nationalistic and jealous of their cultural identity, in conjunction with supporting NAFTA, nurtures in some way the perception that increased economic integration is "not really a threat" to the nation. Indeed, most acknowledge integration's threat to culture as real, but have nonetheless balanced this idea and nationalism with a desire for NAFTA.

Exploring Linkages and Determinants

Turning now to an analysis of the possible linkages and determinants of Mexicans' views regarding the U.S. and the nation, this section examines six hypotheses. Many of these stem from points raised in earlier chapters:

1. Opinion of the U.S., the government and the people, confidence in the U.S., and evaluations of the bilateral relationship all correlate in a positive direction.
2. People with a favorable view of the U.S., more confidence in the U.S., and positive evaluations of the relationship are more likely to support policies of integration like NAFTA or to prefer to live in the U.S.
3. People with greater contact with the U.S. are more likely to have a favorable opinion of the U.S. and to support policies of integration.
4. People identifying themselves politically as right or right-center, with the PRI or PAN, and with a favorable opinion of President Salinas are more likely to have a favorable opinion of the U.S. and the relationship and to support NAFTA.
5. Respondents with higher income and education levels are more likely to have a positive opinion of the U.S. and to support policies of integration.
6. Younger respondents are more likely than older respondents to have a positive opinion of the U.S. and to support policies of integration.

Hypothesis 1: Opinion of the U.S., the government and the people, confidence in the U.S., and evaluations of the bilateral relationship correlate in a positive direction.

Despite the distinct measures, it is possible that a basic, underlying perception of the U.S. exists: a fundamental perception that informs general opinion of the country, the people, the government, confidence, and evaluations of the bilateral relationship. Analytically, the concepts overlap, but they are not identical. To what extent then do Mexicans carefully differentiate the people of the U.S. from the government, or their opinion of the country from issues of trust or their assessments of the bilateral relationship?

Data show that basic opinions of the U.S., U.S. government, and U.S. people are all positively correlated. Data from the 1986 New York Times and the 1991 Los Angeles Times polls, for instance, both show respondents with a positive opinion of the U.S. government or society in general to be more likely to have a positive opinion of the U.S. people (Kendall tau-c $= .531$**

and .181**, respectively).[15] Though positively linked, the relationship is not perfect, however, suggesting that many Mexicans do draw important distinctions in their opinion toward the U.S. country, the government, and the people. Data also uncover a significant relationship between opinion toward the U.S. and assessments of the bilateral relationship. As shown in table 8.6, though not particularly robust, the 1986 New York Times poll shows a significant correlation in the expected direction, with respondents expressing a "favorable" view of the U.S. government to be slightly more likely to assess the relationship as "very friendly" or "friendly," and less likely to believe that the U.S. "runs the Mexican economy." The 1993 MORI poll also shows respondents with a poor opinion of the U.S. to be more likely to see Mexico as "too dependent" on the U.S. Presented in table 8.6, 73% of respondents in this poll expressing a negative opinion of the U.S. felt that the U.S. influenced Mexico "too much" compared to just 54% of those holding a more favorable impression of the U.S.

Analysis of the 1991 Los Angeles Times poll lends further support to the hypothesis. The lower portion of table 8.6 shows a multiple regression of opinion and evaluations of the bilateral relationship using confidence in the U.S. as the dependent variable. It shows opinion of the U.S. and the people, and evaluations of the relationship to be all statistically linked to confidence levels, with an $R^2 = .168$. Respondents with a "very good" or "good" opinion of the U.S., in short, are more likely to have "a lot" or "some" confidence in the U.S. in business than those with a poor opinion of the U.S. In like manner, whereas 62% of those with a favorable view of North American people expressed "a lot" or "some" confidence in the U.S. in business, only 26% with a negative view did so.

Other measures in this area fail to substantiate these findings, however. In the 1993 GEO poll, perhaps because it gauges opinion of the U.S. vis-à-vis Mexico, respondents with a favorable opinion of the U.S. (as measured by "best country in the world") were no more likely to evaluate U.S. treatment of Mexico (economically or politically) in positive terms, or to perceive the U.S. as any more influential in Mexican politics, than those selecting Mexico or some other country as the "best country." The 1993 MORI data, though revealing a relationship between opinion of the U.S. and one measure of a respondent's evaluation of the relationship (dependence) as noted above, shows opinion of the U.S. to be statistically unrelated to perceptions of U.S. influence in Mexican politics. In fact, while 41.2% of those with a poor opinion of the U.S. felt the U.S. would attempt to influence the selection of Mexico's new president, an almost equal percentage (40%) of those with a favorable opinion of the U.S. held this view. This suggests, somewhat surpris-

TABLE 8.6
Correlation-Regression Analysis of Attitudes toward the U.S and
Evaluations of the Bilateral Relationship

1986 New York Times			*1993 MORI*			
Mexico-U.S.	**View of U.S.**		**Dependence**	**View of U.S.**		
Relationship	*Favorable*	*Unfavorable*	**on the US**	*Favorable*	*Regular*	*Unfavorable*
Friendly	72%	61%	Too much	54%	59%	73%
Unfriendly	28%	39%	Adequate	32%	29%	17%
			Insufficient	7%	8%	7%
			None	7%	4%	3%
Kendall tau c = .038*			Kendall tau c = −.100**			

1991 LA Times
Multiple Regression Model
Dependent variable = confidence in U.S. in business

	Standardized Beta
Opinion of the U.S.	.125**
Opinion of U..S people	.188**
Influence of U.S. over Mexico	−.231**
Mexican Dependence on U.S.	−.126**
r2 = .168**	

* p < .05 ** p < .01

ingly, that one's opinion of the U.S. does not necessarily affect whether one sees the U.S. as intervening in domestic affairs or vice versa.

It is possible to hypothesize, of course, that opinion of the U.S. and the nation are linked to more fundamental perceptions about the positive and negative qualities of each of the two societies. Though the data hardly provide much help in evaluating this, it is noteworthy that in the 1986 New York Times poll respondents who felt that the people in the U.S. are happier or that the U.S. has stronger values were more likely to have a favorable opinion of the U.S. and the U.S. people. This was particularly true at the two extremes in both cases. For example, 71% of those believing U.S. people were "a lot" happier held a favorable view of the U.S. people compared to just 39% of those saying the U.S. people were "not at all" happier. This is noteworthy because this pattern would seem to contradict the popular notion that envy of the U.S. feeds resentment and fuels anti-American sentiment. Indeed, an "envy hypothesis" would hold that those viewing the U.S. as "better" (happier, stronger values) would harbor a more negative view of the people or the government; but the data here show the opposite, a positive view of the U.S. Even so, this tendency is difficult to access because of the problem of discriminating the difference between "like" and "envy."

Hypothesis 2: People with a favorable view of the U.S., more confidence in the U.S., and positive evaluations of the relationship are more likely to support policies of integration like NAFTA or to prefer to live in the U.S.

Common wisdom within Mexican business culture holds that Mexicans prefer doing business with friends: people they know, like, and can trust. Extending that logic suggests that people with a more favorable opinion of the U.S. and who trust the U.S. should be more likely to support policies like liberalizing trade or investment or signing a free trade agreement, or even more personal policy decisions like the desire to live in the U.S.

Looking first at an individual's position on free trade or NAFTA, data are relatively consistent in showing a relationship between a favorable opinion toward the U.S. and positive evaluations of U.S. influence, on the one hand, and support for policies of integration like free trade, on the other. In the 1991 Los Angeles Times poll, as indicated in table 8.7, respondents with a good impression of the U.S. are more likely to favor (in whole or in part) a free trade agreement than those with an unfavorable impression of the U.S. They are also more likely to see a trade agreement as "good" for Mexico and to support policies encouraging foreign investment. Data from the 1993 MORI poll also show those with a favorable opinion of the U.S. to be more likely to: (1) believe that a free trade accord will benefit Mexico more than the U.S. or benefit both equally; (2) see free trade as beneficial to Mexico generally; (3) interpret such an accord as less likely to significantly increase Mexican dependence on the U.S.; and (4) support a free trade agreement (table 8.7). Opponents of NAFTA, by contrast, are slightly more likely than proponents to see the U.S. as benefiting more or Mexico as not benefiting at all from an agreement. Opponents are also more likely to grade U.S. influence over Mexico as "too much" (more than 70%). A study by Charles Davis further confirms these findings. In multiple regression models based on the 1991 and 1993 data, he finds attitudes toward the U.S. to be a key determinant of one's position on NAFTA, independent of the influence of other variables. This leads him to conclude that "attitudes toward the United States contribute to an overall positive evaluation of NAFTA."[16]

This same pattern holds in an analysis of the 1993 GEO poll. It shows

TABLE 8.7
Impact of Opinion of the U.S. on Support for NAFTA and Preferred Place of Residence

Position on NAFTA	*1991* LA Times Opinion of U.S.		*1993* MORI Opinion of U.S.		*1993 GEO* Best Country		
	Good	*Bad*	*Good*	*Bad*	*Mexico*	*U.S.*	*Other*
Favor	85%	59%	83%	41%	59%	72%	64%
Opposed	15%	41%	17%	59%	41%	28%	36%
Kendall tau-c	.161**		.266**		− .067		

Prefer to live in the U.S.	*1986* NY Times **Opinion of U.S. People**		Prefer to live in	*1993 GEO* **Best Country**		
	Favorable	*Unfavorable*		*Mexico*	*U.S.*	*Other*
Yes	45%	33%	Mexico	92%	66%	65%
No	55%	69%	U.S.	6%	31%	18%
			All the same	2%	3%	17%
	Kendall tau-c = .114**			Kendall tau-c = .197**		

* p < .05 ** p < .01

respondents with a more favorable opinion of the U.S. (as measured by "best country in the world") are somewhat more likely to see NAFTA as beneficial to Mexico (table 8.7). Consistent with this pattern, it also reveals that those believing the U.S. has significant influence over Mexico and treats Mexico poorly in economic or political terms are less likely to see Mexico as potentially benefiting from a free trade agreement. Ingelhart et al. offer further support for this view. They show a significant, positive linkage between trust of the U.S. and support for closer economic and political ties. In other words, respondents trusting the U.S. are much more likely to support economic integration (i.e., NAFTA) and political integration (i.e., removing the border) than those with limited confidence in their northern neighbor.[17]

Closer analysis of preferences for NAFTA also reveals that support for integration correlates to favorable perceptions of the agreement's economic impact. The 1993 MORI data, for instance, show that respondents believing the U.S. or no country would benefit from NAFTA are more likely to oppose the agreement than those who felt that Mexico would benefit or that both countries would benefit equally. While 46% of those believing the U.S. would benefit the most supported NAFTA and 28% opposed the agreement, 77% of those believing that Mexico would benefit more were in favor and only 7% against the agreement. A similar pattern held with respect to the impact of the agreement on Mexican dependence: those sensing NAFTA would increase dependence on the U.S. were more likely to oppose the accord. Inglehart et al. add yet another dimension to this. As noted earlier, they found respondents were more likely to support political integration (abolishing borders) if they felt that the move would bring economic advantages (better quality of life, higher standard of living, and improvements in health care and the environment), but less likely to support it if it meant a loss of cultural identity.[18]

The desire to live in the U.S. if given the chance represents a type of individual-level preference for integration with the U.S. Again, the expectation is that people liking or trusting the U.S. should be more likely to indicate a desire to live in the U.S. Both polls featuring this question show a weak yet significant association between these variables (table 8.7). In the 1986 New York Times poll, for instance, 45% of respondents with a more favorable opinion of the U.S. people expressed a desire to live in the U.S. compared to 33% of those with an unfavorable view. The 1993 GEO poll also revealed a positive relationship between "best country" and preferred country of residence. Still, it is important to highlight here the fact that even among those viewing the U.S. as the best country in the world, 66% still prefer to live in Mexico.

Hypothesis 3: People with greater contact with the U.S. are more likely to have a favorable opinion and to support policies of integration.

Arguments regarding the effect of contact on perceptions of self and other vary. As outlined briefly in the initial chapter, one view holds that contact reduces stereotypical images and ethnocentrism, instilling a sense of trust toward others. Castañeda, for instance, posits that individuals tied more closely to the U.S. will harbor a more positive view of their northern neighbor and support policies of integration.[19] Erwin Epstein and Catherine Riordan, Jose Lozano, and Alicia Castellanos provide some empirical support for this argument.[20] Others, however, contend that rather than blurring difference and instilling trust, contact actually sharpens the sense of difference, thereby strengthening national identity and distrust. Jorge Bustamante, for instance, argues that contact reaffirms ethnic identity rather than weakening it. His research among border residents demonstrates that though border residents are more likely to use English in their daily discourse, they are also more likely to listen to "Mexican" music and exhibit a stronger sense of national identity and pride than non-border residents.[21]

The polls examined here show a positive relationship between more direct measures of contact with the U.S. and positive opinions toward the U.S. and NAFTA, thus lending some support to the hypothesis. Respondents to the 1986 New York Times poll who had visited the U.S. and those with relatives in the U.S., for example, were both more likely to harbor a favorable opinion of the U.S. than those who had not visited the country or had no relatives living there (table 8.8). In fact, a regression equation showed visiting the U.S. to have the greatest impact on a person's overall opinion of the U.S. However, length of stay and whether the respondent had met a person from the U.S. were unrelated to one's opinion of the U.S. The 1991 Los Angeles Times poll also shows traveling to the U.S. to be a statistically significant determinant of one's impression of the U.S., the U.S. people, confidence in the U.S., and one's position on NAFTA (table 8.8). Both the 1992 CENII and 1995 MORI polls also reveal a significant association between traveling to the U.S. and support for NAFTA. Individuals traveling to the U.S. in the past year were more likely to support NAFTA than others. Data from the 1998 USIA poll also support this view, though the relationship is rather weak. Thus while 73% of those who had traveled to the U.S. held a favorable view of the country, 63% who had not traveled to the U.S. held this view. Similarly, those who had traveled to the U.S. were more likely to agree that Mexicans are for the most part treated well in the U.S. (35% to 19%) The 1998 data also showed that individuals with significant contact with the U.S. (contact with five people or more) were more likely (59% versus 25%) to first mention a positive quality of the U.S. people when asked to describe their northern neighbors.

Geographic proximity represents a somewhat distinct, yet overlapping dimension to contact. Though the pattern varies, data suggest that northerners are generally more likely to have traveled to the U.S. or have relatives there. With regard to opinion of the U.S., trust, and position on NAFTA by region, data from the 1991 Los Angeles Times poll show respondents in the northern region to be somewhat more likely to have a favorable view of the U.S. and the U.S. people, to exhibit more trust in the U.S. in business, and to be slightly more likely to support NAFTA (table 8.8). Whereas more than 30% of the respondents in each of the South, Central, and Mexico City areas considered the North American people as "bad" or "somewhat bad," for example, only 14% of those in the North expressed this view (Kendall tau-c = .064**). The 1993 MORI data also showed respondents from the North to be more supportive of NAFTA than others,[22] while respondents to the

TABLE 8.8
Impact of Travel to the U.S. and Region on Opinion of the U.S. and NAFTA

Opinion of U.S. Government or People	1986 NY Times Been to U.S.		1991 LA Times Been to U.S.	
	Yes	No	Yes	No
Favorable	74%	62%	68%	51%
Unfavorable	26%	38%	18%	34%
Kendall tau- c	.116**		.193**	

	1991 LA Times			
Opinion of U.S.	North	South	Central	DF & Metro Zone
Very good/good	88%	79%	82%	78%
Bad/very bad	12%	21%	17%	22%
Kendall tau c		.042*		
Position on NAFTA	North	South	Central	DF & Metro Zone
Favor	86%	80%	79%	76%
Opposed	13%	20%	21%	24%
Kendall tau c		.073**		

* p < .05 ** p < .01

	1998 USIA						
Opinion of the U.S.	Northwest	Northeast	Bajio	Center	DF	S.Southeast	NATIONAL
Very/fairly good	76%	73%	64%	62%	57%	72%	66%
Fairly/very poor	19%	17%	25%	28%	36%	22%	26%

1998 USIA poll from the northern and southern regions tended to have a more positive opinion of the U.S. compared to those in the Federal District and the Center and Bajio regions (table 8.8). Interestingly, however, despite more positive opinion, perceptions of the U.S. among border residents do not seem to differ all that much from the national perceptions. Though Castellanos found Juarez residents to be more pro-U.S., the traits most and least admired about the U.S. among the border residents paralleled those cited earlier from the national studies: high standard of living (21.5%), salaries and work conditions (16.4%), nothing (15.6%), and consumer goods (10.2%) on the positive side; and racism and discrimination (26.5%), nothing (22%), and customs and family life (8.5%) on the more negative side.[23]

Hypothesis 4: People identifying themselves politically as right or right-center, with the PRI or PAN, and with a favorable opinion of President Salinas are more likely to have a favorable opinion of the U.S. and the relationship and to support NAFTA.

This hypothesis seeks to link an individual's opinion of the U.S. with his or her political outlook. It rests on the tendency for the ideological right to emphasize the policies of neoliberalism, including NAFTA—policies championed by the U.S., the PRI, and President Salinas—combined with the historic tendency for the left, particularly in Latin America and Mexico, to be anti-imperialist and anti-American. Of course, this pattern has never been historically consistent in Mexico. At distinct times, the Mexican right has been just as anti-American as the left, though stressing usually the loss of cultural values and the degrading influence of U.S. materialism in contrast to the left's emphasis on economic imperialism and interventionism.[24] Similarly, the PRI government historically embodied a stridently anti-American, nationalistic tone: a perspective quite different from the post–de la Madrid ideology.

Data generally support the hypothesis. The 1986 New York Times poll, for instance, shows respondents labeling themselves right-wing to be more favorably disposed toward the U.S. government and the people than those considering themselves left-wing. It also shows respondents identifying with the PAN to be more likely to have a favorable view of the U.S. government and U.S. people. Conducted in 1986, this poll, of course, predates the PRI's turn to neoliberalism under President de la Madrid. Data from the 1993 MORI poll further confirm this pattern. It shows respondents identifying themselves as right or center-right to be more likely to have a favorable view of the U.S. and to support NAFTA. It also shows PRD supporters to be more likely to oppose NAFTA and to entertain a less favorable view of the U.S. (table 8.9). Duplicating the findings of Davis, the 1991 Los Angeles Times and the 1993 MORI poll both show opinion of Salinas to be a major determinant of one's position on NAFTA.[25] Not only did one's evaluation of Salinas influence one's position on NAFTA, but it also correlated in a positive direction with confidence in the U.S. and impression of the country (but not the people). As indicated in table 8.9, respondents with a favorable view of Salinas were more likely to have a favorable opinion of the U.S. and support NAFTA.

Hypothesis 5: Respondents with higher income and education levels are more likely to have a positive opinion of the U.S. and to support policies of integration.

As a derivative of modernization theory it is generally held that higher income and education lead one away from local, parochial attachments to

TABLE 8.9
Impact of Political Attitudes on Opinion of the U.S. and NAFTA

Opinion of U.S.	*1991* LA Times			*1993 MORI*			
	Party ID			**Political ideology**			
	PRI	*PAN*	*PRD*	*Left*	*Ctr-Left*	*Ctr-Right*	*Right*
Favorable	87%	73%	68%	41%	44%	41%	56%
Unfavorable	12%	26%	32%	28%	19%	17%	14%
Kendall tau-c	.102**			.116**			

Position on NAFTA	*1991* LA Times						
	Party ID			**Salinas approval rating**			
	PRI	*PAN*	*PRD*	*Very Good*	*Good*	*Bad*	*Very bad*
Favorable	89%	82%	53%	93%	83%	51%	30%
Unfavorable	11%	18%	47%	7%	16%	49%	70%
Kendall tau-c	.165**			.227**			

* p < .05 ** p < .01

the nation, and toward universal values and a sense of cosmopolitanism. This includes greater support for nonnationalistic policies like free trade and integration. Yet literature on Latin America has historically portrayed the elite as nationalistic and even anti-American.[26]

The results are mixed and inconclusive, though some support for the hypothesis can be found. No statistically significant relationship could be found linking income or education to general attitudes toward the U.S., trust, or assessments of the relationship based on the 1986 New York Times, the 1991 Los Angeles Times, and the 1993 and 1995 MORI polls (data from the latter poll is presented in table 8.10). Davis also failed to uncover any significant relationship between education and income, and attitudes toward the U.S.[27] And yet, data from the 1992 CENII, the 1993 GEO, and the two 1998 USIA polls offer a somewhat different pattern, though the relationships are nonetheless quite weak. The 1992 CENII data (shown in table 8.10) find the upper-income group to be more likely to see the Mexican-U.S. relationship as positive and to exhibit no preference for Mexican over foreign goods. The 1993 GEO poll also shows respondents with higher levels of education to be slightly more likely to select the U.S. as the best country over Mexico and their preferred place of residence—though the higher-educated groups were actually more likely to select another country (neither Mexico nor the U.S.)

as the best country. The 1993 MORI and the 1998 USIA data (table 8.10) also exhibit a positive correlation linking education and an individual's opinion of the U.S. Here respondents with a higher level of education are more likely to have a favorable opinion of the U.S. and watch more U.S. TV programs and movies. The report on the 1998 poll, however, does not assess the impact of income or education when controlling for contact as was done for the 1991 and 1993 data. Finally, the 1995 MORI poll, duplicating the finding of the 1992 CENII poll, shows the upper-income group to be somewhat less likely to express a preference for a Mexican product over a foreign product (table 8.10). This is consistent not only with the hypothesis, but also with research presented in chapter 7.

While income and education seem to be at best rather weak determinants of individual perceptions of the U.S., more substantial evidence indicates that both may be more powerful influences of one's opinion toward NAFTA.

TABLE 8.10
Impact of Income and Education on Opinion of the U.S., NAFTA,
and Product Preferences

	1991 LAT			*1998 USIA*		
	SES Index			**Education**		
Opinion of U.S.	*Low*	*Medium*	*High*	*Low*	*Medium*	*High*
Favorable	83%	79%	84%	56%	68%	73%
Unfavorable	17%	21%	16%	39%	25%	24%

Kendall tau c = .009

	1992 CENII						*1995 MORI*					
Position on	**Income**			**Education**			**Income**			**Education**		
NAFTA	*Low*	*Mid*	*Mid*	*High*	*Low*	*Mid*	*High*	*Low*	*Mid*	*High*	*Low*	*Mid*	*High*
Support	66%	62%	76%	79%	59%	74%	80%	40%	41%	63%	35%	44%	50%
Opposition	28%	33%	21%	20%	35%	23%	19%	43%	38%	27%	44%	40%	35%

	1992 CENII				*1995 MORI*		
Product	**Income**				**Income**		
Preference	*Low*	*Mid*	*Mid*	*High*	*Low*	*Mid*	*High*
Prefer Mexican	42%	46%	38%	27%	34%	28%	25%
No preference	42%	32%	34%	37%	39%	41%	43%
Prefer Foreign	14%	21%	27%	35%	nd	nd	nd

Though the strength of the relationship varies across polls, most polls uncover a positive association linking these two variables. Table 8.10 displays this pattern from two polls. But despite their effect on a key policy initiative like NAFTA, class and education seemed to have virtually no impact on the public's perception of the likely consequences of NAFTA or their general concerns for the nation. The 1992 CENII and the 1995 MORI data, for instance, show no link between income and perceptions that NAFTA or closer economic ties with the U.S. would benefit the rich or threaten Mexico's culture or its control over petroleum. In other words, the upper- and middle-income earners may have been more likely to support integration, but they were no more likely to see integration as more or less threatening to the nation than lower-income groups. To the contrary, among the three income groups in the study, more of the higher-income group (64%) feared a loss of control of petroleum than the low- and middle-income groups (54% and 53% respectively). Along these same lines, the 1995 MORI data also show a weak tendency for the higher-income group to see the U.S. and Canada as engaging in unfair competition. Data from the 1998 USIA poll reveal a similar pattern. Though perhaps having a favorable opinion of the U.S. and even offering more support for NAFTA, higher-educated respondents are more likely to have a negative view of U.S. cultural influence over Mexico. While 37% of respondents with a primary school education and 46% of those with secondary education believed U.S. movies had a negative impact on Mexico, 61% of the university-educated sample held this view. Results from Zavala further crystallize the tendency for socioeconomic status or class to correlate with concerns about the influence of integration on the nation's values. He found a slight tendency for higher-income and higher-educated respondents to be more likely to *disagree* with the statement that "we should ensure economic development even at the cost of losing part of our identity and sovereignty."[28] This suggests that higher levels of education and income may diminish the relative importance of economic and material goals—consistent with the idea of postmaterialist values—as promised by a close relationship with the U.S., thus strengthening the relative import of the potential losses to the nation.[29]

In some ways, concern over the impact of contact and integration taps into one dimension of nationalism. According to the broader modernization theory noted earlier, one would expect people with lower levels of income or education to be more concerned about threats to the nation and thus to exhibit a stronger sense of nationalism. Only minimal evidence supports this position, however. The 1992 CENII and 1995 MORI polls show lower-income groups to be more likely to prefer Mexican over foreign products, while upper-income respondents tended to harbor no product preference.

Similarly, Bustamante cites data from the border areas in the early 1980s showing individuals with higher standards of living to measure lower on the scale of Mexicanness.[30] These measures then are in the expected direction. Other measures, however, fail to support the hypothesis. The upper-income group, for example, is equally concerned about the threat to culture as lower- and middle-income groups, as noted above. Hinting at a curvilinear pattern, data from the World Values Survey show that the middle-range income and education groups are slightly less likely to be "very proud" of their national- ity. This too echoes Zavala, who found the lower-middle classes—not the lower classes or the upper classes—to exhibit the lowest levels of pride in being Mexican.[31]

Hypothesis 6: Younger respondents are more likely than older respondents to have a favorable view of the U.S. and to support policies of integration.

A host of arguments can be marshaled to support this hypothesis. Younger people, for instance, are generally more plugged in to a globalized environ- ment featuring consumer values, U.S. entertainment, and U.S. products. They have no firsthand memories of the government's anti-U.S., pro-nation- alistic rhetoric. And they are usually in the process of negotiating their own identities.

Yet, the data reveal no consistent or clear pattern with respect to age. The 1991 Los Angeles Times poll, for instance, shows no relationship between age and opinion of the U.S., yet the 1998 USIA poll finds younger respondents have the most favorable view of the U.S. (table 8.11). It also shows the young to be more likely to like U.S. television, movies, and music by a wide margin (73% of the 18–24 group likes U.S. movies, compared to 58% of the 25–44 cohort and 42% of the 45 + cohort) and to be more likely to see the influence of these cultural devices as positive. With regards to NAFTA, both the 1992 CENII and 1995 MORI polls fail to detect any significant linkage with age. As shown in table 8.11, of the three age cohorts (below 30, 30–49, and over 50), the youngest group was actually more likely to oppose NAFTA than the 30–49 group. And yet, the 1995 MORI poll did show younger respondents to be more likely to prefer foreign products to domestic ones or to hold no preference. This finding is also consistent with the findings from marketing studies presented in chapter 7.

The Issue of Change

Though the nature of the surveys complicates the analysis of change, it is nonetheless possible to question whether there is any empirical evidence to

TABLE 8.11
Impact of Age on Opinion of the U.S. and NAFTA

	1991 LAT					*1998 USIA*		
Opinion of US	*18–24*	*25–29*	*30–39*	*40–49*	*50+*	*18–24*	*25–44*	*45+*
Favorable	84%	86%	79%	75%	85%	70%	69%	55%
Unfavorable	16%	14%	21%	25%	14%	25%	24%	32%

Kendall tau c = .009

	1992 CENII			*1995 MORI*		
Position on NAFTA	*18–30*	*30–49*	*50+*	*18–30*	*30–49*	*50+*
Favor	72%	73%	66%	46%	44%	35%
Neutral	3%	4%	5%	13%	18%	23%
Opposed	25%	23%	30%	42%	38%	41%

suggest that Mexicans' opinions of the U.S., the nation, and related policies have changed in recent years. Since the report of the 1979 poll from Mexico City included comparative polling data going back to the mid-1950s, it is actually possible to plot favorable vs. unfavorable opinion of the U.S. over an extended period. But as shown in figure 8.1, there is no clear indication that opinion toward the U.S. has improved in recent years. If anything, the data hint at a nonlinear pattern with favorable opinion peaking during the 1960s,

Figure 8.1.   Opinion of the U.S. Over Time

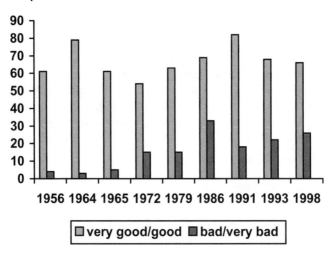

falling during the 1970s, and increasing in the late 1980s and early 1990s before declining somewhat in the subsequent years. Such cycles may correspond to the ebbs and flows in the bilateral relationship and international events, though that issue cannot be explored here.

A closer comparison of current and past studies also seems to suggest continuity rather than change. Ralph Beals's study of Mexican opinion of the U.S. in the 1950s, for example, highlights many of the same traits identified in the studies from the 1980s and 1990s.[32] Back then, Mexicans praised the U.S. for having a high standard of living, respect for the rule of law, and a functioning democracy; but they were critical of U.S. support for fascist regimes and its treatment of Mexico and Mexicans. Mexicans of that time generally considered the U.S. people friendly, but also selfish and irreligious, lacking a respect for culture. The description of one interviewee during the period hardly seems anachronistic: "I still think that almost all the people in the United States think that the only goal in life is to get money, to get work. . . . Besides making money, we have another goal."[33] Such a view clearly parallels those expressed in more contemporary times.

Through interviews with a small group of students during the same period (1950s), Humphrey identified a similar narrative. Hinting at the inherent trade-offs in policy options as discussed above, he found that despite viewing the U.S. tourist as arrogant, most respondents felt that the U.S. tourist should be treated properly because of his or her wealth and power.[34] The 1979 poll in Mexico City also provides some interesting parallels to those of the following decades. Here, respondents viewed a cooperative relationship with the U.S. as important to the nation, and felt that the U.S. treats Mexico and Mexicans poorly and seeks to take advantage of Mexico. And yet, some 63% of respondents held a good or very good opinion of the U.S. In some contrast to the more recent period, a question regarding something akin to integration (interdependence) showed 59% at the time seeing it as a bad thing compared to 40% considering it a good thing.

Figure 8.2, in turn, presents comparisons from a single survey conducted in different years: the World Values Survey. It looks at trends from 1981 to 1995–1997. As shown, the two measures of nationalism actually move in opposite directions, suggesting the complexity of this variable. While slightly more Mexicans considered themselves very proud of their nationality in the 1990s, fewer were willing to fight for the nation.

Longitudinal measures for support of policies of integration like NAFTA focus only on the 1990s. Still, as depicted in figure 8.3, support for NAFTA declined (and opposition increased) during the period. Clearly, the key intervening component here was the economic crisis of 1994–1995. The December 1994 devaluation of the peso threw the Mexican economy into a tailspin.

Figure 8.2.   Mexican Nationalism Over Time

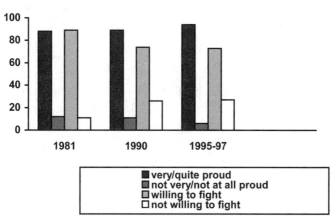

GDP fell 6.9% in 1995 as real wages plummeted, businesses went bankrupt, and banks defaulted.

Among the many effects, this economic earthquake altered the public's perceptions of the U.S., the nation's interests, and NAFTA. As shown in table 8.12, not only did many blame NAFTA for the crisis, but perceptions of the likely impact of economic integration on the country also shifted rather dramatically. By 1995, fewer believed integration would benefit Mexico. More felt the bilateral relationship was detrimental to Mexico and that integration

Figure 8.3.   Position on Free Trade/NAFTA Over Time

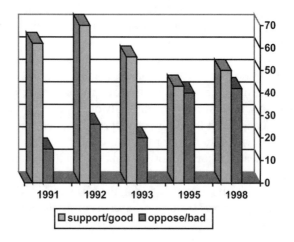

TABLE 8.12
Position on NAFTA Prior To and During the Economic Crisis of 1994–1995

	1992 CENII	1995 MORI	Percentage Change
Position on NAFTA			
Support/some support/continue/			
continue with changes	70%	43%	− 27
Somewhat/completely opposed	26%	40%	+ 14
Relations with the United States are			
Adequate	32%	16%	− 16
Insufficient	42%	32%	− 10
Inadequate	17%	32%	+ 15
Unfair competition favors the United States and Canada			
Yes	39%	55%	+ 16
Mexican products			
Can compete	67%	57%	− 10
Can't compete	28%	41%	+ 13
NAFTA threatens control over petroleum			
Yes	39%	55%	+ 16
Mexico will lose it its culture or traditions as a result of U.S. influence			
Totally	8%	24%	+ 16
Partially	26%	44%	+ 18
Not completely	23%	18%	− 5
No	41%	12%	− 29
Current economic crisis due to NAFTA			
Yes	na	51%	na
No	na	39%	na

threatened such national interests as culture and control over petroleum. When viewed within the context of policy trade-offs, it seems, almost paradoxically, that the concern over noneconomic issues (like threats to culture and petroleum) waxed just as the economic rationale for integration waned. Reintroducing the issue of class, table 8.13 shows that the shift in opinion toward NAFTA because of the economic crisis was more pronounced among middle-class respondents, though support from all income groups fell. This suggests that economic crisis strengthens nationalistic concerns among all social classes.[35]

While a comparison of the 1992 and 1995 data points to short-term changes in opinion attributable to the economic crisis, the short-term shift in opinion just from April to November 1998 recorded by the 1998 USIA poll is perhaps even more striking. It shows shifts beyond the "plus-or-minus" standard for the poll, and all in a consistent direction. Positive opin-

TABLE 8.13
Change in Position on NAFTA 1992–1995 by Income Group

	1992 CENII			1995 MORI			Percentage Change		
	Low	Middle	High	Low	Middle	High	Low	Middle	High
Favor	64%	76%	79%	40%	41%	63%	− 24	− 35	− 16
Neutral	3%	0%	1%	17%	21%	9%	+ 14	+ 21	+ 8
Opposed	31%	21%	20%	43%	38%	27%	+ 12	+ 17	+ 7

ion toward the U.S. climbed from 53% in April to 66% in November, positive evaluations of the bilateral relationship went from 58% to 77%, the view that NAFTA would not benefit Mexico fell from 61% to 42%, and the notion the U.S. was not complying very well or not at all with NAFTA declined from 45% to 30%. While a review of either the events spanning the period or the methodologies of the polls might offer some explanation for these differences, the changes help reiterate the point that opinion is volatile and in flux, and hence descriptive conclusions based on one poll are highly problematic.

Conclusion

Two important conclusions emerge from an analysis of polling data: first, that Mexicans seem to have a more complex and complicated view of the U.S. and the nation than many might have expected; and second, that despite the findings, very little of the variation can truly be explained.

As shown, Mexicans tend to have a favorable view of the U.S., but limited trust; limited trust, but a desire to integrate economically; a desire to integrate economically, but a sense that the rich and the U.S. will benefit more and that the process may threaten Mexican culture or sovereignty. They recognize the need to work with the U.S. to deal with the nation's problems, but feel that the U.S. treats Mexico unfairly or unjustly. They express a favorable view of the U.S., but also a strong sense of nationalism and a preference for and desire to protect Mexican culture. The evidence suggests that contact with the U.S. increases the positive views toward the country, but that mixed emotions about the general effects of that contact persist. And the evidence points to a relatively clear dichotomous pattern in which the positive qualities associated with the U.S. contrast with the negative traits attached to the nation and vice versa. Preference to policies of integration is thus linked to the desire to appropriate (U.S. as opportunity) the positive qualities of the other, while maintaining those associated with the idealized nation.

In terms of explanation, the analysis does reveal a string of statistically significant linkages and patterns. Opinions of the U.S., the U.S. government, and the U.S. people all correlate, while also influencing the feeling of confidence and evaluations of the relationship. Confidence and trust in the U.S. also seem to translate into greater support for policies of integration and even the desire to live in the U.S. Looking at the determinants of these views, traveling to and proximity to the U.S., political attitudes, and to a lesser degree socioeconomic status all seem to influence one's perception of the U.S., assessments of the relationship, and position for or against NAFTA. And yet, despite finding support for most of the hypotheses set out here, very little variation could be explained. Only 20% of the variation in confidence in the U.S. in the 1991 data could be explained by one's opinion of the U.S., the people, and assessments of the relationship. In like manner, the data provide only limited explanation of the variation in perceptions of the U.S. or position on NAFTA. As seen above, only a few of the correlations were particularly strong or robust. In fact, in Davis's study, the extensive, multivariate model—duplicated here—could only explain 13% (1991) and 4% (1993) of the variation in Mexican attitudes toward the U.S.[36] Slightly more robustly, only 32% (1991) and 27% (1993) of the variation in Mexicans' position on NAFTA could be explained. In both cases, but especially with respect to popular attitudes toward the U.S., most of the variation remains unexplained. This suggests, of course, that other untapped, unmeasured, and perhaps even unimagined factors are at play.

Such a conclusion seems somewhat applicable to the issue of change as well. While the data suggest that some change has occurred, particularly in short-term takes, there nonetheless seems to be a relatively consistent range within which opinion fluctuates. Here we see that despite the incredible changes in Mexican society in recent decades, the pattern of opinion toward the U.S. has remained relatively consistent. Past depictions of Mexican perceptions of the U.S. rarely seem anachronistic or out of place. This suggests that perhaps the policy somersaults; the detachment of anti-Americanism from the State's rhetoric, globalization, democratization, and closer integration have had far less an impact on perceptions of *gringolandia* and the nation than one might expect—or that their impact has yet to be fully registered.

Notes

1. Roderic A. Camp, "The Cross and the Polling Booth: Religion, Politics and the Laity in Mexico," *Latin American Research Review* 29 (3) (1994): 69–100.

2. Gilbert, "Rewriting History."

3. Beals, "Mexican Student"; Ulises Beltrán, Fernando Castaños, Julia Isabel Flores, Yolanda Meyenberg, and Blanca Helena del Pozo, *Los Mexicanos de los Noventa* (Mexico City: Instituto de Investigaciones Sociales, Universidad Nacional Autónoma de México, 1997); Bustamante, "Mexico-U.S. Border"; Inglehart et al., *North American Trajectory.*

4. Humphrey, "Mexican Image of Americans"; and Vila, *Everyday Life, Culture and Identity.*

5. Herbert Asher, *Polling and the Public.* 4th edition (Washington, D.C.: CQ Press, 1998), 44.

6. Rivera Velázquez, "Comentario a una encuesta," *Cuaderno a Nexos* 48 (June 1992): iii–viii.

7. While these polls measure differences between the two societies as seen solely by the Mexicans, two studies compare samples of U.S. and Mexican respondents to explore more objective differences between the two cultures. Linda Ueltschy and John Ryans, in "Employing Standardized Promotion Strategies in Mexico," compared the cultural values of a group of students from the U.S. and Mexico, and found significant differences between the two. Most of the difference (they could explain 64% of the variation) centered on the importance Mexicans placed on the "good things in life" (mature love, pleasure, comfortable life, sense of accomplishment, and family security). Such findings parallel the differences described in this chapter. Inglehart et al., in *North American Trajectory,* also focus on a range of values and find similar orientations among the two populations. Their study looks, however, at issues like democracy, free-market economies, globalization, religiosity, confidence in nongovernmental institutions, and autonomy over obedience in child rearing, among others.

8. Vila, *Everyday Life, Culture and Identity,* 309.

9. Pastor and Castañeda, *Limits to Friendship,* 37–38; Judith Alder Hellman, *Mexico in Crisis* (New York: Holms and Meier, 1988), 271.

10. Ivan Zavala, "Valores políticos," in *Como somos los mexicanos,* edited by Alberto Hernández Medina and Luís Narro Rodríguez (Mexico City: Centro de Estudios Educativos, 1987), 107.

11. Daniel M. Lund, "El tratado de libre comercio: Los extremos de la confusión," *Este País,* Julio 1993: 2–6.

12. Judith Alder Hellman, in "Mexican Perceptions of Free Trade: Support and Opposition to NAFTA," in *The Political Economy of North American Free Trade,* edited by Ricardo Grinspun and Maxwell A. Cameron (New York: St. Martin's Press, 1993), 193–204, by contrast, attributes the public's support of NAFTA to the regime's tight control over the media.

13. Inglehart et al., *North American Trajectory,* 142, 146.

14. Vila, *Everyday Life, Culture and Identity,* 393.

15. Asterisks used here and in all tables refer to level of significance: * = .05 level of significance; ** = .01 level of significance.

16. Davis, "Mass Support for Regional Integration," 124.

17. Inglehart et al., *North American Trajectory.*

18. Inglehart et al., *North American Trajectory,* 142–46.

19. Castañeda, *Estados Unidos Affair.*

20. The empirical study by Erwin H. Epstein and Catherine A. Riordan ("Bicultural Preparation and National Identity: A Study of Medical Students at a Mexican University," *Mexican Studies/Estudios Mexicanos* 5 [2] [1989]: 239–63) revealed a negative association between contact with the U.S. and expressed ethnocentrism, while Lozano ("Media Reception," cited in Vila, *Everyday Life, Culture and Identity,* 171–72) and Alicia Castellanos Guerrero, *Ciudad Juarez: la vida fronteriza* (Mexico City: Nuestro Tiempo, 1981) found the residents of Ciudad Juarez to be more pro-U.S. and more "Americanized" (Mexicanidad was measured in terms of identification with traditional family attitudes).

21. Bustamante, "Frontera México-Estados Unidos," and "Mexico-U.S. Border." See also Valenzuela, "Identidades culturales frente al TLC."

22. Davis, "Mass Support for Regional Integration."

23. Castellanos Guerrero, *Ciudad Juarez.*

24. See, for example, Anne Rubenstein, *Bad Language, Naked Ladies & Other Threats to the Nation: A Political History of Comic Books in Mexico* (Durham, NC: Duke University Press, 1998); Zolov, *Refried Elvis.*

25. Davis, "Mass Support for Regional Integration."

26. See Hollander, *Anti-Americanism;* Turner, *Dynamics of Mexican Nationalism.*

27. Davis, "Mass Support for Regional Integration."

28. Zavala, "Valores políticos."

29. It is on this point where the postmaterialist thesis of Inglehart seems to nurture confusion. Parallel to the depiction here, Inglehart defines a postmaterialist ideology as one that deemphasizes material or economic values in favor of more symbolic values. This would seem to include a concern for identity, culture, tradition, morals, and even the nation. And yet, in Inglehart et al., *North American Trajectory,* he seems to portray postmaterialism as antithetical to nationalism and consistent with support for NAFTA and economic opening. But if Mexicans, as the data show, envision NAFTA as primarily an economic opportunity, it would seem that the support would come from those with a more materialist perspective, and that postmaterialists would oppose the agreement.

30. Bustamante, "Mexico-U.S. Border."

31. Zavala, "Valores políticos," 107. The polls offer few direct or indirect measures of nationalism, making it almost impossible to test whether a pro-Mexican versus anti-U.S. dichotomy might exist. The fact that a strong sense of nationalism coexists with favorable opinion of the U.S., however, as noted earlier seems to argue against such a simplistic dichotomy. Interestingly there seem to be only weak associations among the various measures of nationalism. In the World Values Survey, pride in country and willingness to fight were only weakly related ($r = .181$), as were national pride and a person's stance on whether the country should limit imports (Kendall tau-c $= .061**$). Respondents "very" proud to be Mexican were somewhat more likely than others to support a policy of limiting imports, but the relationship was mild at best.

32. Beals, "Mexican Student."

33. Cited in Beals, "Mexican Student," 109.

Chapter 8

34. Humphrey, "Mexican Image of Americans," 118.

35. Stephen D. Morris and John T. Passe-Smith, "What a Difference a Crisis Makes: NAFTA, Mexico and the United States," *Latin American Perspectives* 28 (3) (2001): 124–49.

36. Davis, "Mass Support for Regional Integration."

9

Conclusion: Mexican Images
of Nation and Neighbor

P RIOR CHAPTERS HAVE EXPLORED contemporary political discourse,
school textbooks, political cartoons, the writings of some of Mexico's
foremost intellectuals, national motion pictures, the consumer market, and
public opinion in an effort to shed light on three questions: (1) How do
Mexicans view the U.S.? (2) How do these perceptions relate to perceptions
of the nation? and (3) Are things changing? Despite the reappearance of certain themes and the occasional cross-reference, so far the analysis has not
sought to compare and contrast the findings from the separate foci or pull
them together to offer a more coherent view. Such are the dual tasks of the
concluding chapter.

Mapping the Contexts

In certain ways, different images of the U.S. emerge from the various social
agents examined here. Each context tends to stress different dimensions for
different reasons. The discourse of the politicians emphasizes the political
and economic power of the U.S. and the bilateral relationship. It concentrates pragmatically on defining the national interest, fashioning policies pur-
suant to that interest, and determining acceptable trade-offs. The political
discourse is not monolithic, however, but contains two broad narratives. One
highlights the opportunities stemming from Mexico's proximity to the U.S.;
the other warns of the dangers. The former narrative emphasizes the economic opportunities, envisioning economic integration with the U.S. as the
answer to Mexico's perennial problem of economic development. It envi-

sions a bilateral relationship that has matured in recent years and overcome the difficulties and myths of the past. It portrays a Mexico that is strong enough culturally and nationally to withstand close economic and political ties to the U.S. and a U.S. that now respects Mexico. At the same time, it soberly stresses the imperatives crafted by globalization: Mexico, so it goes, has few if any options. The counternarrative, by contrast, emphasizes the dangers of too close a relationship with the U.S. It underscores the inequitable basis of the relationship, particularly the historic tendency for the U.S. to take advantage of a weak and vulnerable Mexico. And while it acknowledges globalization, it nonetheless sees some room for policy maneuver.

Though both narratives are rooted in the debates of the past, the current discourse is nonetheless different. For one, the State has clearly distanced itself from the rhetoric of much of the post-Revolutionary elite, while the opposition tends to target much of the blame for the adverse consequences of the relationship on the Mexican government. Even Vicente Fox as opposition candidate criticized the Mexican government for not being able to deal effectively with the U.S. Moreover, though somewhat reminiscent of the Revolutionary ideology of the past, the narrative stressing the dangers of the U.S. is hardly anachronistic. The PRD and Cárdenas acknowledge the changes of globalization and do not call for a complete return to the policies of the past, though they do accuse recent governments of violating the historic principles of the nation. Even the EZLN discourse, which goes perhaps the furthest in criticizing the U.S. government and the global capitalist system, envisions a different political context in which some in the U.S. are now seen as potential allies in the struggle.

While the political discourse deals with the political present, privileging the issues of economic prosperity and development, the school texts tend to focus more on the past and the lessons of history. And while some politicians contend that Mexico and the U.S. have overcome that history, having charted a *new era,* the school texts serve to remind students of the difficulties of the past, and to instill the idea that such problems may continue to shape the nation and the bilateral relationship. Perhaps more so than any other context, the school texts go far in portraying the U.S. historically as anti-Mexican and dangerous. More critically from a political perspective, the texts stress the importance of unity in the face of the challenge represented by the U.S. They depict the U.S. as interventionist, the cause of irreparable harm to Mexico, and yet the inspirational source of its national pride. Above all, the texts ensure that no Mexican will ever forget the unjust war perpetuated by the U.S.: an act that serves symbolically to explain Mexico's subsequent failures and its strong sense of identity. At the same time, however, even the texts, like many of the other discourses, acknowledge the internal political freedoms and economic successes of the U.S., and even the benefits to Mexico derived from U.S. trade and investment. To help navigate this paradox, the texts tend to hoist the State up as not just the embodiment of the nation, the symbol of national unity, but also as the only force capable of maximizing the advantages of engaging the potentially dangerous U.S. while keeping it at bay.

In contrast to both the political pragmatism found within the political discourse and the historical and nationalistic teachings found in the school texts, the political cartoons use exaggeration and humor to echo key points within the broader discourse. In many ways, the political caricatures go the furthest in portraying the U.S. in less than flattering terms, providing an important outlet for such sentiments. The cartoons portray the U.S. as being less than friendly toward Mexico, perhaps even to the point of casting the U.S. as incapable of having a friendly relationship. They paint the U.S. as hypocritical and unable to recognize that it treats others differently than itself. The cartoons also depict the U.S. as racist and anti-Mexican, wrapped in its own arrogance and sense of self-worth. The cartoons virtually never admire the internal attributes of the U.S. as is done in other contexts. In many ways, the cartoons reify the historical themes found in the school texts and then apply these to contemporary political and economic problems. Consequently, they offer very little in the way of praising or acknowledging a *new relationship*. The cartoonists, like much of the political opposition, are often critical of the Mexican government's handling of the U.S., viewing the U.S. as an accomplice.

The overwhelming presence of the theme of the U.S. in the writings of important Mexican intellectuals provides an indication of the centrality of the U.S. in defining Mexico and Mexican identity. Mexican intellectuals clearly offer the most sophisticated analysis of the U.S. and the nation, providing insights into the underlying nature of U.S. and Mexican culture and society as well as the political and economic dimensions of the U.S. and the bilateral relationship. The authors focus on history and culture, politics and questions of development. The intellectuals pinpoint key differences between the two societies, and rely on these differences to explain why the U.S. has enjoyed the success that has seemingly escaped Mexico. Most intellectuals also differentiate the admirable internal attributes of the U.S. from its treatment of others, including Mexico. The intellectuals also tend to employ a range of Manichean categories to define Mexicanness in opposition to North Americanness. But in this process of national construction, the intellectuals underscore the key paradox facing the nation: while difference vis-à-vis the U.S. helps define Mexicanness, the country struggles to achieve much of what the U.S. has already obtained domestically (wealth, democracy). However,

Mexico must achieve these without losing those qualities that make it different, without becoming too much "like them." One task embraces imitation;
the other rejects it. Today, Mexican intellectuals continue to lead this historically grounded debate over whether navigating such a paradox is even possible and, if so, how. Paralleling much of the debate over globalization, few
agree, for instance, whether NAFTA impacts national identity and, if so, to
what extent, and what, if anything, can be done about it.

Unlike the other social contexts, Mexican movies focus mainly on the culture of the U.S., usually personifying the U.S. in the form of U.S. characters.
These characters function not only to highlight the negative personality traits
associated with U.S. culture, but also to bring to light the superior qualities
of the Mexican culture. Movies thus provide an outlet, seen in some of the
political cartoons, to reverse the powerful U.S. versus weak Mexican battle
and thus, in the plot's resolution, to reaffirm the superior qualities of the
Mexican. In addition, movies provide a means to attack the idea of the
"American dream," which in Mexico often means going north. Usually, such
movies show migrants suffering at the hands of the anti-Mexican and racist
U.S. On the tragic side, the migrant pays seriously for abandoning his or her
country and culture: loss of life at the hands of the *migra* or a living death,
the loss of identity, and anomie. On the more positive side, the migrant eventually comes to his or her senses, saved in the end by recognizing the inherent
value of family and the national culture (the national family). By showing
the attractiveness of the U.S., the lights, the glitter, the wealth, but suggesting
that these can only be obtained at a price, the movies play on important paradoxes found in other contexts: modernity, but at a cost. They also show that
despite the wealth and the glitter in the U.S., the *gringos* are not nearly as
cunning, caring, or macho as the Mexicans.

In some form or another, most of these contexts underscore the economic
development of the U.S., its wealth and its culture of consumption. Paradoxically, these represent both the attractiveness of the U.S.—the personal desire
for wealth and consumption, and the national desire for development—that
nurtures the desire to imitate, and the hidden danger of assimilating a culture
without meaning, the *pepsicoatl* culture of excessive and unrestrained materialism. Analysis of consumption and marketing peers particularly into this
dimension of the equation only to uncover a mixed pattern. U.S. products
dominate certain sectors of the Mexican economy, but this is not true in all
areas of the economy. Mexicans do associate development and economic
success with the U.S., but again they do not deem all U.S. products superior.
Mexicans still prefer national products in such diverse areas as music, beer,
and food, despite enjoying more choices because of recent economic changes.
A sense of national pride thus seems to temper a tendency to prefer products

associated with the U.S.: a neat parallel to the rejection or acceptance of the origins of Mexico itself as either a rape or a birth. And, it seems, that by highlighting both the U.S. and the Mexican aspects of their products, both Mexican and U.S. companies are aware of this unique mixture.

Data from public opinion polls echo many of these themes, while showing the complexity of Mexican images of the U.S. They show Mexicans to have a generally favorable opinion of the U.S. and the people, but to divide over whether to trust the U.S. or not. Many, of course, do not trust the U.S. Understandably those trusting the U.S. are more likely to support the policies of integration, while those not trusting the U.S. are less likely to support such policies. Such divisions over policy and trust parallel those found in the political discourse and interpretations of history. The polls also confirm many of the ideas found in the intellectual writings about U.S. culture or in the history texts about U.S. behavior: the U.S. is considered materialistic, arrogant, imperialistic—in contrast to the Mexican who possesses meaningful values— and yet the U.S. is also seen as enjoying an admirable political and economic system. The polls also show that people's contact with the U.S. may improve their opinion of and trust toward the U.S. But most importantly perhaps, the opinion polls provide little empirical explanation for the patterns of Mexican opinion toward the U.S. Mexicans' opinions toward the U.S., the relationship, and public policy, in short, cannot be easily explained by such variables as class, geography, political attitudes, or ideology.

In some ways, the competing discourses point in different directions, thus sustaining polar ideological positions. This means, for example, that someone wishing to demonstrate that Mexicans now have a favorable image of the U.S. can easily cite some polling data, the rhetoric of Salinas and Fox, certain passages from the tomes of intellectuals, and consumption patterns. They can combine these with selected statements from the past as proof of the emergence of a *new era* in the relationship. Meanwhile, anyone wishing to demonstrate that Mexicans have a less than favorable opinion can cite other polling data, the Cárdenas and EZLN discourses, the political cartoons, or other passages from the writings of the intellectuals, or just show a movie with a *gringo* character. They can also couple these with historic statements from the elite, a proof of continuity. But despite the seemingly coherent arguments, neither view is any more authentic than the other; instead, the two compete to form a broader and dynamic discourse on self and other. In many ways they are inseparable, flip sides of the same coin. Both have a historic presence and, despite significant political and economic changes, continue to discursively contest and define the nation.

And yet there is evidence to suggest that some change has occurred. The boundaries of the debate regarding the U.S. certainly have shifted in recent years. Mexicans are no longer discussing a free trade agreement *per se* or even foreign electoral observers, but rather a monetary union and an opening of the border. Indeed, the level of contact has increased dramatically in recent years, giving Mexicans a better understanding of the U.S., while at the same time crystallizing the challenges to Mexican culture and identity. Of course, this has happened before, particularly during the early part of the twentieth century, but never to the point of involving so many people within a much more open and internationalized climate. Moreover, the State's (hegemonic?) discourse has changed. Though the political debate remains focused on issues related to Mexico's bilateral relationship with the U.S. and the "art of possible reactions," the State has clearly distanced itself from the rhetoric of past regimes, convincing many of the need to cooperate closely with the U.S. Much of this discourse centers on the idea that it is impossible to escape the demands of the global market.

Of even greater importance, perhaps, is that the equation producing national identity has fundamentally changed. Despite (or concomitant with) the changing rhetoric from the government, the State itself has lost much of the power it once had to construct national identity. As a result of economic changes, globalization, and democratization, the private sector, international forces, consumption, opposition parties, and so on, all play a much larger role today in determining what it means to be Mexican, what defines the nation and its interests than in the past. Such changes portend a more decentered and deterritorialized sense of the nation and national identity, greater degrees of pluralism, and fewer "national" patterns. In many ways, such changes—encapsulated under the term globalization—challenge past notions of identity, prompting the need to "reconstruct" identity, while fundamentally altering the formula used for its construction.

It is within this context of change that the current challenges to Mexico's image of the U.S. and the nation stand as merely some of many other ongoing challenges to national identity. The rise of *neoindigenismo* as a result of the Zapatista uprising in Chiapas, for instance, contests past notions about the Indian, the nature of the country's indigenous past, the indigenous component of *mestizaje,* and the idea of national unity. Above all, *neoindigenismo* challenges Mexico to come to grips with its own racism and construct a pluriethnic nation.[1] Democratization—particularly the PRI's loss of power (Are these the same?)—further challenges fundamental assumptions about the nature of the State and the nation. Though the rhetoric of President Fox parallels in certain ways the views of recent *priista* presidents, the PAN nonetheless debates the need to rewrite the nation's school texts: perhaps to rewrite history in its own image.[2] All these issues—the U.S., the indigenous, the

State—coalesce around the contemporary and yet historic issue of constructing Mexico's sense of nation.

The Imaginary "Mexico" and the Imaginary "U.S."

The nation—an "imagined community," to use Benedict Anderson's celebrated phrase—is a psychological construct crafted through discourses about self and other.[3] In Mexico, these discourses encompass not only an imaginary "Mexico," but an imaginary "U.S.," Mexico's predominant other.

Imaginary "Mexico" is a nation that visualizes a glorious history distorted by the conquest, and yet sees itself as a product of the fusion of the two cultures and the two histories. It is a nation that respects and glorifies the indigenous—as seen through its monuments—but only as a historical artifact. This "Mexico" is a nation characterized by a sense of unity, where racial and even class differences evaporate behind a common sense of belonging and a feeling of historical and providential purpose, "*la raza cósmica*." It is a nation rooted in deep human values stressing family, *virtud*, and the cultural and spiritual essence of the individual. At the same time, this "Mexico" condemns materialism and impersonal institutions. It is a nation scarred by political, economic, and cultural forces beyond its control. And it believes that such forces continue to threaten the nation. It is a nation that considers itself vulnerable, weak, and hence defensive before a powerful neighbor. This "Mexico" aspires to achieve "modernity," to demonstrate to the world its true greatness, but also fears losing that which makes it distinct. Its values and even its primordial legacy make it worthy of greatness, but, for whatever reason, history and God have not been so kind.

Mexico's imaginary "United States," by contrast, is a country lucky enough to have received many of history's and God's blessings. This "United States" enjoys the democratic and developed traits that the imaginary "Mexico" wishes for itself; but the imaginary "U.S." is not worthy of these. For one, the culture of the imagined "U.S." is excessively materialistic, nihilistic, and lacking in "true," "superior" values of family, faith, meaningful human relationships, and high culture. This "U.S." may be rich, but it has paid a fatal price to become so: it sold its soul for riches and those riches cannot buy it back. Even worse, much of its "success" it achieved by exploiting others, including poor imaginary "Mexico." Though internally democratic, this "U.S." treats others with little or no respect, exhibiting an air of arrogance, hypocrisy, and racism that merely invites contempt. This adds even more to its unworthiness: the "U.S." may be rich and democratic, but it achieved these through its (mis)treatment of others. Of course, the "U.S." explains its "success" based on its own attributes, which it then takes as a license to paternalistically dictate to or "help" others, including "Mexico." Even for a Mexican to root for the U.S. in any international sporting event is made difficult because a "U.S." victory merely confirms the worst in it: its arrogance. And yet, its technological wizardry guarantees that it can put on one hell of a show and produce products of incredible quality and attractiveness. Indeed, on the material plane, this "U.S." has no equal.

In many ways, these two imaginary nations serve to define one another. Traits highlighted by one often shadow similar traits of the other, thereby helping to forge difference and hence identity. The perception of the "U.S." as future-oriented, for example, contrasts with and defines "Mexico's" glorious past, while at the same time raising questions about what truly defines greatness. The image of the U.S. as racist similarly contrasts with the Mexican perception of unity and racial purity. At the same time, it makes it difficult for the Mexican to entertain the notion of the Mexican as racist, or the *gringo* as treating the Mexican with respect. The image of the U.S. as lacking in family values contrasts with the self-perception of the Mexican as having strong family values. While rooted in a certain reality, such a view nonetheless hides a portion of that reality. Mexicans may have family problems just like the *gringos,* but the prevailing narrative makes it difficult to recognize such problems, just as it makes it difficult for the Mexican to conceive of a "close" U.S. family.

"Poor Mexico, so far from God and so close to the U.S" implies an imaginary nation abandoned by God and left to suffer from its proximity to another imaginary nation that at times seems to believe itself God or at least God's favorite (i.e., Manifest Destiny). Of course, if either were true in the Mexican imagination, then God would be just as close to Mexico as the U.S. Caught up then in this geographic and seemingly providential inevitability, Mexico is forever torn. Its desire for national fulfillment (development, democracy, etc.) heightens the need to engage the U.S.—the only game in town—to view the U.S. as an opportunity unique in the world; and yet too close a collaboration risks unleashing greater U.S. influence and making Mexico too much like the "*gringo.*" In some ways then, the only way of effectively engaging the "U.S." is to hold on tightly to the imaginary, mythical "Mexico." Even as a portion of it may seem to be slipping away and changing, this imagined "Mexico" cannot be abandoned unless a concurrent and parallel change in the imaginary "U.S." occurs. The two stereotypical images, in short, go hand in hand as a love-hate view of one echoes deep within a love-hate view of the other.

One means of dulling the sharp differences separating the two images is through the growing realization (discourse) in Mexico that the imagined

"U.S." is actually changing and becoming, in a sense, more "Mexican." Such a discourse of change in the imaginary "U.S." helps confirm the "superiority" of the values of "Mexico," while, at the same time, providing an external validation of the country's status and success. However, in stark contrast to interpretations of the "U.S.," Mexico will consider itself worthy of this "success." Within this narrative, Mexico's success—externally validated—will not only ensure respect from others like the "U.S.," but also will nurture a sense of self-respect. Above all, the success will be touted as a demonstration that success can be achieved without mortgaging one's soul: the ultimate solution to the nation's perennial paradox.

Indeed, such cultural shifts on both sides of the border may be occurring, subtly, because of closer contacts, globalization, the growing deterritorialization of the nation, and the beginnings of trilateral political institutions. The altering of the formula determining national identity, particularly the weakening of the role of the Sate, adds to such trends. Increasingly, a common set of global actors influences and shapes individual identity regardless of location. Such changes, however, like the two images themselves, play off one another. In other words, Mexico's quest to reconstruct national identity reflects in some ways a similar quest that is occurring in the U.S. Hence, the growth of things Mexican in the U.S., the changing nature of North American society, helps pave the way for Mexico to perceive its northern neighbor in a different way and hence perceive itself differently. Changes in the national identity in the U.S., now challenged to come to grips with its increasing "Mexicanness," similarly set the stage for the U.S. to reconstruct its image of Mexico. Within this context of mutual influence, hybridity in both cultures and societies seems much more likely than the all-out Americanization of Mexico. And such hybridity pushes beyond the dichotomous, national-based images of the past.

But these postnational trends remain vulnerable and incipient. First, they are vulnerable to the continuing strength of nationalism as an explanatory category and a celebrated cause in both societies. Nationalistic thinking, in short, still frames politics. Both governments still pursue policies that privilege "we the people," and nationalism continues to provide a tried-and-true conceptual device to trace the benefits of integration and globalization. As long as nationalism provides the context for the making of political decisions and for understanding the world, it will continue to reaffirm differences among people and thus shadow the emergence of something new. And though globalization has altered the formula for crafting identity, it has not eliminated the need for identity.

Second, the postnationalistic trends are vulnerable to the continuing asymmetries that ironically divide and at the same time unite Mexico and the

U.S. On the one hand, the asymmetries of power and wealth underlie the paternalistic arrogance of the imaginary "U.S." in its views and treatment of Mexico. They also, on the other hand, force Mexico to deal with the U.S. in order to obtain the fruits of development and globalization, while simultaneously shaping imaginary "Mexico's" reactive posture and inherent need to reaffirm its own identity. Conceiving these asymmetries in national terms ensures the continuation of historic Mexican images of the U.S. and their role in shaping the sense of the nation. It is not that identity is unimportant or fading amid the forces of globalization, but what beyond the imagined nation and its State will anchor identity in the future?

As Jorge Hernández correctly points out, "Mexico continues, as in the beginning, being a nation that is 'made' by the intellect."[4] Indeed, despite changing conditions, Mexico still (re)invents itself on a daily basis, debating the problems and opportunities associated with living beside the U.S. and constructing identity through contrast to its *primos del otro lado* (*del rio!*). The future of the country, its people, and its hemispheric relations all hinge in part upon how Mexicans envision the U.S., how they discursively construct self and nation, and what it means to be Mexican. The question is as important today as in the past: So we are left to ponder, will tomorrow's Mexico be more like the futuristic Mexico described by Carlos Fuentes in *Cristóbal Nonato*, the paradise of the *raza cósmica* imagined by José Vasconcelos, the pluriethnic nation demanded by Subcomandante Marcos, or will it be unabashedly "Americanized" as predicted by some at the turn of both the nineteenth and the twentieth centuries?

Notes

1. See Stephen D. Morris, "Between Neoliberalism and *neoindigenismo:* Reconstructing Mexican National Identity," *National Identities* 3 (3), 2001: 239–56.

2. Pablo Latapí Sarre, "Después del PRI ¿qué historia enseñar?" *Proceso* 1270 (March 4, 2001): 58–59.

3. Anderson, *Imagined Communities.*

4. Jorge Hernández Campos, "México 1995: La Cultura en Crisis," *Cuadernos Americanos* 59 (1996): 216.

Bibliography

Aguilera, Teresa. "Mexican Radio." *Billboard* 108 (39) (1996): 39–41.

Ahmed, Sadrudin A., and Alain d'Astous. "Comparison of Country-of-Origin Effects on Household and Organizational Buyers' Product Perceptions." *European Journal of Marketing* 29 (3) (1995): 35–51.

Almonte, Jaime, Constance Falk, Rhonda Skaggs, and Manuel Cárdenas. "Country-of-Origin Bias Among High-Income Consumers in Mexico: An Empirical Study." *Journal of International Consumer Marketing* 8 (2) (1995): 27–44.

Al-Sulaiti, Khalid I., and Michael J. Baker. "Country of origin effects: A literature review." *Marketing Intelligence and Planning* 16 (3) (1998): 150–99.

Alvarez de Testa, Lilian. *Mexicanidad y libro de texto gratuito.* Mexico City: UNAM, 1992.

Alvear Acevedo, Carlos. *Historia Universal Contemporánea.* Mexico City: Editorial Jus, 1999.

Alves, Abel A. "History, Mexico, the United States and Humanity in the Writings of Octavio Paz." *CLIO* 20 (1) (1990): 53–63.

Anderson, Benedict. *Imagined Communities: Reflections on the Origin and Spread of Nationalism.* Revised Edition. London: Verso, 1991.

Anderson, W. T., and William H. Cunningham. "Gauging Foreign Product Promotion." *Journal of Advertising Research,* February (1972): 29–34.

Andreas, Peter. "The Making of Amerexico: (Mis)Handling Illegal Immigration." *World Policy Journal* 11 (2) (1994): 45–56.

———. "U.S.-Mexico: Open Markets, Closed Border." *Foreign Policy* 103 (1996): 51–69.

Appadurai, Arjun. "Disjuncture and Difference in the Global Cultural Economy." In *Global Culture: Nationalism, Globalization and Modernity,* edited by Michael Featherstone, 295–310. London: Sage, 1990.

———. *Modernity at Large: Cultural Dimensions of Globalization.* Minneapolis: University of Minnesota Press, 1996.

Arredondo, Estela and Ríus. *Los críticos del imperio: La historia de los últimos sexenios a través de la caricatura.* Mexico City: Grijalbo. 1998.

Arriaga, Victor. "El Manejo de la Relación con Estados Unidos, 1990–1994." *Foro Internacional* 34 (4) (1994): 572–91.

Asher, Herbert. *Polling and the Public.* 4th edition. Washington, D.C.: CQ Press, 1998.

Bailey, William, and Sheila Amin Gutierrez de Pineres. "Country of origin attitudes in Mexico: The *malinchismo* Effect." *Journal of International Consumer Marketing* 9 (3) (1997): 25–41.

Bannister, J. P., and J. A. Saunders. "UK Consumer Attitudes toward Imports: The Measurement of National Stereotype Image." *European Journal of Marketing* 12 (1978): 562–70.

Bantjes, Andrian A. "Burning Saints, Molding Minds: Iconoclasm, Civic Ritual, and the Failed Cultural Revolution." In *Rituals of Rule, Rituals of Resistance: Public Celebrations and Popular Culture in Mexico*, edited by William H. Beezley, Cheryl English Martin, and William E. French, 261–84. Wilmington, DE.: Scholarly Resources, 1994.

Barrera, Eduardo. "The US-Mexico Border as Post-NAFTA Mexico." In *Mass Media and Free Trade: NAFTA and the Cultural Industries*, edited by Emile G. McAnay and Kenton T. Wilkinson, 188–217. Austin: University of Texas Press, 1996.

Barron De Moran, Concepción. *Mi libro de Cuarto Año: Historia y Civismo.* Mexico City: Secretaria de Educación Público, Comisión Nacional de los Libros de Texto Gratuitos, 1960.

Bartra, Roger. "Culture and Political Power in Mexico." *Latin American Perspectives* 16 (2) (1989): 61–69.

———. "La venganza de la Malinche: hacia una identidad postnacional." *Este Pais,* Abril (1991): 17–19.

———. *The Cage of Melancholy: Identity and Metamorphosis in the Mexican Character.* New Brunswick, NJ: Rutgers University Press, 1992.

Basave Benitez, Agustín F. *México Mestizo: Análisis del nacionalismo mexicano en torno a la mestizofília de Andrés Molina Enríquez.* Mexico City: Fondo de Cultural Económica, 1992.

Basave Fernández del Valle, Agustín. *Vocación y Estilo de México: Fundamentos de la Mexicanidad.* Mexico City: Limusa, 1990.

Beals, Ralph L. "The Mexican Student Views the United States." *Annals of the Academy of Political and Social Science* 295 (1954): 108–15.

Becker, Marjorie J. "Black and White and Color: *Cardenismo* and the Search for a *Campesino* Ideology." In *Constructing Culture and Power in Latin America*, edited by Daniel H. Levine, 155–70. Ann Arbor: University of Michigan Press, 1993.

Beezley, William H., Cheryl English Martin, and William E. French. *Rituals of Rule, Rituals of Resistance: Public Celebrations and Popular Culture in Mexico.* Wilmington, DE: Scholarly Resources, 1994.

Beezley, William H., Cheryl English Martin, and William E. French. "Introduction: Constructing Consent, Inciting Conflict." In *Rituals of Rule, Rituals of Resistance: Public Celebrations and Popular Culture in Mexico*, edited by William H. Beezley, Cheryl English Martin, and William E. French, xiii–xxxii.

Beltrán, Ulises, Fernando Castaños, Julia Isabel Flores, Yolanda Meyenberg, and Blanca Helena del Pozo. *Los Mexicanos de los Noventa.* Mexico City: Instituto de Investigaciones Sociales, Universidad Nacional Autónoma de México, 1997.

Berg, Charles Ramírez. *Cinema of Solitude: A Critical Study of Mexican Film, 1967–1983.* Austin: University of Texas Press, 1992.

———. "The Cinematic Invention of Mexico: The Poetics and Politics of the Fernandez-Figueroa Style." In *The Mexican Cinema Project,* edited by Chon A. Noriega and Steven Ricci, 13–24. Los Angeles: UCLA Film and Television Archive, 1994.

Berger, Mark T. *Under Northern Eyes: Latin American Studies and U.S. Hegemony in the Americas, 1898–1990.* Bloomington: Indiana University Press, 1995.

Bernstein, Marvin. *The Mexican Mining Industry, 1890–1950.* Albany: SUNY, 1964.

Beverley, John, José Oviedo, and Michael Aronna, eds. *The Postmodernism Debate in Latin America.* Durham, NC: Duke University Press, 1995.

"Big Company Watch," *Latin Trade,* July (1999).

Bilkey, W. J., and E. Nes. "Country of Origin Effects on Product Evaluations." *Journal of International Business Studies* 8 (1) (1982): 89–99.

Bizberg, Ilan, ed. *México ante el fin de la Guerra Fría.* Mexico City: El Colegio de México, 1998.

Blanquel, Eduardo and Jorge Alberto Manrique. *Mi libro de Sexto Año: Historia y Civismo.* Mexico City: SEP, Comisión Nacional de los Libros de Texto Gratuitos, 1966.

Bloom, William. *Personal Identity, National Identity and International Relations.* London: Cambridge University Press, 1990.

Bolaños Martinez, Raúl. *Historia de la Humanidad: De las Épocas Moderna y Contemporánea.* Segundo Curso. Mexico City: Ediciones Pedagógicas, 1994.

Bonfil Batalla, Guillermo. "Dimensiones Culturales del Tratado de Libre Comercio." In *La educación y la cultura ante el Tratado de Libre Comercio,* edited by Gilberto Guevara Niebla and Nestor García Canclini, 157–78. Mexico City: Nueva Imagen, 1992.

Boroujerdi, M. *Iranian Intellectuals and the West: The Tormented Triumph of Nativism.* New York: Syracuse University Press, 1996.

Boulding, Kenneth. "National Images and International Systems." In *International Politics and Foreign Policy: A Reader in Research and Theory,* edited by James N. Rosenau. New York: The Free Press, 1969.

Brading, David. *Los orígenes del nacionalismo mexicano.* Mexico City: Ediciones Era, 1980.

Breuilly, John. *Nationalism and the State.* Chicago, IL: The University of Chicago Press, 1994.

Bruhn, Kathleen. "Antonio Gramsci and the *Palabra Verdadera*: The Political Discourse of Mexico's Guerilla Forces." *Journal of Interamerican Studies and World Affairs* 41 (2) (1999): 29–55.

Buchanan, William. "How Others See Us." *The Annals of the American Academy of Political and Social Science* 295 (1954): 1–11.

Bulmer-Thomas, Victor. *The Economic History of Latin America since Independence.* London: Cambridge University Press, 1994.

Bunker, Steven B. "'Consumers of Good Taste:' Marketing Modernity in Northern Mexico, 1890–1910." *Mexican Studies/Estudios Mexicanos* 13 (2) (1997): 227–69.

Burr, Ramiro. "Mexican music market is booming due to diverse talent and a loyal immigrant audience." *Billboard* 110 (30) (1998): 49–51.

Bustamante, Jorge. "Identidad nacional en la frontera norte: hallazgos preliminares." In *Impacts regionales de las relaciones economicas México-Estados Unidos*, edited by A. Carona Renteria. Mexico City: El Colegio de México, 1984.

———. "Frontera México–Estados Unidos. Reflexiones para un Marco Teórico." In *Decadencia y auge de las identidades*, edited by José Manuel Valenzuela Arce. Tijuana: El Colegio de la Frontera Norte, 1992.

———. "The Mexico-U.S. Border: A Line of Paradox." In *Identities in North America: The Search for Community*, edited by Robert L. Earle and John D. Wirth, 180–194. Stanford, CA: Stanford University Press, 1995.

Calvert, Peter. *The Mexican Revolution, 1910–1914: The Diplomacy of the Anglo-American Conflict*. London: Cambridge University Press, 1968.

Camp, Roderic A. *Intellectuals and the State in Twentieth Century Mexico*. Austin: University of Texas Press, 1985.

———. "The Cross and the Polling Booth: Religion, Politics and the Laity in Mexico." *Latin American Research Review* 29 (3) (1994): 69–100.

Cárdenas, Cuauhtémoc. "Free Trade Is Not Enough." *New Perspectives Quarterly* 8 (1) (1991): 21–22.

———. *Cuauhtémoc Cárdenas: Palabras de Cárdenas*. Prologue by Miguel Ángel Granados Chapa. Mexico City: Grijalbo, 1999.

Caron, André, and Pierre Bélanger. "A Reception Study of American Television in Quebec." In *Small Nations, big neighbor: Denmark and Quebec/Canada compare notes on American popular culture*, edited by Roger de la Garde, William Gilsdorf, and Ilja Wechselmann. Academic Research Monograph, no. 10. London: John Libbey, 1993.

Carrasco Puente, Rafael. *La caricatura en México*. Mexico City: Imprenta Universitaria, 1953.

Castañeda, Jorge G. *Utopia Unarmed: The Latin American Left After the Cold War*. New York: Alfred A. Knopf, 1993.

———. *The Estados Unidos Affair: Cinco ensayos sobre un "amor" oblicuo*. Mexico City: Aguilar, Nuevo Siglo, 1996.

Castellanos Guerrero, Alicia. *Ciudad Juarez: la vida fronteriza*. Mexico City: Nuestro Tiempo, 1981.

del Castillo Vera, Gustavo. "The Cultural Dimension of a Free Trade Agreement: The Case of Mexico." In *North America without Borders?: Integrating Canada, the United States and Mexico*, edited by Stephen J. Randall, Herman Konrad, and Sheldon Silverman. University of Calgary Press, 1992.

Catan, Thomas. "Under the Golden Arches." *Mexico Business*, July/August (1997): 58–60.

———. "I Want My MTV." *US/Mexico Business*, September (1998): 46–48.

Chabat, Jorge. "Mexico's Foreign Policy after NAFTA: The Tools of Interdependence." In *Bridging the Border: Transforming Mexico-U.S. Relations*, edited by Rodolfo de la Garza and Jesus Velasco, 33–47. New York: Rowman and Littlefield, 1998.

"Cinema: Mexico." *Screen Digest* 259 (1999).

Cline, Howard. *The United States and Mexico*. New York: Atheneum, 1973.

"Comidas Rapidas." *US/Latin Trade*, October (1993).

Consumer Mexico 1996. London: Euromonitor PLC, 1996.

Coote, Alice H. *The Images of the Good Neighbor: The Mexican view of the United States as seen in selected Mexican newspapers and periodicals, 1940–1962.* Masters thesis, University of Maryland, 1962.

Cordell, Victor V. "Effects of Consumer Preferences for Foreign-Sourced Products." *Journal of International Business* 23 (2) (1992): 251–70.

Corona Berkin, Sarah. "EUA Para Niños: La imagen de EUA en los libros de texto de las primarias Mexicanas de este siglo." Paper presented at the XIX Congress of the Latin American Studies Association, Washington, D.C., September 28–30, 1995.

Cosío Villegas, Daniel. *The United States versus Porfirio Díaz.* Translated by Nettie Lee Benson. Lincoln: University of Nebraska Press, 1963.

Country Finance: Mexico. London: Economist Intelligence Unit, 2000.

Country Profile: Mexico. London: Economist Intelligence Unit, 2000.

Cremoux, Raúl. *La televisión y el alumno de secundaria del Distrito Federal.* Mexico City: Centro de Estudios Educativos, 1968.

Dávalos Orozco, Federico. "The Birth of the Film Industry and the Emergence of Sound." In *Mexico's Cinema: A Century of Film and Filmmakers,* edited by Joanne Hershfield and David R. Maciel, 17–32. Wilmington, DE.: Scholarly Resources, 1999.

Davids, Jules. *American Political and Economic Penetration of Mexico, 1877–1920.* New York: Arno Press, 1976.

Davis, Charles. "Mass Support for Regional Integration." *Mexican Studies/Estudios Mexicanos* 14 (1) (1998): 105–30.

Dorfman, Ariel and Armand Mattelart. *Para leer el Pato Donald.* Mexico City: Siglo XXI, 1971.

Dornoff, Ronald J., Clint B. Tankersley, and Gregory P. White. "Consumers' Perceptions of Imports." *Akron Business and Economic Review* 5 (1974): 26–29.

Douglas, M., and B. Isherwood. *The World of Goods.* New York: Basic Books, 1978.

Duran, Ignacio, Iván Trujillo, and Monica Verea, eds. *México Estados Unidos: Encuentros y desencuentros en el cine.* Mexico City: Imcine, 1996.

Eberstadt, Fernanda. "Montezuma's Literary Revenge." *Commentary,* May (1986): 35–40.

"En 10 años McD's llegó a representar 39% del total ingreso pro franquisias." *El Financiero,* February 26, 1994.

Epstein, Erwin H., and Catherine A. Riordan. "Bicultural Preparation and National Identity: A Study of Medical Students at a Mexican University." *Mexican Studies/ Estudios Mexicanos* 5 (2) (1989): 239–63.

Erfani, Julie A. *The Paradox of the Mexican State: Rereading Sovereignty from Independence to NAFTA.* Boulder, CO: Lynne Rienner, 1995.

Esteniou Madrid, Javier. "Crisis cultural y desnacionalización: la televisión mexicana y el debilitamiento de la identidad nacional." *Comunicación y Sociedad,* Mayo– Agosto (1990): 97–121.

EZLN. *EZLN: Documentos y comunicados.* Vol. 1. Mexico City: Ediciones Era, 1994.

———. *EZLN: Documentos y comunicados.* Vol. 2. Mexico City: Ediciones Era, 1995.

Featherstone, Mike. *Global Culture: Nationalism, Globalization and Modernity.* London: Sage, 1990.

Fein, Seth. "From Collaboration to Containment: Hollywood and the International Political Economy of Mexican Cinema after the Second World War." In *Mexico's Cinema: A Century of Film and Filmmakers,* edited by Joanne Hershfield and David R. Maciel, 123–64. Wilmington, DE: Scholarly Resources, 1999.

El Fisgón and Helguera. *El sexenio me da risa: La historieta no oficial.* Mexico City: Grijalbo, 1994.

El Fisgón. *Como sobrevivir el neoliberalismo sin dejar de ser mexicano.* Mexico City: Grijalbo, 1996.

Flores, Javier. *The Industry Sector Analysis: Mexico—Satellite Services.* Washington, D.C.: U.S. State Department, 01/95, 1995.

Foster, David William. *From Mafalda to Los Supermachos: Latin American Graphic Humor as Popular Culture.* Boulder, CO: Lynne Rienner, 1995.

Fox, Jonathan. "Assessing Binational Civil Society Coalitions: Lessons from the Mexico-US Experience." Paper presented at Latin American Studies Association Congress, Miami, Florida, March 16–18, 2000.

Fox Quezada, Vicente. *A Los Pinos: Recuento autobiográfico y político.* Mexico City: Oceano, 1999.

"Franchise Faena." *Business Mexico,* September 1999.

Fuentes, Carlos. *La región mas transparente.* Mexico CIty: Planeta, 1958.

———. *Tiempo mexicano.* Mexico City: Planeta, 1971.

———. *Gringo viejo.* Mexico City: Fondo de Cultura Económica, 1985.

———. *Christopher Unborn.* Translated by Alfred MacAdam. New York: Vintage, 1989.

———. "The Decay of Nations." *New Perspectives Quarterly,* Fall (1991): 10–14.

———. *Nuevo Tiempo mexicano.* Mexico City: Aguilar, 1994.

Galceran, Ignacio, and Jon Berry. "A New World of Consumers." *American Demographics* 17 (3) (1995): 26–33.

Ganesh, Jaishankar, and Gillian Oakenfull. "International Product Positioning: An Illustration Using Perceptual Mapping Techniques." *Journal of Global Marketing* 13 (2) (1999): 85–111.

García, Gustavo A. "In Quest of a National Cinema: The Silent Era." In *Mexico's Cinema: A Century of Film and Filmmakers,* edited by Joanne Hershfield and David R. Maciel, 5–16. Wilmington, DE: Scholarly Resources, 1999.

García, Juán Ramón. *Operation Wetback: The Mass Deportation of Mexican Undocumented Workers in 1954.* Westport, CT: Greenwood Press, 1980.

García-Calderón, C. *Para conectarse a Cablevision.* Mexico City: Ediciones El Caballito, 1987.

García Canclini, Nestor. *Culturas Hibridas: Estrategias para Entrar y Salir de la Modernidad.* Mexico City: Grijalbo, 1989.

———. "Cultural Reconversion." In *On Edge: The Crisis of Contemporary Latin American Culture,* edited by George Yudice, Jean Flores, and Juan Franco, 29–43. Minneapolis: University of Minnesota Press, 1992.

———. *Consumidores y Ciudadanos: Conflictos multiculturales de la globalización.* Mexico City: Grijalbo, 1995.

———. "North Americans or Latin Americans? The Redefinition of Mexican Identity and the Free Trade Agreements." In *Mass Media and Free Trade,* edited by McAnay and Wilkinson, 142–56.

————. *La Globalización Imaginada*. Mexico City: Paidos, 1999.

García Castro, María. "Identidad nacional y nacionalismo en México." *Sociología* 8 (21) (1993): 31–41.

García Riera, Emilio. *Breve Historia del Cine Mexicano, Primer Siglo 1897–1997*. Mexico City: Instituto Mexicano de Cinematografía, 1998.

de la Garza, Rodolfo O. "Foreign Policy Comes Home: The Domestic Consequences of the Program for Mexican Communities Living in Foreign Countries." In *Bridging the Border: Transforming Mexico-U.S. Relations*, edited by Rodolfo de la Garza and Jesus Velasco, 69–88. New York: Rowman and Littlefield, 1998.

de la Garza, Rodolfo O. and Jesus Velasco, ed. *Bridging the Border: Transforming Mexico-U.S. Relations*. New York: Rowman and Littlefield, 1998.

Gellner, Ernest. *Nations and Nationalism*. Ithaca, NY: Cornell University Press, 1983.

Ghosh, Amit K. "Brand management in post-NAFTA Mexico." *Journal of Product and Brand Management* 7 (2) (1998).

Giddens, Anthony. *The Consequences of Modernity*. Stanford, CA: Stanford University Press, 1990.

Gil, Carlos B., ed. *Hope and Frustration: Interviews with Leaders of Mexico's Political Opposition*. Wilmington, DE.: Scholarly Resources, 1992.

Gilbert, Dennis. "Rewriting History: Salinas, Zedillo, and the 1992 Textbook Controversy." Paper presented at the XIX Congress of the Latin American Studies Association, Washington, D.C., September 28–30, 1995; subsequently published in *Mexican Studies /Estudios Mexicanos* 13 (2) (1997): 271–98.

Gingerich, Willard. "The Poetics of History: A Defense of the Washington Address of Octavio Paz." *The New Scholar* 9 (1–2) (1984): 13–37.

Gómez Méndez, Sergio Orlando, Silvia Ramírez Campos, Rosa Ortiz Paz, and José Rodríguez Arrvizu. *Historia 2: Edad Moderna y Contemporánea*. Segunda Edición. Mexico City: Prentice Hall, 1998.

Gonzales, Henry Geddes. "Mass media and cultural identity among the Yucatec Maya: The constitution of global, national and local subjects," *Studies in Latin American Popular Culture* 15 (1996): 131–54.

González Navarro, Moisés. "Racism and *Mestizaje*." In *Common Border, Uncommon Paths: Race, Culture and National Identity in U.S.-Mexican Relations*, edited by Jaime E. Rodriguez O. and Kathryn Vincent, 43–67. Wilmington, DE: Scholarly Resources, 1997.

González Ramírez, Manuel. *La caricatura política*. Mexico City: Fondo de Cultura Económica, 1955.

González Sousa, Luis. *Soberanía Herida: México-Estados Unidos en la hora de la globalización*. Tomo 2. Mexico City: Nuestro Tiempo, 1994.

Gordon, David C. *Images of the West: Third World Perspectives*. New York: Rowman and Littlefield, 1989.

Gorka, Barbara Carol. *Images of the United States in the literature of Octavio Paz, Carlos Fuentes, and Jose Emilio Pacheco*. Ph.D. diss., University of Pennsylvania, 1993.

Green, Maria del Rosario. "Mexico's Economic Dependence." *Proceedings of The Academy of Political Science*, 34 (1) (1981): 104–14.

Gregory, Gary D. and James M. Munch. "Cultural Values in International Advertising: An Examination of Familial Norms and Roles in Mexico." *Psychology and Marketing* 14 (2) (1997): 99–119.

Gurría, José Ángel. "La nueva estrategia diplomática de México." In *México ante el fin de la Guerra Fría*, edited by Ilan Bizberg, 21–28. Mexico City: El Colegio de México, 1998.

Gutiérrez López, Roberto, and José Luis Gutiérrez E. "En torno a la redefinición del nacionalismo mexicano," *Sociología* 8 (21) (1993): 87–101.

Haber, Stephen H. *Industry and Underdevelopment: The Industrialization of Mexico, 1890–1940*. Stanford, CA: Stanford University Press, 1989.

Hall, Linda B. *Oil, Banks and Politics: The United States and Postrevolutionary Mexico, 1917–1924*. Austin: University of Texas Press, 1995.

Hall, Stuart. "The West and the Rest: Discourse and Power." In *Modernity: An Introduction to Modern Societies*, edited by Stuart Hall, David Held, Don Hubert, and Kenneth Thompson, 184–228. Cambridge, MA: Blackwell, 1996.

Hampton, Gerald M. "Perceived Risk in Buying Products Made Abroad by American Firms." *Baylor Business Studies*, October (1977): 53–64.

Hanrahan, Gene Z. ed. *¡Abajo el Gringo! Anti-American Sentiment during the Mexican Revolution*. Salisbury, NC: Documentary Publications, 1982.

Hart, John Mason. *Revolutionary Mexico: The Coming and Process of the Mexican Revolution*. Berkeley: University of California Press, 1989.

Hayes, Joy Elizabeth. "Early American Radio Broadcasting: Media Imperialism, State Paternalism, or Mexican Nationalism?" *Studies in Latin American Popular Culture* 12 (1993): 31–56.

Hellman, Judith Alder. *Mexico in Crisis*. New York: Holms and Meier, 1988.

———. "Mexican Perceptions of Free Trade: Support and Opposition to NAFTA." In *The Political Economy of North American Free Trade*, edited by Ricardo Grinspun and Maxwell A. Cameron, 193–204. New York: St. Martin's Press, 1993.

Herbig, Paul and Alain Genestre. "An examination of the cross-cultural differences in service quality: the example of Mexico and the USA." *Journal of Consumer Marketing* 13 (3) (1996).

Hernández Campos, Jorge. "México 1995: La Cultura en Crisis." *Cuadernos Americanos* 59 (1996): 202–27.

Hernández Rodríguez, Rafael. "Melodrama and Social Comedy in Cinema of the Golden Age." In *Mexico's Cinema: A Century of Film and Filmmakers*, edited by Joanne Hershfield and David R. Maciel, 101–22. Wilmington, DE: Scholarly Resources, 1999.

Hershfield, Joanne. "Race and Ethnicity in the Classical Cinema." In *Mexico's Cinema: A Century of Film and Filmmakers*, edited by Joanne Hershfield and David R. Maciel, 91–100. Wilmington, DE: Scholarly Resources, 1999.

Hershfield, Joanne, and David R. Maciel, eds. *Mexico's Cinema: A Century of Film and Filmmakers*. Wilmington, DE: Scholarly Resources, 1999.

Heslop, L. A., and N. Papadopoulos. "But who knows where or when: Reflections on the images of countries and their products." In *Product-Country Images*, edited by N. Papadolous and L. A. Heslop, 39–75. New York: International Business Press, 1992.

Heyman, Timothy. *Mexico for the Global Investor: Emerging markets theory and practice*. Mexico City: Editorial Milenio, 1999.

Hobsbawm, Eric J. *Nations and Nationalism since 1780: Programme, Myth, Reality*. London: Cambridge University Press, 1990.

Hollander, Paul. *Anti-Americanism: Critiques at Home and Abroad, 1965–1990.* New York: Oxford University Press, 1992.

Holleren, Wiebke. "Mexicans fear invasion by U.S. corn tortillas for health, economics." *DPA* (November 3, 2002), reprinted by Global Exchange [www.globalexchange.org].

Holton, Robert J. *Globalization and the Nation-State.* New York: St. Martin's Press, 1998.

Hufbauer, Gary Clyde, W. N. Harrell Smith IV, and Frank G. Vukmanic. "Bilateral Trade Relations." *Proceedings of The Academy of Political Science* 34 (1) (1981): 136–45.

Humphrey, Norman J. "The Mexican Image of Americans." *The Annals of the American Academy of Political and Social Sciences* 295 (1954): 116–25.

Huntington, Samuel P. "The Clash of Civilizations?" *Foreign Affairs,* Summer (1993): 22–49.

The Industry Sector Analysis: Mexico. Washington, D.C.: U.S. Department of State, 1995.

Inglehart, Ronald, et al. *World Values Surveys and European Values Surveys,* 1981-1984, 1990–1993, and 1995–1997. [Computer File]. ICPSR version. Ann Arbor, MI: Institute for Social Research [Producer], 2000. Ann Arbor, MI: Inter-university Consortium for Political and Social Research [distributor], 2000.

Inglehart, Ronald F., Neil Nevitte, and Miguel Basañez. *The North American Trajectory: Cultural, Economic, and Political Ties among the United States, Canada, and Mexico.* New York: Aldine de Gruyter, 1996.

Insch, Gary S., and J. Brad McBride. "Decomposing the Country-of-Origin Construct: An Empirical Test of Country of Design, Country of Parts and Country of Assembly." *Journal of International Consumer Marketing* 10 (4) (1998): 69–91.

Inter-American Development Bank [IDB]. *Economic and Social Progress in Latin America.* Washington, D.C.: Inter-American Development Bank, 1974.

———. *Economic and Social Progress in Latin America.* Washington, D.C.: Inter-American Development Bank, 1990.

———. *Facing Up to Inequality in Latin America: Economic and Social Progress in Latin America.* Washington, D.C.: Inter-American Development Bank, 1998/99.

International Monetary Fund [IMF]. *Direction of Trade Statistics.* Washington: International Monetary Fund and the International Bank for Reconstruction and Development, 1961/65, 1971/77, 1986, 1995, 1997, 1999.

Jaffe, Eugene D., and Carlos R. Martinez. "Mexican Consumer Attitudes Towards Domestic and Foreign Made Products." *Journal of International Consumer Marketing* 7 (3) (1995): 7–27.

Jameson, Fredric. "Notes on Globalization as a Philosophical Issue." In *The Cultures of Globalization,* edited by Frederic Jameson and Masao Miyoshi. Durham, NC: Duke University Press, 1998.

———. Preface to *The Cultures of Globalization,* edited by Fredric Jameson and Masao Miyoshi. Durham, NC: Duke University Press, 1998.

Jameson, Fredric and Masao Miyoshi, eds. *The Cultures of Globalization.* Durham, NC: Duke University Press, 1998.

Jhally, Sut. *The Codes of Advertising: Fetishism and the Political Economy of Meaning in the Consumer Society.* New York: St. Martin's Press, 1987.

Jiménez Alarcón, Concepción. *Historia del Hombre 2. Curso de Historia Universal para Segundo Grado*. Mexico City: Fernández Editores, 1998.

———. *Historia del Hombre en México. Curso de Historia de México para Tercer grado*. Mexico City: Fernández Editores, 1998.

Johnson, John. *Latin America in Caricature*. Austin: University of Texas Press, 1993.

Jusdanis, Gregory. "Beyond National Culture?" *Boundary 2* 22 (1) (1995): 23–60.

Keck, Margaret E., and Kathryn Sikkink. *Activists Beyond Borders: Advocacy Networks in International Politics*. Ithaca, NY: Cornell University Press, 1998.

Keillor, Bruce D., R. Stephen Parker, and Allen Schaefer. "Influences on Adolescent Brand Preferences in the US and Mexico." *Journal of Advertising Research* 36 (3) (1996): 47–56.

Kenworthy, Eldon. *America/Americas: Myth in the Making of U.S. Policy toward Latin America*. University Park: The Pennsylvania State University Press, 1995.

Knight, Alan. "Peasants into Patriots: Thoughts on the Making of the Mexican Nation." *Mexican Studies/Estudios Mexicanos* 10 (1) (1994): 135–61.

———. "Popular Culture and the Revolutionary State in Mexico, 1910–1940." *Hispanic American Historical Review* 74 (3) (1994): 393–444.

———. "Dealing with the American Political System: An Historical Overview, 1910–1995." In *Bridging the Border: Transforming Mexico-U.S. Relations*, edited by Rodolfo de la Garza and Jesus Velasco, 1–31. New York: Rowman and Littlefield, 1998.

Krishnakumar, Parameswar. *An Exploratory Study of the Influence of Country of Origin on the Product Images of Persons from Selected Countries*. Ph.D. diss., University of Florida, 1974.

Laclau, Ernesto, ed. *The Making of Political Identities*. London: Verso, 1994.

Lafayette de Mente, Boye. *NTC's Dictionary of Mexican Cultural Code Words*. Lincolnwood, IL: NTC Publishing Group, 1996.

Lajous Vargas, Alejandra. "Mexico: Culture and Identity in the Information Age." In *Identities in North America: The Search for Community*, edited by Robert L. Earle and John D. Wirth, 101–14. Stanford, CA: Stanford University Press, 1995.

Langhorst, Rick. "Los Estados Unidos vistos por José Vasconcelos." *Los Ensayistas*, March (1981): 117–22.

Lannert, John. "Gringos Are Coming! Tours, Radio and TV Help Swell Sales of Foreign Acts," *Billboard* 106 (48) (1994): 73–75.

Lapid, Yosef, and Friedrich Kratochwil, eds. *The Return of Culture and Identity in IR Theory*. Boulder, CO: Lynne Rienner, 1996.

Lascu, Dana Nicoleta, and Thomas Giese. "Exploring Country Bias in a Retailing Environment: Implications of Retailer Country of Origin." *Journal of Global Marketing* 9 (1–2) (1995): 41–59.

Latapí Sarre, Pablo. "Después del PRI ¿qué historia enseñar?" *Proceso* 1270 (March 4, 2001): 58–59.

Lee, H., C. Kim, and J. Miller. "The Relative Effects of Price, Warranty and Country of Origin on Consumer Products Evaluations." *Journal of Global Marketing* 6 (1–2) (1992): 55–80.

Levin, I., J. Jasper, J. Mittelstaedt, and G. Gaeth. "Attitudes towards 'buy American first' and preferences for American and Japanese cars: a different role for country-of-origin information." *Advances in Consumer Research* 20 (1993): 625–29.

"Life comes back into Mexican Video Market." *Screen Digest* 284 (November 1999).

Lindstrom, Naomi. "The Single-Panel Cartoon." In *Handbook of Latin American Popular Culture*, edited by Harold E. Hinds, Jr. and Charles M. Tatum, 207–27. Westport, CT: Greenwood Press, 1985.

Lippmann, Walter. *Public Opinion*. New York: Hartcourt, Brace and Company, 1922.

Loaeza, Soledad. "The Changing Face of Mexican Nationalism." In *The NAFTA Debate: Grappling with Unconventional Trade Issues*, edited by M. Delal Baer and Sidney Weintraub, 145–57. Boulder, CO: Lynne Rienner, 1994.

Lozano, Jose Carlos. "Media Reception on the Mexican Border with the US." In *Mass Media and Free Trade*, edited by Emile G. McAnay and Kenton T. Wilkinson, 157–86. Austin: University of Texas, 1996.

de Luna, Andres. "The Labyrinths of History." In *Mexican Cinema*, edited by Paulo Antonio Paranaguá, 171–77. London: British Film Institute, 1995.

Lund, Daniel M. "El tratado de libre comercio: Los extremos de la confusión." *Este País*, Julio (1993): 2–6.

Mabire, Bernardo. "El fantasma de la antigua ideología y su resistencia al cambio de la política exterior en el sexenio de Salinas de Gortari." *Foro Internacional* 34 (4) (1994): 545–71.

———. "La utilidad del nacionalismo en el México de hoy." In *México ante el fin de la Guerra Fría*, edited by Ilan Bizberg, 115–38. Mexico City: El Colegio de México, 1998.

Maciel, David, and Norma Iglesias. *El Norte: The US-Mexican Border in Contemporary Cinema*. San Diego: Institute for Regional Studies of the Californias, San Diego State University, 1990.

Maciel, David R. "El Imperio de la Fortuna: Mexico's Contemporary Cinema, 1985–1992." In *The Mexican Cinema Project*, edited by Chon A. Noreiga and Steven Ricci, 33–44. Los Angeles, CA: UCLA Film and Television Archive, 1994.

de Maria y Campos, Mauricio. "Las industrias culturales y de entretenimiento en el marco de las negociaciones del tratado de libre comercia." In *La educación y la cultura ante el Tratado de Libre Comercio*, edited by Gilberto Guevara Niebla and Nestor García Canclini, 235–99. Mexico City: Nueva Imagen, 1992.

Mazza, Jacqueline. "The Dilemma of National Sovereignty in Mexico: The Case of Foreign Electoral Observation." Paper presented at the American Political Science Association meeting, Atlanta, Georgia, September 2–4, 1999.

McAnay, Emile G. and Kenton T. Wilkinson, eds. *Mass Media and Free Trade: NAFTA and the Cultural Industries*. Austin: University of Texas, 1996.

Medina, Jose F., Joel Saegert, and Alicia Gresham. "Comparison of Mexican-American and Anglo-American Attitudes toward Money." *Journal of Consumer Affairs* 30 (1) (1996): 124–45.

Merrill, John C. *Gringo: The American as Seen by Mexican Journalists*. Gainesville: University of Florida Press, 1963.

"Mexican, fast food market in infancy." *Market Latin America*, January 2000.

Meyer, Lorenzo. "Las crisis de la elite mexicana y su relación con Estados Unidos. Raíces históricas del tratado de libre comercio." In *México–Estados Unidos*, edited by Gustavo Vega, 73–93. Mexico City: El Colegio de México, 1992.

Mi libro de Historia de México Sexto grado. Mexico City: SEP, Comisión Nacional de los Libros de Texto Gratuitos, 1992.

Mi libro de Historia de México Cuarto grado. Mexico City: SEP, Comisión Nacional de los Libros de Texto Gratuitos, 1992.

Monroy Gutiérrez, Amelia. *Mi libro de Quinto Año: Historia y Civismo.* Mexico City: SEP, Comisión Nacional de los Libros de Texto Gratuitos, 1964.

Monsiváis, Carlos. "Notas sobre la cultural mexicana en el siglo XX." In *Historia general de México.* Tomo 2, 1375–548. Mexico City: El Colegio de México, 1976.

———. "Muerte y resurrección del nacionalismo mexicano." *Nexos* 109 (1987): 13–22.

———. "Para un cuadro de costumbres. De cultura y vida cotideana en los ochentas." *Cuadernos Políticos* 57 (1989).

———. "Heart of the Mexican Dream." *New Perspectives Quarterly* 8 (1) (1991): 51–52.

———. "De la Cultura Mexicana en Visperas del Tratado de Libre Comercio." In *La educacion y la cultura ante el Tratado de Libre Comercio*, edited by Gilberto Guevara Niebla and Nestor García Canclini, 179–209. Mexico City: Nueva Imagen, 1992.

———. "Interrelación Cultural entre México y Estados Unidos." In *Mitos en Las Relaciones México–Estados Unidos*, edited by Ma. Esther Schumacher, 435–59. Mexico City: SRE y Fondo de Cultura Económica, 1994.

———. "La Malinche y el Primer Mundo." In *La Malinche, sus padres y sus hijos*, edited by Margo Glantz, 139–47. Mexico City: UNAM, 1994.

———. *Los rituales del caos.* Mexico City: Procuradura Federal del Consumidor y Ediciones Era, 1995.

———. "Mythologies." In *Mexican Cinema, Mexican Cinema*, edited by Paulo Antonio Paranaguá, 117–27. London: British Film Institute, 1995.

———. "All the People Came and Did Not Fit onto the Screen: Notes on the Cinema Audience in Mexico." In *Mexican Cinema, Mexican Cinema*, edited by Paulo Antonio Paranaguá, 145–51. London: British Film Institute, 1995..

———. "Will Nationalism be Bilingual?" In *Mass Media and Free Trade*, edited by Emile G. McAnay and Kenton T. Wilkinson, 131–42. Austin: University of Texas, 1996.

———. *Mexican Postcards.* Translated and with an introduction by John Kraniauskas. London: Verso, 1997.

———. "Las caricaturas me hacen llorar." *Proceso* 1198 (October 17, 1999) (electronic version).

———. "Cantinflas and Tin Tán: Mexico's Greatest Comedians." In *Mexico's Cinema: A Century of Film and Filmmakers*, edited by Joanne Hershfield and David R. Maciel, 49–80. Wilmington, DE.: Scholarly Resources, 1999.

Montoya, Alberto, and María-Antonieta Rebeil. "Communication television as an educational and political institution: A case study of its impact on the students of Telesecundaria." In *Communication and Latin American Society: Trends in Critical Research, 1960–1985*, edited by R. Atwood and E. McAnany. Madison: University of Wisconsin Press, 1986.

Moore, Daniel S. "Latin Rockers seek Global Roll." *Variety* 384 (8) (1994): 48.

———. "Mexico Poised for a New Age." *Variety* 384 (8) (1994): 37.

Mora, Carl J. *Mexican Cinema: Reflections of a Society.* Berkeley: University of California Press. 1989.

Morales Moreno, Isidro. "Mexico's National Identity after NAFTA." *American Behavioral Scientist* 40 (7) (1997): 858–83.

Moreno, Julio. "Retail diplomacy in Mexico." *World Trade*, March (2000), 80.

Morris, Stephen D. "Reforming the Nation: Mexican Nationalism in Context." *Journal of Latin American Studies* 31 (2) (1999): 363–97.

———. "Exploring Mexican Images of the U.S." *Mexican Studies/Estudios Mexicanos* 16 (1) (2000): 105–39.

———. "Between Neoliberalism and *Neoindigenismo:* The Reconstruction of Mexican National Identity." *National Identities* 3 (3) (2001): 239–56.

Morris, Stephen D., and John T. Passe-Smith. "Hegemonía cultural o valores posmaterialistas: Resultados preliminares de una encuesta en Jalisco." *Carta Económica Regional* 52 (1997): 10–15.

———. "What a Difference a Crisis Makes: NAFTA, Mexico and the United States." *Latin American Perspectives* 28 (3) (2001): 124–49.

Mraz, John. "Lo gringo en el cine mexicano y la ideologia alemanista." In *México Estados Unidos: Encuentros y desencuentros en el cine*, edited by Ignacio Duran, Iván Trujillo, and Monica Verea, 83–92. Mexico City: Imcine, 1996.

Murray, Frederic W. "The Dynamics of Inter-cultural Dissonance in *Gringo Viejo*." *Chasque: Revista de Literatura Latinoamericana* 19 (1) (1990): 19–23.

Nájera-Ramírez, Olga. "Engendering Nationalism: Identity, Discourse, and the Mexican *Charro*." *Anthropological Quarterly* 67 (1) (1994): 1–14.

Nericcio, William Anthony. "¿Nobel Paz?: A Pre- and Post-Nobel Survey of a Mexican Writer's Evolving Views of Mexico, the United States and Other Na[rra]tions." *Siglo XXI* 10 (1–2) (1992): 165–94.

Neumann, Peter H., and Maureen A. Cunningham. *Mexico's Free Textbooks: Nationalism and the Urgency to Educate.* World Bank Staff Working Papers, Number 541. Washington, D.C.: World Bank, 1982.

New York Times 1998 Almanac, edited by John W. Wright. New York: Penguin, 1997.

Nolan, P. "Making Your Mark in Mexico." *Potentials in Marketing*, September 1994: 34–35.

Noriega, Chon A. "Mexican Cinema in the United States: Introduction to the Essays." In *The Mexican Cinema Project*, edited by Chon A. Noriega and Steven Ricci, 1–6. Los Angeles, Cal.: UCLA Film and Television Archive, 1994.

Noriega, Chon A. and Steven Ricci, eds. *The Mexican Cinema Project.* Los Angeles, Cal.: UCLA Film and Television Archive, 1994.

Ojeda, Mario. *Alcances y limites de la política exterior de México.* Mexico City: El Colegio de México, 1976.

Ordiz Vazquez, Francisco Javier. "Carlos Fuentes y la Identidad de México." *Revista Iberoamericana* 58 (1992): 159, 527–38.

Orme, William A., ed. *A Culture of Collusion: An Inside Look at the Mexican Press.* Miami, FL: North-South Center Press, 1997.

Ortega Pizarro, Fernando. "Gracias a las franquicias, ya esta presente aqui el 'american way of life.'" *Proceso* 824 (August 17, 1992): 18–20.

Oster, Patrick. *The Mexicans: A Personal Portrait of a People.* New York: Harper and Row, 1989.

Otalora, Cristina. "Mexico shows signs of revival." *Music Business International* 8 (4) (1998): 45–46.

Papadopoulos, N. "What Product Country Images are and are not." In *Product-Country Images*, edited by N. Papadolous and L. A. Heslop. New York: International Business Press, 1992.

Papadopoulos, N., and L. A. Heslop, eds. *Product-Country Images*. New York: International Business Press, 1993.

Paranaguá, Paulo Antonio. "Ten Reasons to Love or Hate Mexican Cinema." In *Mexican Cinema*, edited by Paulo Antonio Paranaguá, 1–13. London: British Film Institute, 1995.

Paredes, Américo. "The Anglo-American in Mexican Folklore." In *New Voices in American Studies*, edited by Ray B. Browne, Donald M. Winkelman, and Allen Hayman, 113–28. Lafayette, IN: Purdue University Studies, 1966.

Park, James William. *Latin American Underdevelopment: A History of Perspectives in the United States, 1870–1965*. Baton Rouge: Louisiana State University Press, 1995.

Parodi, Carlos A. "Nationalism and Globalization." Paper presented at the meeting of the Latin American Studies Association, Chicago, Ill., September 24–26, 1998.

Partido de la Revolucion Democratica (PRD) *Programa para el desarrollo económico con justicia social* (n.d.) (electronic version).

———. *1989: Informe de la situación nacional.*Mexico City, 1989.

———. *Propuestas Basicas*. Mexico City, 1997.

Pastor, Robert A., and Jorge G. Castañeda. *Limits to Friendship: The United States and Mexico*. New York: Vintage Books, 1989.

Pastor, Manuel, and Carol Wise. "State Policy, Distribution and Neoliberal Reform in Mexico." *Journal of Latin American Studies* 29 (1997): 419–56.

Paz, Octavio. "The Border of Time." *New Perspectives Quarterly* 5 (1) (1988): 46–52.

———. *One Earth, Four or Five Worlds: Reflections on Contemporary History*. San Diego: Harcourt Brace Jovanovich, 1986.

———. *Labyrinth of Solitude*, 1961. Reprinted as *Labyrinth of Solitude and Other Essays*. New York: Grove Press, 1985.

———. "El Espejo Indiscreto." In *El ogro filantropico, 1971–1978*. Barcleona: Seix Barral, 1979. Originally published in *Plural* 58 (July 1976). Reprinted as "Mexico and the United States" in *Labyrinth of Solitude and Other Essays*.

———. "México y Estados Unidos." In *Tiempo nublado*. Reprinted as "Mexico and the United States" in *Labyrinth of Solitude and Other Essays*.

Pellicer de Brody, Olga. "Viente Años de Política Exterior Mexicana: 1960–1980." *Foro Internacional* 21 (1980): 149–60.

Pérez Montfort, Ricardo. "En contrapunto de la imagen nacionalista. El estereotipo norteamericano en el cine de charros 1920–1946." In *México Estados Unidos: Encuentros y desencuentros en el cine*, edited by Ignacio Duran, Iván Trujillo, and Monica Verea, 93–103. México: Imcine, 1996.

Peterson, R. A., and A. J. P. Jolibert. "A Meta-Analysis of Country-of-Origin Effects." *Journal of International Business Studies* 26 (4) (1995): 883–900.

Pick, James B., and Edgar W. Butler. *The Mexico Handbook: Economic and Demographic Maps and Statistics*. Boulder, CO.: Westview Press, 1994.

Pieterse, Jan Nederveen, and Bhikhu Parekh. "Shifting Imaginaries: Decolonization, International Decolonization, Postcoloniality." In *The Decolonization of Imagination: Culture, Knowledge, and Power*, edited by Jan Nederveen Pieterse and Bhikhu Parekh, 1–20. Atlantic Highlands, N.J.: Zed Books, 1995.

Pike, Fredrick B. *The United States and Latin America: Myths and Stereotypes of Civilization and Nature.* Austin: University of Texas Press, 1992.

"Pitching to Peso-Pinchers." Business Week, May 15, 1995: 82.

Pruneda, Salvador. *La caricatura como arma política.* Mexico City: Instituto Nacional de Estudios Históricos de la Revolución, 1958.

Radcliffe, Sarah and Sallie Westwood. *Remaking the Nation: Place, Identity and Politics in Latin America.* London: Routledge, 1996.

Ramos, Samuel. *Profile of Man and Culture in Mexico.* Translated by Peter G. Earle. Introduction by Thomas B. Irving. Austin: University of Texas, 1962.

"Reel Renaissance." *Business Mexico,* April 2000.

Reierson, Curtis. "Are Foreign Products Seen as National Stereotypes?" *Journal of Retailing,* Fall (1966): 33–40.

de los Reyes, Aurelio. "El gobierno mexicano y las películas denigrantes, 1920–1931." In *México Estados Unidos: Encuentros y desencuentros en el cine,* edited by Ignacio Duran, Iván Trujillo, and Monica Verea, 23–35. Mexico City: Imcine, 1996.

Richey, Brenda E., Patricia B. Rose, and Luis Domínguez. "Perceived Value of Mexican vs U.S. Products in Mexico, Venezuela, and the United States: Implications for Mexican Firms." *Journal of Global Marketing* 13 (2) (1999): 49–65.

Riding, Alan. *Distant Neighbors: A Portrait of the Mexicans.* New York: Vintage Books, 1986.

Ríus [Rio, Eduardo del]. *Un siglo de caricatura en México.* Mexico City: Grijalbo, 1984.

Riva Palacio, Raymundo. "A Culture of Collusion: The Ties that Bind the Press and the PRI." In *A Culture of Collusion,* edited by William A. Orme, 21–32. Miami, FL: North-South Center Press, 1997.

Roberts, James A., and Carlos Ruy Martinez. "The Emerging Consumer Culture in Mexico: An Exploratory Investigation of Compulsive Buying in Mexican Young Adults." *Journal of International Consumer Marketing* 10 (1–2) (1997): 7–31.

Roberts, James A., and Cesar J. Sepulveda M. "Money Attitudes and Compulsive Buying: An Exploratory Investigation of the Emerging Consumer Culture in Mexico." *Journal of International Consumer Marketing* 11 (4) (1999): 53–74.

Rodríguez O., Jaime E., ed. *The Independence of Mexico and the Creation of the New Nation.* Los Angeles: University of California, Los Angeles, 1989.

Rodríguez O., Jaime E. and Kathryn Vincent. *Common Border, Uncommon Paths: Race, Culture, and National Identity in U.S.-Mexican Relations.* Wilmington, DE: Scholarly Resources, 1997.

Roth, Martin S., and Jean B. Romeo. "Matching Product Category and Country Image Perceptions: A Framework for Managing Country-of-Origin Effects." *Journal of International Business Studies* 23 (3) (1992): 477–97.

Rozental, Andrés. "La nueva etapa en las relaciones México-Estados Unidos." *Revista Mexican de Política Exterior* 44 (1994): 7–13.

Rubenstein, Anne. *Bad Language, Naked Ladies & Other Threats to the Nation: A Political History of Comic Books in Mexico.* Durham, NC: Duke University Press, 1998.

Said, Edward. *Orientalism.* London: Routledge, 1978.

———. *Culture and Imperialism.* New York: Alfred A. Knopf, 1993.

Sálazar, Sotelo. "Nación y nacionalismo en México." *Sociologia* 8 (21) (1993): 43–63.

Salvucci, Richard J. "Texas, 'Tyrants,' and Trade with Mexico."Reprinted in *Latin America and the World Economy: Dependency and Beyond*, 60–68. Lexington, MA.: D.C. Heath, 1996.

Sánchez, Rosáura, and Beatrice Pita. "Cartooning and Other Graphic Arts: An Introduction." *The Americas Review* 23 (1–2) (1995): 7–27.

Sánchez-Ruíz, Enrique. "Notas sobre la globalización, el TLC y el espacio audiovisual mexicano." Paper presented at the conference *La comunicación hoy: Escenarios y contraescenarios*, Universidad de las Américas-Puebla, México, November 23–25, 1993.

Saragoza, Alex M., and Graciela Berkovich. "Intimate Connections: Cinematic Allegories of Gender, the State and National Identity." In *The Mexican Cinema Project*, edited by Chon A. Noriega and Steven Ricci, 25–32. Los Angeles, CA: UCLA Film and Television Archive, 1994.

Schmidt, Henry C. *The Roots of Lo Mexicano: Self and Society in Mexican Thought, 1900–1934*. College Station: Texas A & M University Press, 1978.

Schooler, Robert D. "Product Bias in the Central American Common Market." *Journal of Marketing Research* 2 (1965): 394–97.

Schutte, Ofelia. *Cultural Identity and Social Liberation in Latin American Thought*. New York: State University of New York Press, 1993.

Segal, Madhav N., and Lionel Sosa. "Marketing to the Hispanic Community." *California Management Review* 26 (1) (1983): 120–34.

Segovia, Rafael. "El nacionalismo mexicano: los programas politicos revolucionarios 1929–1964." In *Lecturas de Política Mexicana*, 37–53. Mexico City: El Colegio de México, 1977.

Sepulveda Amor, Bernardo. "Objetivos e intereses de la política exterior mexicana." In *México ante el fin de la Guerra Fría*, edited by Ilan Bizberg, 49–76. Mexico City: El Colegio de México, 1998.

Shimp, T. A., and S. Sharma. "Consumer Ethnocentrism: Constitution and Validation of the CETSCALE." *Journal of Marketing Research* 24 (3) (1987): 280–89.

Sinclair, J. *Images Incorporated*. New York: Croom Helm, 1987.

Sklair, Leslie. "Social Movements and Global Capitalism." In *The Cultures of Globalization*, edited by Frederic Jameson and Masao Miyoshi, 291–311. Durham, NC: Duke University Press, 1998.

Smith, Anthony D. *National Identity*. Reno: University of Nevada Press, 1993.

Solis, Leopoldo. "La política económica y el nacionalismo mexicano." In *Lecturas de Política Mexicana*, 55–75. Mexico City: El Colegio de México, 1977.

Sullivan, Michael P. *International Relations: Theories and Evidence*. Englewood Cliffs, NJ: Prentice Hall, 1976.

Tongberg, R. C. *An Empirical Study of Relationships Between Dogmatism and Consumer Attitudes Toward Foreign Products*. Ph.D. diss., The Pennsylvania State University, 1972.

Toussaint, Manuel. "The Political Caricature in Mexico." *Mexican Art and Life*, October 4, 1938.

Tóvar y de Teresa, Rafael. *Modernización y política cultural: Una visión de la modernización de México*. México: Fondo de Cultura Económica, 1994.

Treviño, Javier. "Principios e intereses de la politica exterior de Mexico." In *México ante el fin de la Guerra Fría*, edited by Ilan Bizberg, 39–48. Mexico City: El Colegio de México, 1998.

Triplett, Tim. "Middle-Class Mexicans Share Traits with Their US Counterparts." *Marketing News* 28 (1994): 8.

Tse, D. K., and G. J. Gorn. "An Experiment on the Salience of Country-of-Origin in the Era of Global Brands." *Journal of International Marketing* 1 (1) (1993): 57–76.

Tuñón, Julia. "Una Mirada al vecino. Estadounidenses de celuloide en el cine mexicana de la edad de oro." In *México Estados Unidos: Encuentros y desencuentros en el cine*, edited by Ignacio Duran, Iván Trujillo, and Monica Verea, 103–34. Mexico City: Imcine, 1996.

Turner, Frederick C. *The Dynamics of Mexican Nationalism*. Chapel Hill: University of North Carolina Press, 1968.

Twomey, Michael J. "Patterns of Foreign Investment in Latin America in the Twentieth Century." In *Latin America and the World Economy since 1800*, edited by John H. Coatsworth and Alan M. Taylor, 171–202. Cambridge, MA: Harvard University, David Rockefeller Center for Latin American Studies, 1998.

Ueltschy, Linda C., and John K. Ryans, Jr. "Employing Standardized Promotion Strategies in Mexico: The Impact of Language and Cultural Differences." *The International Executive* 39 (4) (1997): 479–95.

United Nations. *Economic Survey of Latin America 1957*. New York, 1959.

"US film exports hit a record $5.7 B." *Hollywood Reporter,* August 26, 1999.

Valenzuela Arce, Juán Manuel. "Las identidades culturales frente al TLC." *Sociología* 8 (21) (1993): 103–29.

Vasconcelos, José. *La raza cósmica: Misión de la raza iberoamericana*. Ninth edition. Mexico City: Espasa-Calpe Mexicana, 1948.

———. *Obras completas*. Mexico City: Libreros Mexicanos Unidos, 1957.

Vázquez, Ignacio. "Mexicans are buying 'Made in USA' food." *Marketing News* 32 (18) (1998): 14.

Vázquez, Josefina. *Ciencias Sociales: Sexto Grado*. Mexico City: SEP, Comisión Nacional de los Libros de Texto Gratuitos, 1974.

Vázquez de Knauth, Josefina. *Nacionalismo y Educacion en Mexico*. Mexico City: El Colegio de México, 1975.

Vázquez Segura, Ma. de la Luz and Meyra Egremy Pinto. *Historia de Mexico*. Mexico City: Limusa Noriega Editores, 1996.

Vega, Gustavo, ed. *México–Estados Unidos*. Mexico City: El Colegio de México, 1992.

de la Vega Alfaro, Eduardo. "The Decline of the Golden Age and the Making of the Crisis." In *Mexico's Cinema: A Century of Film and Filmmakers*, edited by Joanne Hershfield and David R. Maciel, 165–92. Wilmington, DE.: Scholarly Resources, 1999.

Velázquez, Rivera. "Comentario a una encuesta." *Cuaderno a Nexos* 48 (June 1992): iii–viii.

Vila, Pablo Sergio. *Everyday Life, Culture and Identity on the Mexican-American Border: The Ciudad Juarez-El Paso Case*. Ph.D. diss., University of Texas at Austin, 1994.

Wang, Chih-Kang. *The Effect of Foreign Economic, Political and Cultural Environment on Consumers' Willingness to Buy Foreign Products*. Ph.D. diss., Texas A&M University, 1978.

Wang, Chih-Kang, and Charles W. Lamb, Jr. "The Impact of Selected Environmental Forces Upon Consumers' Willingness to Buy Foreign Products." *Journal of the Academy of Marketing Science* 11 (1983): 71–84.

Weinert, Richard S. "Foreign Capital in Mexico." *Proceedings of The Academy of Political Science* 34 (1) (1981): 115–24.

Weintraub, Sidney. "Mexico's Foreign Economic Policy: From Admiration to Disappointment." In *Changing Structure of Mexico*, edited by Laura Randall, 43–54. New York: M. E. Sharpe, 1996.

Whitehead, Laurence. "Mexico and the 'Hegemony' of the US: Past, Present and Future." In *Mexico's External Relations in the 1990s*, edited by Riordan Roett, 243–62. Boulder, CO: Lynne Rienner, 1991.

Whiting, Van R., Jr. "Markets and Bargains: Foreign Investment and Development Strategies in Mexico." In *Mexico's Economic Crisis: Challenges and Opportunities*, edited by Donald L. Wyman, 57–78. Center for US-Mexican Studies, University of California, San Diego, 1983.

Wilt, David Edward. *Stereotype Images of United States Citizens in Mexican Cinema, 1930–1990*. Ph.D. diss., University of Maryland, College Park, 1991.

Witt, Jerome, and C.P. Rao. "The Impact of Global Sourcing on Consumer: Country-of-Origin Effects on Perceived Risk." *Journal of Global Marketing* 6 (3) (1992): 105–28.

Woodward, Kathryn, ed. *Identity and Difference*. London: Sage, 1997.

Zamudio-Taylor, Victor, and Imma Guiu. "Criss-Crossing Texts: Reading Images in *Like Water for Chocolate*." In *The Mexican Cinema Project*, edited by Chon A. Noriega and Steven Ricci, 45–51. Los Angeles, CA: UCLA Film and Television Archive, 1994.

Zavala, Ivan. "Valores políticos." In *Como somos los mexicanos*, edited by Alberto Hernández Medina and Luís Narro Rodríguez, 93–111. Mexico City: Centro de Estudios Educativos, 1987.

Zebadúa, Emilio. "Del plan Brady al TLC: La lógica de la política exterior mexicana, 1988–1994." *Foro Internacional*, 36 (4) (1994): 626–51.

Zolov, Eric. *Refried Elvis: The Rise of the Mexican Counterculture*. Berkeley: University of California Press, 1999.

Zuño, Jose Guadalupe. *Historia de la Caricatura en México*. Mexico City, 1967.

Index

Index

About the Author

Stephen D. Morris (Ph.D. Arizona 1988) is the Director of the International Studies Program and Professor of Political Science at the University of South Alabama, and Director of the Guadalajara Summer Program for Thunderbird, The Garvin School of International Management. He has taught at La Universidad de las Americas in Puebla and as a Fulbright Lecturer at the Universidad de Guadalajara. He is the author of *Corruption and Politics in Contemporary Mexico* (1991) and *Political Reformism in Mexico* (1995) and numerous articles on Mexican politics, corruption, and nationalism appearing in the *Bulletin of Latin American Research, Corruption and Reform, The Journal of Interamerican Studies and World Affairs, The Journal of Latin American Studies, Mexican Studies/Estudios Mexicanos, National Identity,* and *Third World Quarterly.* In addition to his research on political corruption in Mexico, Morris is working on a companion volume to *Gringolandia* exploring U.S. perceptions of Mexico.